AN INTRODUCTION TO FINNISH LAW

AN INTRODUCTION TO FINNISH LAW

Edited
by
Juha Pöyhönen

FINNISH LAWYERS' PUBLISHING
Helsinki 1993

© 1993 FINNISH LAWYERS' PUBLISHING and
The writers

Cover: Jukka Mäkelä

ISBN 951-640-622-X

Gummerus Kirjapaino Oy
Jyväskylä 1993

All rights reserved. No part of this publication may
be reproduced, stored in a retrieval system, or transmitted
in any form by means, electronic, mechanical, photocopying,
recording or otherwise, without the prior written permission
of the publisher.

Writers

I Introduction
Professor Aulis Aarnio

II Constitutional Law and Human Rights
Dr. Martin Scheinin

III Contracts and Torts
Dr. Juha Pöyhönen

IV Company Law
Mr. Gerhard af Schultén, Attorney at Law

V Labour Law and Non-discrimination Law
Professor Niklas Bruun

VI Property Law
Professor Leena Kartio

VII Family Law and Inheritance Law
Professor Urpo Kangas

VIII Legal Procedure
Professor Antti Jokela

IX Administrative Law
Professor Olli Mäenpää

X Environmental Law
Dr. Kari Kuusiniemi

XI Tax Law
Dr. Timo Viherkenttä

CONTENTS

Preface 1

I Introduction. By Aulis Aarnio 3
   1. General View 5
   2. On the Legal Thinking 8
   3. The Nature of the Legal Order of Finland 15
   4. The Organization of the Judiciary 15
   5. Law in the Welfare State 20
      5.1 A Finnish Point of View 20
   6. The Future Needs 25

II Constitutional Law and Human Rights. By Martin Scheinin 27
   1. Four Distinctive Features of the Finnish Constitution 29
      1.1 More than One Written Constitutional Document 29
      1.2 A System of Exceptive Enactments 30
      1.3 Strong Presidential Powers 30
      1.4 A Parliamentary System of Constitutionality Control 31
   2. The Structure of the Constitutional System 32
      2.1 The Electoral System 32
      2.2 Parliamentary Competencies and Procedures 33
      2.3 Presidential Powers 35
      2.4 The Cabinet and the Administration 36
      2.5 The Judiciary and Legality Control 37
      2.6 Self-government 37
   3. The Individual and the Constitution 38
      3.1 Constitutional Rights in the 1919 Constitution Act 38
          3.1.1 Contents 38
          3.1.2 Citizenship 39
          3.1.3 The Role of Parliament's Committee for Constitutional Law 40
          3.1.4 The Right to Work 42
          3.1.5 Constitutional Rights in Courts 44

		3.2	International Human Rights Treaties	46
			3.2.1 Ratifications	46
			3.2.2 Domestic Status	48
			3.2.3 Court Cases	49
			3.2.4 Supreme Court Case KKO 1993:58	50
	4.	Revision of the Constitution		52
		4.1	The Procedure	52
		4.2	The Plan for a Total Reform	53
		4.3	The Strategy of Partial Amendments	53
		4.4	The Rights Reform Project	54
		4.5	Effects of European Integration	55
		4.6	Further Reform of Presidential Powers	56
	Bibliography			57

III	Contracts and Torts. By Juha Pöyhönen		59
	Contracts		61
	1.	Introduction	61
	2.	The Sources of Finnish Contract Law	65
	3.	Offer and Acceptance	66
	4.	Interpretation of Contracts	67
	5.	The Invalidity of Contracts	69
		5.1 Duress	70
		5.2 Fraud	72
		5.3 Undue Influence	73
		5.4 Mistake	73
		5.5 The Small General Clause, Good Faith and Honesty	74
		5.6 The Big General Clause, Unfair Contracts	75
	6.	Specific Areas of Contract Law	80
		6.1 Agency	80
		6.2 Consumer Contracts	80
		6.3 Standard Form Contracts	80
		6.4 Commercial Law and Civil Law	81
	Torts		82
	1.	General Overview	82
	2.	Some Areas of Strict Liability	85

	Bibliographical Essay	86
IV	Company Law. By Gerhard af Schultén	87
	1. The Corporate Structure	89
	2. The Choice of Corporation Form	90
	3. Partnerships	91
	4. Cooperatives	94
	5. Companies Limited by Shares	95
	5.1 Scope of Application	96
	5.2 The Formation of a Limited Company	97
	5.3 Share Capital, Shares and Capital Issues	99
	5.4 The Book-entry Securities System	100
	5.5 Securities Regulations	102
	5.6 Organization	104
	5.7 Minority Protection	107
	5.8 Creditor Protection	108
	5.9 Groups	109
	5.10 Reorganizing Companies	110
	5.11 Bankruptcy and Restructuring	112
	6. Foreign Ownership and Participation	113
	7. The Company Law Reform	115
	References	117
V	Labour Law and Non-discrimination Law. By Niklas Bruun	119
	1. The Finnish Industrial Relations System	121
	1.1 History	121
	1.2 Organizational Structure	121
	1.3 Incomes Policy	122
	1.4 Distinctive Finnish Features	123
	2. Finnish Labour Law	124
	2.1 Historical Roots	124
	2.2 New Developments	125
	2.3 Leading Principles of Finnish Labour Law	125
	2.4 Legal Sources of Labour Law	126
	2.5 Jurisprudence	127
	Bibliographical Essay	128

3. The Individual Employment Relationship 129
   3.1 Employment Contracts – the Employment Relationship 129
       3.1.1 The Form and Period of Validity of an Employment Contract 130
       3.1.2 Duties of the Employee 131
       3.1.3 Wages 131
       3.1.4 Wages where the Completion of Work is Prevented 132
       3.1.5 The General Applicability of Collective Agreements 133
       3.1.6 Other Employer Duties – Working time, Free time, Annual Vacation, and Health and Safety 134
       3.1.7 Temporary Lay-offs 137
       3.1.8 Termination of an Employment Contract 138
       3.1.9 Termination by Notice 139
       3.1.10 Rescission of an Employment Contract 141
4. Collective Labour Relations 142
   4.1 Background 142
   4.2 Structure of the System of Collective Agreements 142
   4.3 The Form and Parties to Collective Agreements 144
   4.4 Contents of Collective Agreements 144
   4.5 Legal Effects of Collective Agreements 145
   4.6 Industrial Peace 146
   4.7 The Labour Court 147
   4.8 Mediation in Labour Conflicts 148
   4.9 Co-operation Within the Enterprise 148
   4.10 Representation on the Board 151
5. Non-discrimination Law 152
   5.1 Background 152
   5.2 Protection of Union Activities 152
   5.3 General Ban on Discrimination 153
   5.4 The Act on Equality between Men and Women 154
6. The Future 158

VI	Property Law. By Leena Kartio	161
1.	Property Law as a Legal Discipline	163
	1.1 Property Law as a part of Finnish Legal System	163
	1.2 Future Prospects of Property Law	166
2.	Property Rights and their Classification	168
3.	Sources of Law and Legislation in Property Law	170
	3.1 General	170
	3.2 The Examination of Legislation	171
4.	Objects and Property	177
	4.1 Immovables and Movables	177
	4.1.1 General	177
	4.1.2 Immovables	179
	4.1.3 Movables	181
	4.2 Constituent Parts and Appurtenances of an Object	184
	4.3 Real Property and Personal Property	185
5.	Ownership	186
	5.1 The Concept of Ownership	186
	5.2 Joint Ownership	188
6.	Principle of Publicity, Possession and the Registration System	189
	6.1 Principle of Publicity and Protection of Good Faith in Property Law	189
	6.2 The Concept of Possession and its Significance Generally	192
	6.3 Registration in Real Property Law	194
	6.3.1 General	194
	6.3.2 The Registration of Title to Real Property	195
	6.3.3 Registration of Rights other than Ownership	196

VII	Family Law and Inheritance Law. By Urpo Kangas	199
1.	The Myth of a Uniform Family and Inheritance Law	201
2.	The Classic Paradigm of Family and Inheritance Law	204
3.	The Alternative Paradigms of Family and Inheritance Law	208
4.	The General Doctrine of Family and Inheritance Law	211
5.	Principles Pertaining to the Fields of the Law	213
	5.1 The Code of Inheritance 1965	213

XI

5.2	The Law of Wills 1965	218
5.3	The Marriage Act	221
	5.3.1 Conclusion and Dissolution of Marriage	221
	5.3.2 Property Rights during the Marriage	223
	5.3.3 Distribution of Matrimonial Property	225
	5.3.4 Maintenance of the Spouses	226
5.4	Cohabitation	226
5.5	Child Law	227
	5.5.1 Paternity Act 1975	227
	5.5.2 Adoption	229
	5.5.3 The Child Maintenance Act of 1975	231
	5.5.4 Child Custody and Right of Access Act 1983	234
	5.5.5 Child Welfare Act 1983	237
	5.5.6 The Guardianship Act	238
Bibliographical Essay		239

VIII Legal Procedure. By Antti Jokela ... 243

1.	Historical Overview	245
2.	The Principal Sources of Procedural Law	246
3.	The Foundation of Procedural Law	248
4.	Divisions of Procedural Law	249
5.	The Main Principles of Procedural Law	251
6.	The Finnish Court Organization	253
	6.1 The Foundations and the Division	253
	6.2 The General Lower Courts	254
	6.3 Appeal Courts	255
	6.4 The Supreme Court	256
	6.5 The Special Courts	257
7.	The Advocates	258
	7.1 The Use of an Attorney and Trial Counsel	258
	7.2 The Qualifications and Duties of an Advocate	259
	7.3 The Advocates' Duties and Their Supervision	260
	7.4 The Advocate's Fee	261
	7.5 General Legal Aid	261
8.	The Procedure in a Civil Case in the Lower Court	262
	8.1 The General Contents of the Lower Court Reform	262

	8.2	The Institution and Preparation of a Civil Action 262
	8.3	The Main Hearing 264
	8.4	The Minutes of the Proceedings and the Judgment 265
9.	The Processing of Non-contentious Civil Cases 266
10.	The Processing of Criminal Cases 267
	10.1	Preliminary Investigation and Coercive Means 267
	10.2	The Complainants, the Prosecutors and the Consideration of Charges 270
	10.3	The Regular Criminal Procedure 271
	10.4	The Reform of Lower Court Proceedings in Criminal Matters 273
	10.5	The Special Forms of the Criminal Procedure 275
11.	Appeal 275
12.	The Compensation of Litigation Expenses 278
	12.1	The Imposing of Expenses 278
	12.2	Liability to Recompensate in Civil Matters 278
	12.3	Liability to Provide Compensation in Criminal Matters 279
	12.4	Liability to Provide Compensation in Non-contentious Civil Cases 279
	12.5	Plans of Reform 280
13.	Cost-free Legal Proceedings 281
	13.1.	The Scope of Cost-free Legal Proceedings 281
	13.2	Persons Eligible for the Benefits and their Material Qualifications 282
	13.3	Applying for the Benefit and the Procedure 282
	13.4	The Appointment of a Counsellor 283
	13.5	The Relationship to General Legal Aid 283
14.	Arbitration 284
15.	Enforcement 287
	15.1	The Administrative Organization 287
	15.2	The Enforcement of Domestic Judgments 288
	15.3	The Enforcement of Foreign Judgments 289
16.	Bankruptcy Law and the Regulation of the Debtor's Insolvency 290
	16.1	Bankruptcy Procedure 290

		16.2	The Creditors' Order of Priority to Receive Payment 292

        16.2   The Creditors' Order of Priority to Receive
              Payment 292
        16.3   The Rearrangement of Private Persons' Debts 292
        16.4   The Reorganization of an Enterprise 293
    Bibliography 294

IX   Administrative Law. By Olli Mäenpää 295
     1.   Introduction 297
        1.1   Theoretical and Conceptual Evolution 297
        1.2   Sources of Administrative Law 299
     2.   Scope and Forms of Administrative Action 304
        2.1   The Duties of Public Administration and their
              Fulfillment 304
        2.2   Administrative Law Relationships 308
        2.3   The Use of Decision-making Power and Decision-
              making 309
     3.   Public Administration 312
        3.1. Structural Elements and Principles 312
        3.2. State Administration 312
        3.3   Municipal Administration 315
        3.4   Indirect Public Administration 321
        3.5   The Civil Service and Public Employment 321
     4.   Administrative Procedure 322
        4.1   Basic Principles of Administrative Procedure 322
        4.2   Scope and Application of Procedural Rules 324
        4.3   Grounds for Establishing Bias 325
        4.4   Preconditions for Taking the Case into
              Consideration 327
        4.5   Means of Investigation 329
        4.6   Administrative Decision: Formal Requirements 329
        4.7   Self-correction 330
     5.   Public Control of Administrative Activity 331
        5.1   Access to Administrative Documents 331
        5.2   General Control of Legality 335
        5.3   Legal Responsibility of Public Employees 337
     6.   Review of Administrative Action 337

		6.1	Administrative Appeal	338
		6.2	Special Legal Remedies	342
	Bibliography			344

X	Environmental Law. By Kari Kuusiniemi	345
	1. Environmental Law as a Legal Discipline	347
	1.1 The Development of Environmental Law in Finland	347
	1.2 Characteristics and Structure of Environmental Law	348
	2. General Background	349
	2.1 Development and Structure of Environmental Legislation	349
	2.2 Systems of Regulation	349
	2.3 Landowner's Position and the Environment	351
	2.4 Citizens' Influence and the *Locus Standi*	353
	3. Planning of the Use of the Environment	354
	3.1 Land Use Planning	354
	3.1.1 The Bases of the Planning System	354
	3.1.2 General Planning	355
	3.1.3 Detailed Planning	356
	3.1.4 Shore Area Planning	357
	3.1.5 The Authorities and the Procedure	358
	3.2 Sectoral Planning Affecting Land Use	359
	3.3 Environmental Impact Assessment	360
	4. Regulation of the Use of Natural Resources	362
	4.1 Nature Conservation	362
	4.2 Soil Excavation	365
	4.3 Water Management Projects	367
	4.4 Road Construction Projects	369
	4.4.1 Public Roads	369
	4.4.2 Private Roads	369
	5. Environmental Protection (Pollution Control)	370
	5.1 The Structure of the System	370
	5.2 Air Pollution Control	371
	5.2.1 The System of the Air Pollution Control Act	371
	5.2.2 The Control System According to the Public Health Act	373

		5.2.3 The Nuisance Rules of Neighbourhood Law 375

    5.3 Noise Abatement 376
    5.4 Water Pollution Control 377
    5.5 Waste Management 378
    5.6 Environmental Permit System 380
    5.7 Compensation for Environmental Damage 381
    5.8 The Impacts of EC Rules on Finnish Environmental Law 382
  Bibliographical Essay 385

XI Tax Law. By Timo Viherkenttä 387
  1. Introduction 389
  2. Income Taxation 390
    2.1 Background and General Structure 390
    2.2 Capital Income 393
        2.2.1 General Aspects 393
        2.2.2 Interest 393
        2.2.3 Dividends 394
        2.2.4 Capital Gains and Losses 395
        2.2.5 Interest Expenses 396
    2.3 Earned Income 398
    2.4 Taxes Payable 399
    2.5 Business Taxation 401
        2.5.1 The Calculation of Business Income 401
        2.5.2 The Division of Business Income into Earned Income and Capital Income 402
        2.5.3 Corporate Tax 404
    2.6 International Aspects of Income Taxation 404
        2.6.1 Residents and Non-Residents 404
        2.6.2 Tax Treaties 404
        2.6.3 The Taxation of Foreign Income 405
        2.6.4 The Taxation of Non-Residents 405
        2.6.5 The Arm's Length Rule for International Transactions 406
    2.7 Anti-Avoidance Clause 407
    2.8 Procedure and Appeals 407

3.	The Net Wealth Tax, the Inheritance and Gift Tax and the Property Tax	408
4.	Value-Added Tax	409
5.	Other Taxes and Levies	410
6.	Future Aspects	411

Preface

The aim of this book is to give for foreign readers a general description of certain central areas of Finnish law. This volume is not, however, a comprehensive book on Finnish law, and many areas, e.g. public and private international law, criminal law, and copyright law, were omitted in order to keep the book of manageable size. Each section included is aimed to be solid in the sense of giving the author's personal view on that field. Together these articles should provide a many-sided starting point for a more detailed study of Finnish law.

This book does not have direct predecessors. Some useful material, with the normal caveats concerning possible essential changes in legislation and other legal sources, can be found in "The Finnish Legal System" (Finnish Lawyers' Publishing Company: Helsinki 1985).

In the preparation of this volume, special thanks are due to Ms. Päivi Rotola-Pukkila for her technical assistance, and to Professor Henry Fullenwider for his contribution in the final revision of the manuscript. The greatest debt, of course, is to the authors of the essays included here; it is their ideas and analyses the reader will benefit from.

Rovaniemi, November 1993

The editor

I INTRODUCTION

By Aulis Aarnio

1. General View

Finland has been an independent and sovereign state since 1917. Before that, Finland first belonged to the Kingdom of Sweden for more than 650 years (1150–1809). A natural consequence of this was a strong cultural association with the Swedish intellectual life, and thus, all the Swedish laws were valid in Finland.

From 1809 to the achievement of full political independence in 1917, Finland had an autonomous position, as a Grand Duchy, in connection with Czarist Russia. This period of more than 100 years was the first real step towards independence. Finland received its own parliament, currency, basic education, and own legal institutions. However, old Swedish laws were still followed also in the Grand Duchy of Finland which was a rare, even an exceptional situation seen from an international point of view.

All this means that the Finnish legal culture has from the very beginning been deeply and profoundly Swedish coloured. The most important influences came naturally from the western mother country. On the other hand, also some features of the own and independent Finnish legal culture were to be seen from time to time. Quite many Finnish scholars, mainly theologians, studied in German universities and received thus directly the Central European, especially German impulses. Since 1640, Finland also had its own university in Turku having many contacts not only with the University of Uppsala but also with German and French universities.

One of the prominent figures of that time was Michael Wexionius (Gyldenstolpe after having been awarded a noble title). He was a theologian but also a legal philosopher who wrote several books on natural law and had influence not only in Finland but in Sweden as well.

In Sweden, old local traditions were the solid basis of written law. Already in the Middle Ages, Sweden received its first law books (some kind of codifications), separately for the towns and for the countryside. The common codification for the whole country, from 1734, was the oldest in the whole Europe. It continued the Swedish (Scandinavian) traditions in an important way. The reform work took closely 50 years and it was based on very careful and detailed discussions among the leading intellectuals, administrators and judges of the country. The language of the statutes is not only economic but also beautiful like the biblical language. No wonder that some parts of it have survived for more than 250 years.

In the beginning of the 1734 codification, there were printed the guidelines of the judges, collected by the reformer *Olaus Petri* in the middle of 16th century. These guidelines were an official part of the law book only for two years (1734–36) but after that (1736) they have been some kind of an introduction of the Swedish and Finnish law books. The guidelines contain elements from the old Roman Law, Jewish legal tradition, ius commune, as well as German and Swedish (Germanic) traditions. They tell, for their own part, which are the criteria of a good and moral judge and a good and moral law. In this very sense, they also give important hints of a classical Nordic conception of ideal law and of the ideal judge. The guidelines are therefore like a measure or standard expressing the deepest expectations of Nordic people what is law.

Despite of strong national traditions, the codification was not solely Swedish as far as its origins are concerned. During the catholic time (until 16th century) some traces of canonical law had influence on the Swedish courts. The most important factor was, however, the reception of Roman Law by the courts of Appeal in the 17th century. It opened routes for *ius commune* in Sweden and Finland, too. Thus, it is well founded to say that the old Finnish law since the beginning of 18th century was essentially an European law.

As it was earlier referred to, the codification of the year 1734 was followed in the Finnish courts also after 1809, that is during the period of autonomy. Some elements of it are even now formally valid, as is partially the case in in the real estate law.

However, an intensive reform activity began towards the end of the 19th century. It was possible because the Czar accepted to call the meeting of the Finnish parliament in 1863. This event opened a real and quite independent possibility for the legislative work in Finland although the Czar had a formal veto. He did not, however, use this veto during the most flourishing period of the Finnish autonomy, that is between 1863 and the beginning of the repression period at the turn of the century.

For example, the Marriage Act was enforced in 1889, the Act of Guardianship in 1892, and the Penal Code 1898. Many other reforms were ready to be realized. At that time, however, the hold of the Czarist government in Finland began to be very tight and the independent possibilities to direct basic legislation of Finland were diminished all the time. The period of the so-called Russianization began in Finland, and it was not over until 1917 when Finland, partially guaranteed by V. I. Lenin, received full independence (December 6, 1917).

After 1917, the next most intensive reform period in the Finnish legislation took place in the 1920s and the beginning of the 1930s, about 50 years after the first legislation period in the end of 19th century. Finland of that time was an agrarian country which began to industrialize quite rapidly. However, the dynamics of society let to wait itself until the years after World War II. The values and legal traditions in pre-war Finland were typical of an agrarian culture. Very few really modern reforms were realized. One exception is, however, the Marriage Act (1929) which followed the common Nordic lines and could also be called in its own time radically modern if compared to many European laws. The formal equality between the spouses was accepted, and in this sense, for example, the dissolution of the matrimonial property relations was organized so that the wife received better legal protection than before.

In general, however, the Finnish legal life was during the first half of this century more stable and more conservative than in other Nordic countries. Yet, the societal change and the economic growth in Finland after World War II belonged to the most rapid ones in the world. Agrarian Finland became a highly industrialized country in less than 30 years since 1945. Finally, Finland became one example of the Scandinavian Welfare States comparable in this very sense with Sweden, Denmark and Norway.

Especially the period since the 1960s has been labelled by the Nordic legislative co-operation, and the reform co-operation between Finland and Sweden has been so intensive that many central laws, such as the Marriage Act, central parts of contract and consumer laws, law of Estate and the Act of Inheritance are close to identical.

An important reason for this is the intensive immigration from Finland to Sweden especially in the 1960s when the economic situation of Sweden was clearly better than that of Finland. The rapid diminishing of agriculture pushed people from the northern and eastern Finland, first, to south of the country, and finally, to Sweden. Many of them married in Sweden, rooted in the Swedish culture and therefore there is a practical need to have similar laws in both countries.

However, also the very active economic co-operation and some common goals in the European market have been important reasons for the common legislation.

In this very respect, the modern Finnish law has as few really original features as had the legal order of the Swedish period. The reception of the Nordic and now especially of the ETA laws has made the Finnish law as well as the Finnish legal thinking a form of European law and thinking. The negotiations of receiving a membership status in EG do not thus mean radical changes in Finland as far as the central principles of law are concerned.

2. On the Legal Thinking

Hegelian philosophy achieved a reasonably firm hold in Finnish philosophy in the first half of the 19th century. This is rather surprising in view of the fact that the philosophical position Hegel sought to refute, namely the Kantian foundationalist approach to philosophy as a basic discipline centered in epistemology and underlying the sciences, actually never gained a significant footing in Finnish intellectual life in the early 19th century. Although the philosophy of law holds a rather important position in the Hegelian conception, Hegel's ideas did not have a permanent or even a significant effect on Finnish philosophy of *law*. This was the case even though the noteworthy Finnish philosopher and statesman, *Johan Wilhelm Snellman*, published in 1840 his principal and strongly Hegelian work on the philosophy of law, *Rättsläran* (The Doctrine of Law). Snellman's central role in strengthening Finnish national identity has been acknowledged to be incontestable, but his thoughts on the philosophy of law have not met with a sympathetic response among jurists. For example, *Rättsläran* was never accepted as a textbook in the Faculty of Law at the University of Helsinki, while Snellman's principal work in political theory, *Läran om staten* (The Doctrine of the State, 1842), was a mandatory textbook also for jurists till the end of the century.

Natural law had a greater influence in Finland than Hegelianism, although it cannot be regarded as having been a permanent major trend in Finnish philosophy of law, either. At that time, the theoretical frame of reference for legal thinking was something like a secularized natural law. This can be seen both in the requirements for a law degree, which included *Heinrich Ahren*'s famous exposition on natural law as mandatory reading, and in various treatises, for example in *Johan Philip Palmen*'s much-used *Juridisk Handbok* (The Legal Handbook).

As time went on, however, both Hegelianism and natural law were shunted aside. Various shades of the so-called conceptualist legal dogmatics (*Begriffsjurisprudenz*) gradually won ground. As is well known, the main idea in conceptualist legal dogmatics is to find out those conceptual categories that every legal order requires in order to be a legal order. The conceptualist tradition started by Puchta held that the task of legal systematics is to point out those "necessary relationships" that are carried into effect within the legal order. At the end of the 19th century, the leading representative of this trend in Finland was *Robert August Montgomery*, whose doctoral dissertation in 1870 on articles of incorporation already bore some signs of its influence. Later on, Montgomery, who was influenced by, among others, *Bernhard Windscheid*, published a treatise on civil law which was strongly marked by the tradition of conceptualist legal dogmatics. This treatise held a key position in all Finnish jurisprudence for a long time at the end of the 19th century.

Montgomery was certainly not the only scholar leaning favorably towards conceptualist legal dogmatics. For example, in 1878 *Robert Hermanson* published a profound treatise on conceptual structures in the law of the state. Also Hermanson had close ties to Germany; during the 1870s he studied under *Paul Laband*.

The explanation which the scholars representing conceptualist legal dogmatics gave to the question of why natural law was pushed aside is interesting. *Rabbe Axel Wrede*, who was a key figure in Finnish jurisprudence at the turn of the century and for several years on, emphasized the role of conceptualist legal dogmatics in mastering legal relationships which were becoming increasingly complex. Natural law could provide sufficient guidance in dealing with the simple problems of a static society. A complex societal situation, however, called for more advanced conceptual instruments, such as those offered by conceptualist legal dogmatics.

It is clear that in time also Finnish conceptualist legal dogmatics became the focus of the same type of re-evaluation as its German prototype. One of the most significant sources of this criticism was so-called interest jurisprudence. It is worth observing that *Rudolph Ihering's Der Kampf um' s Recht* was translated into Finnish already in 1902. This did not mean, however, that interest jurisprudence would have reached an official position in Finnish legal thinking. On the contrary, one could say that it served as a warning signal: the idea was to avoid the radical versions of conceptualist legal dogmatics. It has been said that, despite the voiced criticism, conceptualist legal dogmatics retained its position as a latent background theory in Finnish science of law up to the years following World War II.

The matter could perhaps be expressed by saying that interest jurisprudence and related schools primarily served as a background philosophy for legal policy, at the same time as they shed a light on the foundations of law and legal concepts. The methodology of legal research proper, on the other hand, was colored by conceptualist legal dogmatics and by its theoretical assumptions.

At the end of the 19th century and the beginning of this century, the atmosphere in Finland was indeed favorable for conceptualist legal dogmatics. The tendency, referred to in passing above, of emphasizing the autonomous position of Finland in relation to the centralist Russian state must first be remembered. Later on, it led to ever-strengthening attempts to break away. The repression of the Czarist government and the so-called Russianization attempts were resisted by appealing to the need to obey the law in all matters. One had to go by the rules of the game. This strong legalist spirit naturally brought with it a need for constructive thinking. Thus conceptualist legal dogmatics also came to serve the needs of politics and state. However, there were also other reasons for this tendency.

First, a specific feature of this time was the dissolution of the previously static society. This was connected with the strengthening of the position of the peasantry and the upspring of industrialization. Liberalism became the prevailing ideology. All this brought about the relatively rapid development of railways, mail services, telephone and telegraph connections, bank activity, and the like. This, in turn, initiated among other things the growth in the number of administrative offices. On the other hand, a powerful body of civil servants was of great importance in regard to the autonomous position of

Finland and the subsequent struggle for independence. Therefore, it is understandable that gradually a development began which strongly emphasized the study of law in higher learning.

The first half of the 20th century was also characterized by a politically shaded conflict between two language groups. A demand for the enlargement of the Finnish-speaking school system and university education was presented, in order to level off linguistic inequality. In these circumstances, also the strengthening of the Finnish national movement at the turn of the century improved the position of the academic and humanistic trend of education in higher learning. Moreover, the Finnish national movement adopted an anti-industrialist attitude, which in its turn gave rise to a reluctancy to advance technological and commercial education. As the rise of industry, for several reasons, did not take place in Finland until relatively late in the 20th century, humanistic and legal subjects retained their dominant position in higher learning for up to the 1930s.

Secondly, we cannot pass without mention the fact that the acute development of social conflicts at the turn of the century led to a civil war in 1918. After the war, many legislative measures directed at stabilizing social conditions were taken. This resulted in a universal emphasis on legality and was well in harmony with the line taken before this.

All this had far-reaching consequences in view of the teaching and the study of law. University education was mainly considered to lay the foundation for the performance of the traditional civil office duties. A degree in law was the key to government positions, making one qualified for legislative as well as administrative offices. In view of the content of teaching, this put the emphasis on teaching activities directly serving praxis. On the other hand, because university studies and research were always connected with teaching and *vice versa*, also research was clearly accentuated in the direction of the practical study of law.

The constructivist way of thinking was in keeping with conceptualist legal dogmatics somewhat loosened its grip at the turn of the century, but it seems to have regained a firm position after the 1918 Civil War. This was no doubt due to more than one reason, and obviously a legalist tendency again was one of the most significant of them. The legalization of social conditions required a strongly constructivist grip in research: given legal norms had to be interpreted and systematized. In other words, the content of the valid legal order had to be uncovered by means of research. It was German constructivist research employing exact legal concepts, which provided an excellent (technical) model as well as equipment for doing this. In some cases, the conceptual system of the German *Bürgerliches Gesetzbuch* even provided a systematic model.

In this phase, legal thinking was a means of working out the tasks and foundations of legal policy rather than a theory of research. The already mentioned fact that Ihering's famous book was translated into Finnish in 1902 shows us in which direction the key issue of legal philosophy at that time were deemed to lie. On the other hand, for instance the already emerging Scandinavian realism (the Uppsala philosophy) did not gain much attention from Finnish legal scholars except in some scattered cases.

It would be wrong, however, to consider the beginning of this century some sort of a vacuum in other legal thinking than the conceptualist one. The situation was quite the opposite; in the 19th century, for instance, a fertile discussion took place, rich in content, dealing with theoretically relevant problems of law and jurisprudence. In addition to the already mentioned prominent figures, for example, the following scholars took part in the discussion: *Robert Lagus, A. W. Boisman, Jakob Wilhelm Chydenius, and Allan Serlachius*. The debate continued on the arrival of this century, although not quite as forcefully as before. However, one should not overlook, for example, the writings of *F. O. Lilius*, published in the early years of this century.

During the first decades of the 20th century, the situation in legal thinking proper was in somewhat disarray. Although conceptualist legal dogmatics was still strongly present as the methodological frame of reference for legal research (legal dogmatics), it had no significant representatives in the field of jurisprudence. On the contrary, one could say that theoretical study had a reserved or a negative attitude towards conceptualist legal dogmatics and its background metaphysics of law. No common front in opposition to conceptualist legal dogmatics was formed, however. Finnish legal thinking, in the modern sense of the word, was in search of itself.

After World War II, the political constellation of Finnish society changed completely, and at the same time an unprecedented economic change began. The industrialization of the country proceeded far more rapidly than before, and this soon brought along its effects, that is, its usual compound phenomena such as urbanization, regional differentiation, organization, a rise in the level of education, and so on. This societal change relatively soon also gave rise to new problems to which the legal order had to respond. Not only did this result in a continuous increase and social widening in the application of statutory material, it also signified the fact that the need to reform the law was becoming more and more urgent also in traditional areas. Legal norms tailored for an earlier society could no longer solve the problems created by a changed social structure.

Perhaps this can also be put by saying that a lag occurred between legal provisions and the structural development of society. This remark needs a few qualifications. The intention is not to suggest that society mechanically proceeds from one state to another, irrespective of its cultural institutions and their influence. Neither can the lag in legal development be offhand closed by humans, since they cannot, by the means of legal regulations at their disposal, guide the development of society in the desired direction. Instead, the concept of lag is specifically intended to point out that law is one of the instruments by means of which, within certain limits, it is possible to guide and intervene in social development. In the course of the social change discussed above, the objective conditions of social planning had changed essentially. At the same time, the problems that legal provisions were to settle underwent a change. Now, the lag consisted of the fact that the juridico-technical tools practicable at earlier times were no longer sufficient to master the problem created by the altered situation. As this lag grew more severe, the pressure for changing the law naturally increased. As time went on, this pressure was relieved in the form of reform bills and new laws.

In a situation like this, there usually also emerge demands that research into the legal order should be directed in new ways. The more dynamic social change is, the more forceful attempts usually are made to reform legal research. Earlier objects and patterns of research are seen as unsatisfying, and previous answers are considered insufficient in the view of new problems and needs.

Simo Zitting, one of the pioneers of Finnish analytical legal theory, in his discussion of property rights observes that social factors are easily reflected in the position of the owner, especially the real-estate owner. For instance, when the limitations of property rights by public law increase, a growing pressure for reforming the concept of ownership itself emerges. In other words, the dynamics of social development posit new challenges for traditional patterns of legal thinking. Legal research in itself must undergo a renewal, and this implies a revision of its basic theoretical frame. Being clearly conscious of this, Zitting says that in a dynamic development phase of society "there is some reason to take a critical stand on the traditional concept of ownership".

The new line of thought had in fact begun much earlier: in the time before World War II. The German legal philosopher *Hans Fehr* had stated in his work *Recht und Wirklichkeit* (translated into Finnish as early as 1934) that as the static conception gives way to dynamic-functional view, there necessarily emerge new concepts, including a new concept of ownership. On the other hand, in Finland the effects of social development began to accumulate and be acutely felt only after the middle of the century. This accumulation, on its part, prepared the ground for the arrival of an essentially new way of thought. This alone, however, does not suffice to explain why this way of thought emerged in this very form, that is, as *analytical* legal dogmatics.

The main target of the criticism put forth by analytical legal theory was traditional legal dogmatics. The proponents of the analytical trend argued that constructive legal dogmatics, strongly influenced by the German tradition, was theoretically vacuous and unable to adequately meet the needs of the day. The tenor of this criticism is characteristically shown in two essential objectives of analytical legal theory. Irrespective of their mutual ranking of importance, they may be put as follows:

(a) Superfluous factors and elements that obstruct legal thinking must be eliminated as far as possible from the language of legal dogmatics. In particular, the essentialist speculations characteristic of German-influenced legal dogmatics must be obliterated;

(b) On the other hand, legal theory must be able to provide legal dogmatics with conceptual equipment exact enough to make it possible to grasp the internal dynamics of the legal system. Above all, the solving of problems aroused by trade was an important practical motive for this argument. As I have already said, questions related to trade naturally were not new as such, but earlier they had remained in the shade of the static conceptual frame in legal research. It was from now on that the problems of trade were considered truly significant, and their solution seemed to require an analytical examination of the problems.

3. The Nature of the Legal Order of Finland

Finland has a statutory law system, but the law has not been codified in the proper sense of the term (cf., the 'Code Civil' of France or the BGB of Germany). An 'Act of Parliament' is adopted when parliament approves a Government Bill for the act and the President of the Republic signs the law into force. The act enters into force (at the earliest) after it has been published in the Statutes of Finland. Most acts contain a provision specifying the date of entry into force.

According to the Constitution, the President of the Republic has the power to issue decrees on the implementation of acts. The Council of State has the power, in certain cases specified by law, to issue statutes ('decisions of the Council of State') that are to be followed as legal norms. Furthermore, either a statute or a decree may empower a lower authority, such as a county government or a municipal council, to enact by-laws binding the administrative sector in question of by-laws binding a local area. Statutes enacted in this manner are official sources of law. An example is municipal by-laws.

4. The Organization of the Judiciary

The Constitution of Finland is based on a tripartite division of powers (Constitution Act, Art. 2). Parliament and the President of the Republic exercise the legislative function, the Council of State and its subsidiary administrative structures exercise the judicial function. The independent courts consist of two separate branches, the general courts and the administrative courts. Each of these two court organizations has three levels.

The general courts are divided into the lower courts of general jurisdiction

– the district courts and the city courts, the six courts of appeal and the Supreme Court. The district courts, which operate in rural areas and in some urban areas, are chaired by a professional judge or by junior lawyers undergoing court training. In addition to the judicially trained chairman, the district courts have a lay board of at least seven laymen. The members of the lay board are selected for a four-year term by the municipal council, generally on political grounds. In both questions of law and questions of fact, the position of the lay board becomes the decision of the court if the lay board is unanimous. Otherwise the issue is determined by the chairman. It is very rare for the lay board unanimously to vote against the chairman and in this way decide the case. So-called non-contentious civil cases, such as the probating of a will, are decided by the chairman without the lay board.

Most towns and cities have a city court. The members of the city court are generally judicially trained judges although, primarily in small towns, laymen also may serve as members of the city court. The city court generally functions in divisions of three members each. Each division is chaired by a judicially trained judge.

Each court of appeal has a president and ordinary or extraordinary justices, as well as senior secretaries to prepare the cases for decision. All of them are judicially trained. The court of appeal is the first appellate level for decisions of the lower courts. In addition, the court of appeal hears appeals against decisions of the executor in chief (the county government and the city administrative court). The court of appeal is the court of first instance in cases involving treason or high treason, and in certain cases involving charges for an offence committed in office.

Most appeals are decided by the court of appeal as the final authority. This is due to the provisions limiting the right of appeal. The reform of these provisions in 1980 has considerably increased the efficiency of the system. Except where the court of appeal has considered the case in the first instance, a decision of the court of appeal can be appealed to the Supreme Court only if the latter grants leave to appeal.

Leave to appeal can be granted in three cases: (1) if the hearing of the appeal is important for other similar cases, or if the decision of the Supreme Court could be important in order to secure uniformity of legal practice; (2) if there are special grounds for granting leave to appeal because of a procedural or other error that has been made in the case; or (3) if there are other important grounds for granting leave to appeal. Land and water rights can be taken to the Supreme Court without leave to appeal.

As a result of the amendment of the law on the right of appeal, the position of the Supreme Court in guiding legal practice has strengthened, since it deals solely with matters that are important for legal practice and for due process. The granting of leave to appeal can be illustrated by the following figures. During 1989, the Supreme Court received a total of 2 630 applications for leave of appeal; of these 275 (12 per cent) were accepted. The lowest rate of acceptance (5 per cent) was for insurance cases. The figures show that more than eight cases out of ten in which leave to appeal is sought from the Supreme Court are left to stand on the basis of the decision of the court of appeal.

The amendment referred to above has made it possible to avoid the large backlog of cases that has weakened due process up to the 1980s. For example during 1979, the Supreme Court decided a total of 3 200 cases, but at the end of the year almost 6 000 cases were still waiting for a decision. At present there is no backlog, which has also improved the quality of the decisions and speeded up the hearing of the cases.

The Supreme Court has a president and at least 21 justices. The work of this court is usually carried out in divisions of five members, each chaired by the senior justice present. If the proposed decision is at odds with an earlier decision of the Supreme Court on a similar case, the case can be decided by a so-called enlarged division (11 members) or by a plenary session (so-called change of practice: *'Praxisveränderung'*).

Precedents are not legally binding in Finland, either horizontally or vertically, even though the Supreme Court, owing to its standing orders, may not go against an earlier precedent except on the basis of so-called qualified procedure. In cases where the law was ambiguous, lower court judges deciding against precedent are not guilty of misconduct in office.

In particular since the reform of the system of appeal in 1980, an attempt has been made to strengthen the role of the Supreme Court as a court of precedent. The intention is for decisions of the Supreme Court to be as binding as possible on lower courts. The head-note of a decision (a short description of the legal issue decided in the case) is taken to be an essential component of the guiding effect of the decision. In practice, the writing of the head-note requires the formulation of the legal norm(s) applied in the decision. We may speak of 'head-note norms' which, after the publication of the case, remain in force as independent legal guides. However, no system of sanctions in the proper sense has been adopted in cases where a lower court has deviated from a precedent.

The decisions of the Supreme Court are published both in separate annual reports and in the 'FINLEX' data bank. The data bank provides the possibility of obtaining up-to-date information on decisions through a terminal. The data bank is regularly used by judges, lawyers and legal scholars.

The Supreme Court has adopted a relatively conservative approach to the publication of decisions. The bulk of the decisions are not published, and can be read only in the archives of the Supreme Court. The published decisions are divided into two categories: (1) 'reports' which deal with decisions made in a plenary session as well as the decisions that the Supreme Court deems of particular significance, and (2) 'notes' which deal with the other decisions that are published. The decision regarding publication is made by the division that decided the case in question.

In administrative cases, a citizen who finds that the decision of an authority violates his or her right may appeal the decision as high as the Supreme Administrative Court, unless the law stipulates another avenue of appeal, such as to a Ministry, the Supreme Court of Office, the Rector of the University of Helsinki (for certain cases involving the University) or another authority. Decisions of senior administrative authorities, such as national boards, are subject to appeal either to the Council of State (in cases involving an appointment) or to the Supreme Administrative Court (in all other cases).

The first level of appeal for most decisions of lower administrative authorities is the county administrative court which, in administrative law matters, corresponds to the court of appeal. The county administrative court, for example, deals with all appeals in taxation cases. The normal channel of appeal from decisions of the county administrative court goes to the Supreme Administrative Court.

Restrictive provisions similar to those that apply to appeals to the Supreme Court do not apply to appeals to the Supreme Administrative Court. However, many acts prohibit appeals to the Supreme Administrative Court on the issues covered by the statute, thus easing its docket of cases. The Supreme Administrative Court hear about 6 500 appeals each year, over 40 per cent of which deal with taxation.

The Supreme Administrative Court has president and at least 13 justices. The cases are presented for decision by judicial secretaries and senior secretaries. Special experts may, on the basis of certain special provisions, participate in the hearing of a case as extraordinary members.

The competence of the Supreme Administrative Court is limited to questions of law. If the appeal concerns an issue that primarily requires consideration of questions of expediency (policy), the Supreme Administrative Court must transfer the case to the Council of State for decision. In practice, about one per cent of the appeals made to the Supreme Administrative Court are transferred to the Council of State. The decisions of the Supreme Administrative Court are published in accordance with the same principles as the decisions of the Supreme Court. However, in respect of the Supreme Administrative Court, there has not been the same discussion of the binding effect of decisions as there has been in respect to the Supreme Court. The decisions of the Supreme Administrative Court are not legally binding, although in many cases they have a binding effect as a practical matter.

The High Court of Impeachment deals, on the basis of Art. 59 of the Constitution Act, with charges raised against a member of the Council of State, a justice of the Supreme Court, or the Supreme Administrative Court, or the Chancellor of Justice for an offence in office. The president of the High Court of Impeachment is the president of the Supreme Court, and the members are the presidents of the Supreme Administrative Court and of three courts of appeal, a professor elected by the Faculty of Law of the University of Helsinki, and six persons elected by parliament. During the entire period the Constitution Act has been in force (some 70 years), the High Court of Impeachment has been convened only three times.

Finland does not have a separate constitutional court that would consider the constitutionality of an act of parliament or interpret the constitution. Responsibility for the constitutionality of acts is held not only by the President of the Republic but also by the Constitutional Committee of Parliament, which exercises advance control of constitutionality during the legislative process. If a legislative bill marks a break with the constitution, a special, qualified legislative procedure must be followed. In the absence of a specific provision to the contrary, not even the Supreme Court or the Supreme Administrative Court have been deemed to have the right to interpret the constitutionality of acts of parliament. However, the law states that the general courts and administrative authorities are responsible for deciding whether or not decrees and other lower regulations are compatible with acts of parliament.

5. Law in the Welfare State

5.1 A Finnish Point of View

The rule of law ideology has been widely accepted in Finland, and partially due to it, the Finnish jurisdiction has for decades been quite legalistic (formalistic) as to its nature. On the other hand, Finland can, on several criteria, be classified as one member of the Scandinavian Welfare States, and thus in Finland, one easily can see signs indicating the changing role of the rule of law ideology in the Welfare State.

The formal rule of law ideology is consisted, for example, of the following elements:

(A) The *separation of state powers* into three parts: the legislation, adjudication and the executive power. Furthermore, the rule of law stresses the necessity for clear *ex ante* legislation which regulates the use of coercive power. It is also commonly understood as the frame which sets the conditions for the proper *exercise* of legislative power and stipulates reasonable generality, clarity and consistency in the law. From the *judicial* point of view it is essential that all three powers ought – according to the doctrine – to be independent of each other. This principle gives to the judge that formal and independent position they ought to have in solving legal cases (competence, power, and also the obligation to give a solution);

(B) There is a special *legal profession* that is concentrated to take care of the legal issues in society. The origin of this profession can particularly be identified in the area of the rule of law as protection against absolute monarchism or, in general, against the legislative as well as executive power;

(C) The idea of *legal protection* became a core of the whole rule of law idea. An individual citizen has to be legally protected not only against another citizen but also against the state. From this idea also grows up the above-mentioned expectation for legal protection (or more specifically: expectation for legal certainty) among the citizens. The maximal realization of this expectation is an inviolable virtue of the rule of law state;

(D) Legal certainty, in its turn, is guaranteed, on the one hand, by the formal *discursive principles*, such as "Nullum crimen sine lege" (no crime without law). On the other hand, legal *procedure* itself is organized so that it gives a strong guarantee for an objective hearing of the case (cf., such principles as "Reformatio in peius" and "audiatur et altera pars");

(E) A certain structure of legal norms is also typical of a formal rule of law notion. The basic norm category is normally consisted of *rules*, either regulative ones (commands, prohibitions, permissions) or constitutive norms (for example, different kinds of competence norms). Legal *principles* are mainly understood as an "umbrella" that covers the system of rules. If there is a gap in the rule system, one can, by means of legal induction (or by using some other accepted methods), fill that gap with a norm inferred from a certain principle. However, the *role* of principles according to the rule of law ideology is subordinate to the rules. The principles are complementary to the rules;

(F) Also the *structure of the argumentation* is formal as to its nature. A legal decision is often described as a *syllogism* in which the conclusion can be deducted from two premises. The first one is normative, for example a statute, whereas the second premise refers to the facts of the case. The conclusion is inferred deductively from the premises (so-called subsumption);

In some extreme forms of syllogistic thinking, this formula is presented both as a heuristic (in the context of discovery) and as a justificatory formula (in the context of justification). Most often, however, the syllogism idea refers only to an *ex post* justification. The judge "clothes" his decision in a logical form when he writes down the justification (reasoning) of his solution. Nevertheless, the syllogism is typical exactly of a formalistic rule of law notion;

(G) Finally, the rule of law ideology emphasizes *formal justice* as the purpose of legal arrangements. The legal order does not guarantee the substantial equality or other substantial forms of justice. It takes into account only the formal side of legal phenomena, for example, the formal equality of spouses (cf., Kelsen's "pure theory of law").

In regard to this notion of the rule of law, all kinds of *formal* requisites are essential.

In his theory of European rationality, *Max Weber* often told about the materialization of law. Such being the case, all kinds of substantial criteria which begin to define the contents of the formal law destroy something essential in the very notion of law. This tendency is quite evident in the so-called Welfare State. On could even say that, at least, the Scandinavian Welfare States are school examples how the materialization of the rule of law idea functions. The minimum social security for everybody and a "good life" as the goal of social policy are essential (and necessary) elements of the Welfare State ideology.

That is the reason why the situation in all of the Scandinavian Welfare States is so illuminating as far as our them is concerned. *The separation of the state powers* has become blurred in many ways in such a Welfare State as, for example, Finland is. One of the most interesting phenomenon is the strengthened position of the executive power in relation to the legislator. Considering the state budget the legislator (the Parliament) often delegates some authority directly to the Departments of State without defining how this power should be used. This concerns cases when resources are given to a Department to be further allocated.

In Finland, there also exist problems in the relation between the legislator and the Supreme Court. The latter has taken more than before the role of a precedential court. From this it follows that the decisions are prospective guidelines to other (especially lower) courts. Furthermore, then the decision is no more a mere solution of a single case, as it ought to be according to the Finnish Constitution, but a general norm applicable to similar cases. The borderline between a solution of a concrete case and the general norm is blurred which means that the position of the legislator as a norm giver becomes – at least partially – problematic.

In the Welfare State, there is no longer a clearly identifiable *legal profession* for the application of law. Different kind of other professionals, like economists, sociologists, polititologists, and people who have an administrative education are responsible for such functions that earlier belonged to lawyers (jurists) only. These new groups do not have the legal education of the same quality as the lawyers have. This is a problem due to the changed law application situations (see (i) below).

On the other hand, also in the Welfare State important features of the formal rule of law idea are still valid. No one underestimates, let us say, the significance of the legal protection or of the general principles of legal certainty. As obvious is the necessity of court system applying the procedural rules as well as the possibility to appeal.

However, as far as our topic is concerned, the most remarkable changes, typical of the Welfare State, lie in the above mentioned points E, F, and G.

Here one really finds the true core of the materialization of law. Let us take two problems under consideration:

(i) First, the *structure of statutory norms* has been radically changed. The bulk of the legal order is still consisted of statutory rules as well as of the classical principles. In recent years, however, several other types of statutory norms have been placed on a par of the traditional ones. Some examples elucidate the situation:

- Especially in the field of social welfare, statutes which only define the *goals* (policies), not exactly the means, are used in the planning policy;
- The so-called *resource norms* give certain financial possibilities to the officials without exact prescriptions how the resources have to be allocated. Sometimes the resource norms have also some features of the policy norms;
- From the viewpoint of our theme, all kinds of *general clauses* and statutes of *open texture* are most interesting. They are typical of the Scandinavian Welfare States. By means of such "open" statutes, society tries to produce *material justice*. For example, the general clauses are one of the most important symptoms about the materialization of law.

The material (substantial) justice and reasonableness cannot always be reached by means of strict rules. On has to *weight and balance* different types of factors, for example, the interests of the parties. An elucidating example is § 36 in the Swedish and Finnish Act of Contracts. According to this statute, the court has the right to adjust the unreasonable terms of the contract. The statute means that the old Roman principle "Pacta sunt sevanda" (one has to keep the contract) is not unconditionally valid any more. It is sacrificed to the main goal of the Welfare State, that is to the protection of the weaker part. The other feature, worth mentioning here, is the strengthened role of so-called human rights due to the European Treaty of Human Rights, justified also in Finland in 1990. This means that the courts much more often than before have to deal with basic principles of the Constitution and the human rights manifested in them.

(ii) From the above-mentioned results that *thinking operation* cannot any more be simply a logical one. In the modern Welfare State, even in Finland, all kinds of *discursive* methods are becoming ever more relevant. Weighting and balancing is, as one might sat, *built in* the modern post-industrialized statutory interpretation.

The classical elements of the *formal* rule of law ideology have thus not at all disappeared in the development towards the materialized law. On the contrary, the core concepts and principles are in the full sense of the word valid also in the modern law. The forms and formalities are still *the* bond that keeps the elements of legal order together (as a whole). On the other hand, the materialization tendency has been so strong that some ideas, such as the idea of formal justice, have lost a great deal of their significance as bearing principles.

Hence, two distinct tendencies *meet* in the modern law: (a) the tendency to formal qualifications (as formal justice), and (b) material qualifications (as material justice and reasonableness), and the problem is how to *balance* them.

In many statutory law countries, as in Finland, the doctrine of the separation of powers leads to quite a closed judiciary system. The Supreme Court has a strong influence on the procedure where the judges are appointed. That procedure does not follow the normal democratic ways because, so goes the argument, the independence of the judges would be in danger.

The possibility to control the *content* of the decisions becomes thus extremely important. However, the only *means* to realize that kind of control is to open the decision to well-founded and coherent reasoning. That is why the court decisions *have to* be argued in a proper and public way, and why it also *is*, in a Welfare State type of a country, often argued according to these principles.

6. The Future Needs

In the Welfare State the theory of legal reasoning, especially the theory of legal decision-making, faces necessarily such demands that were unknown in the formal rule of law ideology. These new and challenging features are:

> (1) New standards for rational legal discourse: the standards of communicative rationality;
>
> (2) New discussions about the *substantial criteria* for reasonable decisions, which means new doctrine of the source of law, a deepened discussion on law and morality as well as further analysis of such crisis tendencies that can be identified in the legal orders of the Welfare States. They are, for example:
> - the complexity of the order;
> - the weakening of general doctrines (Allgemeine Lehre: in German), or more generally: the weakening role and significance of all kinds of forms and formalities;
> - excessive specialization of the legal profession and, as a result of all of these phenomena,
> - the possible alienation of ordinary people (who are not specialists) from the legal reality.

In the future, legal research cannot avoid to take into account changing features of the modern world such as these. Despite of the possibility that the Scandinavian Welfare States lose some traditional features due to the economic crisis, the Welfare State is also in the future an interesting challenge for the lawyers.

II CONSTITUTIONAL LAW AND HUMAN RIGHTS LAW

By Martin Scheinin

1. Four Distinctive Features of the Finnish Constitution

1.1 More than One Written Constitutional Document

Amongst present-day Western constitutions the Finnish one has at least four distinctive features. Representing the heritage of the period when Finland was part of the Kingdom of Sweden (until 1809) the Finnish Constitution is composed of more than one written enactment with constitutional status. Today, there are four Acts of Parliament including an explicit declaration of their constitutional status. They are the Constitution Act of 1919 (CA), the Parliament Act of 1928 (PA), the Ministerial Responsibility Act of 1922, and the Act on the High Court of Impeachment, also of 1922. Of these four enactments the Constitution Act covers most of the provisions usually included in written constitutions, namely the form of government, constitutional rights, distribution and definition of legislative, executive and judicial powers, state finance etc. The composition and election of Parliament and the procedure for enacting legislation is, however, stipulated in the Parliament Act. Therefore, also the procedure for amending the Constitution Act is prescribed in the Parliament Act (Section 67). In addition, the Parliament Act includes very detailed provisions on the internal organization and functioning of Parliament, matters that in most countries are covered by regulations of lower hierarchical status than constitutional enactments.

In addition to the four above-mentioned constitutional enactments the Act of the Autonomy of Åland (1991) has a quasi-constitutional status as it may be amended, explained, repealed or exceptions to it made only through the same procedure as is used for amending the Constitution and, in addition, with the consent of a two thirds majority of the Åland Legislative Assembly (Section 69).

1.2 A System of Exceptive Enactments

After the Swedish period, Finland became an autonomous grand-duchy within the Russian Empire (1809–1917). Finland was assured, among other features to be preserved, its own Constitution. According to the understanding of the Finns this meant that 17th and 18th century Swedish constitutional enactments remained in force in Finland through the Russian period. Finland had its own legislative body which gradually developed a procedure for enacting exceptions from the old Swedish constitutional documents without, however, amending their wording. What has resulted from this tradition is the system of exceptive enactments, the second distinctive feature of the Finnish Constitution. Both the Constitution Act (Section 95) and the Parliament Act (Section 94) include a provision on the possibility to make exceptions to these constitutional enactments, through the procedure prescribed for amending the Constitution itself. The legislator has the power to enact Acts of Parliament which clearly stand in conflict with the Constitution, provided that a sufficient qualified majority is reached.

1.3 Strong Presidential Powers

Also the third distinctive feature, the relatively strong position of the President, has its historical origins. When Finland, in 1917, declared its independence there were strong social and political controversies which in the winter of 1918 escalated to a civil war between the "Whites" and the "Reds" (socialists). After the victory of the former, a controversy between republicans and monarchists emerged among the victors. The defeat of Germany in World War I settled this controversy, as the German Prince Friedrich Karl, already elected King of Finland by Parliament, decided to withdraw. The 1919 Constitution Act became republican, but several features concerning the distribution of powers were maintained as they stood in the monarchist drafts. Therefore, the powers of the President are quite far-reaching compared to other West-European countries. Quite paradoxically, the fact that Finland became a republic and not a monarchy has to certain extent prevented or at least slowed down the process towards a clearly parliamentary system, a development well-known in West-European monarchies where executive power gradually has shifted from the monarch to the Cabinet, politically responsible to Parliament. Also the strong personalities and long terms of President J. K. Paasikivi (1946–1956) and President U. K. Kekkonen (1956–1982) have contributed to the fact that wide presidential powers, markedly in the sphere of foreign affairs, have remained a reality. During the term of President Mauno Koivisto (1982–1994), however, a shift towards parliamentarism is visible.

1.4 A Parliamentary System of Constitutionality Control

After World War II, judicial review of Acts of Parliament has become a regular feature of West-European constitutions. Also former East-European countries have established Constitutional Courts as a part of their efforts towards Rule of Law. Against these developments the absence of judicial review of Acts of Parliament, combined with the existence of a quasi-judicial body supervising the observance of the Constitution, is to be mentioned as the fourth, and final, distinctive feature of the Finnish Constitution. The prohibition for courts to examine the constitutionality of Acts of Parliament is derived from Section 92 of the Constitution Act, and it is closely linked to the above-explained system of exceptive enactments. As it is within the competence of Parliament to enact laws that are in conflict with the Constitution, provided that appropriate procedural rules are respected, the decision on the choice of procedure is understood as a matter decided by Parliament itself. In this decision-making Parliament's Committee for Constitutional Law has, as a political body, a unique role serving a quasi-judicial function.

2. The Structure of the Constitutional System

2.1 The Electoral System

Until the approval of the 1906 Parliament Act, Finland applied the old Swedish system of having a Diet composed of representatives of the four estates, altogether incorporating the political influence of a small minority only. The reform of 1906 was rather radical, as Finland with one leap adopted the system of unicameral Parliament, elected through universal suffrage extended to both men and women. This shift was, however, softened by far-reaching minority protection in enacting new laws. Even ordinary laws, not requiring the procedure for constitutional enactments, became subject to the right of one third of Parliament's members to hold a bill over the next parliamentary elections.

Since 1906, the electoral system has remained principally the same. Gradually, restrictions for the right to vote have been removed, and the voting age has been lowered. According to the present wording of 1928 PA, Section 6 (as amended in 1972), every citizen of Finland who has reached the age of eighteen years before the year of election is entitled to vote, except persons who have been convicted of electoral fraud or of disturbing electoral freedom by violence or threat.

The system of representation is based on direct and proportional elections within fourteen electoral districts, each having 7–30 seats corresponding their proportional share of inhabitants with Finnish citizenship. The Åland Islands, however, constitute an electoral district of their own, having one seat out of the total 200 in Parliament irrespective of their rather low population. The term of Parliament is four years. The electoral system places big political parties in a somewhat advantageous position compared to small ones as there is no system of equalizing seats on the basis of the total national vote.

Until the presidential elections of 1991, a system of indirect elections was used in electing the President. Citizens elected, through proportional elections, 300 electors who, in turn, elected the President with a majority of votes. In 1991, a system combining features of direct and indirect elections was used as citizens voted both for President and for electors. As President Koivisto did not quite achieve a majority of direct votes, the electors were needed to confirm his election for a new six-year term.

According to CA, Sections 23 to 23 b (as amended in 1991), the presidential elections will, beginning with the 1994 election, be direct, closely following the French model. Citizens vote for presidential candidates, and in case none of them achieves a majority, a new election is held between the two candidates who received the greatest number of votes in the first election.

2.2 Parliamentary Competencies and Procedures

Section 2 of the Constitution Act expresses both the doctrine of parliamentary supremacy and the doctrine of separation of powers. According to paragraph 1, sovereign power in Finland shall belong to the people, represented by Parliament convened in session. Paragraphs 2 to 4 then list the functions of the legislature, the executive and the judiciary, respectively. In paragraph 2, parliamentary supremacy is relativized by stipulating that legislative power shall be exercised by Parliament "in conjunction with the President of the Republic".

Irrespective of the last-quoted clause, Parliament has sovereign legislative power. The scope of matters falling within the sphere of legislation is decided by Parliament. All members of Parliament have the power to submit legislative bills (PA, Section 31), which may be approved by Parliament irrespective of the opinion of the Government. Parliament itself is responsible for choosing the appropriate legislative procedure and for supervising the constitutionality of Acts of Parliament. The President has the power not to ratify a bill passed by Parliament, but Parliament has the power to break the *veto* of the President by approving the same bill again in its next regular session, i.e., next year (CA, Section 19).

In practice, the role of the Government is strong in enacting new legislation. Usually laws are enacted on the basis of Government bills, prepared by the Cabinet and given to Parliament by the President (CA, Section 18). In the Committees of Parliament, Government bills have priority in relation to bills made by M.P.s (Procedure of Parliament, Section 18 b).

Parliament decides on the State budget, which does not require ratification by the President (CA, Section 66). The budget proposal is prepared by the Cabinet and submitted to Parliament by the President. Parliament formally has the power to make any amendments it wishes to the budget, but at least during Cabinets representing a parliamentary majority the opinion of the Cabinet is in practice decisive.

According to the main rule foreign relations are a matter of the President. Consent of Parliament is, however, needed for the President's ratification of treaties falling within the legislative sphere, and in certain other cases as well (CA, Section 33).

The principle of parliamentarism is expressed in Section 36 of the Constitution Act, according to which the members of the Cabinet (the Council of State) must enjoy the confidence of Parliament. This general clause is entrenched by the duty of a new Cabinet to present Parliament its programme (CA, Section 36 a, as inserted in 1991) and by the duty of the President to release a Cabinet or a Cabinet member from service if Parliament has expressed its lack of confidence (CA, Section 36 b, as inserted in 1991). The Parliament Act includes detailed stipulations on written and oral questions and other institutions aimed at enabling parliamentary control of the Cabinet and its members.

In addition to parliamentary political control, Parliament participates in the control of the legality of Cabinet members' actions. Complementing the functions of the Chancellor of Justice and the President, also Parliament has the possibility to institute charges against a Cabinet member in the High Court of Impeachment.

Non-legislative matters are decided by Parliament through majority vote. Previously, almost all types of legislation were subject to power of one-third of the members to hold a bill over the next elections. This rather unique phenomenon caused a need for obtaining a two-thirds majority for any stable Cabinet. It was abolished as late as in 1992 through an amendment of Section 66 of the Parliament Act. Therefore, most bills can now be approved through majority vote.

The qualified procedure for amending the Constitution or enacting exceptions to it remained, however, intact. According to Section 67 of the Parliament Act, there are two alternative procedures for amending the Constitution or enacting an exceptive Act. The main rule, as established in paragraph 1, is that such a bill must be approved by a majority of votes and then be left in abeyance until the first regular parliamentary session following an election. After the election the same bill must be approved by a decision that has received the support of no fewer than two thirds of the votes cast. Paragraph 2 stipulates an alternative procedure for "urgent" cases. According to it a constitutional amendment or an exceptive enactment may be approved without intervening elections, if it is declared urgent by five sixths of the votes casts and then immediately approved by two thirds of the votes cast.

Section 69, paragraph 1, of the Parliament Act prescribes a shortened constitutional procedure for the incorporation of international treaties conflicting with the Constitution. Neither a declaration of urgency nor elections are needed. Therefore, a treaty that is in conflict with the Constitution can be incorporated into Finnish law by a two-thirds majority. An identical procedure is available for temporary exceptive Acts that contain provisions for the supervision and regulation of the economy during severe disturbances in the national economy (PA, Section 67 a, as amended in 1992). So far, this possibility has never been resorted to.

2.3 Presidential Powers

As has been mentioned above, the powers of the Finnish President are wide in comparison to those contained in most Western constitutions. After consulting the Speaker of Parliament and parliamentary parties the president appoints the Prime Minister and the other members of the Cabinet (CA, Section 36). On the basis of a reasoned initiative by the Prime Minister and after consulting the Speaker of Parliament and parliamentary parties the President may dissolve Parliament by ordering new elections (CA, Section 27, paragraph 2). Government bills are proposed to Parliament by the President (CA, Section 18 and PA, Section 28), who also has the power to withdraw a Government bill (PA, Section 28, paragraph 2). Acts of Parliament must be ratified by the President before they can be published and enter into force. In case the President, however, refuses to ratify, Parliament has the power to approve the same bill again during its next regular session, in which case presidential ratification is not needed (CA, Section 19).

According to Section 33 of the Constitution Act the relations of Finland with foreign powers shall be governed by the President. The President is also Commander in Chief of the Armed Forces (CA, Section 30). He has the power to issue Decrees that include more detailed stipulations on the implementation of Acts of Parliament. A Decree shall not contain a provision that would effect an amendment to an Act of Parliament (CA, Section 28). The President appoints a great part of all public officials (CA, Sections 87 to 90).

The President is not politically responsible to Parliament for his decisions or other actions. Even the legal responsibility of the President is quite limited, as he can be charged, on the basis of unlawful acts in office, only with treason and high treason (CA, Section 47, paragraph 2).

In spite of recent constitutional amendments strengthening the position of Parliament and also of the Cabinet, acting under parliamentary responsibility to Parliament, the powers of the Finnish President remain a reality. Especially the President's strong role in foreign affairs and in the appointment of Cabinet members continues to demonstrate the importance of the Presidency as a powerful and independent State body.

2.4 The Cabinet and the Administration

The Cabinet (the Council of State) is responsible for preparing the matters decided by the President. An important limitation to the exercise of presidential powers is in Section 34 of the Constitution Act, requiring that the President makes his decisions "in the Council of State on the basis of a presentation by the competent Minister". This clause does not, however, mean that the President would not have the power to make another decision than the one presented by the Minister. Through recent amendments to the Constitution the role of the Prime Minister has been strengthened by making the President's possibility for action depend on the initiative of the Prime Minister in the dissolution of Parliament and the dismissal of a Cabinet member in other cases than lack of confidence by Parliament.

Independently of the President, the Cabinet has some norm-giving powers in the form of Decrees (CA, Section 28) and the power to appoint, mostly lower, public officials.

2.5 The Judiciary and Legality Control

Chapter V of the Constitution Act establishes the basic features of the court system. The Supreme Court exercises the highest jurisdiction in general legal proceedings and supervises the administration of justice (Section 53). In the field of administrative law the Supreme Administrative Court exercises the highest appellate jurisdiction (Section 56). The Presidents and Justices of these two Courts are appointed by the President of the Republic (Section 90). All judges are secured the right to remain in office (Section 91).

All courts, as well as administrative authorities, are, according to CA, Section 92, paragraph 2, under an obligation not to apply a Decree that is in conflict with the Constitution or another Act of Parliament. From this provision a prohibition for courts to examine the constitutionality of Acts of Parliament is derived. The role of courts of law in protecting constitutional rights is discussed later on in this essay.

In addition to the court system there are two institutions with general competence to supervise the legality of the actions of all public authorities, namely the Parliamentary Ombudsman and the Chancellor of Justice. The Ombudsman is elected by Parliament for four years, and each year he reports to Parliament (CA, Section 49). The Chancellor of Justice is appointed permanently by the President, but he reports annually to Parliament as well (CA, Sections 46 and 48). The Ombudsman and the Chancellor of Justice cannot issue punishments or repeal administrative decisions. They can, however, decide that criminal charges shall be instituted against public officials, in addition to expressing their opinion on the legality of certain acts or omissions and to initiating extraordinary remedies for the purpose of reversing an administrative or judicial decision.

2.6 Self-government

The Swedish-speaking Åland Islands enjoy a wide autonomy within the Finnish constitutional system. The 1991 Autonomy Act of Åland is not formally one of the constitutional enactments of Finland, even though its amendment or repeal has been made even more difficult than the repeal of the Constitution itself. An amendment to the Constitution Act, explicitly giving constitutional guarantees to the self-government of Åland, is pending in Parliament.

According to Section 51, paragraph 2, of the Constitution Act the administration of municipalities shall be based on self-government according to specific Acts of Parliament. Also the Lutheran Church (CA, Section 83, paragraph 1) and the University of Helsinki (CA, Section 77) are guaranteed self-government in the Constitution Act.

3. The Individual and the Constitution

3.1 Constitutional Rights in the 1919 Constitution Act

3.1.1 Contents

The Constitution Act of 1919 includes a separate chapter on the "General Rights and Legal Protection of Finnish Citizens". According to present-day comparative standards, it is a rather old-fashioned and limited catalogue of constitutional rights that mainly fall within the category of "negative" liberty rights.

The rights listed in CA, Chapter II include *equality before the law* (Section 5), *protection of life, honour, personal liberty and property* (Section 6, paragraph 1, complemented with a clause requiring full compensation in case of expropriation in paragraph 3), *protection of labour and the right to work* (Section 6, paragraph 2), *liberty of movement and freedom to choose one's residence* (Section 7), *freedom of religion and prohibition of discrimination based on religion or belief* (Sections 8 and 9), *freedom of expression, freedom of association and freedom of assembly* (Section 10), *privacy of the home and of postal, telegraph and telephone communications* (Sections 11 and 12), *the right to be judged by a court of law having legal jurisdiction* (Section 13) and *equal linguistic rights for Finnish-speaking and Swedish-speaking persons* (Section 14). In addition, Chapter II includes a prohibition for conferring titles of nobility or other hereditary dignity (Section 15) and a clause on the possibility to enact necessary restrictions to constitutional rights through ordinary Act of Parliament in times of war or rebellion (Section 16).

The provisions on constitutional rights are short and general. In most cases they include a clause, according to which the exercise of the right in question may be prescribed by Act of Parliament. Other Chapters of the Constitution Act complement Chapter II. The right to primary education free of charge, as well as features of some other cultural rights as well, are covered by Chapter VIII on education. Section 60 complements Section 13 with a prohibition of temporary courts. Similarly, Section 83 extends freedom of religion, Section 8, to the right to establish new religious communities. Section 61 defines the constitutional requirements for tax liability. Section 93, finally, secures every individual the right to sue a government official in case of damage or unlawful behaviour.

3.1.2 Citizenship

As a rule, the Constitution guarantees rights to Finnish citizens only. Ordinary laws and international human rights treaties have extended the exercise of most fundamental rights to foreigners as well. Nowadays this holds true for, e.g., freedom of expression, association and assembly, as well as for social rights and benefits. The right to vote and eligibility for Parliament (PA, Sections 6 and 7), the right to freely enter the country (CA, Section 7) and some areas of economic life, falling within the scope of the property clause in CA, Section 6, remain as rights of Finnish citizens. In some of these matters, citizens of other Nordic States or of EEA States receive preferential treatment in comparison to other non-citizens.

The rules on citizenship are set forth in CA, Section 4 and in the Citizenship Act of 1968. Everyone born of two Finnish citizens as parents, of a Finnish mother or of a Finnish father married to the child's mother becomes a Finnish citizen. In addition a child born in Finland and not becoming a citizen of another country becomes a Finnish citizen. A foreigner may be granted Finnish citizenship on the basis of an application, usually after living five years in Finland. Neither the Constitution nor the Citizenship Act establishes any ethnic or linguistic criteria for acquiring citizenship.

3.1.3 The Role of Parliament's Committee for Constitutional Law

The Finnish system of protection of constitutional rights is unique, and a source for continuous scholarship and debate. As was mentioned already in the introductory part of this essay, there is no system of judicial review of the constitutionality of Acts of Parliament. The task of protecting constitutional rights in relation to new legislation is entrusted to Parliament itself. The main bodies exercising this task are the Speaker of Parliament, authorized to refuse presenting for voting any matter contrary to the Constitution (PA, Section 80, paragraph 1), and, in particular, the Parliament's Committee for Constitutional Law.

According to the 1928 Parliament Act, the Committee for Constitutional Law has formally binding decision-making power only in the case of a conflict between Parliament and its Speaker (Section 80, paragraph 2). In addition, the Committee operates as one of the standing Committees of Parliament, submitting for consideration in the plenary its report on any matter sent to it by the plenary. The Committee for Constitutional Law exercises this task in matters relating to the enactment and amendment of constitutional enactments and other enactments with a close substantive connection with a constitutional enactment (PA, Section 46).

The unique role of the Committee for Constitutional Law in protecting constitutional rights, and other parts of the Constitution as well, relates to a third function of the Committee. In addition to deciding any conflicts between the plenary and its Speaker and to submitting reports to the plenary, the Committee issues *opinions* to other Committees of Parliament. These opinions, based on Section 18 a of the Procedure of Parliament, are generally understood as *de facto* binding, highly authoritative interpretations of the Constitution. In issuing such opinions the Committee for Constitutional Law, composed of M.P.s, i.e. politicians, operates as a quasi-judicial body.

In practice the system of parliamentary control of the constitutionality of new legislation operates as follows. If doubts concerning the constitutionality of a bill are raised in the media or in Parliament, Parliament sends the bill to one of its Committees, at the same time instructing this Committee to ask for an opinion by the Committee for Constitutional Law. The latter Committee invites experts on the substance of the bill in question, as well as experts on constitutional law, notably university professors to a hearing. After hearing experts, the Committee issues its opinion, through majority vote if necessary. The primary issue in these opinions is, whether the bill in question is in harmony with the Constitution and can be approved as an ordinary Act of Parliament, or whether the bill conflicts with the Constitution and can be approved only through the qualified procedure for enacting amendments or exceptions to the Constitution. In both cases the Committee may complement its conclusion with suggestions how to amend the bill in order to achieve better harmony with the Constitution or how to avoid an eventual conflict with the Constitution.

Previously, the right to property (CA, Section 6) has been by far the constitutional provision most often subjected to scrutiny by the Committee for Constitutional Law. Several hundred Acts of Parliament have been enacted as exceptions to the property clause in the Constitution Act, as the line of interpretation developed in the Committee's practice has been very strict by comparative standards. From the beginning of the 1970s, however, the Committee has gradually paid more attention to other constitutional rights as well.

There are several weak points in the system described. The control of the constitutionality of new laws is abstract and preventive in nature. The possibilities of experts and M.P.s to identify possible constitutional problems is therefore limited, and in the application of the law in concrete cases totally new problems might emerge. The actual parties of (future) constitutional controversies are not necessarily heard. The matter is submitted to the Committee for Constitutional Law by a majority vote, and the Committee expresses its opinion through majority vote, irrespective of the fact that these decisions are of great importance from the point of view of the need to achieve a qualified majority (5/6 or 2/3) in the plenary consideration. And of course the integrity of M.P.s in the exercise of a quasi-judicial function may be questioned.

Much has been written concerning these, and similar, problems. Still, the general understanding among Finnish constitutional law scholars is that the system is functioning relatively well. Parliament does not turn down, through majority vote, proposals to ask the opinion of the Committee for Constitutional Law. The members of the Committee try to base their judgement on the previous practice of the Committee, as systematized and interpreted by constitutional law professors heard as experts. And, as far as possible, the Committee refrains from voting on the constitutionality or unconstitutionality of a bill.

In recent years there have, however, occurred several instances of politically controversial matters becoming controversial also in constitutional terms. The number of bills sent to the Committee for Constitutional Law has grown, and in relatively many cases the Committee's opinion has been divided. Below, one of such issues is presented as an illustration.

3.1.4 The Right to Work

The right to work is so far the only social and economic right explicitly covered by Chapter II of the Constitution Act. Originally, Section 6, paragraph 2, of the CA was a general clause on the labour of the citizens enjoying "special protection of the State". In 1972, a new clause explicitly guaranteeing the right to work, was inserted: "If necessary, it shall be the duty of the State to provide a citizen of Finland with employment, unless otherwise prescribed by Act of Parliament". The amendment did not bring about any sudden factual changes. Unemployment seemed to continue its fluctuations, depending on the economy.

From the beginning of the 1980s, however, Parliament's Committee for Constitutional Law adopted a position of interpreting the clause on the right to work as binding, at least on the legislature and the Government. The Committee stated that the then-in-force Employment Act was not fully in harmony with the Constitution and emphasized the Government's obligation to prepare a new Act, securing the constitutional right to work. This position was emphasized by repeating it several times (see, in particular, the Committee's Report No. 10 of 1980, Opinion No. 4 of 1984 and Report No. 9 of 1985). In 1987, finally, a new Employment Act was enacted. It was based on the State's obligation to provide either work or unemployment benefits, and certain categories of unemployed persons were secured the right to a working-place. Such a subjective right to work was promised, after a specified period of unemployment, to persons belonging to groups whose possibilities to find employment within the labour market were considered limited, namely long-term unemployed and young persons.

During the favourable economic trends of the late 1980s the individual right to work seemed to function relatively well. Especially in the worst unemployment areas in Northern and Eastern Finland, a functioning machinery to provide temporary employment to persons belonging to the groups in question was created. The Committee for Constitutional Law continued to emphasize the binding character of CA, Section 6, paragraph 2, by deriving from it a constitutional prohibition to "go back" on the legislative and other measures introduced to implement it (see, Opinion No. 2 of 1987).

The deep recession in the beginning of the 1990s, however, brought a drastic change. The expenses of unemployment benefits and unemployment services exploded. The authorities in Southern areas were not prepared to cope with the obligation to provide work for people filling the criteria established in the Employment Act of 1987. As unemployment figures continued to grow, Parliament was, in 1992, presented a Government bill aimed at repealing the clauses on a subjective right to work in the Employment Act (Government bill 305 of 1992).

The Committee for Constitutional Law decided, after a vote closely corresponding the line between government and opposition parties, to capitulate in front of the factuality of an unparalleled economic recession. According to its opinion (No 32 of 1992), the clause on the right to work in CA, Section 6, paragraph 2, was "generally programmatic" and its obligations were more of "political" than of "juridically precise" nature. The Employment Act was amended through the normal legislative procedure, i.e., not as an exceptive Act.

The experience with CA, Section 6, paragraph 2, has been a source for serious critical remarks in the discussions on constitutional law in Finland. Some politicians, scholars and authorities have used the example as evidence of the fact that social and economic rights cannot or should not be guaranteed as genuine constitutional rights. Some others, including the present author, have taken the position that the experience in itself has given proof of the suitability of economic and social rights being constitutionally secured, but the existing system for protecting constitutional rights has suffered a great loss of its legitimacy.

3.1.5 Constitutional Rights in Courts

As was explained above, courts are in Finland not allowed to examine the constitutionality of Acts of Parliament. Even though the provisions in CA, Chapter II are understood as part of the legal order binding also judicial bodies, courts have been markedly cautious in making any mention of constitutional provisions in their rulings. It would, however, be wrong to assert that constitutional rights have been irrelevant for Finnish courts. This is mainly due to two factors.

Firstly, especially the Supreme Administrative Court has relatively often based its decision on the requirement of equality or the prohibition of discrimination, asserted also in CA, Section 5. Through its case law the Court has controlled the exercise of discretionary powers by administrative and municipal authorities. The cautiousness of the Court, in relation to the legislature, is illustrated by the fact that only in one of these approximately 50 cases has the Supreme Administrative Court explicitly referred to CA, Section 5 (case KHO 1979 I 4).

Secondly, the late 1970s and the 1980s indicate a gradual but real change in the judiciary's position of extreme restraint. When the Supreme Court in 1973 found three first-instance judges guilty of misconduct in office because they had treated two accomplices manifestly differently in sentencing, the Court made a reference to "the principle of equality" and not to CA, Section 5 (KKO 1973 II 73). Some ten years later, in a case relating to the position of illegitimate children, the Supreme Court explicitly based its ruling on CA, Section 5 (KKO 1984 II 95).

In the author's opinion the last-mentioned judgment is quite remarkable as the equality clause in the Constitution was applied *directly,* not only as an additional source of law affecting the *interpretation* of an ordinary Act of Parliament. This distinction relates to a scholarly debate within Finnish constitutional law on the proper role of constitutional rights in Finnish courts. Some authors, especially the late Paavo Kastari, then professor of constitutional law in the University of Helsinki and his successor, Mikael Hidén have spoken for a more active role of the courts in securing constitutional rights. Another school, represented, i.a., by Antero Jyränki, professor of constitutional law in the University of Turku, has defended the supremacy of the legislator and the primacy of Parliament's Committee for

Constitutional Law in the interpretation of the Constitution. Of younger scholars Veli-Pekka Viljanen has explicated a *constitution-oriented interpretation approach* in defending a position that courts are allowed to use constitutional provisions in their reasoning, the wording of an Act of Parliament, however, forming the limit for such use. The present author, in turn, has defended a *direct application approach* according to which the wording of an ordinary Act of Parliament should not form an absolute limit to the influence of constitutional provisions. According to this approach the prohibition for examining the constitutionality of Acts of Parliament is respected as long as the courts limit their reasoning to the circumstances of the concrete case and avoid any assessment on the competence of the legislature.

CA, section 6, paragraphs 1 and 3, on the right to property has been referred to by the Supreme Court in the case KKO 1979 II 28 and by the Supreme Administrative Court in the cases KHO 1975 II 53 and KHO 1982 I 2. Section 10, on freedom of expression, freedom of association, and freedom of assembly, has been invoked by the Supreme Administrative Court in the cases KHO 1974 II 31, KHO 1980 I 2, KHO 1982 II 2 and KHO 1982 II 6. Maybe the most important of these cases is the judgment KHO 1980 I 2, giving protection to the constitutional right to freedom of expression against the power of municipal authorities to subject street vendors of political publications to licensing.

A new change in the judiciary's attitude to the application of the provisions of CA, Chapter II seems to be emerging. In recent years references to CA, Chapter II seem to have, again, become almost nonexistent in the case law of the Supreme Court and the Supreme Administrative Court. *International human rights treaties* seem to provide the courts a less problematic source of fundamental rights, in relation to CA, Section 92, paragraph 2. This development is illustrated below.

3.2 International Human Rights Treaties

3.2.1 Ratifications

Finland is a State Party to most international human rights treaties, and in most cases the ratification has taken place without reservations. Due to reasons of foreign policy, Finland was, until early 1990s, a State Party to most United Nations and ILO conventions but not to the European Convention on Human Rights or the European Social Charter, two instruments open for Council of Europe members only. Below, a list of human rights treaties ratified by Finland is given, in chronological order based on the point of time when they were internationally opened for ratification.

Slavery Convention (1926, Finnish Treaty Series 27/27)
Forced Labour Convention (1930, ILO Convention No. 29, FTS 44/35)
Charter of the United Nations (1945, FTS 1/56)
Freedom of Association and Protection of the Right to Organize Convention (1948, ILO 87, FTS 45/49)
Convention on the Prevention and Punishment of the Crime of Genocide (1948, FTS 4–5/60)
Right to Organize and Collective Bargaining Convention (1949, ILO 98, FTS 32/51)
Geneva Convention for the Amelioration of the Condition of the Wounded and Sick in Armed Forces in the Field (1949, FTS 7–8/55)
Geneva Convention for the Amelioration of the Condition of the Wounded, Sick and Shipwrecked Members of the Armed Forces at Sea (1949, FTS 7–8/55)
Geneva Convention relative to the Treatment of Prisoners of War (1949, FTS 7–8/55)
Geneva Convention relative to the Protection of Civilian Persons in Time of War (1949, FTS 7–8/55)
Convention for the Suppression of the Traffic in Persons and of the Exploitation of the Prostitution of Others (1950, FTS 33/72)
European Convention on Human Rights (1950) and Protocols No. 1–8 (FTS 18–19/90)

Equal Remuneration Convention (1951, ILO 100, FTS 9/63)
Convention relating to the Status of Refugees (1951, FTS 77/68)
Convention on the Political Rights of Women (1953, FTS 30/58)
Protocol amending the Slavery Convention of 1926 (1953, FTS 8/54)
Convention relating to the Status of Stateless Persons (1954, FTS 80/68)
Supplementary Convention on the Abolition of Slavery, the Slave Trade, and Institutions and Practices Similar to Slavery (1956, FTS 17/59)
Convention on the Nationality of Married Women (1957, FTS 32/68)
Abolition of Forced Labour Convention (1957, ILO 105, FTS 17/60)
Discrimination (Employment and Occupation) Convention (1958, ILO 111, FTS 63/70)
Convention against Discrimination in Education (1960, FTS 59/71)
European Social Charter (1961, FTS 43–44/91)
Equality of Treatment (Social Security) Convention (1962, ILO 118, FTS 48/69)
Convention on Consent to Marriage, Minimum Age for Marriage and Registration of Marriages (1962, FTS 50/64)
Employment Policy Convention (1964, ILO 122, FTS 64/68)
Convention on the Elimination of All Forms of Racial Discrimination (1965, FTS 37/70)
International Covenant on Economic, Social and Cultural Rights (1966, FTS 6/76)
International Covenant on Civil and Political Rights, and (First) Optional Protocol (1966, FTS 7–8/76)
Protocol relating to the Status of Refugees (1967, FTS 78/68)
Protocol Additional to the Geneva Conventions of 1949 and relating to the Protection of Victims of International Armed Conflicts (1977, FTS 81–82/80)
Protocol Additional to the Geneva Conventions of 1949 and relating to the Protection of Victims of Non-International Armed Conflicts (1977, FTS 82/80)
Labour Relations (Public Service) Convention (1978, ILO 151, FTS 15/81)
Convention on the Elimination of All Forms of Discrimination against Women (1979, FTS 67–68/86)
Workers with Family Responsibilities Convention (1981, ILO 156, FTS 72/83)

Convention against Torture and Other Cruel, Inhuman or Degrading Treatment or Punishment (1984, FTS 59–60/89)
European Convention for the Prevention of Torture and Inhuman or Degrading Treatment or Punishment (1987, FTS 16–17/91)
Additional Protocol to the European Social Charter (1988, FTS 43/91 and 84/92)
Convention on the Rights of the Child (1989, FTS 59–60/91)
Second Optional Protocol to the International Covenant on Civil and Political Rights (1989, FTS 48–49/91)

3.2.2 Domestic Status

The Constitution does not give human rights treaties, or international treaties in general, any special status in relation to the domestic legal order. In the Finnish Constitution there is no priority clause, comparable to Article 94 in the Dutch Constitution. In comparison to other Nordic countries, however, the domestic status of international treaties is strong. Although Finland, similarly to Denmark, Norway and Sweden, basically applies the dualist doctrine concerning the relationship between domestic and international law, incorporation of international treaties has, since the early years of independence, been a standard practice in Finland. Therefore, the Finnish system, although basically dualistic, is described as "half-monistic" or as "*de facto* monism". A consequence of the standard practice of incorporation is that all the human rights treaties listed above are, in addition to being internationally binding in relation to Finland, also part of domestic law.

One distinction is, however, to be made. Only those international treaties that were, at the time of ratification, understood as falling "within the legislative sphere" (CA, Section 33, paragraph 1) have required the consent of Parliament and incorporation through an Act of Parliament (PA, Section 69 paragraph 1). Other treaties were incorporated through a Presidential Decree only, and hence they enjoy formally the hierarchical rank of Decrees within the domestic sphere. Since the mid-1980s incorporation through an Act of Parliament has become a regular feature in the ratification of all human rights treaties except ILO treaties, which are a special case. The list given above illustrates this distinction, because all treaties incorporated through an Act of Parliament have in the list two, usually consecutive FTS (Finnish Treaty Series) numbers, whereas treaties incorporated through Decrees only are identified with one FTS number. For example, the European Convention on Human Rights (ECHR), the European Social Charter and the UN Covenant on Civil and Political Rights (CCPR) all were incorporated through an Act of Parliament. According to the prevailing doctrinal understanding, confirmed by the Committee for Constitutional Law (Opinion No. 2 of 1990), normal rules of interpretation, including the *lex posterior* rule, are applicable in possible instances of conflict between international treaties incorporated through an Act of Parliament and other Acts of Parliament. According to the Committee, in the case of human rights treaties such rules must, however, be complemented with a rule of "human-rights-friendly" interpretation of domestic enactments.

3.2.3 Court Cases

The prohibition for courts to examine the constitutionality of Acts of Parliament, derived from CA, Section 92, does not relate to possible conflicts between international human rights treaties and domestic enactments. Therefore, the relatively strong formal status of international treaties within the Finnish legal system entails a possibility of international human rights treaties becoming the real "Bill of Rights", enforceable by courts of law. In this respect the situation of Finnish judges is similar to that of their Dutch colleagues, who have, in spite of Article 120 of the Dutch Constitution, prohibiting judicial review of Acts of Parliament, developed a rich case-law on the basis of international human rights treaties, especially the ECHR and the CCPR.[1]

It is, in fact, true that Finnish courts have, starting as late as in 1988, invoked international human rights treaties more and more often. The first cases were decided by the Supreme Administrative Court, which quashed an expulsion order on the basis of the 1967 Refugee Convention (KHO 1988 A 49) and examined an allegation of the cancellation of a passport being in

---

1 Concerning the Dutch development, see the article by P. van Dijk in Festschrift für Felix Ermacora, N. P. Engel Verlag, Kehl am Rhein 1988, pp. 631–649.

conflict with the CCPR, Article 12 (KHO 1988 A 48). After the ratification of the ECHR this instrument has become the most often cited human rights treaty. The provision most often invoked by the Supreme Administrative Court is article 8 on the right to family life, referred to especially in expulsion cases.

For the part of the Supreme Court, criminal procedure and Article 6 of the ECHR and Article 14 of the CCPR constitute the largest group of human rights cases. In one of the most recent of these cases (KKO 1993:19), the Supreme Court clearly stated that these two treaties are "part of the law of the land". In another recent case, not relating to criminal procedure, the Supreme Court relied on international human rights treaties in deviating from the actual wording of an Act of Parliament. A closer analysis of the case illustrates the differing present understandings of the judiciary's role in protecting constitutional and/or human rights.

3.2.4 Supreme Court Case KKO 1993:58

The case dealt with the establishment of paternity. As Mr A was married to Mrs B in 1975 when the child C was born, he was regarded as C's father on the basis of a legal presumption. Actually Mrs B had already in 1975 lived together with Mr D, and the couple was married in 1976, two months after A and B were divorced. In 1977, Mr D died.

There existed medical evidence, strongly suggesting the paternity of D. In 1990, A's paternity was nullified by a court. Because of the fact that C was born before the 1975 Paternity Act entered into force, the death of D precluded, according to the wording of the Implementing Act of the said Act, the possibility of instituting paternity proceedings. Such a conclusion would be problematic in light of several human rights treaty provisions, including those of non-discrimination, the right to family life and the child's right to know his or her parents.

The majority, President Olavi Heinonen together with two other Justices in the five-member Chamber of the Supreme Court, classified the problem as one of *interpretation.* According to them, a literal interpretation of the Implementing Act would cause "unjustified inequality". The *ratio legis* of the Act could be realised only by deviating from its wording, that is, by allowing C to institute court proceedings for the establishment of the paternity of the late D. According to the majority, such an interpretation was "in harmony with the principle illustrated by" Article 7 of the Convention of the Rights of the Child and with Articles 8 and 14 of the ECHR.

Supreme Court Justice Lauri Lehtimaja, *concurring,* first referred to the *ratio legis* and to the general equality clause in CA, Section 5. Then he made a reference to Articles 8, 6 and 14 of the ECHR and to Articles 7 and 8 of the Convention of the Rights of the Child, and continued: "On the basis of what has been said above and taking, in particular, into account the provisions of the above-mentioned conventions, falling within the legislative sphere and having been incorporated into domestic law through Acts of Parliament, Nos. 438 of 1990 and 1129 of 1991, which have been enacted later in time than the Implementing Act of the Paternity Act, I am of the opinion that Section 7, paragraph 2, of the Implementing Act of the Paternity Act, restricting action in cases of death [of the potential father] is inapplicable in the case of C".

Supreme Court Justice Per Lindholm, also *concurring,* would have decided the case without any reference to human rights treaties or to the CA. According to him the Implementing Act of the Paternity Act related to a certain transitory period and its Section 7, paragraph 2, was therefore not applicable in a case in which the preconditions for instituting paternity proceedings had emerged only after the Paternity Act had entered into force.

These three opinions, all coming to the same conclusion, indicate that the Supreme Court is perhaps unanimous in recognizing the need to comply with international human rights treaties but the Justices have differing opinions concerning the appropriate juridical construction needed for this end. Justice Lehtimaja followed a *"direct application approach"* and laid emphasis on the *lex posterior* rule. A similar direct applicability approach was, with less dramatic consequences, used in the above-mentioned case KKO 1993:19. The majority, headed by President Heinonen, resorted to the *"interpretative effect approach",* emphasizing neither the formal domestic status of human rights treaties nor the formalistic *lex posterior* rule. A similar approach was used also in the case KKO 1991:84, relating to criminal procedure.

One additional feature of the majority opinion deserves attention, namely the absence of references to the domestic Constitution. As explained above, in the late 1970s and the early 1980s the Supreme Court and the Supreme Administrative Court made references in some of their cases to the provisions in the Constitution Act. One of these previously mentioned cases, representing in the author's opinion, the direct applicability approach to *constitutional* rights, related to CA, Section 5 and the Implementing Act of the 1975 Paternity Act (KKO 1984 II 95). In this case, as well as in most other cases where the Supreme Court made a reference to CA, Chapter II, the Court was divided in the issue. In the new case (KKO 1993:58), only Justice Lehtimaja made a reference to CA, Section 5.

In the late 1980s and the early 1990s international human rights treaties have gradually received attention by Finnish courts, especially by the highest ones. An observation of the author, albeit based on the rather small empirical evidence of existing cases, is that the number of references to the Constitution seems to *decline* together with this trend. It is fully understandable that the doctrine concerning CA 92 makes it more problematic for judges to use constitutional rights in their argumentation than to use international human rights treaties. Therefore, the Dutch experience of human rights treaties, especially the ECHR, becoming "the real Bill of Rights" might become true for Finland, as well. Of course, a different path of development might be chosen through constitutional reform.

4. Revision of the Constitution

4.1 The Procedure

As was explained above, there are two alternative procedures for amending the Constitution. Either an amendment must be approved by two Parliaments, with intervening elections, and by a two-thirds majority in the latter one. Or, alternatively, the Constitution can be amended through an urgent procedure requiring a five-sixths majority in Parliament, without the need for new elections. Until the late 1970s political coalitions were rather unstable, and the term of Cabinets was less than one year on the average. This explains why the "slow" method of amending the Constitution was seldom used. The 5/6 requirement of the "fast" method, in turn, was not too high for often temporary exceptive enactments, but was more unlikely to be reached for the purpose of amending the Constitution itself. Until the late 1970s, the 1919 CA and the 1928 PA remained rather intact.

4.2 The Plan for a Total Reform

During the temporary Socialist majority in Parliament (1966–1970), a plan for a total revision of the Constitution was made. In 1970, a governmental commission was established for the purpose. The political tensions involved turned out to be too high, and by 1975 it had become clear that the project could not become successful. Still, the *1970 Constitution Commission* and the *Second Constitution Commission* of 1974 produced useful reports on various possibilities for constitutional reform, and later on these reports have become valuable sources for inspiration in the more piecemeal reform work.

4.3 The Strategy of Partial Amendments

In 1987, the first partial reform concerning presidential powers and the system for presidential elections was finalized. In the same connection the institution of consultative referendum was inserted as Section 22 a of the Constitution Act. In 1991, presidential powers and elections were, again, reformulated. On both occasions the intention has been to give citizens a more direct role in the election of the President, and to balance such a change with some mitigation of the comparatively wide presidential powers.

In 1991, Chapter VI of the Constitution Act, concerning State finances, was rewritten *in toto*. Amendments have also been made to the Parliament Act, concerning, e.g., the Committees of Parliament and the questioning hour.

Below, a table on the number of amendments to the 1919 Constitution Act and the 1906 and 1928 Parliament Acts is given. It illustrates the fact that, since late 1970s, amendments have become quite frequent in comparison to the earlier period when especially the Constitution Act remained almost intact.

period	1919 CA	1906/1928 PA
1918–1975 (58 years)	9	23
1976–1992 (17 years)	20	21

4.4 The Rights Reform Project

After several unsuccessful efforts to renew CA, Chapter II on constitutional rights, a Government commission chaired by Mr K. J. Lång, general director of the Prison Administration *and* the chairman of the Finnish League for Human Rights, was established in 1989. After two and a half years the commission presented its 482-page report, including for the first time via such reform efforts a comprehensive proposal for a "Bill of Rights", i.e. both a new catalogue of constitutional rights and provisions for its implementation. International human rights treaties served as an important source of inspiration for the commission. Compared to existing CA, Chapter II, two new substantial categories of rights were covered, namely the right to fair trial, extended to the right to good governance, and economic and social rights. For both extensions to the existing catalogue the influence of international human rights treaties is evident. Other rights, already traditionally covered by the CA, were defined in more precise terms than previously. The right to work, however, was worded more softly than in the existing Constitution, now explicitly approving vocational training and unemployment benefits as alternatives to work.

The commission did not propose a system of judicial review, i.e. authorizing the courts to examine the constitutionality of Acts of Parliament. But in another respect the proposal was quite far-reaching in relation to the 1919 CA. The commission proposed the abandonment of the system of exceptive Acts, not totally but in relation CA, Chapter II. Therefore, a clause on permissible limitations to be enacted through an Act of Parliament (proposed Section 16 a), as well as a derogation clause for states of emergency (proposed Section 16 b), were necessary. As a consequence, the normative force of the Constitution, in relation to the legislature, would have been strengthened.

At the moment the prospects for materializing this intention do not seem very favourable. Soon after the Government commission presented its report a new commission chaired by Supreme Administrative Court Justice Pekka Hallberg (who now has been nominated President of the Court) was established by the Ministry of Justice, apparently because of public criticism concerning the expenditure of new social and economic rights. The second commission came with a report including "softer" provisions on economic and social rights and a less ambitious reform to the implementation machinery. Draft Section 16 b on derogation during state of emergency was preserved, but the distinction between prohibited exceptions and admissible limitations was excluded by maintaining the system of exceptive Acts and by deleting draft Section 16 a on limitations.

Another structural feature of the rights reform, deserving attention in this connection, is constituted by direct references to international human rights treaties to be inserted to CA, Chapter II on constitutional rights. As a consequence, international human rights and domestic constitutional rights could become a more harmonious system. The report by the Lång commission included several such references, and the Hallberg commission maintained most of them. The Constitution Act would be complemented by a general clause on the duty of all public authorities to promote human rights and constitutional rights. Parliament's Committee for Constitutional Law, the Parliamentary Ombudsman and the Chancellor of Justice would be entrusted with the task of securing human and constitutional rights in performing their tasks, and the emergency clause would include a direct reference to Finland's international human rights obligations as one of the necessary conditions all emergency measures must meet.

A Government bill on the rights reform, based on the proposal by the Hallberg commission, is expected still during the year 1993.

4.5 Effects of European Integration

Finland has signed the Porto Agreement on the European Economic Area and is negotiating on a full membership in the European Community (or the European Union). Some constitutional consequences of the integration process are already visible.

Because of its system of exceptive enactments Finland does not necessarily need to amend its Constitution in order to delegate some of its sovereign powers to an international organization. The EEA Agreement or the EC Accession Agreement can be approved as exceptions to the Constitution by a two thirds majority in Parliament and without any amendments to the wording of the Constitution. Parliament already has approved such an exceptive enactment relating to the EEA Agreement. According to this Act – still awaiting official publication after the EEA Agreement itself enters into force – new rules of priority will be instituted for courts. Finnish judges are given the task to examine whether Finnish Acts of Parliament are in conflict with "sufficiently precise" EEA and EC rules and to decide not to apply a Finnish enactment in case a conflict is found.

Finland's participation in the European integration process puts the parliamentary system of constitutionality control into a new light. It is by no means a coincidence that Parliament, as it approved the exceptive Act on the EEA Agreement, simultaneously instructed the Government to prepare a report on the need for a system of examining the constitutionality of Acts of Parliament *ex post facto*.

European integration poses challenges also to the distribution of powers between Parliament, the President and the Cabinet. In connection to the EEA Agreement, an amendment to the Constitution Act and several amendments to the Parliament Act will be soon approved by Parliament in order to enable Parliamentary participation in the EEA decision-making structures already during the preparatory phases.

4.6 Further Reform of Presidential Powers

In April 1993, the Constitutional Drafting Commission, chaired by M.P. Paavo Nikula, presented its report with several new proposals for strengthening the role of Parliament through adjustments of presidential and executive powers. The role of Parliament would become crucial in the appointment of a Cabinet as Parliament would make three efforts to elect the Prime Minister through majority vote before the matter would be given to the hands of the President. The President's power to issue Decrees, as well as a great part of the President's power to appoint public officials would be transferred to the Cabinet, politically responsible to Parliament. In most of the matters that would still be decided by the President the role of the Cabinet would be strengthened by a clause according to which the President can only approve the proposal made by the Cabinet or return it to further preparation.

Another Constitutional Drafting Commission, chaired by Mr Seppo Tiitinen, General Secretary of Parliament, is at present considering the need for amendments concerning the distribution of powers in foreign affairs.

Bibliography

Constitutional Laws of Finland, Procedure of Parliament. Parliament of Finland, Ministry for Foreign Affairs, Ministry of Justice, Helsinki 1992.
The Finnish Parliament, Helsinki 1990 (see, in particular, the articles by Bengt Broms and Mikael Hidén)
Hannikainen, Lauri, Cultural, Linguistic and Educational Rights in the Åland Islands. An Analysis in International Law. Publications of the Advisory Board for International Human Rights Affairs, No. 5 (1992). (Includes an English translation of the 1991 Act of the Autonomy of Åland)
Hidén, Mikael, Constitutional Rights in the Legislative Process: the Finnish System of Advance Control of Legislation. Scandinavian Studies in Law 1973, pp. 97–125
Joutsamo, Kari, The Direct Effect of Treaty Provisions in Finnish Law. Nordisk Tidsskrift for International Rett 1983, No. 3–4, pp. 34–52
Jyränki, Antero, Constitutional Definition of Rights and Freedoms, in The New Constitutional Law, Editions Universitaires Fribourg Suisse, Fribourg, 1991, pp. 3–25
Kastari, Paavo, The Constitutional Protection of Fundamental Rights in Finland. Tulane Law Review 1960, pp. 695–710
Myntti, Kristian, The Protection of Persons Belonging to National Minorities in Finland. 2nd Revised Edition. Publications of the Advisory Board for International Human Rights Affairs, No. 2 (1992)
Sakslin, Maija (ed.), The Finnish Constitution in Transition. The Finnish Society of Constitutional Law, Tampere, 1991. (includes articles by

following scholars: Antero Jyränki, Teuvo Pohjolainen, Kaarlo Tuori, Martin Scheinin, Veli-Pekka Viljanen, Pekka Länsineva, Sami Manninen, Lars D. Eriksson, Kauko Sipponen and Olli Mäenpää)

Scheinin, Martin, English Summary in Ihmisoikeudet Suomen oikeudessa [Human Rights in Finnish Law]. Suomalainen Lakimiesyhdistys, Jyväskylä, 1991, pp. 349–364

Tuori, Kaarlo and Scheinin, Martin, Emergency Legislation in Finland. In Buure-Hägglund, Kaarina – Mattila, Heikki S. – Kilpeläinen Karla (eds.), The Finnish National Reports to the XIIIth Congress of the International Academy of Comparative Law, Helsinki 1990 (pp. 97–115)

Uotila, Jaakko (ed.), The Finnish Legal System. Finnish Lawyers Publishing Company, Helsinki 1966 (see, in particular, articles by Veli Merikoski, Paavo Kastari and Jan-Magnus Jansson)

Uotila, Jaakko (ed.), The Finnish Legal System. Second, completely revised edition. Finnish Lawyers Publishing Company, Mikkeli, 1985. (see, in particular, articles by Mikael Hidén, Jaakko Uotila and Jan-Magnus Jansson)

III CONTRACTS AND TORTS

By Juha Pöyhönen

Contracts

1. Introduction

There are several on-going discussions which give a picture of the background values in Finnish contract law. I refer to two of them. The first one is that concerning loyalty between the contractual – and even negotiating – parties. It shows the force of reliance thinking, and the way this principle has been developed into concrete rules. A party in a building contract possessing relevant knowledge has to inform the other party about significant things related to the latter's building work. Persons suffering damages must do their utmost to minimize these. In a contractual relation where the other party is weaker, this duty of loyalty is even stronger extending to include active information duties about the content and legal significance of clauses containing heavy obligations to the weaker party. This idea of reliance resembles to some extent those views laying emphasis on contracts more as a long term co-operation than a single and unique phenomenon between the parties.

The second discussion concerns adjustment. Up to the 1970's the problem of unfairness was dealt with in specific legal rules only in certain contract types, such as labour contract, sale-and-lease-back contracts, and in the law of bills of exchange. In the legal literature a discussion took place on whether the courts had a general authority to adjust every contract and not only contracts of these specific types. This discussion held to some extent in the shadow the more characteristic feature in the adjustment, i.e. that of seeing contract as an exchange of mutually reciprocal things or values. In Finnish contract law this tendency means an effort to avoid as far as possible results leading to the enforcement of unbalanced contracts. And the last resort for the courts today is the use of the adjustment clause now included in the Contracts Act (originally 1929, but amended in this respect 1983). Supreme court cases after the introduction of this sec. 36 show a clear tendency to see the application area of this principle as being rather wide, although the differing circumstances of those cases have meant that an adjustment in that specific case has not always been the end result. Under sec. 36 a court may set aside or modify a contract term, or the whole contract, if it is improper with regard to the contents of the contract, the circumstances of the formation of the contract, subsequent events, the characteristics and position of the parties, and other circumstances. The effort to keep the possibility of an adjustment open has been significant when comparing for example the use of unconscionability in English contract law, or 2-302 of the Uniform Commercial Code in various states of the United States of America. The nickname used for sec. 36, the "Big General Clause", should therefore be taken very much by the letter.

One *caveat* must be said, however. There is no such thing as a uniform Finnish contract law. There are different ways to see and read the legal sources, i.e. the short Contract Act and other legislation, supreme court cases, preparatory works for legislation, and consequential (sometimes called also realistic) arguments. Especially the habit of our supreme court not to give extended legal reasoning in its cases – even if the reasoning now is much more thorough than one decade ago – means that those different possibilities are very often open. And the label of an exception can be used now and then to countervene some decisions, which do not fit the observer's paradigm. This multiplicity of paradigms is a resource in the further development of contract law, especially when Finland is experiencing new pressures in connection with the European integration.

The different paradigms (contract theories) mean that the non-formal definitions of contract are different. Formally contractual obligations arise out of the meeting of two expressions of wills that are not essentially different. But the next question is of course how this formal definition is to be read. The will paradigm lays emphasis on the idea that the several parties have to know that they are representing their own individual wills, and tries to see the definition as exclusive in its reference to the wills of the parties. The reliance paradigm takes into account that the definition, as a working definition is easy to apply in easy cases but in need of further elaboration in hard cases. And this elaboration is then done in the light of the principle of reliance, very often concretely meaning that decisive significance is given to what the party knew or should have known. There is a famous dispute about "second parts" of certain sections, and whether these are exceptions, as the will theorists say, from the definition, or showing how the system works in more elaborated areas, as the reliance theorists say. For example if the two expressions are not identical, contractual obligations can still arise. For a will theorist this needs to be explained, and it is done either by saying that there was a silent will, or by defining these obligations as not really contractual but arising directly from the behaviour. For a reliance scholar this is a sign of the underlying significance of reliance, which is also present (but not needed) in the easy case but must be juridically worked through much more clearly in a difficult situation.

The idea of reliance is often combined with the general aim of contract as a legal institution to further the interests of exchange. One concrete doctrine which can be understood from that point of view is the legal evaluation of contractual damages. If a party suffers losses because of the contract (e.g. due to the breach of the other party), negligence is presumed, and damages have to paid to the suffering party if the other party cannot show the lack of negligence on its side. This arrangement clearly increases the use-value of contracts for economic activities because in practice it is the burden of proof that is often decisive in court cases.

The idea of balance refers to one further paradigm. Here the search for a definite threshold to divide the relations of the parties into fully non-contractual and fully contractual is seen as unnecessary. A contract is a process where the overall principle is that of respecting the reciprocity of the give-and-take, of the gains and the losses. Then the definition of contract referring to the expression of will, or in certain situations to the reasonable reliance of the other party, is only seen as an indirect easy-to-apply hunch in the legal construction of a balanced result. But if it can be shown that these *prima facie* criteria would lead to unbalanced results, a different solution can be based directly on the principle of reciprocity. The termination of a contract because of a breach by the other party has as a necessary requisite that the breach was essential. This can be seen as a concrete instance of the idea of reciprocity: only minor breaches do not entitle a party to terminate the contract but the breaches must be "in balance" with their consequences. The principle of balance is, as already mentioned, strongly at hand in situations where there is an inequality of the bargaining powers of the parties.

It is natural to start a description of Finnish contract law with the idea of freedom of contract. Although it is not formally stated in the Contracts Act it is clearly prevailing, and it is used as a background argument in court cases. There are formal definitions stating that this freedom means several "subfreedoms" such as the choice to make or not make a contract, freedom for the parties to determine the content of the contract, free choice of the form if no legislative restrictions are given (sale of real estates must be in writing, like consumer credit agreements, etc.), and free choice in respect of the type and variation of clauses used. A material analysis of this principle can lead to different directions, however. A will theorist emphasizes the connection to the use of free will, a reliance theorist sees no necessary conceptual link to will but a continuous scale of different ways to use one's freedom. A balance theorist would link the freedom more to the social nature of the institution used by the parties, and try to see the concrete contract as an instance where the social institution is used to further the positive freedom, i.e. freedom to realize some values and goals of the individuals.

To the three principles mentioned so far, freedom of contract, reliance (and loyalty), and balance, must be added a fourth one, the protection of the weaker party. One central aim in the contract law policy in Finland during the whole period after the Second World War is the protection of the weaker parties. This is connected, if not always directly, to the creation of the Nordic type of welfare state. Some new legal areas, such as consumer protection, with corresponding legislation, have emerged. The method of protection has been two-fold. On the one hand special state agencies have been established to survey, direct, and give decisions in the field. Normally these offices have a special duty to look for the interests of the weaker parties, and to give these parties advice and guidance if asked to. Good examples are the consumer ombudsman and the consumer complaint board, dealing with problems in the consumer area. On the other hand the relevant legislation in this area is usually mandatory in the sense that contract clauses depriving the weaker party any of his or her rights in any respect are void. Even the old institution of compulsory contracting (common callings) has its natural application area in consumer relations (post, telecommunications, heating, railways).

2. The Sources of Finnish Contract Law

Seen from the point of view of the sources of law I would characterize the Finnish contract law system as semi-continental. This system is continental in the sense of sharing a legal culture based on the idea of written laws, and thus a certain way of differentiating the characteristics of legal reasoning (e.g. through a doctrine of the sources of law where legislation is seen as the principal source). Even more, the content of the Finnish Contracts Act has been influenced especially by the German private law discussions and theories. On the other hand, the Finnish contract law system is only semi-continental because it lacks a comprehensive civil code in the sense of the German Bürgerliches Gesetzbuch or the French Code Civil. Important parts of private law are codified in several more or less independent acts, such as the Contracts Act, the Bill of Exchange Act, the Sale of Goods Act, etc. Other parts, and especially the general principles of private law, are uncodified. This has meant that the primacy of legislation has not had as central an effect on legal practice as in countries with a code. Another effect is that the role of court decisions as a source of law is more important.

One type of material presented as an argument in favour of certain interpretations may be seen in the preparatory works for the Contracts Act. This is a clear difference from the common law tradition, in which parliamentary discussion and committee work has had only a limited role. The preparatory works are reflecting a way of thinking which dates back to the beginning of this century. Therefore the role of other sources, especially court cases and realistic arguments (i.e. arguments concerning the consequences of a decision), but also academic literature, has become more prominent. For the later modifications of the Act, and especially for the introduction of the new general clause on unfairness one decade ago, the preparatory material is of central importance.

The hierarchy of legal sources is very informal, reflecting the generally low degree of formality in Finnish private law. There exists no binding rule that would establish an internal balance between different authoritative and substantive arguments in Finnish law apart from legislation, which is normally considered to be the primary source.

3. Offer and Acceptance

The first chapter of Contracts Act contains rules about offer and acceptance. They state that offers, and correspondingly also acceptances, are already binding, and not only contracts. Offers have to be sufficiently definite statement of terms so that an acceptance may be made without suggesting new terms. There are specific rules for situations which do not follow the simple model of the law. For example, the offeror must react if he or she gets an acceptance which is not identical to the offer but through which he or she realizes that the offeree thinks that a contract was concluded.

The Contracts Act does not contain any rules about contractual negotiations. In legal practice the idea that negotiations must be conducted in good faith has developed, meaning a duty to pay damages for certain expenses (restitution) if the negotiations are broken in bad faith, or are not used for the purpose of reaching a contract at all. Especially complicated long term contracts are made through different phases, such as preliminary negotiations, letters of intent, concrete negotiations, and signing the documents, with normal alterations during the activities. This seems to reflect an idea that the threshold no contract / contract is not as clear-cut as the rules of the Contracts Act presuppose. Binding elements, even some resembling those in a fully developed contract, emerge throughout these phases. Their concrete content cannot easily be defined in a court case, however.

In the formation of contract, but also in other respects, passivity can have significance. Passivity is also one of those institutions of Finnish contract law that have different meaning from different points of view. (Of course, these points of views are not only inventions of the theorists but sometimes clearly match with the facts of concrete cases as well.) A will theorist tries to see passivity as a silent will, a silent approval of the situation. If no such thing can even be constructed, or if the intentions of the party are contrary to an approval (a free rider in a tram), then passivity must be seen as an independent source of obligations. For a reliance theorist the systematization of passivity poses no great difficulties. If one party remains passive in some respect, and if the other party is acting in good faith, the effect of contractual obligations is natural and follows the general line of the emergence of such kind of obligations.

4. Interpretation of Contracts

Words, whether written or spoken, never fully express what is intended. Furthermore, the parties making a contract may well not have thought of certain matters which later prove to be relevant. Judges are therefore constantly faced with the task of deciding the rights of parties who have expressed themselves unclearly or incompletely. This process of determining the meaning of ambiguous or incomplete expression is governed by a number of unwritten rules to guide the court. These principles are laid down by the practice of Supreme Court in its cases. In the proposal for new amendments to the Contracts Act (1993) it was not thought appropriate to codify these principles, mainly because it would disturb the vulnerable balance between different principles of interpretation. Only some of them have a meaning clear cut enough to be written down as legal rules.

A difference on a general level is made between subjective (will based) and objective (reliance based) paradigms of interpretation. They lay emphasis on different sides of contract, or even more: they have a different concept of contract. The main idea of the subjective alternative is to see contract as a use of private autonomy and of free will, and consequently the aim of interpretation is to reconstruct the meeting of minds reached by the parties. The objective paradigm has its justification in the idea of reliance as a basis for contractual obligations. Language and expressions used in contracts must reflect this idea, and thus linguistic expressions should be given their common meaning.

Subjective paradigms of interpretation are often seen to lead to impractical results. Disputes arise just because the parties did not have common goals or ideas about the contract. Objective paradigms improve the usefulness of contract as an instrument for economic planning because they reduce the area which a contracting party has to find out about the other parties' aims. Expressions can be taken as they normally are understood without a need to find out possible specific meanings. If the objective line is followed a court procedure seems better suited as a means to decide on questions of evidence. One does not have to go through material where no objective evidence is normally possible, i.e. the state of mind and aims of an individual at a certain time, but the court can concentrate on evidence about the general meaning of expressions.

Although it is true to say that in Finnish contract law interpretation is based on a combination of both paradigms, the reasons just mentioned mean that this compromise is leaning towards the objective paradigm. Only such kind of subjective evidence about the state of mind and aims of the contracting party is allowed which the other party knew. This combination of different paradigms makes it understandable why Finnish law respects the principle *falsa demonstratio non nocet* even if it favours objective interpretation of contracts. If, but only if, both parties mean the same specific thing with an expression does it form the basis of their mutual contractual rights and duties.

Contract interpretation can in practice come very near the phenomenon of constructing, i.e. adding something new in the agreement. Principally the difference is clear. Constructing comes into question only if the contract does not contain a clause applicable to the dispute at hand. The arguments for constructing are derived from non-mandatory legislation, business practice, previous practice between the same parties and so forth.

The court will, however, pay attention not only to the actual words of the contract but also to the extrinsic circumstances. The interpretation of legal transactions is much less strictly bound by the letter of the transactions than is the case under English law. The court may refer to all the circumstances surrounding the making of the declaration. Words may have a very different meaning not only according to the context in which they are found but also according to the circumstances in which they are employed. A general point is that an interpretation in line with other expressions is to be favoured.

There are also such legal principles of interpretation which are not directly connected to language. Often the result of an interpretation is that some legal consequences are attached to the contract, affecting the position of the parties. In this situation the interpretation should respect the functionality of the contractual relation, seen also from the point of view of the effect of the consequences on the parties. Among different possibilities one should choose that one which furthers the common aims and goals of the contract. This results also from the more general principle of *favor contractus*. In interpretation one should avoid alternatives that are unjust or unreasonable towards either of the parties. If there is a continuing court practice on the question, that should not be neglected, and respect should also be given to legislation in an analogous area.

If the linguistic principles and the legal principles do not lead to an unambiguous result some supplementing rules are to be used. The rule *in dubio contra stipulatorem* means that the risk of an ambiguity in a contract clause is on the side of the party which drafted that clause. This favours the general aim of clarity in contracts by giving the sanction on that side which had better possibilities to avoid the unclarity. This rule is very strong in the field of standard form contracts (adhesion contracts) where a consumer always has a good case if he or she can show an ambiguity in the standard clauses used by the merchant. Elsewhere the supplementary nature of this rule means that it can be applied only if the application of the primary rules have not produced a result. A further supplementary rule is that which favours that alternative which is least onerous to the party obligated under the clause. One natural area for this rule are unilateral promises, such as gifts.

There is a range of a more technical type of rules for situations of internal tension between different parts of the same contract. The text is to be favoured over the headings, corrections over the original text, hand written clauses over printed clauses, important clauses over less important clauses and specific clauses over general clauses. If different contract documents would lead to different results, younger ones are to be preferred to older ones, documents concerning essential parts of the contract to those dealing with less essential parts, individual clauses to general clauses, and a detailed document to a general document.

5. The Invalidity of Contracts

The invalidity of a contract is traditionally conceived of as an "all-or-nothing" situation. It has not been considered possible that, for example, a buyer chose to elect for the contract to subsist and get the price reduced when an invalidity rule is applicable. This feature has been criticized in the contract law literature, and there have been even some cases where a contrary view has been argued for. The discussion has lost most of its significance because of the new big general clause, sec. 36, which expressly makes it possible to leave the contract in force while adjusting only some of the contract clauses.

When the invalidity rules in the third Chapter of the Contract Act were prepared, i.e. in the first three decades of this century, the possible background assumptions of contractual liability were normally centred around two of the theories or contract paradigms mentioned previously. The will theory was emphasizing the protection these rules would give to the free will of the parties. The adherents to this theory saw it as an important change in the old law that now, for example, an offeror could make use of many new types of claims related to the non-conformity with his or her actual will. These new rules could be understood actually as giving meaning to what is the proper use of freedom in contracting, e.g. that when duress was used against the offeror, his or her her will was not a real one, and not suitable as a basis of contractual liability. Those in favour of the reliance theory saw a breakthrough in the growing attention paid in the sections to the good faith demand on the side of the receiver of the expression of will. Very often the sections have a reference to the criterion of the receiver's bad faith as a necessary requisite for a successful claim from the innocent party. The reliance theory systematized this as a sign of a strengthening of the main rule of contract law, i.e. the protection of good faith and reliance.

5.1 Duress

28 § and 29 §

Sections 28 and 29 regulate situations where a contracting party was forced to contract. In the old system all contracts made through force were null and void. The Contracts Act made a significant change to previous law when it introduced an area of protection for a party acting in good faith. Thus, a distinction is made between the use of, or threatening with, physical force, and other types of force. When the contract came about by the use of physical force against the contracting party (I shall call him or her the innocent party) or by threatening with physical force the contracting party or anybody near to him or her, the contract is voidable even if the party knew nothing about the force and was thus acting in good faith. On the contrary, if the force in question was something less than physical force, a criteria of bad faith was set up. Bad faith means that the party knew, or at least should have known, that such force was being used by somebody else against the injured party. Otherwise, the contract is valid.

A detail which has received much theoretical attention is the requirement that even in the case of physical force there is a limited protection for the good faith of a contracting party. If the party is acting in good faith, meaning that it was not using or even aware of the force, the injured party has to give notice of the use of the force without undue delay after the use of force has ended. If this is not done the injured party may be bound to the contract as made. This is a radical change from the old law where rendering the contract null and void was the only possible consequence.

However, the Finnish legal academic literature of the 1950's developed a popular, and successful, analysis to break down the old classification of contracts into on the one hand totally valid contracts and on the other hand contracts which are null and void. It was based, being deeply influenced by some ideas of the analytical philosophy of concepts forming a part of Scandinavian Realism, on a distinction between three perspectives of invalidity. Firstly, a defect can have significance automatically and be recognized by a court without the need for a court ruling, or someone must react in some way (e.g. make a claim or bring about a case or give a notice to someone else) before the defect has any legal significance. Secondly, an invalidity may be definite and not curable at all, or it might be cured by some factor (the running of time, passivity, etc.). Thirdly, the invalidity may have consequences to all possible holders of rights, i.e. to both contract parties as well as to third parties, or it may be limited to certain persons. Now the null and void situation is seen as a combination of these three perspectives, where the invalidity is functioning automatically, is final, and effects all persons. And as is easily found in the text of the Contracts Act, the invalidity meant there demands a reaction, is curable, and is normally only applicable to the contract partner.

In English contract law there is one trend which does not seem to have a direct counterpart in Finnish contract law. I refer to the problem of economic duress. Principally, there is nothing in the Finnish statutes or in the preparatory works to prevent that kind of pressure labelled economic duress from having an impact on the legal evaluation of a case. In the academic discussion a supplementary requisite of unlawfulness is set up. This means that normally either the means or the aims have to be unlawful (but not strictly criminal). An example of the latter type, i.e. where aims make a contract voidable, is at hand if a contract party threatens to go to court to get some extra benefit, even if the claim as such is fully permitted and has a reasonable basis. In some exceptional cases a comparison between the means and the aims can lead to the result that their relation is considered to be unlawful. To threaten to force the other party to bankruptcy to get its shares (e.g. in a take-over situation) for a lower price is a kind of borderline case.

The topic of economic duress can be discussed under some other sections besides sec. 29. As is seen in the next pages, both sections 31 and 33 may be applicable in cases of economic duress, the former if the relationship is one of one-sided dependence or trust, and the latter if the stronger party does not give some information considered to be in those circumstances significant for the decision of the weaker party. And at least after the amendment of sec. 36 in 1983 the Finnish courts might see the problem of economic duress always in relation to the inequality of bargaining power. The effectiveness of at least some types of economic pressure seems to be based on the unequal division of economic resources etc. And normally, economic pressure is used in order to gain some benefits so that even if the unfairness reasoning demands some internal criteria, they are normally at hand as well so that sec. 36 is applicable.

5.2 Fraud

30 §

The paradigm case of fraud is when an innocent party is induced to make a contract because of some false information. In some extreme cases even the non-disclosure of information may be considered to constitute fraud, but normally the non-disclosure is systematized under sec. 33. The clear difference between the two sections is that fraud is at hand only if the party behaves fraudulently, i.e. intentionally or recklessly. There is also a criterion of causation: it must be the false information that induced the innocent party to make the contract. This criterion is eased by the division of the burden of proof, i.e. the fraudulent party is presumed to have caused the formation of the contract unless he or she cannot prove the opposite.

5.3 Undue Influence

31 §

Historically, the first form of this type of regulation was the rules against usury, i.e. excessive interest charged by money-lenders. It was the idea of the authors of the Contracts Act to widen this defence to cover all forms of misuse of a party's weak position. The criteria of sec. 31 can be divided into two. (i) Firstly, the stronger party must be shown to have taken undue advantage of the weaker party who is in a situation of distress, lack of understanding or experience, imprudence, or special relationship of dependence. These circumstances are to be understood subjectively. The court should place itself in the position of the innocent party, and try to imagine his or her own sense of the situation. An example used in the *travaux preparatoires* are young expectant heirs making bad bargains. In practice also salvage services rendered to a vessel in distress were mentioned as a type of contract suitable for evaluation on this ground. This section has been used in practice also in the cases of transactions between the solicitor and a client. (ii) Secondly, the contract must be internally appreciably unbalanced. This is usually understood to mean a significant difference between the parties' rights and duties in the context of the circumstances when the contract was made.

The behaviour of the stronger party must amount to a misuse of his or her position. In other words, the imbalance must be a result of the blameworthy behaviour of the stronger party. From the point of view of the innocent party, there must be a victimization.

5.4 Mistake

32 §

A basic distinction is made between mistake in motives and mistake in expression. There is no general relief for mistakes in those motives which led to the contract. Every one has to look after his or her own interest, and also to bear the responsibility of any inadequacy thereof.

There are two different lines of thought with different divisions of risk in the case of an expression mistake. In the first part of sec. 32 a mistaken party is bound if the other party acted in good faith. This section is not considered to be applicable if a party signs a contract with a different content than that expected. These problems must be dealt with not by the law of mistake but rather under the principles developed for the evaluation of standard clauses, or the principles of interpretation of contracts. The situations meant in the first part are for example cases where the party expresses himself or herself in a language or with technical terms he or she does not know well enough. And in these cases the expression mistake invalidates the contract only if the receiving party knew or should have known about the mistake.

The paradigm case of the second type of expression mistakes at the time the Contracts Act was written is a "wiring mistake". It means that the behaviour of neither party has any connection to the mistake. In these cases the offeror's real will is respected and no contract is formed. At the time the Contracts Act was drafted the wiring companies had limitation clauses. Therefore the division of risk was put totally on the receiver. The argument was that anyone who makes contracts through wiring or other type of indirect system takes a risk of technical and similar defects. The development of modern technology has not as such changed this line of reasoning. There is however a tendency to lay responsibility for any damages caused by technical and similar errors to the organization maintaining the system (e.g. a bank was liable on a paying mistake caused by a false account number given to it because the name of the receiver was correct and such a mistake should be detectable by a well-planned computer system).

5.5 The Small General Clause, Good Faith and Honesty

33 §

There was a discussion of the need for this kind of general clause in the third part of the Contracts Act. It was included in the Act to prevent the conclusion that the enacted invalidity rules would be an exhaustive list. Sec. 33 does not contain any direct reference to the will of a party. Therefore, from a theoretical perspective there are at least two different ways of reading it. A will theorist would claim it to be only an exceptional complementary provision to the main area where the will of the innocent party plays the major role. A scholar in favour of the reliance theory sees this section as unveiling a perspective which dominates the previous sections, i.e. the respect for a well-founded reliance.

According to its text, sec. 33 invalidates contracts made under such circumstances that an invoking of the contract would be contrary to good faith and honesty. There are some types of contract making that have caused a reaction by the courts based on this section. Firstly, those protected by the section have been very old people or people who have only a limited sense of understanding although they are not contractually incapable. Secondly, a clear duty of disclosure has been established through this section.

The focus of the reasoning must clearly be based on the circumstances when the contract was made. There must also be at least a possible knowledge by the other party about these circumstances. The evaluation of the dishonesty is an objective one, so no respect is given to the opinion of the other party.

In fact sec. 33 gives a limited amount of protection to the motives of contracting, an area of evaluation left out from the mistake institution. If one notices, or is supposed to have noticed, a misunderstanding of some sort by the innocent party, this misunderstanding must be corrected or else there is a risk of invalidity. On the whole, legal practice and even academic literature have been rather careful in the application of this section.

One discussion with a more theoretical flavour has been that about loyalty duties for contractual parties, as mentioned in the beginning. The connection with sec. 33 is somewhat indirect. The argument is that there are some loyalty duties between parties who have just entered in the contracting phase, the more reason for upholding these duties after the contract has been made.

Brief mention should be made of the fact that sec. 34 concerns a forgery contract, and sec. 35 the validity of a negotiable instrument or a receipt.

5.6 The Big General Clause, Unfair Contracts

36 §

The most significant single amendment to the Scandinavian Contracts Acts has been the almost total change of the old sec. 36 to a new one, which has been valid since 1983. The old section from 1929 provided for the possibility to adjust unfair penalty clauses, and typically a comparison was made between the amount of damages and the penalty.

Because of the very wide expressions used in the new clause there was some discussion whether the old invalidity rules, i.e. sections 28–33, should be altered or repealed. It was noted, however, that there was a difference in scope for judicial intervention under the new provision and that the application of the new section was also in some senses more demanding. It seemed that not all the cases which could be brought under some of the old sections would be unfair in the sense of sec. 36. As shown below, this results from the fact that no substantive element is present in some of the old sections, whereas substantial unfairness is a necessary condition when applying sec. 36. Actually, the real overlap was in the case of secs. 31 and 33. These sections were not changed or removed, and the main reason was because there was not a total overlap. There were also references made to the informative character of a code. In practice there are some signs of a move towards using the unconscionability section even when one of the older institutions of invalidity would also be applicable. This attitude can be criticized from the point of view of the problem-solving logic of sec. 36, which could benefit from making the old doctrines applicable to modern problems.

There is a kind of external structure of reasoning created by the adjustment section. This reasoning has seven phases:

(i) The preliminary phase. The binding force of the contract in question is decided upon. This is done according to the normal rules of the system, including the invalidity sections. A contract can be adjusted only if it is considered to be binding. This means that if the claimant is making reference to the old invalidity sections and also sec. 36, the court has to decide first the applicability of the old sections.

(ii) The imbalance of the contract. The possibility of adjustment exists, according to a specific statement in the *travaux preparatoires*, for the prevention of unfair contracts in the sense of unbalance. Therefore, in a case where the party claims adjustment, he or she must show that the contract is unbalanced, i.e. the party is paying for more than he or she is getting. For the court this is a problem of relative measuring from the notion of just price, normally the price-level or the so-called dispositive norms of law (i.e. in the case of exclusion clauses). Adjustment is impossible without the unbalance of the contract.

(iii) The reason for the imbalance. As a necessary condition for the adjustment clause, the imbalance must be caused by a factor which is considered relevant in contractual matters. These factors vary, but can generally be said to adhere to something generally known to have significance in contract law reasoning. Thus one group of reasons is those having characteristics similiar to the circumstances mentioned in the specific invalidity sections. The strength of the cause for imbalance need not, however, be strong enough to make the contract void or voidable. The cause must only have some similarity to the regulation of void or voidable contracts. One possible explanation could be that the party shows that it was in a take-it-or-leave-it situation. Another type of explanation would be to show that the other party was in a superior bargaining position. Other factors than imbalance get their values, or weight, through contractual principles. Therefore, this phase can be described through other institutions and doctrines of contract law. The logic of adjustment in relation to these other institutions can be characterized as an "almost-logic". Adjustment is possible even if the conditions of these other institutions are not fulfilled, but in circumstances where they are almost fulfilled. Only exceptionally is the adjustment claimed for in a situation where the party could claim the contract avoided. Normally the facts of an adjustment case do not give enough arguments for the total ineffectiveness of the contract or the section in question but would only, to some extent, support such a claim. In this situation adjustment is possible.

(v) The overall evaluation of unconscionability. In this phase the weight of arguments supporting and opposing the adjustment claim are considered as a whole. The results of the first and third phase are summed up. The final result can be called the unconscionable value of the contract.

(vi) The comparison of the unconscionable value to the adjustment threshold. The *travaux preparatoires* of the amendment are not very clear in this matter. However, it seems that some kind of threshold must exist in order to keep the system workable. Thus, the adjustment threshold is the result of the value given to formal legal rules of contract law. Every deviation from them has an initial negative weight. Therefore, the unconscionable value must be higher than this threshold. Otherwise adjustment is not possible.

(vii) The effects of the adjustment. According to sec. 36, there are four possible types of adjustment. Firstly, only the unreasonable clause can be changed. Secondly, that clause can be considered as totally ineffective. Thirdly, another clause of the same contract can be changed and, fourthly, the whole contract can be declared void. The general assumption still held in Finnish contract law is the old idea of *favor contractus*. This idea means that the last way of reaction is to be used only after careful consideration, and where another kind of consequence would not be able to bring about a fair contract. The court practice in all the Scandinavian countries is also in accordance with that principle, and the normal way to adjust has been to change the unfair term to comply better with the dispositive rules or normal prices (although the adjustments have rarely been exhaustive in the sense of trying to reach full compliance of the contracted price and the normal price), or when a change is not possible, to leave the term unapplied.

The basic idea in the preparatory works was that adjustment should always be possible if not explicitly forbidden. It is only forbidden in cases of wages, the argument being a somewhat naive supposition that the system of collective agreements will take care of the fairness issues, including wages, in labour relations. In addition to wages, there seems to be also some other types of contracts and clauses where adjustment does not seem to be possible. Firstly, there are, of course, many relations that are not contractual by nature. The more detailed analysis would lead us to the question of the privity of contract. Although I cannot develop the theme here, I want to remark that some legislative decisions, e.g. in the area of responsibility for marketing information, as well as some court cases open perspectives to rethink the somewhat rigid and formal understanding of the concept of contract. Another example of relations based on the by-laws of companies (or articles of association) are in this sense problematic but have been seen as possible targets for adjustment. There are also areas of "contracting" with authorities included in the application area of adjustment, such as hunting licenses. Secondly, there are situations that lack a measure for unconscionability. Two specific cases of wages and rents can be mentioned. Unconscionability can be controlled by the special rules of the validity of such a contract or clause so that only reasonable contracts are valid. They have a system of their own for the control of fairness. It is also possible that there is no measure for imbalance, as in gifts.

Sec. 36 can be read as containing another legal rule in addition to adjustment on a basis of an overall evaluation of the contract. Namely the text makes a difference between contracts and terms that are (*per se*) unfair and those ones where the unfairness is related to their application. The former situation means that a clause or the whole contract is void because of its type-unconscionability. This evaluation is made on the level of typicality, and reminds one of the distinction in the German Law on Standard Contract Terms 1977 between (a) void conditions which are unfairly prejudicial in any type of contract and (b) conditions, where a test of reasonableness is to be applied. But it is based on reasoning characterized as fairness as balance. Type-unconscionability means the average imbalance of the contract or the clause. Therefore, this rule raises substantial questions about how this rule can be systematized as a part of the contract law system. Taking the average balance as the decisive criterium for contractual responsibilities is a challenge for the will or reliance paradigms. These paradigms cannot easily combine any kind of direct contentual, or material, evaluation of (possible) contractual relations with their ideas of overreaching significance of free will or reliance. Thus, type-unconscionability based directly on a material evaluation of the situation can give rise to discussions leading towards a new paradigm having reciprocity and balance as basic starting points instead of will or reliance.

There are some invalidity rules not included in the Contracts Act. The most important ones are rules invalidating unlawful contracts or contracts against "*bonnes mores*" (e.g. clauses concluded for the sole purpose of avoiding taxes) and rules concerning incapacity. From a systematical point of view the difference between common law and Scandinavian thinking is that (traditionally) minor age makes a contract null and void, and the possible duties of the minor in such situations are based on specific legislation. The results in practice seem to differ very little, because of exceptions enabling minors to enter ordinary small contracts but not to take on debt. For example, hire-purchase contracts with minors are invalid but cash sales of necessities normally lead to full responsibility. Even in cases of invalidity, damages must be paid if the goods were used for the benefit of the minor.

6. Specific Areas of Contract Law

6.1 Agency

The Contract Act contains a second chapter dealing with agency. Its basic solutions are similar to those in the continental systems. An agent is somebody acting on behalf of his or her principal with the authority of the latter, and the contractual relation is created between the third party and the principal. If the agent exceeds his or her competence, e.g. sells another piece of the principal's property that he or she was supposed to, no obligations are created to the principal. If the agent, however, only sells the property cheaper than agreed upon with principal, the latter is bound to the contract. There is specific legislation in certain important areas such as in contracts concluded with insurance agents and sales agents.

6.2 Consumer Contracts

Consumer contracts are normally regulated by mandatory rules. The parties cannot exclude their application. These rules also contain many restrictions for a termination of contract. The acquisition of a merchandise for recreational purposes does not as such exclude the application of the Consumer Protection Act (1978). There have been opinions in the legal literature that the principles of that act should also find application when contracts are made between big companies and small firms.

6.3 Standard Form Contracts

Standard form contracts are in Finnish scholarly writings defined as contracts in which one party, who is, e.g. because of a monopoly situation, or where a branch organization has unilaterally made the formula, the strongest, fixes in a unilateral way the content of the contract, so that the other party, if it really wants to enter the contract, can only adhere to the proposed clauses. There is no separate act on standard form contracts but the legal practice has developed some specific rules applicable to these types of contracts, e.g. concerning the validity of such clauses, and their interpretation (e.g. interpretation against that party who drafted the clause, i.e. the rule of *in dubio contra proferentem*.

6.4 Commercial Law and Civil Law

Finnish private law does not contain a clear-cut distinction between civil law and commercial law. Commercial transactions are only to some extent governed by special legislation, such as the Sale of Goods Act (1987). There are no special commercial courts. The general principles, concerning e.g. the formation and interpretation of contracts, are applicable in contracts made in various areas. The Contracts Act is applied in private and commercial contracts alike.

Torts

1. General Overview

The rules for paying damages were until 1974 only included in the Criminal Code. This old connection is one reason for the fact that even today some questions of criminal law and tort law fall under same type of legal analysis, e.g. intentional and negligent acts, and the problem of causality. The Act of Damages (1974), like the whole tort system, has two basic functions: restitution and prevention. Restitution should correct the harmful effects of the party suffering losses. That party should have compensation for personal injury or damages to his or her property. The preventive function means that individuals and companies are more careful when dealing with other parties when they act under the threat of a duty to compensate damages their activity causes for third parties. In situations where strict liability is applied the aims of regulation function so that it tends to discourage dangerous activities while not entirely prohibiting any social benefit they may have.

One idea of the welfare state was that the community (state or municipality) has to take responsibility for providing basic security to every citizen. This is one of the background reasons why the level of compensation in Finland for personal injuries is seen internationally as being rather low. The welfare state system was also fulfilled through obligatory insurance, e.g. to cover the working accidents or traffic accidents. To be insured is often better for the party suffering losses because he or she can apply for compensation from a solvent company. Also from the point of view of the parties causing damages, the possibility to avoid unexpectedly high compensations is of value. Contractual damages are to some extent regulated by their own principles, especially when we speak of economic losses, and the burden of proof.

For these reasons the core area of torts is limited. Its significance is indirect, meaning that if no specific rules or regulations are found it is applicable. This character applies also to contractual damages although a clear rule of application in the Act of Damages states that it applies only to non-contractual situations.

There are some development tendencies in the Finnish law of obligation, e.g. contracts and torts, which I want to emphasize. In the beginning of this century it was common to stick very strictly to the written word and to require the fulfillment of contractual obligations with the utmost harshness. This feature changed through the development of rules favouring the weaker party, first in specific legislation and then also in the Contracts Act. In tort law there has been a tendency to make the responsibility of certain businesses strict, i.e. not bound to proof of negligence. On the other hand the responsibilities of private individuals seem to be smoothed so that somebody else bears the primary responsibility, e.g. the employee or insurance company, or in such a way that the amount does not cover the whole damage.

However, it is still the starting point in the Finnish tort law system that each party must take responsibility himself or herself for damages which he or she may have suffered. There must be some ground to require somebody else to pay for the damage, either showing that the damage was caused by purpose or by negligence. One is purposefully causing the damage if it was intentional or at least thought as a possible consequence of the action, or when the conduct was recklessly disregardful of the interests of others in a situation where it was probable that the consequence might occur. For negligence, or for the concretization of the notion "a reasonable man", there is no single unambiguous criteria. One needs to have a measure for the behaviour, e.g. in the area of medical treatment or traffic rules. Sometimes the occurrence of the damage is itself a sign of negligence somewhere in the activity, such as in uncontrolled explosions in construction work.

In certain situations a duty to pay damages is hindered by certain counter-arguments. If one causes damage when protecting oneself against a non-justified physical attack, no responsibilities arise. The same holds true if one grants permission for some acts, such as medical treatment. Sometimes it is a question of an official acting on a basis of competence norms, e.g. imprisoning a suspected person. All these situations have some limits, actions must be well-founded, and some very radical actions do give rise to a duty to pay damages. In sporting activities the permission covers only normal play according to the rules and spirit of the game.

Damages are usually divided into physical and material. An important specific group is what is called in Finnish tort law pure economic loss. The Damages Act has a strong limitation in the sense that pure economic losses are compensated only when caused by a criminal act, by a governmental authority, or when very strong arguments can be given for the compensation. The last expression have given rise to court practice which has been rather reluctant. For example in a case where the damage was caused by unfair marketing compensation was ordered, but not where the loss was caused by a boycott in connection to a labour dispute.

Employers and state officials have only a secondary responsibility, meaning that the employee or the state can, after having paid, by a regress demand that the sum be payed by the employee or official that caused the damage through gross or normal negligence (but not through mild negligence).

The evaluation of the causal connection is done on the basis of the idea of *conditio sine qua non*. Had the effect not taken place without the action, then the action is the cause of the effect. This evaluation becomes problematic when the chain of causes becomes complex or when a hypothetical chain has to construed for future events.

The English doctrine of remoteness has its resemblance in Finnish tort law with the idea of adequacy. The chain of causes has to be broken somewhere not to widen the area of responsibility too much. So only such acts give rise to a duty to compensate which are adequate to the effect. These principles are under ongoing discussion. One situation is where the circumstances have become normal in the meanwhile, or when control of events has been achieved. Another criteria is not to let disrespect of certain norms cause compensation duties when the effects have nothing to do with the policies of these norms, such as when breaking parking rules causes a material damage to another property. One cannot free oneself from the argument that the damage would have taken place anyway (burning a house just before a storm hits and would have destroyed it). When responsibility is based on the activity itself and its dangerous features, the damage has to be in the direction of the danger to be compensated. If a tree falls on a parked car the damages are not paid out of the traffic insurance because the compensation systems aims to deal with the risks of cars used in traffic. Sometimes the idea of foreseeability may hinder the compensation in such a way that if unexpected consequences arise from a conduct, a party is not deemed to be negligent.

2. Some Areas of Strict Liability

Product liability has been introduced to Finland, and it follows the European Community directive. The manufacturer, importing company, and a company marketing the product as its own are strictly liable for any damage caused by the article if the article was not as safe as could reasonably be expected when it was placed in the market. The damage may follow from a defect in the product or from misleading or lacking manuals for use. The responsibility is limited to personal injuries and damages to private property only. There is a three-year time limit for claims arising out of such damages, counted from the date when the information about the damage and about the rights to compensation reached the injured party.

Finland is a part of the international network for nuclear damages. The nuclear power companies are responsible also without any acknowledgement of negligence on their side for damages caused by radiation, poisonous or other dangerous character of the nuclear material.

There are special rules for associations and companies keeping personal registers. Their possibilities to give out the information are regulated and often restricted. If the information is false or given without competence, damages, including mental suffering if it is not to be considered as minor, has to paid.

The state is responsible for damages to person arrested or imprisoned without legally acceptable reason. No compensation is paid if the person has himself contributed to his or her imprisonment, for example by a false confession. Compensation is to be paid for expenses, for loss of income, and also mental anguish. The victims of crimes have also a limited possibility to be compensated by the state if the offender lacks resources. This covers mainly personal injuries. Any damage to property is compensated only in special occasions, such as when a prisoner on a leave or an escaped prisoner or mental patient has caused the damage, or there were special reasons connected to the victim's personal characteristics that made him or her particularly vulnerable to it such as old age or sickness, and a compensation is socially arguable.

Bibliographical Essay

Up to date presentations of Finnish contract law are rare. Useful material, but from a specific point of view, is found in Thomas Wilhelmsson, Critical Studies in Private Law (Kluwer: Dordrecht 1992). The author tries to show the possibility and grounds for a change in the traditional doctrines of the law of obligation. Discussion on Welfare State and contract law is found in (Dartmouth 1994, in print). The book is an Anglo-Finnish comparison on different topics. Y. J. Hakulinen's Obligationenrecht (Berlin 1936) provides background material to understand especially the possibilities of applying German doctrinal thinking also in Finland. It should be balanced by other material, however. Kluwer Publishing Company is including is its series also a book on Finnish Contract law, written by the author of this essay.

The discussion of the law of torts follows quite closely the presentation in Finnish by Professor Eero Routamo in: Johdatus Suomen oikeusjärjestelmään s. 271–288 (Lakimiesliiton kustannus: Helsinki 1993).

IV COMPANY LAW

By Gerhard af Schultén

1. The Corporate Structure

Business, trade or professional activities may be carried out in Finland by individual enterpreneurs as well as by corporate entities. In principle freedom of occupation prevails, which means that no special permit needs to be obtained for the right of establishment. There are of course a number of specific business activities which are licensed or otherwise restricted. Competition policy in Finland aims, however, to do away with or diminish legal obstacles to free competition also within home market industries. To a certain extent the rules concerning foreigners are different; these rules will be explained in greater detail in chapter 6 of this article.

The most important forms of incorporation for business enterprises are General Partnerships (avoin yhtiö), Limited Partnerships (kommandiittiyhtiö), Companies Limited by Shares (osakeyhtiö) and Cooperative Societies (osuuskunta). To some extent foundations (säätiö) may be engaged also in business activities, primarily as holding entities.

Legal form	Statute	*Number* (1992)*
General Partnership	(1988)	21 318
Limited Partnership	(1988)	64 822
Limited Companies	(1978)	157 654
Cooperatives	(1954)	2 007

* registered in the Trade Register

These figures should be compared with the total number of individual entrepreneurs, which in 1992 amounted to 50 540.

A type of company peculiar to Finland is the so-called Housing Company. Most privately owned apartment houses and terrace houses are organized as companies limited by shares under a separate Act, revised in 1991 (Asunto-osakeyhtiölaki).

When examining the statistics above, it should be born in mind that a considerable number of registered companies – maybe as many as one half – have in fact ceased their activities or are mere paper companies.

It should also be noticed that Finnish companies in general are small when measured in terms of own capital, number of employees or turnover, with a small number of big companies that employ a considerable part of the labor force. In 1990 45 % of all business enterprises employed less than 100 persons and 0,05 % more than 2 000 persons.

Most limited companies too are small enterprises. Of all companies with a registered turnover in 1990, almost 70 % had a share capital of less than FIM 50 000 and only less than 5 % had a share capital of FIM 1 million or more. About half of all limited companies had an annual turnover of less than FIM 1 million and 1,3 % of all companies a turnover of FIM 100 million or more.

At present there is no legislation concerning joint ventures and similar arrangements. Within the framework of the Agreement on establishing an European Economic Area (EEA), the European Economic Interest Grouping (2137/85 O. J. 1985 L 199/1) will be introduced in our domestic legislation making it possible to establish such groupings in Finland and for Finnish enterprises to join groupings established within the EC.

Joint ventures are nevertheless well known in Finland. Reference can be made to shareholders' agreements, joint construction projects and various pooling arrangements between enterprises. Joint ventures are not treated as separate legal entities. They cannot acquire rights or enter into obligations on their own. A joint venture has no assets of its own, decisions have to be taken unanimously and all profit belongs to the partners.

2. The Choice of Corporation Form

In general, the form of the business may be freely determined by its owners. Within certain regulated areas, such as financial services, this choice is restricted to certain forms, accepted by the law.

In practice there are sometimes few options as to how to organize a business. If the owner must turn to the public in order to raise risk capital, the limited company is the obvious choice. Otherwise the choice between existing options can be a rather complex issue. It is a well known fact that tax considerations are often decisive. Here I refer to a separate presentation of Finnish tax law in this book.

There are also other important aspects that should be taken into consideration. There is the question of ownership and liability for the obligations of the enterprise. If one wishes to avoid personal liability, one has to choose the limited company (or the cooperative society). In reality, however, the owners and operators of small limited companies usually will have to give personal guarantees and/or pledge securities for company debts.

If one wants to retain the possibility of disposing company funds, one should choose either of the two forms of partnership. Money invested in a partnership can be withdrawn at any time. In a limited company on the other hand only net profit may be distributed to the shareholders. Strong rules protect the paid-up share capital against unlawful redistribution.

Business operators search for legal frameworks that on the one hand are flexible and adjustable to their specific needs and on the other hand do not create uncertainty about what can lawfully be done and what not. The Finnish Companies Act has always been reasonably easy to cope with also in the context of small business, whereas until the enactment of the 1988 Partnerships Act the legal framework for partnerships was old-fashioned and incomprehensive. Yet the popularity of limited companies seems to be unchallenged.

Finally it should be observed that the Partnership Act contains specific rules which make it possible to convert a general partnership or a limited partnership into a limited company, whereas a conversion the other way around is not possible without dissolving the company.

3. Partnerships

A general partnership is a legal person formed by an agreement between two or more founders. The partners are jointly and severally responsible for the commitments and other liabilities of the partnership. A partnership that wishes to carry on a trade has to be registered in the national Trade Register.

The entry of the partnership in the Register has, however, no constitutive effect, as it exists from the moment the agreement is made. The Partnerships Act of 1988 (Laki avoimesta yhtiöstä ja kommandiittiyhtiöstä), which resembles the corresponding Norwegian and Swedish acts, is based on the principle of contractual freedom for the partners. This means that, as far as the mutual relations between the partners are concerned, they may make whatever arrangement they see fit concerning, among other things, the division of power between the partners, the management of the company and the right of a veto. The stipulations of the law are not mandatory except for the right granted to all partners to investigate company accounts and books and to bring a legal action against the annual accounts. Partnerships in general are organized in quite a simple way owing to the fact that in most cases there are only two partners (who often are members of the same family).

In relation to third parties each partner may represent the company and sign the name of the company within the framework of the objects of the company. However the partnership agreement can stipulate, that a certain partner has no right of representation or that the company can be represented only by two or more partners jointly. These restrictions have to be registered in the Trade Register.

The partners may agree on their investments in the partnership as they like. Thus a partner may contribute for example by working in the firm instead of investing money in it. There are no legal requirements as to the capital of the partnership. Partners working actively in the company usually receive a salary. According to a non-mandatory rule profit, as shown in the balance sheet, is distributed to the partners in the following manner. At first interest is paid on the prevailing amount of the invested capital. What is left shall be distributed evenly between the partners. In practice profit sharing is normally dealt with in the partnership agreement. Profits can, of course, be left undistributed to increase the own capital. From a creditor's perspective it must be observed that partners can at any time loan money from the company or otherwise take out money or other assets from the company, even to the extent that the balance sheet will show a negative own capital.

A general partnership has to prepare annual accounts consisting of a profit and loss statement and a balance sheet. If a partnership has more than 30 employees on an average, the accounts have to be audited by a professional

auditor. The annual accounts have to be made public when two of the following criteria are met:
1) the turnover is FIM 20 million or more,
2) the balance sheet total is FIM 10 million or more,
3) the average number of employees is at least 50 persons.

As was said earlier every partner is responsible for all the debts of the company, not only with his or her capital contribution but with all his or her personal property. A creditor can demand full payment from any of the partners for a claim that is due. The liability of the company and of its partners is hence identical. The creditor must, however, get a separate title against each party from whom payment is sought.

A new partner is personally liable for company debts existing on the date of entry into the company. A resigning partner is not responsible for debts that have come into existence after the resignation has been registered and given public notice.

The Partnership Act contains comprehensive stipulations on the dissolution of the partnership, the redemption of shares, on conversion to a limited partnership or to a limited company and on amalgamation with another general partnership or a limited partnership.

A limited partnership differs from a general partnership primarily in the fact that the former has two kinds of partners: general partners with unlimited liability and so-called silent partners, whose liability is limited to the amount of their investment. The position of the general partner is the same as that of partners in a general partnership. A limited partnership must always be registered.

The silent partners have neither managerial power nor a right to block decisions or a right to represent the company. Their interests focus on their share of the profit according to the provisions of the law and/or the partnership agreement. Certain decisions of great significance can not be made without their approval. Such is the case for instance when the general partner wishes to go beyond the objects of the company, or assign his share in the partnership, or merge with another company.

When a general partnership is dissolved, the silent partners have a priority right to repayment of their capital contribution out of the company's net assets.

The limited partnership is the most popular corporation form next to the limited company. It has proven to be particularly handy for the running of family businesses and for professionals such as attorneys and architects.

4. Cooperatives

A cooperative is the most important kind of trade society. Under the Cooperative Societies Act of 1954 (Osuuskuntalaki), a cooperative is a society whose number of members and amount of capital is not determined in advance and whose purpose is to carry on business operations in order to support the finances or trade of its members by having the members use the services of the society. A cooperative therefore does not have as its purpose the generation of profit to its members.

The members of a cooperative society are not personally liable for the debts of the cooperative; the by-laws may, however, stipulate a so called additional fee to be paid by them in case of liquidation or bankruptcy.

Membership in a cooperative carries two types of rights: membership rights and financial rights, in particular the right to a share of the annual surplus and the right to refund of the membership fee in case of resignation. In many cooperatives there is an open access to membership. In others on the other hand the by-laws may contain detailed rules on membership qualifications. Every member has only one vote, unless the cooperative is a so-called central cooperative, in which the majority of the members are societies or other associations. The members are at all times entitled to resign from the cooperative by written notification, but membership as such is not transferable, only the right to the refund of the membership fee.

The organization of a cooperative society is quite similar to that of a limited company. One peculiarity is the Assembly of Delegates, a body that replaces the general meeting of the cooperative in the largest cooperatives.

Members have to pay a membership fee in accordance with the stipulations in the by-laws. The paid membership fees constitute the subscribed capital of the cooperative. This capital is not fixed but rather depends on the number of members. From the point of view of the creditors, the reserve fund is more important. The reserve fund must be increased until it is equal to triple the amount of the subscribed capital. No less than 5 per cent of the annual surplus must be transferred to the reserve fund each year until the full amount has been reached.

Over the past 20 years the issue of raising risk capital in cooperatives has been a tricky one. New alternatives for equity funding have been developed in Finnish legislation. Thus the by-laws may prescribe that members can participate in the cooperative by paying additional fees. Such members do not thereby receive any additional voting power but have a preferential right to an annual interest paid out of the surplus. Another new instrument for funding is the placement fee or share. These fees constitute an investment share capital and they are designed very much like company shares. Even non-members can acquire such shares since they have no voting power. From the beginning of 1990 it has also been possible for a cooperative to convert to a limited company.

Cooperative societies, although not large in number, play an important role in the agricultural sector, where producers of dairy products and meat as well as other foodstuffs are frequently organized in cooperatives. Two of the four leading retail chains are consumer cooperatives, and cooperatives can be found in the production of telecommunication, financial and transport services and of electricity. On the other hand there are also limited companies with a cooperative structure.

5. Companies Limited by Shares

The Finnish Companies Act of 1978 (Osakeyhtiölaki), which replaces an old act of 1895, is the result of Nordic legal cooperation. Preparatory work took place in cooperating national committees of experts during the 60s and later on at the intergovernmental level, with the aim of achieving as much similarity in substance as possible. As a result of this cooperation the Finnish, Norwegian and Swedish Companies Acts form a common pattern in substance as well as in form. This is not to say that there are no national varieties as far as details are concerned. The Danish Companies Act is based on common Nordic principles as well. When Denmark became a member of the EEC in 1972, she had to implement the first EEC Directive on the Harmonization of Company Law and to take into consideration further directives under preparation. It was felt advisable to divide Danish limited companies in two categories; ordinary limited companies and companies of the German GmbH-type. Over the years the Danish Companies Act has been amended in order to implement new EC directives. For reasons that will be explained in chap. 7. below, this does not necessarily mean that Danish company law could not be regarded as a member of the Nordic company law family.

5.1 Scope of Application

The Finnish Companies Act of 1978 applies basically to all sorts of limited companies, private and state-owned, family enterprises as well as enterprises listed on the stock exchange. For banks and insurance companies limited by shares there is specific legislation that to some extent overrules the general Companies Act.

Public and private companies

Contrary to the tradition in most Continental European countries and nowadays in the European Community at large, Finnish company law has not recognized two separate forms of limited-liability companies, one for public/ large companies and another for private/small companies. Neither has a distinction been made between companies limited by shares and limited-liability companies without shares. The reasons for not following this path at least until the present time, can be summed up as follows:

> 1. The number of limited companies that would qualify as public or real limited companies is too small to justify exclusive and comprehensive legislation. In 1992 only a total of 109 companies had introduced their shares on the Helsinki Stock Exchange and the OTC list.

2. The need to protect investors should be met through mandatory and self-disciplinary stock exchange regulations.

3. In order to attribute any real significance to the division of companies into small and large, private and public, the legislature must grant appreciable relief to small companies, in particular with regard to the preparation and publication of annual accounts. Since increasing importance is being attached to satisfactory public accounts and qualified auditing also in the case of smaller companies, it would be difficult to make separate rules in this respect for different companies.

4. The Companies Act itself has been drafted in such a manner as to offer companies a variety of alternatives, particularly with regard to the organization of management and the acquisition of equity capital. This flexibility minimizes the risk that companies are forced into impractical solutions in particular cases. I shall illustrate this with an example. A company needs to have a Board of Directors consisting of a minimum of three members and, in addition, a Managing Director, if the share capital or the minimum share capital is FIM 1 million or more. If the capital is less than that, the company – a company owned by one person for instance – can be run by a board with only one member, who also will be in charge of the day-to-day management of the company affairs. On the other hand, such small companies may not set up a Supervisory Board to supervise the activities of the management.

5.2 The Formation of a Limited Company

The rules of the formation of a company are quite detailed and generally similar to those to be found in modern company laws. This is true in regard to most of the various chapters in the Finnish Act. As a result I will concentrate on the broad lines of the Act and point out a few rules that are specific to it and might be of particular interest for international readers.

A limited-liability company can be founded by one person and it can from the start function as a company in which all the shares are owned by the same private person or legal entity. The Act separates the role of the founder from ownership.

The Act requires a minimum paid-up share capital of FIM 15 000. The Act strives to make stringent requirements concerning capital contribution in kind. It seems, however, that it has not been able to abolish bad or illegal practices, such as simulated cash payments immediately followed by the acquisition from an insider of assets or a business.

The resolution concerning the formation of the company shall be adopted at the constituent meeting of shareholders. This meeting may be convened without any notice if all shares are subscribed for and all subscribers agree thereto. Unless it is shown at the constituent meeting that the subscription and allotment of shares correspond to at least the minimum share capital set forth in the deed of formation, the question concerning the formation of the company shall be considered abandoned.

Application for registration of the company shall be submitted within six months after the date of signing the deed of formation. The registration carries constitutive effect and the company is not considered a legal entity before the registration has been effected. The registration will not be granted unless half of the above-mentioned share capital has been paid and the board of directors have produced a written statement declaring that the legal requirements concerning the formation of the company have been observed and that the paid-up capital is in the possession of the board. Registration takes place in the national Trade Register – a common (computer-based) register for all business enterprises – and is published in a special Trade Register Bulletin.

Prior to registration the company can not acquire rights or enter into obligations. The persons who have taken part in a measure or a decision on behalf of the company are jointly and severally responsible for any obligations entered into prior to the registration. At the time of the registration, the obligation shall pass to the company provided that the obligation results from the deed of formation or has arisen subsequent to the constituent meeting. The latter rule gives rise to quite a few legal disputes.

The formation of a limited company is a swift and inexpensive transaction, assuming that the proposed name of the company does not create problems concerning distinctiveness etc.

5.3 Share Capital, Shares and Capital Issues

The Companies Act requires, as was already mentioned, a very modest minimum share capital of FIM 15 000. This is to be compared with the requirement of a minimum share capital amounting to FIM 10 million as a precondition for listing on the Helsinki Stock Exchange. Shares are indivisible and must be of equal face value. The share capital must be paid up in whole within a year after the registration of the company.

A company may, through a provision in the articles of association, divide its share capital into various classes, e.g. so that one class has preference to a dividend while another has greater voting power at the general meeting. In that case, the number of votes carried by any one share may not be more than 20 times the number of votes carried by another share. Neither bearer shares nor non-voting shares are allowed.

The shares are entered both in a numeric Share Register, kept by the board, and an alphabetical Shareholders Register. Both registers are open for inspection by any interested party. There is no obligation for a shareholder to have his or her shares entered in the register. In order to be eligible for the exercise of voting rights, share holdings have to be registered.

The par value principle is applied under Finnish law, meaning that the amount to be paid for each share must always be at least the nominal amount of the shares. The Act, however, accepts a so-called mixed issue of share capital, in which, for instance, 80 % of the nominal amount shall be paid in cash and 20 % by transferring the necessary funds from other equity capital sources such as the reserve fund or distributable profits.

Although a share is freely transferable in principle, the transferability may be restricted by a provision in the articles of association. The most common restrictions include various types of redemption or first refusal clauses giving to the other shareholders and, under certain conditions, to the company itself, the option to buy any shares transferred to outsiders. The purchase price is usually established by reference to the price the third party has offered for the shares, but the price may alternatively be fixed for instance to the book value or the tax value. Particularly in cases where the redemption price is favourable, the buyer may try to object to redemption especially on procedural grounds, and litigations based on redemption clauses are not rare.

The share capital may be raised at any time after the company has been registered. Most companies use the possibility to operate with a minimum and a maximum share capital, in the ratio of 1:4. Within these limits the general meeting can, by simple majority vote, raise the share capital, or for a period of one year authorize the board of directors to do so. A decision to depart from the shareholders' preferential right to subscribe for new shares – for instance to permit a takeover to be financed with equities – must be taken with a qualified majority.

In 1992 the Act was – due to reported abuses of the authorization power – amended in such a way, that a deviation from the shareholders' preferential right must be based upon weighty economic reasons from the point of view of the company's interest. Furthermore the authorization to the board to decide on such a share issue is restricted to 20 % of the registered share capital. The board can never be authorized to decide on a deviation from the shareholders' preferential right in favour of certain insiders such as other shareholders with a holding of at least 1 % of the shares, members of the board, the managing director and close relatives to the above-mentioned persons.

The general meeting can also decide to issue convertible bonds and option loans. The same principles of authorization and shareholders' preferential right of subscription prevail.

The share capital is in principle untouchable unless reduced under certain specific conditions that protect the interests of the company's creditors. Furthermore, a company is not allowed to buy its own shares or sponsor such an acquisition by a third party. There are some exceptions as regards the acquisition of own shares e.g. in connection with a takeover or a merger. It is also possible to stipulate in the articles of association that the company may, with non-restricted equity capital, acquire shares that are offered to it, and that shares might be redeemed in accordance with a predetermined amortization plan. In the latter case the share capital has to be reduced.

5.4 The Book-entry Securities System

In the mid-1980s the volume of securities that (physically) changed hands increased in step with the growth in the trading volume on the Helsinki Stock Exchange. Dealing in shares and promissory notes often creates an enormous amount of paperwork, where hundreds of thousand of certificates and coupons have to be checked and transferred. On certain occasions lorries loaded with share certificates were driving back and forth between sellers and buyers. Rationalizing the systems for processing securities required dematerialization of physical certificates and therefore new legislation. In August 1991 the Finnish book-entry system for securities entered into force. The principal laws are the Book-entry Securities System Law (Laki arvo-osuusjärjestelmästä) and the Book-entry Account Law (Laki arvo-osuustileistä) and a new chapter 3a in the Companies Act.

The core of the book-entry-system consists of book-entry registers maintained primarily by banks and other stock brokers. The securities accounts, to which each investor's holdings of securities are entered, are kept in these registers. All legal rights previously tied to physical share certificates etc. are now evidenced only by entries in securities accounts.

The centralized lists of shareholders in each issuing company will be maintained in a Central Share Register, which is open for inspection by the public. Foreign investors can be registered through a nominee. Each time a holding is traded or changes hands, the register of owners is updated. The book-entry registrar must immediately notify the accountholder of entries made on the account. Book-entry securities are traded in the Helsinki Stock Exchange's automatic trading system and trades concluded are settled in a automatic settlement system. The settlement period is three register days from the trading day.

In the book-entry securities system a right to dividend is held by the party registered in the company's shareholder register kept by the Central Share Register on the record date specified by the company. Dividend is paid via the book-entry register to the bank account of the authorized dividend recipient or as a money order.

In connection with an issue of new shares the company determines the record date for ownership thus forming the basis for the allotment of subscription rights. Subscription rights are considered as separate book-entry securities from the commencement of a share capital issue, when they are registered in the relevant book-entry account, and they may be traded in the same way as other book-entry securities.

A shareholder of a company belonging to the book-entry securities system may not exercise voting rights under the Companies Act until he or she is registered as a shareholder in the shareholder register kept by the Central

Share Register. Only a shareholder registered in the said register not later than 10 days prior to the general meeting is entitled to attend the meeting. This reduces the risk of coups at the general meeting.

A pledge may be registered in a book-entry securities account at the request of the beneficiary with the written permission of the account holder. Unless otherwise agreed, dividend shall be paid to the account holder, the right to subscribe for new shares and other such payments considered as capital to the holder of the pledge.

Changeover to the computerized book-entry securities systems will be compulsory for the shares quoted on the Helsinki Stock Exchange and optional for other shares. Each company decides to join the system at a general meeting. It is estimated that all listed companies will have joined the system by the end of 1994 and that they will be followed soon by the OTC companies.

The performance of the book-entry registers and the Central Share Register is supervised by the Bank Inspection Office and, as far as the technical functioning is concerned, also by a self-disciplinary body, the Securities Association.

5.5 Securities Regulations

The Companies Act does not contain specific provisions on the protection of investors in securities nor does it regulate such stock market abuses as insider trading. In 1989 the Securities Markets Act (Arvopaperimarkkinalaki) entered into force. This Act contains detailed provisions on the preparation of share issue prospectuses, flagging, disclosure of sensitive information, official tenders, redemption and insider trading.

Under the provisions on flagging, a shareholder whose holding in a listed or an OTC company exceeds one-tenth, one-fifth, one-third, one-half or two-thirds of voting rights, must immediately declare such ownership.

Shareholders who have acquired more than two-thirds of the voting rights in a listed or an OTC company are required to redeem other shareholders' shares at their current price.

The Act obligates the above-mentioned companies to immediately disclose any information that substantially affects the price of their shares, such as financial statements, the payment of dividends, share issues, corporate acquisitions or divestitures and any other decisions or events materially affecting their operations. Such information is to be provided simultaneously to all interested parties.

The misuse of price-sensitive information is a criminal offence. The prohibition extends to anybody who has gained such information by virtue of his position, office or commission. By the law the following insiders in listed or OTC companies are obliged not to trade with company shares on a shorter perspective than six months:
- members and deputy members of the board of directors and supervisory board,
- the managing director and his deputy,
- the auditor and deputy auditors.

This ban also affects companies or other associations in which any of the said persons alone or jointly with members of his or her family has a decisive influence.

The Bank Inspection Office is the supervisory authority in security market issues.

The Securities Market Act is being amended so as to correspond to EC legislation. A bill to this effect is pending in Parliament. This amendment extends the disclosure obligation to companies subject to other public trading (companies on the brokers' list). The approval of the authorities is to be obtained for all the prospectuses to be distributed in the primary market. The basic regulations on the financial statements and interim reports will be transferred from the Rules and Regulations of the Stock Exchange to The Securities Market Act. Regulations on the obligations of flagging and redemption are more precisely defined in the proposed bill. The bill also tightens the insider regulations (and widens the concept of insiders) by providing that market information and price-sensitive statistics are also to be treated as insider information and disclosed simultaneously to all parties.

5.6 Organization

The compulsory company organs are the general meeting, where the shareholders exercise their supreme authority as owners, the board of directors as the executive body conducting the company's activities, and the auditor. Companies with a maximum share capital of at least FIM 1 million must have a managing director, who is in charge of the day-to-day management of the company. Such a company may also have a supervisory board composed of at least five members.

Small companies with a maximum share capital of less than FIM 1 million may appoint a one-member board; otherwise the board must consist of a minimum of three members.

The most common organization pattern for companies – other than companies or subsidiaries owned by one person – is a board with 3 to 9 outside members and a managing director, who sometimes, but not as a rule, is also a member of the board. When the supervisory board is used, the board of directors is often composed of company insiders, with the managing director as the chair. All possible varieties, however, exist in practice.

The general meeting of shareholders elects the members of the board and the auditor(s), approves the annual accounts, decides whether profits shall be distributed or not, discharges the board from liability, and makes extraordinary decisions with respect to amendments of the articles of association, increases in the share capital, dissolution of the company and amalgamation with another company. Here it should be noted that the general meeting cannot decide to distribute more profit than the board finds acceptable.

Discharge of liability covers only decisions or measures that have been brought to the attention of the shareholders in the annual report, or the auditors' report or otherwise at the general meeting.

The board of directors usually elects the managing director, issues guidelines and instructions regarding the performance of the day-to-day management of the company, supervises that the management properly pursues the objects of the company and the goals set by the board and takes (or should take) active control of company affairs in critical situations. The managing director, assisted by a staff, may enter into transactions which with regard to the scope and nature of the company's operations are unusual or of great importance only with the board's approval or where the decision to be made by the board can not be delayed without considerable inconvenience to the company.

The board of directors represent and sign for the company. The board may, when stipulated in the articles of association, authorize a member, the managing director or any other person to represent and sign for the company, alone or jointly with an other person. The managing director may always represent and sign for the company with regard to measures which are within his or her duties pursuant to the law.

The task of the supervisory board is to elect the members of the board of directors and to supervise the board and the managing director. The supervisory board is sometimes a rather large body, composed of people representing shareholders, customers, creditors, public authorities, political and other interest groups, individual expertise, and sometimes the employees. In the articles of association it can be stipulated that the supervisory board takes decisions in matters which concern a substantial extension or reduction of the company's activities or an essential change in the organizational structure of the company.

A limited company need not have more than one auditor. In companies with a restricted own capital exceeding FIM two million at least one auditor must be an accountant authorized either by the Central Chamber of Commerce or by a (local) chamber of commerce. Certain companies, such as companies listed on the Stock Exchange and companies with more than 500 employees on the average must have an auditor or an auditing company authorized by the Central Chamber of Commerce. The audit, which is conducted in accordance with good auditing standards, is completed in a written report to the general meeting. In the report the auditor makes a statement as to the approval of the annual accounts, the issue of discharge and the proposed allocation of the company's profit or loss as made in the directors' report. If the auditor has found that a director or the managing director has acted or omitted to act in a way which may entail liability for damages, or is otherwise contrary to the Companies Act or the articles of association, this fact shall be mentioned in the auditor's report.

Unlike many other European company laws, the Finnish Companies Act contains no provisions concerning workers' participation on boards. This issue has been regulated in a separate Act of 1990 on Personnel

Representation in the Management of Business Enterprises (Laki henkilöstön edustuksesta yritysten hallinnossa). This law applies to all limited-liability companies, cooperative societies, banks and insurance companies with a personnel of not less than 150 persons on the average.

According to the Personnel Representation Act the social partners in a particular business firm may agree on how to arrange the participation right of the employees. If an agreement can not be reached, a majority of the employees representing at least two personnel groups can demand representation either in the supervisory board, if any, the board of directors, or such management groups that together cover the various profit centers within the firm. The choice of allocation belongs to the employer.

The representatives of the employees are chosen in addition to those members of the chosen body that the firm itself has elected. Employees' representation can constitute as much as 20 per cent of the total representation. The number of employees' representatives shall be one as a minimum and four as a maximum. To give an example, it is decided that participation shall take place within the supervisory board, which is composed of 13 persons elected by the general meeting. In that case 1-3 employees' representatives can be nominated to the board. Personnel representatives have basically the same rights and obligations as other members of the said body and they are nominated for the same term of office.

So far in a majority of all cases the participation system has been adopted through an agreement at the corporate level. The most popular solution seems to be to allocate personnel participation (and influence) to a management group under the leadership of the managing director. Membership in the supervisory board is chosen almost as often as representation in the board of director. In many instances participation is granted both in a management group and at the corporate organ level.

Reference should also be made to the Act of 1989 on Personnel Funds (Henkilöstörahastolaki). According to this Act business enterprises employing at least 30 persons may decide after negotiations with the labour representatives to establish a profit-sharing system according to which a profit bonus is paid into a fund, which will be owned and administered by the personnel. A profit share is calculated on the basis of the operating margin or some similiar basis that reflects the profitability of the business activities, and it is treated as a tax-deductible cost, not as a dividend. In 1992 43 business enterprises had established personnel funds and these funds had approximately 100 000 members.

5.7 Minority Protection

The core of minority protection is, in addition to a number of provisions requiring decisions at the general meeting to be made with qualified majority, the so called "general clause", which provides that the general meeting may not pass a resolution whereby certain shareholders or third parties manifestly obtain an unjustifiable benefit at the expense of the company or other shareholders. Any shareholder who considers that the majority has infringed his or her rights in this way may appeal to the court to have the resolution declared null and void.

The general clause does not afford sufficient protection against a systematic oppression of a minority since legal proceedings, even if successful, have no effect for the future. Therefore the Companies Act contains a special rule giving shareholders the right to apply to the court to have the company rounded up if other shareholders have cooperated in a decision conflicting with the general clause or have otherwise wilfully misused their influence in the company. It provides that an order to wind up the company can be made only if there are exceptional grounds for making the order. Alternatively the court may, upon the request of the aggrieved party, order the company to redeem the shares held by the plaintiff at a reasonable price.

Shareholders representing 10 % of all shares in the company may demand that an extraordinary general meeting shall be held to discuss a certain matter. The same qualified minority has the right at the general meeting to demand that at least half of the profit of the financial period shall be distributed as dividends. The right to a minimum dividend may not entail that more than 5 % of the equity capital of the company shall be distributed as profit. A minority of the said size, alternatively representing one-third of the shares present at the meeting, may also request a public authority to appoint an auditor in addition to the ordinary auditors appointed by the general meeting, or to appoint special inspectors, with the task of examining the administration and the accounts of the company for a specific past period or of a specific measure or matter relating to the company.

The right to demand a special investigation is important particularly in cases where the minority wishes to initiate a claim for damages against members of the board, the managing director or an auditor who has committed negligence. Such an action is instituted on behalf of the company. Those who initiate the proceedings are themselves responsible for their legal costs, but have the right to be compensated by the company to the extent that the costs are covered by the amount recovered by the company in the court action. The right to conduct a derivative suit accrues to shareholders with an aggregate 10 % of the company's share capital or one-third of the shares present at the general meeting, provided that they opposed the granting of a discharge from liability.

In case of an amalgamation (fusion) with another company, shareholders, who at the general meeting voted against a decision to amalgamate may request the company to redeem their shares at their current price (generally understood as the price at the time of the request). Disputes arising out of this right are submitted to arbitration, with the company normally paying the costs of the procedure.

5.8 Creditor Protection

The fact that the shareholders are not personally liable for the obligations of the company calls for strong guarantees that the restricted equity capital is paid up properly and that it can be repaid only if the creditors' interests are duly observed.

As far as payment control is concerned there are some shortcomings in the present law; fictitious payment of the share capital is not an unknown phenomena. The share capital and the restricted reserve fund can be repaid to the shareholders only by means of a reduction of the share capital or the dissolution of the company. In both cases the court as a rule issues an official proclamation inviting creditors to give notification of their claims and to safeguard their interest.

Dividends to the shareholders may not exceed the amount which, according to the adopted balance sheet for the last financial year, has been reported as the company's non-restricted equity capital. Violation of this rule is a criminal offence. The Finnish Companies Act contains detailed provisions restricting the granting of cash loans or the furnishing of a security or a guaranty to insiders such as directors and members of their families as well as shareholders holding more than one percent of all shares in the company. The main principle is that such transactions are lawful only within the framework of the non-restricted equity capital and providing that the debtor lodges a sufficient security. The company may not grant a loan for the purpose of acquiring shares in the company or a subsidiary.

5.9 Groups

In the meaning of the Companies Act a group exists when one limited company holds an absolute voting majority in the general meeting of another limited company. The most typical example is where one company holds more than 50 % of all shares of another company. To prevent the evasion of the rules it is also provided that a group exists when a company in any other way, e.g. by contract, has a decisive influence over another company and a significant share in its results. This complementary rule has proven to be of minor importance.

The statutory regulation of groups in Finland aims at the protection of the creditors. A parent company may not distribute as profit an amount exceeding the aggregate amount of the annual profit of the group and the non-restricted consolidated equity capital; that is to say losses by subsidiaries decrease the amount payable as dividend in the parent company. A subsidiary may not acquire shares in the parent company and such shares owned by a subsidiary have no voting power in the general meeting of the parent company.

The concept of the company group is based on rather formal criteria. This can be at least partly explained by the fact that, with one exception, the statute does not contain provisions relating to the position of minority shareholders in groups, to the legal relations between group companies particularly as regards the administration of subsidiaries, and to similar issues.

The exception referred to grants the parent company the right to acquire compulsorily the remaining shares in a subsidiary when the parent holds more than 90 % of the shares and they represent more than nine-tenths of the votes. A minority shareholder has a corresponding right to require the parent company to purchase his or her shares. In case of a dispute the value of the shares is determined by special arbitrators and the company has normally to bear the costs of the arbitration procedure. The redemption option is frequently used as a preparatory step for a merger between the parent company and the subsidiary.

Originally only limited company groups were subject to the obligation of preparing a consolidated profit and loss statement and a consolidated balance sheet for each financial year. Due to a 1993 amendment to the Finnish Accounting Act of 1973 (Kirjanpitolaki), all groups of some economic significance – according to the same standards as apply to the requirement to publish the annual accounts (see above p. 119) – are under the said obligation, regardless of whether the parent company is a limited company, a partnership or a cooperative society and regardless of the mixture of various company forms among the subsidiaries. Also the accounts of a foreign subsidiary have to be consolidated. The concept of a group is somewhat different from the definition in the Companies Act in order to fit the requirements of the relevant EC Directives on Group Accounts. The consolidated accounts shall show the result of the group for the financial year after deduction of inter-company incomes and expenses as well as of inter-company dividends. The consolidated balance sheet shall show the group's equity capital after deduction of inter-company receivables and debts and inter-company holdings.

5.10 Reorganizing Companies

As in all other Western economies, business enterprises in Finland reorganize themselves in search of synergy and more competitiveness. Companies merge and divide, sell out sectors, and establish joint ventures with others. Company law provides the actors with the necessary legal frameworks, whereas labour law and tax law have a decisive impact on the course of action.

Sometimes ownership has to be reorganized. A change-of-generation scheme for instance could be carried out in such a way that the company redeems the shares, provided that a redemption clause is inserted in the articles of association, and that there are sufficient distributable profits to dispose of. A withdrawal can be achieved also through a reduction of the share capital, but that requires the consent of the creditors.

The Companies Act offers a flexible set of options for the merging of companies. Companies may amalgamate through absorption or through combination, in which case a new company comes into existence. If a parent company holds all shares in a subsidiary, decisions to merge can be taken by the boards of the companies. Normally such decisions require the approval of the general meeting in all merging companies. The consideration to be paid to the shareholders in the transferor company consists often of shares in the absorbing company, but nothing prevents the parties from using convertible bonds or cash or a combination of these instruments. A shareholder in a transferor company who is opposed to amalgamation may, as has been mentioned, demand that the company acquire his or her shares at their current price.

Amalgamation can as a rule take place only between associations with the same legal constitution. A wholly-owned limited company, however, can be absorbed through amalgamation by a parent with a different corporate structure, e.g. a cooperative or a savings bank. A Finnish company can not amalgamate with a company that has its domicile in another country. International mergers have to be accomplished for instance through a holding company.

As has been pointed out, a general partnership as well as a limited partnership can be transformed into a limited company according to the principles of "going concern". A cooperative society can transform itself into a limited company and a savings bank into a savings bank limited by shares or a commercial bank limited by shares.

The Finnish Companies Act contains no rules on the division of companies. Finnish tax law, however, has recently introduced the concept of partial splitting. If a company wishes to set up a subsidiary and transfer a part of its assets to this new company, it can do so without any adverse tax effects. The rule also applies when two companies set up a joint company for the purpose of carrying on a part of their former activities. The share capital in the new company is paid in kind.

5.11 Bankruptcy and Restructuring

When less than one-third of the share capital is covered, the board of directors have to decide either on measures to reconstruct the capital basis or else they must wind up the company. If the board fails to act, directors can be held liable for any damages caused to the creditors of the company. In order to save the company new equity capital may be raised (after a reduction of the original share capital to cover losses) or creditors may agree to subordinate their loans.

More and more companies, limited by shares as well as partnerships, become bankrupt. The number of business enterprises going into bankruptcy doubled in three years and totalled 7 207 in 1992. Bankruptcy proceedings are dealt with in this anthology in more detail in an article on procedure.

On February 8, 1993 new legislation entered into force, providing business firms an alternative to bankruptcy proceedings. The Restructuring of Companies Act (Laki yrityksen saneerauksesta) establishes the legal conditions for the restructuring of companies that are viable, but are currently in financial difficulties. The restructuring procedures laid down in the Act are to be applied in the preparation of a programme for the restructuring of a company with the goal of placing it on a healthy foundation and undertaking the necessary restructuring of its debts. Application for restructuring proceedings can be made either by the company itself, or by one or more creditors, or by the debtor and the creditors jointly, when the company is in insolvency or is threatened by insolvency.

If the competent district court approves the application, the company enters into a period of protection during which no debts that arose before the proceedings may be paid, collected or enforced. The court appoints an independent administrator with the task of preparing a report on the financial situation of the company, monitoring and supervising the company's operations during the proceedings and preparing a proposal for the restructuring programme. The management retains the right to decide on the normal day-to-day operations of the company. However, the consent of the creditors is necessary for significant decisions, such as agreements on new loans.

The restructuring programme should stipulate all the measures that are required for placing the company on a healthy footing. Among the conditions that may be set for approval of the programme are further investments in equity capital, changes in the management, or measures improving the efficiency of operations. The restructuring programme may alter the schedule of payment of debts, order that the installments shall first be credited as payments on the capital, reduce the interest rate on the remaining period of credit or reduce the amount of the unpaid debt. Debts secured by collateral have a privileged position to the extent that the value of the collateral at the time the proceedings began is sufficient to cover them. Such debts can not be settled (compulsory) as a part of a restructuring programme.

The restructuring programme has to be approved by the court provided that it is sufficiently supported by the creditors. The Act contains detailed provisions on the basic conditions for approval. An application for the restructuring of a company takes precedence over an application in bankruptcy until a decision is made on initiating restructuring proceedings.

6. Foreign Ownership and Participation

In Finland a foreigner always needs a permit granted by the county government to carry on a trade. The same applies to a foreigner who wishes to operate as a personally liable partner in a partnership. A permit is also required when a foreign company establishes a branch in Finland. For a foreign bank to set up a branch in Finland a licence is needed.

Under current legislation, foreigners can freely invest in Finnish shares and purchase real estate in Finland. The previous Restricting Act was rescinded in December 1992. The only remaining general restrictions apply to the ownership of real estate for holiday use, which is still subject to special permission. The liberalization of foreign ownership took place automatically by virtue of the law; existing clauses restricting foreign ownership lost their validity effective January 1, 1993. In the same connection, foreign ownership of banks and insurance companies was also liberalized. Foreign owners can no longer be discriminated against on the basis of a company's articles of association, nor can any limitations be imposed on their voting rights at shareholders' meetings.

For the time being until the end of 1995, the Ministry of Trade and Industry retains limited control of corporate acquisitions. Under this control, large companies – with a turnover exceeding FIM 1 billion and more than 1 000 employees) – are required to inform the Ministry of any transaction involving the transfer of more than one-third of their voting power to foreign owners. The Ministry can refuse approval of any such transaction if it is deemed to endanger Finland's national interests.

At least half of the ordinary and deputy members of the board of directors of a limited company as well as the managing director must be permanent residents of Finland and they also must be citizens of Finland or another Nordic country. However, a maximum of one-third of the members of the board can be resident outside the Nordic countries or citizens of other countries than Finland or the other Nordic countries. The Ministry of Trade and Industry may grant the company an exeption from these requirements. At least one of the auditors in a limited company or a partnership has to be a Finnish citizen residing in Finland. Cooperatives can not have foreign auditors at all.

The above-mentioned restrictions concerning participation in boards etc. will be abolished as soon as the Agreement on the European Economic Area enters into force. References to citizenship in Finland or the other Nordic countries and to residence in Finland will be replaced with a reference to residence within the European Economic Area, that is to say e.g. that at least half of the members of the board of directors of a limited company and the managing director must have their residence in any of the 19 countries forming the said Economic Area. In partnerships residents within the EEA will no more need any permission to act as a partner.

7. The Company Law Reform

On May 1992 the European Communities, the Member States of the EC and the Member States of EFTA signed the Agreement on the European Economic Area. According to Article 77 of this Agreement the Company Law provisions in force in the EC are part of the so-called "aquis communitaire" and are thus binding also in the EFTA countries. Within a transition period of two years from the entry into force of the Agreement all the existing ten EC Directives on the Harmonization of Company Law must be incorporated into Finnish company law. In 1992 a state committee issued a report (Komiteanmietintö 1992:32) in which it makes proposals for the implementation of the said directives, and for the amendment of the Companies Act based on domestic reasons.

In this context it is not possible to explain in detail all the proposals made by the Committee. In general one may claim that there are no fundamental differences in substance between the Finnish Companies Act and the EC rules, that the present Finnish Act already reflects European legal thinking in general. Nevertheless numerous amendments are required to meet the demands of the EC Directives.

A major reform is the proposed division of limited liability companies into Public Limited-Liability Companies and Private Limited-Liability Companies. The reason for this division relates to the implementation of the EC Capital Directive with the goal that Finnish companies would also be able to assume the form of public companies, as recognized in all the EC states. Also the development of the securities markets and the new demands of investor protection point to such a division.

Only a public limited company may have securities offered to the general public and only such securities may be subject to public trading. The minimum share capital of a public limited company must be at least FIM 500 000, whereas the capital requirement for a private limited company is proposed to be FIM 50 000. Technically the Committee proposes the British solution, that is to say, that the division of limited-liability companies is realized within the framework of one and the same law. Most of the provisions of the Act will apply to both private and public companies.

Other more remarkable proposals are

- liability of the shareholders, the board members and the managing director for the commitments of a private-liablity company during two years after the beginning of its operations (unless the company has a share capital of at least FIM 500 000);
- a more extensive definition of groups to correspond with the definitions in the Accounting Act (making the power to appoint the majority of board members equal to the majority of voting rights), and more extensive application of group regulations to foreign members of a group;
- voting by share series, meaning that certain important decisions by a shareholders' meeting are valid only if they have received the support of the required majority of the votes cast in each share series represented in the meeting;
- the introduction of preference shares with a priority right to the profit and assets of the company and with a very restricted voting right;
- a restricted right to acquire own shares; in a public limited company the shareholders' meeting may decide to acquire or authorize the board to acquire through the stock exchange, the contractual market or by a public offer own shares to a number not exceeding five per cent of the share capital of the company;
- provisions regarding equitable subordinated loans, which may be raised for instance to avoid the compulsory winding up of the company due to insufficient coverage of the share capital;
- new rules on payment of the share capital, whereby among other things payment in cash should be transferred to a specific bank account to be opened by the company;
- the introduction of a set of provisions on the division of a company into two or more companies, designed in accordance with the rules laid down in the EC Division Directive;
- an obligation for public limited companies to prepare and publish interim accounts at least once a year;
- an obligation for all limited companies, regardless of their size, to deliver the documents relating to their annual accounts to the Trade Register, where they are open for inspection by the public;
- non-mandatory provisions on postal voting at shareholders' meetings.

Additionally the Committee identified a number of company law issues that from a domestic point of view need to be further examined. The Committee makes special reference to group subsidies, cross holdings and the question of liability identification or disregarding the corporate identity.

References

The Finnish Companies Act of 1978 including amendments as of October 31, 1987; Hannes Snellman, Attorneys at Law, Helsinki

Establishing a business in Finland, Ministry of Trade and Industry, 1990. This booklet will be revised as soon as the EEA Agreement enters into force.

Developments in Nordic Company Law by C. G af Schultén, Legal Problems of an Enlarged European Community, British Institute Studies in International and Comparative Law No. 6, London 1972.

How to Trade in Finland – A Guide to the Securities Market '93, issued by the Finnish Foundation for Share Promotion.

The Finnish Book-Entry Securities System, a brochure issued by the Securities Association, Helsinki.

V LABOUR LAW AND NON-DISCRIMINATION LAW

By Niklas Bruun

1. The Finnish Industrial Relations System

1.1 History

The breakthrough of industrialization in Finland is usually taken as going back to the 1890s with the formative period of collective bargaining going as far back as the years 1896–1909. This period saw not only an increase in the growth of organized labour and the commonality of strikes and collective agreements but also the founding in 1907 of the first central employee organizations and the corresponding employer organizations.

The hundred-year history of the Finnish industrial relations system has been marked by discontinuity and violent upheavals. From the end of the civil war in 1918 until the conclusion of peace in 1944 very few collective agreements were made as the employers were opposed to them in principle. After 1944 the situation changed when collective agreements were again negotiated. Nevertheless to a large degree during the post-war years wage policies have been subject to state regulation. In 1955 the loosening of wage controls triggered a general strike which was followed by the split-up of the central labour union organizations into two competing bodies. The year 1969 saw their reunification and the 1970s witnessed the rapid development of what can best be described as a Nordic model of industrial relations.

1.2 Organizational Structure

The Finnish labour market is characterized by a high level of organization of both the employers and employees. The figure usually quoted for employees is 86.7 %, including officials and civil servants. However, if pensioners and other special groups are excluded, the figure drops to a significantly lower 71.8 %.

The largest labour union organization, with 1.1 million members, is the SAK, or Central Organization of Finnish Trade Unions. It is organized primarily according to the principle of industrial federations. Precise figures for the next largest central organization, are at the moment difficult to ascertain as the 300 000 member TVK, filed for bankruptcy during the autumn of 1992 as a result of extensive losses from speculative investments. Nearly all of the member organizations of the TVK, however, have decided to apply for membership in the STTK, or Confederation of Technical Employees Organizations in Finland. As a result the STTK, which formerly had 150 000 members, has now almost quadrupled in size. The other central organization, the Confederation of Unions for Academic Professionals in Finland (AKAVA) currently has approximately 250 000 members.

On the employer side there are four important central organizations. The TT or Confederation of Finnish Industry and Employers is made up of over 7 000 member firms with over 500 000 employees. The TT is the result of the fusion in 1992 of the STK, an employer organization, and the TKL, an industry interest organization. The Employers Confederation of Service Industries (LTK) covers firms in the retail trade, the hotel and restaurant branch, banking and insurance, and other areas within the service industry. Within the public sector there are two central negotiating partners, the Department of Public Personnel Management (VTML) for the state administration and Local Authority Employers' Commission (KT) for the municipal administration.

1.3 Incomes Policy

Since the end of the 1960s wages and working conditions have been covered by a national incomes policy. From a legal point of view, the central incomes policy agreements do not constitute a collective agreement but only establish a central framework within which each branch or federation must come to an agreement. In other words the agreements negotiated between the central labour market partners and the state establish a framework for wage, tax and social policy for the period under negotiation. Since 1968 only a small number of these negotiating rounds have resulted in a failure to reach agreement at the central level.

The incomes policy has encouraged the emergence of a neocorporatist political regime. It has also resulted in the increased centralization of the central labour market organizations and in their holding seats on many state agencies and boards. Power and importance have to a large degree been concentrated within the central organizations, with the central leadership of the confederations exercising direct power from within the top level of the central confederations.

1.4 Distinctive Finnish Features

The Finnish economy, including the metal and electronics industries, stands and falls with the paper and wood processing industry. It is the need for forestry workers which partly explains why Finland's industrial structure has for so long been characterized by the large percentage of small independent farmers who work in the forests during the winter.

An active labour market policy has been pursued by Finland to a significantly lesser degree than by Sweden. The result has been an increase in unemployment during times of recession, the severity of the 1992–1993 economic crisis in Finland being revealed by official unemployment figures nearing 20 %. However, while a higher level of unemployment has been accepted in Finland than in Sweden and Norway, from the end of the Second World War until the beginning of 1990s the level of unemployment never exceeded 7 %.

The exceptionally large number of women in the Finnish labour market came about in response to the shortage of labour at the end of the Second World War. In 1950 the number of gainfully employed women, who for the most part were engaged in full-time work, amounted to 41 % of all wage earners. In 1990 the number had risen to 50 %.

During the entire post-war period the Finnish labour market has experienced a high rate of strikes, and especially in the 1970s there were frequent strikes within the metal and paper industries. However, although the level of labour conflict has been high, Finland has experienced relatively moderate demands for industrial democracy, with the 1978 legislation on industrial democracy having limited practical import. Nevertheless, at the local union level within industry in particular, shop stewards do have a strong position.

The public and private sectors of the Finnish labour market are not subject to the same regulations. On the individual level civil servants are subject to a separate set of regulations. On the collective level the central part of the regulations governing the civil service do not markedly deviate from the Collective Agreements Act. The system for the public sector is more centralized with somewhat different regulations than the private sector: the right to strike is clearly more limited and the right to collective bargaining is more restricted than in the Collective Agreements Act. Therefore, while the following presentation only treats the non-public sector, it nevertheless has much bearing for the public sector. In addition, it should be noted that the employment relationship of extensive groups of employees on the state and municipal levels comes under the provisions covering private employment relationships.

2. Finnish Labour Law

2.1 Historical Roots

Finnish labour law has its roots in both continental Europe, among other countries Germany and Austria, as well as in the other Nordic countries, Sweden and to some degree Denmark. During the first decades of the twentieth century the Finnish legal system was influenced among other things by the fact that Finnish legal scholars generally received their education in Germany, whereas since the Second World War the Scandinavian influence has been much stronger.

The predominant legal tradition in Finland is reflected in the detailed and comprehensive regulations in Finnish labour law – labour relations in Finland are very closely regulated by law. The foundation of individual labour law in Finland was laid in 1879 with the introduction of the law on the freedom of trade. Detailed proposals from 1908 formed the basis for the Employment Contracts Act, passed in 1922 after the end of the civil war and the establishment of Finnish independence. The Collective Agreements Act was passed in 1924 at a time, paradoxically enough, when collective agreements were quite rare. The 1924 legislation was largely based on a proposed German law never implemented in Germany that had been drawn up by the well known German labour expert Hugo Sinzheimer, and the current Finnish Collective Agreements Act in its central parts is still based on a modernized version of Sinzheimer's proposal. The Mediation of Labour Conflicts Act, which has been later amended, was passed in 1925.

The legal regulation of the labour market in Finland has always been strongly influenced by international models. The shape of Finnish legislation has been influenced by many ILO conventions – in the 1920s the only forum where Finnish labour market partners were able to cooperate was the International Labour Organization. Likewise, the largely informal cooperation between the Nordic countries has been important.

2.2 New Developments

The regulations on social policy of the European Community have been important for Finnish labour law in recent years. In compliance with the EEA agreement, Finland is in the process of harmonizing its legislation with EC rules, which has led to the introduction of a number of new labour protection regulations within the areas of health and safety.

The increasing internationalization of firms has accentuated the practical importance of problems in the area of international private law with the result that a number of new regulations have been added to the Employment Contracts Act (Paragraph 51 a-d) concerning the national law to be applied in international employment relations.

2.3 Leading Principles of Finnish Labour Law

Today legislation in the area of labour law is still guided by the policy of trying to provide legal protection to the weaker party in an employment relationship, i.e. the employee. A clear expression of this policy can be seen in the legislation establishing mandatory legal minimums for the protection of employees. The principle of protection is even relevant as a principle of interpretation in labour law.

The principle of advantage in Finnish case law constitutes a special application of the principle of protection. The principle of advantage means that the norm which is the most advantageous to the employee is to be applied in cases where for the same question there are different stipulations within the many-faceted hierarchy of norms in labour law.

The principle of neutrality is followed by the state in the area of collective labour law. This means as a main rule that the state is to remain neutral in conflicts of interest between the parties.

The tripartite principle means that the parties are to be given the opportunity to present their views during the preparation of laws and administrative procedures concerning the labour market.

Also of relevance to labour law is the strong Finnish constitutional protection of private property, which among other things protects earned pension rights and prevents legislative encroachments upon earlier agreements in the labour market. Likewise the Form of Government Act, a part of the constitution, guarantees the right to work, a guarantee that in practice means only the right to subsistence money in situations of unemployment.

2.4 Legal Sources of Labour Law

The hierarchy of legal norms in Finnish labour law is complicated by the large number of different sources of rules that regulate the conditions in specific employment relations. The normal order of priority in cases involving a conflict of norms is as follows:

(1) the absolute rules of law;
(2) the norms in a collective agreement which are generally applicable according to the Employment Contracts Act;
(3) the norms in a collective agreement which are to be followed on the basis of the Collective Agreements Act;
(4) the absolute statutes from which one can deviate through a collective agreement;
(5) the provisions in an employment contract;
(6) the labour regulations covered in Paragraph 6 of the Co-operation within Undertakings Act;

(7) the conditions in a collective agreement from which one can deviate in an employment contract;
(8) optional statutes;
(9) norms in customary law (and the established practices which often have the same status as the conditions in an employment contract); and
(10) employer's orders.

2.5 Jurisprudence

"Modern" labour law research in Finland dates back to the end of the Second World War. It began as a result of the new situation in the labour market, which saw the enormous expansion of the labour movement, the establishment of collective bargaining, the creation of a labour court and the renewal of legislation on labour law. The guiding principle in the "modern" concept of labour law was based on the assimilation of the legal positivist view of law already accepted in other fields of jurisprudence and on the establishment of labour law as an independent field of study (the postwar period saw the establishment of a chair of labour law at the University of Helsinki). The changes were accompanied by serious efforts to interpret and systematize labour law legislation. Collective agreements were the subject of two studies published in the 1950s, Kopponen's study in 1954 and Vuorio's classic work in 1955. Vuorio introduced the analytical method of legal studies inspired by what can be called the Scandinavian realist approach (Alf Ross and the Uppsala school of thought) and logical empiricism, which began to exert considerable influence on Finnish labour law. This analytical labour law can be described as the prevailing paradigm in postwar Finnish labour law, with Kaarlo Sarkko and Kari-Pekka Tiitinen as the scholars explicitly following the Vuorio tradition. A somewhat broader concept inspired by the social sciences is represented by Martti Kairinen and Niklas Bruun. Pirkko K. Koskinen has been a pioneer in studying womens' legal position on the labour market. There are currently two chairs in labour law in Finland, one at the University of Helsinki and one at the University of Lapland. In addition the University of Helsinki and the University of Turku each have one assistant professorship in labour law.

Bibliographical Essay

Not many works on Finnish labour law are available in major languages. The most important, by Antti Suviranta, was written for the International Encyclopaedia for Labour and Industrial Relations (ed. Blanpain). The second edition was published in 1987 and an off-print has been separately published in Finland by Lakimiesliitto. A brief description of industrial relations in Finland and the basic figures and facts are presented in the leaflet "Labour Relations in Finland" published by the Ministry of Labour. An almost up-to-date analysis of the Finnish labour market system can be found in the work "Unemployment and Labour Market Flexibility: Finland" by Lilja, Santamäki, Vuori and Standing (ILO, 1990) and in the chapter "Finland: No Longer the Nordic Exception" by Kari Lilja in the book "Industrial Relations in the New Europe" by Ferner and Hyman (Basil Blackwell, 1992, pp. 198-217). A Nordic and European perspective on Finnish labour law can be found in "The Nordic Labour Relations Model" by Bruun, Flodgren, Halvorsen, Hydén and Nielsen (Dartmouth, 1992). A general introduction to labour law research in Finland is presented by Bruun in the work "Labour Law Research in Twelve Countries" edited by Edlund (Stockholm, 1986, pp. 31–45).

Official versions of Finnish labour legislation are published in Finnish and Swedish only. English and French translations of the most important pieces of labour legislation are published in the Legislative Series of the ILO. In many cases unofficial translations are also available in the government ministries. Selected Finnish case-law is reported in English in the annually published "International Labour Law Reports" edited by Margenstern.

3. The Individual Employment Relationship

3.1 Employment Contracts – the Employment Relationship

Finnish labour law pertaining to individuals is heavily influenced by the Employment Contracts Act of 1970, parts of which have been since amended. Section 1 of the Employment Contracts Act defines an employment contract as an agreement "in which one of the parties, the employee agrees with the other party, the employer, to carry out work under his direction and supervision in return for wages or other remuneration". The definition is important not only for the application of the Employment Contracts Act. In accordance with the prevalent theory of the so-called basic relationships in Finnish labour law, it also establishes the definition of a comprehensive area of application for the whole system of rules in labour law. This occurs via the criteria laid down in Section 1 of the Employment Contracts Act which have come to constitute the necessary conditions of the employment relationship. The difference between an employment contract relationship and an employment relationship is that the former commences when one enters into an employment contract, whereas an employment relationship commences at the time when the work that has contracted to be done in fact begins. Whereas only the conditions that have been agreed upon by the employer and the employee are covered by the employment contract, different types of norms (law, a collective agreement, etc) come into effect in an employment relationship (see below). In addition, the concept of an employment relationship also indirectly defines the concepts of employee and employer.

The definition of an employee in Finnish law is broad. Even work done at home and work done with the employee's machines may directly fall within the application of the law. Moreover, the requirement that the work be done under the supervision and direction of the employer has been given a liberal interpretation. The mere right of the employer to supervise the work has been taken to suffice, regardless of whether the employee is de facto supervised.

A special legal authority, the Labour Council, renders decisions that are binding on the courts concerning questions related to the application of labour legislation. The Labour Council also renders opinions on the interpretation of various statutory labour laws. In accordance with the tripartite principle, the Labour Council is composed of impartial civil servant representatives (including the chairperson) and representatives of the employees and employers.

3.1.1 The Form and Period of Validity of an Employment Contract

Every person who has reached the age of 15, may enter into an employment contract as an employee. The employer may be either a physical or a legal entity.

A contract of employment may be concluded in any form. It may be written or oral, or it may even based on a conclusion of fact. In cases where the conditions of employment are oral or a conclusion of fact, each of the parties is obligated upon request to give the other party a written confirmation of the agreed conditions. An employment contract concluded for a specified period in excess of one year should be in writing. A contract of employment which has not been drawn up in writing becomes a contract for an indefinite period one year from the date when the contract began.

An employment contract may be concluded for a specified period, or for an indefinite period with the possibility of termination by giving notice. By an employment contract for a specified period is understood a contract for the completion of a particular job or a contract whose time limit is apparent from its purpose (for example a leave-of-absence on account of illness). These limitations are to prevent the circumvention of the employee's protection against unfounded dismissal. According to the Employment Contracts Act an employment contract may only be concluded for a specified period at the initiative of the employer if the firm's operations or the work to be carried out constitutes a justifiable reason for concluding a contract for a specified period. An employment contract for a specified period that conflicts with these limitations is deemed valid for an indefinite period of time.

An employment contract for a specified or indefinite period may contain a trial period of not more than four, or in some cases, six months. An agreement on a trial period may not however, without good reason, be entered into if the employee is concluding an employment contract with a previous employer concerning employment which is equivalent to previous employment where the employment begins within a reasonable time of the expiry of the previous contract.

3.1.2 Duties of the Employee

An employee is, under the Employment Contracts Act, responsible for carrying out the assigned tasks conscientiously and in accordance with the employer's directions and instructions provided that the employer acts within his or her competence. In addition the employee is to observe the precautions required by safety at work, is not to divulge any of the employer's business or trade secrets that have been entrusted to the employee or otherwise come to the employee´s knowledge and is not to accept bribes. The employee is not to conclude a contract with an employer engaged in a competing activity nor in any other way engage in competitive activities which could cause damage to the employer. Contracts restricting competing activities after the end of the employment relationship are separately regulated in the law.

3.1.3 Wages

In an employment relationship remuneration for work performed is the main obligation of the employer. The amount of remuneration is not fixed by either the Employment Contracts Act or any other law. The Employment Contracts Act on the other hand does contain general provisions on the different kinds of wages, the basis for fixing the wage, the time and place, and manner of payment, as well as the employee's right to a wage during the time he or she has been unable to work on account of causes brought about by the employer, or on account of unavoidable or comparable hindrances or on account of the employee's illness. The size of the remuneration is either fixed in the employment contract, or more often, determined according to the provisions in a normally or generally binding collective agreement (see below).

Agreement may be made for remuneration to be paid either in money, or in kind or in a combination of the two. If nothing else has been agreed, however, remuneration must be made in the country's legal tender. The basis for calculating the size of the remuneration may be freely agreed. In practice the size of the remuneration is decided acording to the time spent on the work on the basis of an hourly, weekly or monthly wage, on the basis of the amount of work done or piece-work, or on the basis of a combination of these two.

The wage must be paid at the agreed time. Upon the cessation of an employment relationship the payment of the wage is generally due as of the last day of work. A separate legal clause entitles the employee to a wage for the waiting days in the case of the late payment of an uncontested wage.

3.1.4 Wages where the Completion of Work is Prevented

Exceptions to the principle that a wage need only be paid for work done have been legislated for the most part on account of social reasons. The employer must pay a wage where in accordance with a contract the employee has been at the employer's disposition even if the employee has been unable to carry out the work for reasons that depend on the employer. In addition the employee has the right to a wage if he or she has been prevented from working on account of fire or exceptional acts of God which have struck the work place or on account of similar impediments that do not lie within the control of the employee or employer. In such cases the employee has the right to a wage for the duration of the impediment for a maximum period of two weeks. According to legal practice the impediments covered by this paragraph in the law include measures taken by other employees in labour conflicts that prevent an employee from working where the employee or the employee´s organization is not a party and has in no way contributed to the labour conflict, or if the aim of this measure is not to improve the employee's terms of employment or work conditions.

An employee also is entitled to wages for the time he or she is ill if after the employment relationship has lasted one month the employee is prevented from working on account of illness or accident which he or she has not brought about intentionally or through gross negligence. The employee is entitled to wages until the end of the seventh working day after the disability began, after which the employee begins to draw the daily sickness benefit from the compulsory sickness insurance. If the employee has the right to draw the benefit earlier, the period for which wages must be paid is shortened accordingly.

3.1.5 The General Applicability of Collective Agreements

With respect to the minimum obligations of an employer, the principle of the general applicability of collective agreements is of central importance. The principle of general applicability means that even employers who are not members of an employer organization and are not a party to any collective agreement are nevertheless obliged in certain cases to follow the terms of the relevant collective agreement. The Employment Contracts Act specifies that the minimum requirement concerning employment relationships is that the employer follow the terms found in the concerned branch's nationwide general collective agreement. However, although the obligations specified in the Employment Contracts Act have several points in common with the collective agreement which are made binding by the rules on collective agreements (see below), the principle of general applicability needs to be kept separate from the "ordinary" system of collective agreements. In the Employment Contracts Act collective agreements are a means of guaranteeing the minimum conditions in employment relations for employees who may freely agree with their non-organized employer on their wages and other conditions of work.

The duty to follow the general binding stipulations of the collective agreement applies only to the employer. Generally binding collective agreements do not impose any duties on an employee but instead give the employee the right to demand that the employer apply those stipulations in the general collective agreement which are more advantageous to the employee than the stipulations in other provisions (e.g. labour contracts or law) which treat of the same question. Generally applicable collective agreements do not bring about any labour peace obligation. Disputes that arise are disputes involving work contracts and, they fall within the general competence of the courts. Where questions arise on the interpretation of a general collective agreement, the regular courts may request an opinion of the Labour Court.

The generally binding rule in the Employment Contracts Act has often been classified as a minimum wage law. Its legal bearing however is not limited only to wage conditions. It also means that an employer must apply all the stipulations (norms) in the general collective agreement that are applicable in an "employment contract" as well as all the regulations applicable to an "employment relationship". These are clauses in Employment Contracts Act is automatic and mandatory for all employment relationships, viz. a stipulation in an employment contract that is less advantageous to an employee than the corresponding stipulation in the general collective agreement is null and void and is superseded by the stipulation in the collective agreement.

Where no general collective agreement exists for an area and the employer is not obliged to abide by a generally binding collective agreement, the right of freedom of contract is not very restricted. It is restricted only by the absolute statutes of labour law and the general principles and rules of contract law. The Employment Contracts Act contains no explicit rules on how the conditions of an employment relationship are to be decided in cases where there has been no agreement on any question, e.g. questions concerning the wage or questions concerning the stipulations for some agreed wage that for some reason appears to be null and void. Where such questions arise an attempt should be made to ascertain whether the wage is in accordance with what is reasonable and acceptable within the concerned branch.

3.1.6 Other Employer Duties – Working time, Free time, Annual Vacation, and Health and Safety

The employer's other duties, e.g. the right to maternity, paternity and parental leave as well as child-care leave, are based on separate statutes in the Employment Contracts Act. The Annual Holidays Act which guarantees the right to an annual holiday, the Hours of Work Act, the Protection of Labour Act, and other acts impose a number of legal duties on the employer and grant a number of rights to the employee. The following is a very brief summary of the main contents of these acts.

According to the Employment Contracts Act an employee has the right to a maternity, paternity or parental leave during the time which the Sickness Insurance Act grants the right to a maternity, paternity or parental benefit. A maternity benefit is paid to the child's mother for 105 weekdays. The right to a maternity benefit generally begins 30 weekdays before the calculated date of confinement and ends 75 weekdays after the starting date for the first payment. A pregnant employee who through her work is exposed to chemicals or radiation or is at risk of contacting a contagious disease that may be expected to threaten the development of either the fetus or the pregnancy has the right to a special maternity benefit together with the corresponding maternity leave in principle from the beginning of the pregnancy. A condition for the special maternity benefit is that it is neither possible to relocate the employee during the time prior to the normal maternity leave nor to remove the cause of risk.

With a number of restrictions, including the approval of the mother, a father who is not working on account of the birth has the right to a paternity benefit for a minimum of 6 and a maximum of 12 days. This paternity benefit reduces by a corresponding amount the time for the parental benefit. In addition the father has the right to a paternity benefit for 6 weekdays which does not shorten the period for the parental benefit. The father can take time off according to his own choice either during the maternity leave or during the time for the parental benefit.

The right to a parental benefit and therewith also to parental leave begins immediately upon the expiry of the period for the maternity benefit. The parental benefit is paid out for 170 weekdays either to the mother or, with the consent of the mother, to the father if he remains absent from work in order to look after the child. If more than one child is born at the same time the period for the parental benefit is extended by 60 weekdays. Parental leave may be taken two times for a minimum of 12 weekdays. Also an employee adopting a child under 6 years of age has the right to a parental benefit and to parental (adoption) leave. In addition to parental leave an employee has the right to childcare leave for two periods of time. The length of time is related to the age of the child, 2 and 3 years respectively. The minimum length of a period of of childcare is 2 months. In certain cases when a child under the age of 10 years of becomes ill, the parents have the right to temporary childcare leave in order to take care of the child. By means of a part-time childcare leave the parents of small children can also shorten their work time in a way that is agreed upon between the employer and the employee.

The Hours of Work Act gives detailed rules on the regulation of working time. Working time for specific branches, including most importantly commerce and offices, is regulated by several other laws. The maximum normal working time is an 8-hour day and a 40-hour week. It is possible to exceed the weekly limit where the employer lays down a schedule in advance, providing that working hours do not exceed 40 hours a week on average over a period of one calendar year. For certain kinds of work the normal working time can also be organized as periodic work with a maximum of 120 hours over three weeks or a maximum of 80 hours over two weeks. Further deviations from these working hours are possible as agreed in the collective agreement of a nationwide labour market organization. A proposal for a total revision of the legislation on working time, is anticipated to be accepted by parliament in 1994.

The Annual Holidays Act of 1973 is based on the principle of earnings-employees earn their holiday in the same way as their wage. The holiday time earned is usually two and a half vacation days per month with a wage being earned for the holiday period. A minimum of 14 days of work for the same employer in one calendar month entitles the employee to holiday time. In addition there are detailed provisions for those days of absence counted as work days that give the right to holiday time. The law also contains detailed rules concerning the time of the holiday, which can be decided by the employer after having heard the employee's representative. The holiday must be given during the holiday period of 2 May through 30 September; holidays exceeding four weeks may be given as a holiday during the winter. In addition an employee has the right to save six days of the annual holiday until a later date. A separate law on study leave guarantees the employee a longer period of time-off for studies. For this time however the employer does not have the duty to pay out a wage.

The Protection of Labour Act regulates the physical environment. Under this act the employer has the duty to continually attend to the work environment and to immediately attend to shortcomings in order to avoid dangers. The basic principle gives the employer primary responsibility to organize the work, the work conditions and the work environment so that there is no damage or risk to health. This should be attended to already in the planning of the work conditions. As a secondary measure steps towards personal protection should be taken. In the last instance an employee has the right to refuse to carry out a task which may bring about serious danger to the employee's or another employee's life or health. The labour protection representative – the employee's statutory representative in questions involving labour protection – has the right to stop work that may result in immediate or serious danger to the life or health of an employee. The employer or the employer´s representative is responsible for assuring that the Protection of Labour Act is followed. Responsibility for violations of the Protection of Labour Act may rest with producers, importers and sellers as well as, with those who, in violation of the law, remove a safety or warning installation or sign. Violation of the law is punishable by criminal procedure. The duties of combating health hazards connected with employment are covered in the Work Health Care Act of 1978.

3.1.7 Temporary Lay-offs

The rights and duties in an employment relationship may be temporarily "suspended" in the case of a temporary lay-off. Where an employee is laid off for economic reasons or causes related to production, an employer covered by the Co-operation Within Undertakings Act must follow a number of procedural rules enumerated in this act.

According to the Employment Contracts Act an employer may, under the conditions under which an employment contract may be terminated or rescinded, unilaterally temporarily lay off an employee so that the work and the wage is stopped for a specific or indefinite period (entirely) while the employment relationship otherwise continues. This also covers cases where the employee's work has temporarily diminished and the employer is unable to reasonably arrange other work or training which corresponds with the employer's need. In such cases an employee may be temporarily laid off for a maximum period of 90 days. The lay-off may also be given in the form of a shortening of the ordinary working time per day or per week, e.g., a six-hour workday or a four-day work week. In practice the question of a temporary lay-off most often arises when the requirement for dismissal on account of economic reasons or causes related to production has been fullfilled, i.e., when the work has seriously or permanently fallen off or been temporarily reduced.

An employer must announce a unilateral temporary lay-off at the latest 14 days in advance. In addition to the time when the temporary lay-off is to begin, the announcement must also state the reason and the anticipated length of time. Failure to announce a temporary lay-off is subject to payment for damages. In the event that a temporary lay-off is a reduction in the work on account of economic reasons or causes related to production, the employer must give the shop steward advance notification immediately when the employer knows of the temporary lay-off and if possible no later than three months prior to the lay-off. If a minimum of 10 employees are affected by the planned temporary lay-off, the employer must also inform the local manpower authorities. Failure to give advance notification is independent of the duty to provide compensation. The employer's unilateral right to make temporary lay-offs may be extended through a collective agreement.

3.1.8 Termination of an Employment Contract

An employment contract that has been concluded for a specified period terminates when the time period has expired, when the agreed-upon work has been completed or when the grounds for a specified-period employment contract have expired. As a rule the ending of a specified-period employment contract does not take place through the termination of employment. Termination before the agreed time may take place only by rescission for the reasons listed below. An employment contract for an indefinite period may be terminated by notification in accordance with the required period of notice or without a period of notification if such has been agreed or if specially provided for in the Employment Contracts Act. The period of notification may be agreed to amount to a maximum of six months. Under the Employment Contracts Act, one may also agree that the employer's period of notification is longer than the employee's period of notification. A contract of employment may be rescinded if one of the parties is guilty of a breach of contract so that the other party cannot reasonably be expected to continue the contract relationship. When an undertaking is transferred or leased, the employment relation does not cease to exist but the rights and duties within the employment relation pass to the new owner in accordance with the Employment Contracts Act.

3.1.9 Termination by Notice

The grounds for termination by notice are provided in the Employment Contracts Act. The act gives the rules for the individual grounds for termination, i.e., those grounds relating to the employee's person or behaviour, and the collective grounds, i.e., those grounds relating to a reduction of work on account of economic reasons or causes related to production. These two categories of the grounds for termination, which in practice are not always easy to distinguish, have a quite central importance for the procedures used in the termination and above all for the compensation in cases of unjustified termination.

According to the covering clause in the Employment Contracts Act an employer may not terminate an employment contract without an especially weighty reason. The act also lists the grounds which under no circumstances may be considered to constitute such a reason. An employee may not be terminated on the grounds of illness or injury unless it is accompanied by significant and permanent decline in the employee's capacity to work. The legal practice in deciding whether the work capacity has significantly and permanently declined is to consider among other things whether it will be restored and whether the employer has any practical means for avoiding termination. The participation of an employee in a strike or other labour dispute does not constitute an especially weighty reason for termination of employment. In addition, an employee's political, religious or other opinions or an employee's participation in community or association activities do not constitute an especially weighty reason for termination, in accordance with the principle of protection of the employee's freedom of opinion and action. Where these opinions or association activities seriously affect the carrying out of the work, decisions made must observe the requirements for dismissal.

The Employment Contracts Act does not give examples of an employee's person or behaviour which may be considered to constitute sufficient grounds for termination. In legal practice sufficient reason is constituted by carelessness, failure to follow instructions which fall within the area of competence of the employer, gross negligence, dishonesty or absence without reason.

Decisions on the seriousness of an employee's omissions or faults must take into account the nature of the work, the position of the employee within the undertaking, the specific characteristics of the work, the circumstances under which the neglect took place, as well as the result of the neglect or mistake on the employer or other employees. In the event that the employee's behaviour is not especially serious, the general expectation is that the employer give the employee a clear warning about the omission and in this way give the employee the chance to improve his or her behaviour.

The reasons for collective terminations are separately provided in the Employment Contracts Act. A general provision also gives the conditions which an employer must meet in exercising the right to give a termination. This provision also gives examples of situations where the employer is not considered to have the right to give a termination. The purpose for giving these examples was in part to describe situations where the collective grounds do not constitute sufficient grounds and in part to avoid the situation where the individual reasons are circumvented or hidden by a reference to economic reasons or causes related to production.

An important and long-term reduction of work in general is sufficient grounds for termination except in the case where an employee with appropriate work skills and abilities could reasonably be relocated. It is the duty of the employer to offer work where proper training and adequate experience would enable the employee, with pertinent education, general skills and experience to carry out the work. The point of departure is that the requirements, responsibility etc. for the work offered be as similar as possible. It is the responsibility of the employer to investigate what kind of work the employee can do. The Employment Contracts Act also includes a provision making it the duty of the employer to reemploy an employee during a nine-month period from the date of termination in the event that the employer again wishes to increase the labour force.

The Employment Contracts Act also contains special provisions on terminations resulting from the transfer of an undertaking, the bankruptcy or death of an employer, as well as detailed provisions on the procedure for termination.

The protection of an employee against termination is clear: an employment relationship ceases when the period of notification expires.

Challenging the grounds for termination or taking the matter to court does not change the situation. Neither can an employment relationship that has been illegally terminated be reinstated without the agreement of both parties. In general the sanction for an illegal termination is compensation. The termination rules attempt to assure that the employer, as a very minimum, is forced to carefully consider whether to continue or reinstate an employment relationship which has been terminated without weighty reason.

An employer who has without reason terminated an employment contract must pay compensation to the employee for a minimum amount of three and a maximum amount of 24 months' wages. The compensation provided for in the Employment Contracts Act is not related to damages but has the special character of a sanction; the minimum compensation must be paid even though no material damage to the employee has occurred.

3.1.10 Rescission of an Employment Contract

According to the Employment Contracts Act both an employment contract for a specified time as well as a contract for an indefinite period can be rescinded to take effect immediately "if it is justified by an important reason". The grounds for rescission must always be weightier than for termination even though the somewhat inconsistent wording of the Employment Contracts Act might appear to give rise to a different interpretation. Recission requires especially important reasons. Important reasons have generally been defined in law as the kind of neglect or behaviour of one of the parties or the kind of change in conditions belonging to the risks of this party on account of which the employment relationship cannot reasonably be expected to continue. Changes which occur in one's own area of risk do not give the right to rescind an employmemt contract. The act contains quite detailed descriptions of examples of the most typical situations where one of the parties may rescind the contract. In such cases the general reasons for rescission must be satisfied.

Before an employment contract is rescinded by an employer or an employee, the other party must be given the opportunity to respond to the reasons for the rescission. The penalty for illegal cancellation is the liability to pay damages.

4. Collective Labour Relations

4.1 Background

The current Finnish system of collective agreements dates back to the years 1945-46 when Finnish employers reconsidered their negative attitude to collective agreements after Finland's loss of the Continuation War with the USSR and the legalization of the Finnish Communist Party. Within a short time the level of union activity increased markedly.

From the year 1946, when the Collective Agreements Act was amended, the Finnish collective agreement system has been characterized by a high degree of centralization with the system being built "from above" through central labour market agreements and the directives of the central organizations. Both wages and the economy were highly regulated by the state with labour market policy being influenced by the intense power struggle between social democrats and communists within the unions.

4.2 Structure of the System of Collective Agreements

Since the end of the 1960s the Finnish labour market system has consisted of a hierarchy of four different levels. At the first or top level, the central organizations enter into both incomes policy agreements and general agreements. The incomes policy agreements include comprehensive agreements on wages, agricultural income, tax policy and questions concerning economic policy. The labour market organizations, other interest organizations, the Government and the Bank of Finland are all involved in the process. Although often formulated in writing, in strictly legal terms the incomes policy agreement is best characterized as an informal agreement. At times a comprehensive incomes policy has not been formalized but instead one has remained satisfied with a centralized labour market agreement that been based on more or less clearly documented expectations of the Government's economic policy for the period covered by the agreement.

The central labour market agreements and the incomes policy agreements together establish a framework or guidelines for the collective agreements that are concluded by each confederation and do not directly legally effect the parties to a collective agreement. In addition to the framework or guidelines which give the agreements something of the character of an incomes policy for the development of earnings, a so-called general agreement concluded by the central organizations often covers questions to be resolved over a longer period of time. Such general agreements have been concluded concerning the protection of employees against dismissal as well as the rationalization of and cooperation within the firm. In practice the general agreements have been implemented by making them part of the collective agreement individually accepted by confederations for different branches.

The most important level for concluding an agreement on the labour market, is at the level of the nationwide industrial federations, where in practice, the collective agreements described in the Collective Agreements Act take place. The comprehensive and detailed agreements at this second level are of great importance in the regulation of the work conditions at the different places of employment within the various branches.

While is fully possible to conclude a valid collective agreement at the level of the local workplace, the third level, such agreements are more common for large firms, such as Finnair and the Finnish Broadcasting Corporation, which do not belong to an employer organization. Otherwise, even though during the last few years both the interest in and need for local solutions appear to have increased, local agreements are most often still concluded with the support of a delegating clause within a confederation agreement (for a further method of concluding an agreement on the local level see below the Co-operation Within Undertakings Act).

On the fourth or individual level it is always possible within the framework of individual employment contracts to agree on more advantageous conditions over and above the minimum level established by the collective agreement.

4.3 The Form and Parties to Collective Agreements

A collective agreeement must be written and may be concluded between the employer or the employer association and the employee organization. The collective agreement is an agreement on the norms which apply to the conditions to be applied to "a collective agreement or other relationships of employment". This means that by definition a collective agreement must regulate individual conditions of employment in order to enjoy the juridical effects regulated by law.

4.4 Contents of Collective Agreements

The Collective Agreements Act grants the parties an exceptional authority to establish the duties and rights of individuals who are not individually party to the agreement. This authority or power to regulate is narrowly interpreted.

While the power to regulate covers above all the right to regulate the individual conditions or norms in an employment relationship, in practice the power to regulate has been expanded to include other matters. The extension has in a classic German manner come to cover not only so-called solidarity norms (norms about the social facilities at the work place and shop stewards) but also certain other questions which de facto may circumscribe the employer's right to lead and organize the work. The de facto discrepancy between theory and practice in the Finnish collective labour law, i.e. the solidarity norm, continues to exist in a form which does not appear to have an especially large relevance for the actual functioning of collective agreements.

The collective agreement as a rule includes those conditions which are intended only to have legal effect on the contracting parties. These kinds of conditions are normally referred to as obligatory clauses in contrast with normative clauses, which may be included in the agreement under the power to regulate provisions in individual employment relationships.

4.5 Legal Effects of Collective Agreements

The Collective Agreements Act lays down that the individual norms of a collective agreement have an automatic and obligatory effect on employment relationships. This means that where the stipulation in an employment contract is in conflict with a stipulation in a collective agreement to the disadvantage of the employee, it is invalid. In such cases the stipulations of the collective agreement apply.

There are two different ways to guarantee that the normative stipulations in a collective agreement are followed in the work place. In the first instance an employer who is bound by a collective agreement and who has knowingly broken one of the normative clauses in the agreement or who has good reason for having understood that he was breaking such a stipulation may be sentenced to a pay a maximum fine of FIM 121 000. An employee who is bound by a collective agreement may under the same conditions of the violation of individual norms be sentenced to pay a maximum fine of FIM 1 200. This latter sanction has little importance in practice as the majority of the conditions in a collective agreement involve the duties of the employer. Moreover in a collective agreement it is the association which is responsible for seeing to that its members follow the stipulations in the collective agreement. An association which neglects its duty of control may be sentenced to pay a maximum fine of FIM 121 000.

Section 4 of the Collective Agreements Act gives a list of the parties bound by a collective agreement. They are on the one hand the parties to the agreement themselves, i.e., the employers or associations which are party to the collective agreement together with those who have in writing joined the agreement and on the other hand those who are bound by the agreement without being a party to it, i.e., the registered member associations of associations who are party to the agreement together with the employers and employees who during the period of the validity of the agreement are or have been members of an organization which is bound by the agreement. In other words resignation from an organization during the period of the validity of the agreement does not mean that the employer or employee is no longer bound by the agreement for the duration of its effect. On the other hand an organization which is bound by a collective agreement without being a party is not bound by the agreement if it ceases to belong to the member organization.

An employer who is bound by a collective agreement also has the duty to apply the conditions of the collective agreement to employees who themselves are not bound by the collective agreement. However, this provision in the Collective Agreements Act is optional. Under the Employment Contracts Act, irrespective of the restraints in the the collective agreement under the Collective Agreements Act, the employer is also obliged to observe the wage and other conditions which have been decided for the work in question in the collective agreement that is common to the branch in question.

The legal effects of the collective agreement are generally applicable for the period for which the agreement has been concluded. In addition, doctrine and practice support the conclusion that the conditions of a collective agreement have a certain effect that extends beyond the end of the agreement period, i.e., the conditions of a collective agreement are also to be applied during a situation where there is no collective agreement, viz. the individual employment conditions, if nothing else is agreed.

4.6 Industrial Peace

A collective agreement fills two classic functions. First, it guarantees certain minimum standards in the conditions of employment during an agreement period. Second, it operates to guarantee industrial peace during an agreement period.

The provisions on industrial peace in the law on collective agreements is based on the principle of parity. Conflicts are to be formally and impartially regulated, i.e., in law the measures taken by employers and employees are to be treated in the same way.

The point of departure recognizes that the legally enforced duty of industrial peace is relative. The only kinds of industrial actions forbidden are those directed at particular stipulations in the collective agreement or at the agreement as a whole. In practice the duty to maintain industrial peace has been given an all-encompassing interpretation. The only two important exceptions to the main rule that the duty to maintain industrial peace is absolute are so-called political actions and, under certain conditions, so-called sympathy actions. However, the duty of industrial peace ceases with the expiry of the period of the collective agreement.

The duty to maintain industrial peace is divided in general into an active and passive duty to maintain peace. The passive duty involves the duty not to resort to forbidden measures in disputes; it applies to employers and associations who are parties to or who are bound by the agreement but does not apply to individual employees who can never be sentenced for breaking the duty to maintain peace. The active duty involves the duty to assure that members, i.e., organizations and individuals, do not resort to the use of forbidden actions in disputes.

The economic sanction that may be imposed for breaking industrial peace is a maximum fine of FIM 120 000. The fine is levied, instead of damages, with due consideration to the assignment of blame and to the circumstances described in the law.

4.7 The Labour Court

The regulation of industrial peace in Finnish law is based on a fundamental division of disputes into disputes of interest and disputes of rights. Disputes of interest are resolved in open negotiations where the parties may even resort to industrial action in order to realize their goals. Disputes of rights refer in contrast to the application of a pertinent collective agreement and may be brought before the Labour Court, whose decisions are final, i.e., its decisions may not be appealed.

The Labour Court has a tripartite composition consisting of employers, employees and impartial representatives who are appointed for three years. As a rule the court sits in two departments of six judges but it also may sit in plenary session. The plaintiff and the defendant before the Labour Court, are in general organizations who are party to an agreement.

The Labour Court settles 150–200 disputes a year involving a collective agreement's validity, existence, content or comprehensiveness. The Labour Court not only decides whether an action has violated the Collective Agreements Act or one of the stipulations of an agreement but also considers and passes sentence on cases involving the breaking of industrial peace.

4.8 Mediation in Labour Conflicts

The system of collective bargaining is based on the freedom of negotiation and the freedom of contract. The state however may intervene in disputes of interest and negotiations during a period not covered by an agreement so as to prevent the development of a strike or a lockout.

According to the Mediation in Labour Disputes Act a work stoppage, i.e., a strike or a lockout, may not take place over a labour dispute without a minimum two-week written notification of the work stoppage being given to a mediator. Mediation is the responsibility of a national mediator and six regional mediators. The purpose of the two-week period is to give the mediator the possibility to begin negotiations with the parties in order to resolve the dispute. In certain exceptional cases when it is in the general interest the Ministry of Labour may in addition delay the time for the commencement of the work stoppage.

Although the Mediation in Labour Disputes Act makes it obligatory for the parties to take part in the negotiating process led by the mediator, according to Finnish law a settlement cannot be made compulsory. Neither of the parties is obliged to accept the proposed mediated settlement.

4.9 Co-operation Within the Enterprise

The Co-operation Within Undertakings Act which entered into force in 1979 applies to firms which normally have a minimum of 30 employees and functionaries; the law does not apply to non-profit associations. The original act was amplified in 1990 with provisions on cooperation within firms having the structure of groups of companies. These provisions are to be followed by Finnish corporate groups with a personnel in Finland of a minimum of 500 persons.

The aim of the act is to expand cooperation within the firm as well as to increase the possibilities for the personnel to exercise an influence on the consideration of matters which relate to their work and workplace. It is anticipated that in this way the activities of the firm and the conditions of work will be developed.

Measures of cooperation are in the first instance based on the local rules for negotiation which have been agreed in the collective agreement. The employer's representative is chosen within the organizational framework of the firm in accordance with the character of the issue which is to be taken up in each separate case. In questions concerning an individual employee the measures of cooperation in the first instance are started between the employer and the concerned person. Both parties in the employment relationship may in addition demand that the matter be taken up in negotiations between the employer and the representative of the personnel, i.e., by the shop steward, who, on the basis of the provisions in the collective agreement, is elected by various groups of the personnel, and the labour safety official who represents the employees in questions concerning labour safety. In addition non-organized employees have the right to elect their own representative in situations where they constitute a majority of the group of personnel. Lastly, within individual firms one may agree to appoint a delegation for one year at a time to consider questions concerning cooperation.

The measures on cooperation involve the duty of the employer to inform the personnel of important questions as well the duty to negotiate. The duty to inform means the duty to regularly present accounts of the firm's economic situation and statistics on its profits, among other things. In addition the information needed must be separately given each time a concrete measure of cooperation is begun.

The duty to negotiate covers questions concerning the means of co-operation. Section 6 of the Co-operation Within Undertakings Act includes a description of such questions. The question here is of the circumstances which effect the position of the personnel such as important changes in work tasks, work methods and work arrangements, the movement from one task to another, important acquisitions of machines and equipment which effect the personnel, important arrangements involving the work space and changes in the range of products and services, as well as the closing down of the firm or a part of it or its relocation or an important increase or decrease of its operations. Measures on cooperation must also be followed in cases of a dismissal, a temporary lay-off and with the reassignment to part-time work brought about for economic reasons or reasons of production or with the transfer of ownership of a company or a merger, as well as with connected training and transfers. Measures also included within the area of cooperation concern the plans for the firm's personnel and education as well as questions concerning rationalization, the setting of work time schedules over a twenty-four hour period and the principles concerning the employment and use of outside labour. Also included are the firm's internal information, the work regulations, education on cooperation, housing connected with one's employment and a number of questions touching upon social activities.

The measures on cooperation are not only limited to the means of negotiation, that is to the employees' participation. According to the Co-operation within Undertakings Act the employees have the right of co-determination and in a number of questions the right to unilaterally decide a question. For example the work regulations can be put into effect only if agreement to do so has been secured in accordance with the procedures for cooperation. One must also agree on the content of the education for cooperation and what it shall encompass, as well as questions concerning social activities. Here the representatives for the personnel have the right to decide in cases where it is not possible to agree via the measures on cooperation.

In certain cases the employer's duty to negotiate is time-bound. Such is the case when those measures which are the object of negotiation clearly can lead to the employee being given notice, temporarily laid off or given part-time work. The length of this obligatory negotiating period – which can be shortened only in the case where this has been agreed through negotiations – varies from one week to three months, for the most part depending on how many employees are affected by the notice, temporary lay-off, or reduction to part-time work. Section 9 of the Co-operation Within Undertakings Act gives provisions for concrete cases involving the use of outside workers.

In the procedures on cooperation the planned measure's grounds, effects and alternatives must be taken up in a manner that gives the representatives of the employees a real possibility of affecting the outcome. Although the aim of the procedures on cooperation is to reach an understanding, the employer has the right to decide the matter after the duty of negotiation has been fullfilled.

Through an agreement on cooperation a nationwide employer organization and employee organization may deviate from what is otherwise prescribed in the act. Such an agreement acquires the same legal effect as a collective agreement. The consequences of breaking the act are in general a fine. When a violation of the act results in an individual employee being given part-time work, being temporarily laid-off or being given notice, the employee has the right to receive punitive damages from the employer up to a maximum of 20 months' wages.

4.10 Representation on the Board

The Act on the Representation of the Personnel in the Management of the Firm came into force in 1990. Compared with the other Nordic countries, representation of the personnel on the board has been introduced into Finland quite late.

The act, which covers Finnish companies with a minimum of 150 employees in Finland, presupposes that board representation will be implemented primarily through the support of agreements on the level of the firm. In cases where an agreement has not been concluded, the act applies in full. However, it is not possible to reach an agreement that violates certain central rules, and representation of the personnel must be implemented if at least two personnel groups together representing a majority so demand.

The act gives detailed provisions on the election of representatives of the personnel, on their authority and on their rights, duties and responsibilities. Among other things it provides that the representatives of the personnel must have an employment relationship with the firm. Furthermore, while the act states that the employer may decide to which body the representatives are to be appointed, the representatives are in the first instance to be independently appointed by the personnel. The number of representatives must be at least one and at most four. According to the law the representatives of the personnel may not participate in the consideration of certain matters, such as the choice or dismissal of the heads of the firm, their conditions of employment, the conditions for the hiring of employees and measures to be taken in cases of conflict.

To date the experience of this legislation has for the most part been positive.

5. Non-discrimination law

5.1 Background

Finland does not have a developed tradition of the legal protection of the individual against discrimination. The country's strong legalistic tradition has for the most part meant that the law has carefully regulated the authority of civil servants and officials rather assuring citizens the means to protect their rights.

Historically, Section 5 of the Form of Government Act of the Finnish Constitution, according to which all Finnish citizens are equal before the law, forms the basis of the legal principle of equality in Finland. More narrowly, the Employment Contracts Act of 1922 provided that both of the parties to an employment contract were to respect the freedom of association of each side.

Later, in the 1970s protection against discrimination against unions was increased in various ways while ILO conventions provided the basis for the enactment at this time of legislation forbidding discrimination. Still later, in the 1980s detailed special regulations were introduced to prevent gender discrimination, above all in working life, the latter being a reflection of Nordic legislation which in turn had been influenced by the EC.

5.2 Protection of Union Activities

The freedom of association has been guaranteed in the Finnish Constitution since independence. Even if the Finnish central union organization was dissolved in 1930 on the grounds of engaging in activities hostile to the state and of being under the domination of communists, freedom of association has traditionally been a generally accepted basic right in Finland. The duty to respect the freedom of association has been a part of the Finnish law of employment contracts since the passage of the Employment Contracts Act in 1922.

The current law on employment contracts provides that if there is a minimum of 10 employees at a work place the employer must grant them and their union organizations the free use of the appropriate space in possession of the employer for union meetings outside of working hours with the provison that such meetings take place without disturbance to the operations of the firm.

Special rules on the position of the shop steward attempt to prevent discrimination against employees who are active in a union. In addition, the general agreement concluded between the central organizations in 1946 included a special clause that on account of the responsibility of elected shop stewards they could not be dismissed or moved to a poorer paid job. The 1969 shop steward agreement between the central organizations further strengthened the position of the shop steward against dismissals for collective reasons to the effect that the shop steward is to be the last person to be dismissed. The Employment Contracts Act of 1970 provided similarly that a shop steward may only be dismissed if a majority of the employees whom the shop steward represents agree or if the work completely finishes and other similar work which corresponds with his or her professional skills cannot be arranged.

The Employment Contracts Act contains a number of rules which indirectly protect union activity. One major rule is that actions taken during a dispute by a union organization are not to be considered as a breach of contract by an individual. In addition, a non-unionized employee also has the right according to legal practice to remain neutral in such disputes and is not obliged to perform the work of strikers.

5.3 General Ban on Discrimination

The provisions of the current Employment Contracts Act were formulated with the aim of satisfying ILO conventions No 98 and No 111. The act includes a general provision stating that an employer must treat his employees impartially and that no person is to be given a different position on the grounds of ancestry, religion, sex, age, political activities or union activities or other similar grounds without good reason. The courts have applied the provisions relatively seldom on account of the problem of the burden of proof. The penalty for a violation of the provision is a fine or imprisonment for a maximum of three months.

The prohibition of discrimination is also found in other provisions. The rules on termination explicity state that an employee's political, religious or other opinions or his participation in community or association activities do not constitute sufficient grounds for termination. Likewise an employment relationship during a trial period cannot be terminated for undue or discriminatory reasons.

The prohibition of discrimination originally only applied to an employment relationship which had already begun. For example, in the event a person was passed over in new hiring, the rule could not be applied since the discrimination was not directed towards a person in an employment relationship. In 1986 however the act was amended so that it also contains a separate provision which forbids discrimination in hiring. Similar prohibitions against discrimination are also included in the legislation concerning civil servants.

5.4 The Act on Equality between Men and Women

The Act on Equality between Women and Men, which came into force in the beginning of 1987, was passed on the basis of examples of European and Nordic regulations on equality and in satisfaction of the requirements of the UN Convention on the Elimination of All Forms of Discrimination against Women. At the same time the prohibition against discrimination was altered in the Employment Contracts Act with the removal of "sex" in the list of prohibited forms of discrimination being replaced by a reference to the Act on Equality.

Although the central aim of the Act on Equality between Men and Women is to improve especially the position of women in work life, it is not an act which only applies to women and gives protection against discrimination only to them. The improvement of the position of women includes also an attempt to realize the equality between men and women in other areas as well.

The act includes general provisions forbidding discrimination in all areas of social life which have not been expressly excluded from the area of application of the act. Areas which have been expressly excluded are activities connected with the exercise of religion within religious societies, the relations between family members or other relations in private life or certain positions and posts within the defense establishment and the border guards for which there exist separate provisions with the understanding that exceptions are to be narrowly interpreted. In addition the act does not regulate advertisements which degrade and demean either of the sexes.

The provisions in the Act on Equality can be divided into three main groups: programme requirements, the prohibition of discrimination and supplementary provisions, and the rules on the enforcement of the act and its sanctions.

Unlike the laws on equality in some countries, the Finnish Act on Equality between Men and Women not only regulates conditions in work life but also includes provisions on various agreements, the selection of people to positions of trust, the selection of students and textbooks and other educational material, and the mass communications. In addition unless compelling reasons dictate otherwise the act mandates the participation of both men and women on state committees, delegations and other similar bodies, and municipal boards. The programme requirements enjoin employers, officials, educational institutions and associations involved in education to take measures to promote equality. The programme provisions differ from the prohibition of discrimination in that they are directed not only at prohibiting discrimination but also at promoting equality. The provisions are of a general nature and neither favour nor protect particular persons. Likewise the Act on Equality does not provide for any sanctions which could strengthen the effect of the programme provisions except for the caveat that the Equality Ombudsman may give instructions and advice on their implementation.

The Act on Equality defines discrimination as the placing of women and men in different positions on the basis of gender. By discrimination is also understood any measure whereby women and men are de facto placed in clearly different postions in relation to each other. The meaning of "discrimination" in work life has been defined in relatively clear terms in the Act on Equality with actual examples of discriminatory practices. Although the kinds of discriminatory practices described in the Act on Equality are also illegal under the general prohibition of discrimination in the Act on Equality, it has nevertheless been taken as justified to give a more detailed definition in the act.

The Act on Equality originally only prohibited discrimination on the basis of gender: a man may not be placed in a better position than a woman only because he is a man; neither may a woman be favoured only because she is a woman. When the Act on Equality came into force it was not clear in the text of the act if discrimination based on gender related factors, such as motherhood or pregnancy, was prohibited even if the preparatory work did express such an understanding. In answer to this question the Supreme Court (case 1992:7) decided in 1992 that the revocation of an employee's employment contract during the trial period had taken place on account of pregnancy, and not gender, for which reason the gender discrimination in the law on equality did not apply. Following criticism of the court decision, the law was amended in 1992 to the effect that gender discrimination also exists when a person is treated differently on account of pregnancy or childbirth or is placed in a different position on account of parenthood or family responsibility or some other cause which indirectly is related to gender.

Despite this amendment to the Act on Equality, it is legal to take matters of gender into consideration in work life and to place one of the sexes before the other even though the applicant or the employee is less qualified. Such a measure is not considered to be discriminatory if it can be demonstrated that there is some weighty and acceptable reason in the nature or character of the work or if there is some acceptable reason for different treatment other than the gender of the employee. Examples of such different treatment in the preparatory report to the bill cite reasons which remove the presumption of discrimination: one may look for a male or female dancer for a ballet group or an actor or actress in a theatre group; likewise one may without the hindrance of the prohibition select either a man or a woman as a home-helper or as a minder for the ill or the aged etc. Likewise formal competence need not be the only deciding factor. An employer may among other things consider test results which show if the applicant is suitable for the task. Nevertheless, it is clear that the reason why a more qualified applicant is passed over in favour of a less qualified applicant of the opposite sex must be acceptable. The limitations on equality as found for example in provisions in the Act on Bakeries must be observed even when they are discriminatory; however, collective agreements may not include extra limitations on equality.

According to the Act on Equality the following are not considered to be discriminatory:

1) special protection of women on the grounds of pregnancy and childbirth;
2) military service for men only;
3) acceptance of either only women or only men as members in an association if this is based on an express clause in the association's article of association; or
4) actions founded on a plan and goal of implementing the objective of the Act on Equality.

Consequently, the Act on Equality grants the possibility of affirmative action. In addition a separate decree has been issued concerning the plans of action for implementing equality within the state admininstration – a number of public bodies have accepted such plans.

The Equality Ombudsman and the Equality Board have been established as independent authorities not only to monitor how the act is followed but also to take active measures to ensure that it is observed. The Equality Ombudsman has the right to obtain information from various authorities as well as from persons in possession of information which is of importance for the supervision of the act. The ombudsman may conduct inspections of work places as well as obtain assistance from other officials where supervision of the act so requires. Failure to provide documents or information is punishable by law.

Where necessary the Equality Ombudsman may bring a matter concerning the violation of the prohibition of discrimination or discriminatory job advertisements before the Equality Board. Different sanctions apply for different kinds of violations of the act. The Equality Board has the right to prohibit continuous or repeated illegal behaviour. It may prohibit discrimination or discriminatory advertising under threat of a fine and the Equality Board may impose fines as issued by either the Equality Ombudsman or the Equality Board.

An employer who violates the prohibition of discrimination may receive a court order to pay a minimum compensation of FIM 11 100 to the victim of discrimination and a maximum of FIM 35 000 depending on the nature of the discrimination. The amount of the compensation may be adjusted every three years to take into account any change in the value of the money.

The Act on Equality has given rise to 200 to 300 complaints yearly. Court cases have also been brought concerning the interpretation of the act: many cases have involved the question of appointments within the public sector. At the moment a number of smaller revisions of the Act on Equality are under preparation.

6. The Future

Two features above all mark the future prospects of the Finnish labour market system. The first is the current deep economic crisis in Finland, which is the worst since the Second World War. The nearly 20 % unemployment rate and the pronounced drop in tax revenues have created large problems in the public sector, including the system of social security, while the large supply of labour has simultaneously given rise to the demand for more flexibility in collective agreement rules on working hours and wages. The second is internationalization. The "large" Finnish firms now operate in a number of countries and their relationship to and dependence on the Finnish nation state have changed to a decisive degree. European integration together with the EEA agreement and EC membership negotiations are symbolic of this internationalization; the legal work regulations set by the EC and the EEA agreement are relatively well met by Finland. Another new feature is the availability of cheap labour in Russia and Estonia.

These two features have changed the view of labour market policy of Finnish employers, of both the large firms and the employer organizations. A result is their discussion of the need for decentralization, local agreements, and increased flexibility in legislation concerning, among other things, working hours and holidays.

The Government has of late prepared a series of proposals aimed at meeting the demands of employers and has prepared proposals for a reform of the Collective Agreements Act, the Hours of Work Act and the Annual Holidays Act. Although in the current difficult economic situation two wage agreements have been accepted without any nominal increase in wages, the labour union movement has not accepted the proposals. In the meantime the

Government has been twice forced to withdraw planned legislative reforms under threat of a general strike.

The big question within the coming years is how the needed decentralization and flexibility of the labour market system can take place in a controlled and gradual manner. The labour union movement, which has increased its membership during the crisis on account of the unemployment benefit fund system, wants to maintain the status quo and takes an ambivalent or negative stance to proposed changes. For the unions it in part is a question of the level at which negotiations and agreements shall take place: on the central organization level, the federation level or locally. There is a not altogether insignificant risk of a large conflict during the immediately coming years. Legislation will undoubtedly reflect the necessary changes that take place in labour market relations. The legal structures are however surprisingly robust and have a high capacity for adapting to new conditions, which is why decisive changes in Finnish labour law are scarcely to be expected in the near future.

VI PROPERTY LAW

By Leena Kartio

1. Property Law as a Legal Discipline

1.1 Property Law as a Part of Finnish Legal System

The roots of Finnish property law are to be found, on one hand, in the old Swedish-Finnish legal tradition and, on the other hand, in German law, based on the reception of Roman law.

In Finnish civil law one of the main distinctions is the distinction between *the law of obligations* and *the law of property*. This distinction is based on influences adopted from German law and, ultimately, from the German Civil Code (BGB). This distinction, which has been very important up until the last decades, has functioned as the basis for the whole system of property rights. The law of obligations as a legal discipline has been deemed to concern (subjective) rights to a claim, in other words, rights to obligations; the law of property, on the other hand, concerns property rights. This distinction might have been used in legal reasoning, when legal effects have been pursued in order to derive a distinction between private law seen as the law of property or obligations. Property rights have been deemed to relate to objects and to be rights protected with regard to everybody.

Nowadays the distinction between the law of property and of obligations is not given the same significance as earlier. The "compartmentalization" of rights into property rights and rights relating to the law of obligations has been seen as unnecessary and even misleading. In this respect, Finnish law has followed the development which took place in Nordic law – especially in Danish and Norwegian civil law – already early in this century. Occasionally, it has been held that all property rights pertain to both to the law of obligations and the law of property. The first mentioned applies to the relationship between contracting parties, in other words, to the relationship *inter partes*. The property law side of the rights, on the other hand, appears as the rights of a holder of a right in relation to a third person, who is outside the original contractual relation. Thus, sometimes reference is made to the protection of the holder of a right pertaining to property law when it is meant e.g. that the other contracting party is protected against the claims of the other party's successors and debtors. This way of thinking is connected with a concept that will be mentioned later, according to which property law should deal only with questions pertaining to the protection given to holders of a right in exchange and its grounds.

On the whole, property law as a legal discipline is defined in Finnish law in two different ways at the moment:
1) Property law is a legal discipline with reference to property rights in a subjective meaning, and
2) Property law is a legal discipline with reference to questions concerning the protection given to a third party, in other words, to an outsider in an exchange or, to be more precise, concerning the preconditions and contents of this kind of third-party protection.

The first (1) definition is connected with the traditional distinction, described above, of rights pertaining to the law of property and obligations. In accordance with this definition, the research on property law earlier applied to provisions concerning various property rights and especially to the examination of the contents of property rights. The general doctrine of property law, which contains the basic definitions of that field of law and general principles, has concentrated, especially, on studying the concept of an object and distinctions between different kinds of objects. In addition, an emphasis has been put on the concept of possession and on the institution of registration; possession and registration fulfil the requirement of publicity, which is important in property law. The essential, "fundamental", subjective property right in property law, on the other hand, has been and still is *ownership*. It has received a lot of attention in property law literature. Other rights dealt with have been different kinds of *limited property rights*.

Beginning in the 1950's, property law has been seen partly in a new way. The problems relating to the contents of property law have been set aside and development has gone in the direction mentioned in definition number two (2). This definition means the adoption of a way of looking at things from a point of view that emphasizes *exchange* as the basis for systematics. Then, for example, the question of establishing property rights and their contents remains outside property law. The same applies to judicial problems between contracting parties, or *inter partes,* relating to private law. The objects of examination will be only the problems relating to the *third party protection pertaining to property law,* in other words, problems *relating to dynamic protection in a conflict.*

Simo *Zitting*'s studies started this development in Finland. His dissertation "Change of ownership, with special reference to the effects of registration of title to property" (1951) took the concept of ownership as its object, in contrast to earlier research. Zitting saw that ownership consisted of three different elements; the possession right of the owner, the competence of the owner, and the dynamic protection that the owner enjoyed vis-à-vis certain outsiders. This kind of research method, based on a classification of concepts, is characteristic of the analytical civil rights trend in the Nordic countries that Zitting's research purely represents.

The question of access to dynamic protection in a conflict and its preconditions arises in situations when two rights conflict and both of them can't be carried out at the same time. A good example of this is the sale of the same object to two persons. The right that remains permanent in a conflict is said to enjoy dynamic protection. Talking about *third-party* protection is well-motivated because a conflict does not arise between contracting parties but between persons that are strangers to each other – in the example mentioned previously – between the former and the latter purchaser.

It is important to notice that questions mentioned in connection with definition (2) relating to third-party protection are not restricted to the property rights mentioned in definition (1). Questions relating to third-party protection become relevant also e.g. in respect of rights to a claim, rights to a share (partnership shares, such as shares of a limited company) or in the exchange of incorporeal rights. Incorporeal rights are also to be thought of as individual objects, even if they are not physically tangible objects. The question of a better right to them can become the object of a dispute, just as a corresponding conflict can arise in situations relating to tangible objects.

The analytical research method has prevailed quite clearly in property law research in Finland during the last decades. Researchers' interest has concentrated on various kinds of conflicts appearing in property exchange and credit granting. The emphasis of this kind of view corresponds at the same time to the needs of today. It may be observed here that the same kind of development has occurred in recent property law research, for example, in Sweden.

The second above-mentioned definition of property law does not however prevail in Finland. The research done in the field of property law and also the leading text books understand property law in the meaning of definition (1) as well as in the meaning of definition (2). For example, the clarification of the contents of possession, ownership, and limited property rights is now also a part of property law. As property rights are to be considered then – irrespective of their applicability to outsiders – all such rights whose contents typically pertain to the actual legal use or disposition of objects.

1.2 Future Prospects of Property Law

Problems relating to the contents and to the field of property law, as well as to the future trends of property law have recently given rise to even more lively discussion among the researchers in the field. An emphasis has been put, among other things, on the fact that the analysis of the problems relating to third-party protection might turn out to be an unproductive undertaking in the long run. The examination of legal conflicts should therefore be deepened and developed further. An emphasis should be put, apart from circumstances in single decisions, on the general doctrine of conflict protection and especially on the basic principles on which decision rules in different kinds of conflicts are based.

The problems relating to the exchange of different kinds of intangible property rights, like partnership shares and rights to a claim have not been given much consideration in relation to their importance in present property law. Furthermore, property law and the research relating to property law should quite evidently extend further than before to bankruptcy law and execution law, in other words, to the material norms of enforcement law. The position of the holders of property rights and stability of their rights is, in practice, very dependent on the legal rules of procedural law. Some researchers moving along the border line between property law and procedural law have expanded property law research also to the scope of procedural law.

Apart from the questions relating to third party protection, it is still important to pay attention to the problems relating to property rights as a whole and, thus, to questions relating to the subjects and objects of rights, claims and their termination and the contents of rights. For example, legal rules of the contents, transfer and protection of ownership can vary, depending on who the owner is, what is owned, and how the object of ownership is used. Also, the effects of public law regulation on the basic institutions of property law should be clarified in property law.

Within the framework of the analytical study method *contractual questions* have not been paid much attention to in property law. Various legal types have often been analyzed rather stereotypically. However, it is precisely a contract which influences in an essential way the position of the holder of a right, even in property law. The relationship, *inter partes*, must be evaluated, basically, on the basis of the contracts that have been entered into. A starting point in the relation between contracting parties is the freedom of contract, which is otherwise the case in all private law. It is restricted also on the same grounds as the freedom of contract between private entities generally. Also the general rules and principles of contract law relating to the interpretation and invalidity of contracts and adjustment of contractual terms become applicable.

From the freedom of contract and its restrictions, *inter partes,* must be distinguished the question of whether contracting parties can bindingly determine the effects that extend to *third parties that are outside the contract.* In this respect, the starting point is that no freedom of contract exists. If A for example establishes a limited property right to his object in favour of B, he or she can not bindingly agree with B with regard to his or her own creditors, that B's right remains permanent in regard to them. The question of the permanence of B's right is settled solely in accordance with the pertinent obligatory rules of conflict. By restrictions to the freedom of contract in property law are meant often precisely the restrictions to determine the effects that extend to outsiders.

The requirements of new *social civil law* can not be set aside in the current discussion of the freedom of contract. When inspecting the significance of social civil law in property law, a distinction must be made between the relationship, *inter partes,* in property law contracts and the effects of the contracts on an outsider, on a third party. In neither respect is the influence of social viewpoints great in property law. When it comes to third party relations, it has not been deemed possible to adjust, for example, the conflict rules of property law even if they would be unreasonable with respect to the third party in a conflict. An interesting question for the future is whether and how property law should give more importance to personal qualifications and conditions relating to the contracting parties.

2. Property Rights and their Classification

The amount and types of such rights that, according to the prevailing view, can be qualified as property rights have not been restricted in Finnish law. The *"numerus clausus"* principle, adopted in German Civil Law Code, is currently unknown to Finnish property law. However, the classification of property rights, on one hand, to *ownership* and, on the other hand, to *limited property rights (jura in re aliena)* is well-founded. This is the case despite the fact that the borderline between ownership and other similar rights has sometimes been difficult to define. However, ownership is in some respect a general right compared to limited property rights.

The traditional sub-classification of limited property rights to *rights of use* and to *rights of value* is principally appropriate in Finnish law, as well. Characteristic of the rights of use is the power to use an object belonging to somebody else in one way or another. Value rights, on the other hand, give the holder of a right the power to receive a certain performance from the value of the object (a typical example is a right of lien), or then their purpose is in some other way to secure a claim, for example, a right of retention, which gives its holder a right to keep an object belonging to another in his or her possession as long as he or she receives payment for the claim.

Rights of use might presuppose the possession of an object or the entitlement to use an object only in some respects. In practice, the most important right of use that presupposes possession is lease, which means a fixed term right of use of an object that belongs to somebody else against payment. It is based on a contract. No "eternal" rights of possession that would be in force for an unlimited period of time, e.g. to a real estate belonging to somebody else, can be established through a contract.

Close to the rights of use are the *rights of severance,* in other words, rights based on legal acts to sever from an object something belonging to it, like timber from a real estate or different kinds of land resources. It is very common – especially outside planning areas – to convey a parcel of real estate, in other words, an area the borders of which have been defined, from one piece of real estate so as to form a piece of new real estate. The right of the beneficiary of a parcel before it is formed to a new piece of real estate has also been considered the right of severance in Finnish legislation; nowadays, however it is considered to be more like ownership. The legal position of the beneficiary of a parcel is in many respects very close to the legal position of the beneficiary of a whole piece of real estate. The revision of real estate legislation under consideration in Finland, will, when enacted, draw a closer parallel between the position of the holder of a parcel and that of the owner of a whole unit of real estate.

The most important group of the *value rights* mentioned above are real security rights. Essential to them is that a certain individualized object secures the claim of the holder of a right. In new Finnish literature security rights are divided into ownership securities and encumbrance securities. In ownership securities the security object is owned by – at least for the present and nominally – the creditor. The most common ownership-based real security system is the sale with a provision for reservation of title. In order to secure the purchase price, it is agreed that the ownership of a sold good is to be transferred after the whole purchase price has been paid. The starting point is that a provision regarding a reservation of title binds, in addition to a purchaser, also the purchaser's successors and creditors. Also *financial leasing,* which has become more common in recent times, belongs among the ownership securities. It is closer to provisions regarding a reservation of title than the traditional lease of a movable object. There is no special law on financial leasing in Finland. In Finnish law the assignment by way of security of a movable object is regarded *ultra partes* as invalid if the provisions relating to the pledge have not been followed. The assignment by way of security of a real estate is not binding even *inter partes.*

In encumbrance securities the owner of the security object is normally the debtor. The most important encumbrance security and, at the same time, the most important of all real securities is a right of lien. The objects of lien can be, apart from concrete physical objects, certain rights, such as rights to a claim, rights to shares of a company or certain incorporeal rights. The establishment of a right of lien occurs only in different ways, depending on the object of the right. In order to create legal effects by a pledge, a necessary act to create publicity is, severally, delivery, registration or notice of pledged property. Close to pledge of a claim is *factoring,* which is a form of business financing which became customary in Finland in the 1970's.

3. Sources of Law and Legislation in Property Law

3.1 General

Legislation is the most important source of law in Finland. However, legislation in force does not cover property law, by far, as a whole. As legislation in force in property law is for many parts very old, not even preparatory materials are of great help in questions of interpretation. Legal practice and legal science, instead, have had considerable influence on the formulation of legal rules in property law.

Although the precedents of the highest courts in Finland don't have a formally binding effect on lower courts, especially the published decisions of the Supreme Court have, in fact, a great significance in forming the legal rules of property law. This applies e.g. to the regulation of the rights of a purchaser and a seller in a real estate deal. On the basis of legal practice so-called customary law can originate, as the established legal practice develops into binding norms. This has occurred, for example, with respect to legal norms relating to constituent parts and appurtenances of an object as well as in many questions relating to the rights of use and of severance from a real estate which are not regulated by law. Also legal practice and juridical doctrine operate in these cases in close interaction.

Apart from other sources of law, *legal principles* are sometimes used to support legal decisions. They are legal rules, accepted by a community governed by law, which have not been written in law as such. As a matter of fact, they form the basic framework of the contents of the Finnish legal system. Legal principles are in force although they are not fully followed for various reasons. As examples of such legal principles that are effective in property law can be mentioned the principle of publicity and the principle of good faith.

European integration must also briefly be referred to when talking about the sources of law. The Agreement on European Economic Area, which was concluded in 1991 and Finland's possible joining the EC are to cause changes in sources of law and to the rules under which they would apply in Finnish law. This is true also for property law, although not to the same extent as for other fields of law, in the short run at least. The European Convention on Human Rights, which affects the member states of the Council of Europe, on the other hand, has become binding on Finnish authorities due to a law that entered into force in 1990. Among other things, the regulations relating to the legal protection of ownership on the basis of this agreement also fall to some extent under the purview of property law.

3.2 The Examination of Legislation

Legislation in property law is on average older than in many other fields of private law. For example, the provisions of the Land Law Code of 1734 Codification of the Kingdom of Sweden – to which Finland belonged to until 1809 – still regulate the real estate transactions in Finland although, understandably, quite insufficiently. In recent years legislation relating to property law has also been considerably revised. Furthermore, many legislative revisions are under consideration. The broadest of them is the already-mentioned complete revision of legislation relating to real estate law, which means the total revision of the Land Law Code of 1734 Codification. The purpose is to include in the new Land Law Code detailed provisions on the conveyance of a real estate, the registration of title to real estate, the contest of a real estate acquisition, the registration of limited property rights to a real estate and the establishment of a right of lien to a real estate. At the time of writing this article a proposal for a new Land Law Code is under preparation in the Ministry of Justice on the basis of a commission report, which was presented in 1989.

On the other hand, property law also includes unregulated areas which are not even meant to be governed by law. Thus, *ownership* is presupposed to be recognized in Finnish legal order without specific legislation; there are no general provisions governing it. However, the right of joint ownership is regulated by a separate law (1958). In addition, many statutes contain provisions restricting an owner's legal status. They apply mostly to the relationship between the owner and the public authorities. The objects of the regulation are mostly real estates. For example, the Building Act of 1958, which applies to planning and construction, regulates and restricts construction on a real estate.

The concept of *an object* and the distinction between movable and immovable objects is essential in Finnish property law. Consequently, property law is concerned with fundamental principles relating to the formation of units of real estate as well as to parcels of real estate. Provisions relating to these matters are scattered in various statutes. The basic features of real estate formation are clarified in chapter 4.1.2.

The regulation of the *acquisition and transfer of ownership* belongs, with certain exceptions, to property law. In Finnish legal order provisions relating to the delivery of movable objects (sale and gift) are not included in property law, except for certain matters relating to third-party protection – such as protection vis-à-vis an assignor's creditors. Matters relating to movable objects are regulated in the Commercial Code of 1987, an important legislative achievement, which is based on inter-Nordic legislative preparation.

Legislation on *real estate transactions and other conveyances of real estate* are, on the other hand traditionally the core subject of property law. In a real estate transaction the object of the sale is always individual. In addition, real estates are considered to be very valuable financial objects. The legal relations relating to real estates must strive to be as clear as possible. For these reasons, among other things, the regulations on the sale of movable and immovable objects can not be at all monolithic.

The general provisions on the sale, exchange and gift of real property are set forth in the Land Law Code of the 1734 Codification. Only some of its provisions are still applicable. One of the most important of them is the formal requirement relating to the sale, exchange and gift of real estate. Moreover, the Land Law Code contains special provisions, among other things, on the permanency of the first conveyance of a real estate in double conveyances, on a seller's liability for the legality of a purchase, and on a real owner's right to have a real estate returned to him or her.

The specific form of a real estate transaction was already originally prescribed in the Land Law Code. The Land Law Code of 1933 set the requirement that one of the two witness to a written contract of conveyance of a real estate must be an authority, a notary public. The seller and the purchaser or their agent and both witnesses have to be present simultaneously at the confirmation of the contract of sale. All the essential conditions of the sale must be stated in the deed of conveyance, and any conditions that have been informally agreed upon are principally not binding. The form, prescribed by law, has been interpreted very strictly in legal practice and negligence in following it results in the invalidation of the whole conveyance. This invalidation can be cured only if the conveyance with a formal error has been registered and the period of enjoyment for one year prescribed in the Title Registration Act has elapsed. The period of enjoyment is calculated both from the date of the legal confirmation of possession of a real estate and from the date of the transfer of ownership possession.

The system of notarization has been considered functional and important for many reasons. There is no intention to abolish it in new legislation, either. According to a decree currently in force concerning the obligations of the notary public, he or she is required to inform certain authorities within a short fixed time of the conveyances of real estates, in particular those authorities which for various reasons need to be informed of these conveyances. The obligation to inform applies also with respect to the conveyance of parcels of register units of real estate. With the help of reports the exchange of land property can be supervised publicly. This has significance both for the registration of different kinds of real estate information and for the overseeing of exchanges of land.

Also the old Decree on Improper Clauses in a Real Estate Transaction of 1864 applies to real estate transactions. A provision in it which forbids the rights of repurchase in a transaction involving rural real estate is interpreted in Finnish law, on a regular basis, to mean that all dissolving clauses in a real estate transaction are forbidden. Instead, suspensive provisions are valid. The existence of a distinction between dissolving and suspensive clauses has begun to be considered unsatisfactory. The reform proposal of the Land Law Code, similarly to Sweden's new Land Law Code, has started from the principle that both dissolving and suspensive provisions would be permitted provided that they are limited in duration.

The provisions of the Consumer Protection Act that relate to sale do not apply to real estate transactions. However, the provisions of the act on the regulation of marketing and the validity of contract terms must be applied to the marketing of a residential real estate if a merchant markets it to a consumer. The fairly new Act on Consumer Protection in a Real Estate Agency (1988) demonstrates the strengthening of consumer protectionism in questions relating to real estate transactions. It is applicable when a real estate agent arranges the conclusion of a transaction involving a real estate or an apartment which is used as a residence or otherwise primarily for private purposes. Although the Act does not directly apply to real estate transactions, its provisions have a significance for the purchaser of a real estate if there is a defect in the object of a sale. The real estate agent must, among other things, provide to the purchaser, under the threat of liability to pay compensation, all the information concerning a real estate that he or she knows or should know which bears on the decision to conclude a contract of sale.

For the time being, the *exchange of land is overseen* by many statutes. *The Act on Pre-emption* provides that a municipality has, with certain exceptions, the right of pre-emption in a real estate transaction in a municipality. By a right of pre-emption is meant the right of a municipality to redeem a real estate by the purchase price that the seller and the purchaser have agreed on. The right of pre-emption can be used to acquire land for community construction and for the purposes of recreation and protection. In practice the Act on Pre-emption has so far had little significance. *The Act on the Right to Acquire Agricultural and Forestry Land* has made the sale of these kinds of land, with certain exceptions, subject to a permit. The act has aimed at restricting the transfer of agricultural and forestry land from the ownership of farmers. The act does not, thus, apply e.g. to contracts of sale of land that is used as a residential area or as a construction site, and not at all to contracts of sale in which the area of the sold land does not exceed two hectares.

The Act on the Monitoring of the Right of Persons Living Abroad and Foreign Corporations to Acquire Real Estates entered into force in the beginning of 1993 as a consequence of the obligations that the EEA Agreement imposes on Finland. According to earlier legislation, foreigners, foreign corporations and foundations needed, principally, the permission of the Council of State to acquire real property. The new act, instead, entitles authorities to restrict only the transfer of real estates that are important for national defence, and the transfer of leisure time real estates and recreation areas to the ownership and possession of persons living abroad. In these cases the permission of the relevant county government is needed. Otherwise, the acquisition of real estates is basically free for persons living abroad. The Act contains, on the other hand, an authority to restrict this freedom with a decree under certain conditions, unless the provisions of the EEA Agreement otherwise state.

The registration legislation relating to real estates is considered to be a part of property law. By registration in property law is meant the registration of *rights* relating to objects in registers kept by a public authority. The registration forms currently in force in real property law are registrations of title to property and the registration of other rights to a real estate including mortgages. In addition, on the basis of special legislation different register entries are made in registers.

The legislation relating to the registration of real estates includes provisions relating both to material law and to registration procedures. By far the basic statute on the confirmation of possession of real property is the Title Registration Act of 1930. The corresponding statute relating to mortgages, the Mortgages Decree of 1868, is even older, and it has the status of a law. Special legislation has been enacted on the registration of limited rights on a real estate in some cases. A new act relating to a uniform, data-based register concerning rights relating to real estates was passed in 1987. It also provides for a new registration procedure. This new act will be gradually implemented by Finnish registration authorities, and it has been anticipated that it would be in use in the whole country by 1995.

Most *rights of use and rights of severance* are not regulated by law. The taking of certain extractable land resources (stone, gravel, sand, clay and soil) and the obtaining of a permit for such purposes has been prescribed by law, but this law does not apply to questions relating to property law. The most important laws relating to rights of use are the Tenancy Acts of 1987 and of 1966. Special legislation relating to the rental of a flat has been in force already from the beginning of the century. The Tenancy Act of 1987 applies to letting a building or a part of it (flat) irrespective of the purpose of use. Flats are divided into dwellings and other apartments. Most of the provisions of the act apply to dwellings. The Tenancy Act of 1966 is the first act to apply to all leases of land in Finland. Before it came into force the leasing of land was not regulated by law in city areas. The regulations of the Tenancy Act provide for a partial differentiation based on whether the leased area is used as a permanent residence, for agriculture or for other purposes, such as for business use or for use as an industrial area.

Loan, deposit and hire of movable objects are still regulated by the old provisions of the Commercial Code of 1734 Codification. These provisions do not have very much practical meaning under the present conditions.

Nevertheless, an exception to this is to be found in provisions which apply to a bona fide title (protection against loss of title) with respect to a movable object that has been lent or deposited. These provisions have a remarkable general significance in current property law. They express the general rule on protection against loss of title, which must be applied in all cases except when the real owner has been deprived of a movable object owing to petty theft, theft, robbery or extortion. In other cases a transferee, acting in good faith, is protected if the transferor has had the possession of the object and he or she, acting as an owner, has transferred the object to the possession of a transferee. However, the general protection against loss of title is restricted by the real owner's redemption right.

Legislation relating to *personal property assigned by way of security* is mostly quite new in Finland. The right of lien to vessels and aircrafts by registration has been regulated already since the 1920's. A representative of newer legislation is the Law on Motor Vehicle Mortgage (1972), which permits mortgage as a security for debt on vehicles as specified more exactly in the law.

The establishing of a lien by registration is possible in principle with respect to all personal property of an enterprise within the framework of the Law on Enterprise Mortgage, enacted in 1984. Enterprise mortgage is available for enterprises carrying on a trade that has been entered into the Trade Register. The registration authority is the National Board of Patents and Registration of Trademarks. The objects of the enterprise mortgage are, in addition to the the movable property of the enterprise, among other things, funds, receivables, securities and incorporeal rights, leases and other rights of use and rights of severance. The property under mortgage can be transferred and used as normal business activity requires. According to the new Law concerning Creditors' Preferences to Payment from Estate under Bankruptcy, enterprise mortgage will, as of the beginning of 1995, after certain other preferential claims, have a preferential claim to 50 per cent of the value of the property under mortgage in the bankruptcy of an enterprise.

The old provisions of the Commercial Code of 1734 Codification relating to the conversion of a pledge were revised in 1988. The selling procedure of a pledge corresponds to a procedure which has been prescribed in a new Law on the Entrepreneur's Right to Sell an Unredeemed Object, enacted at the same time.

In new property law, an effort has been made to place more emphasis on certain questions relating to execution. These kinds of questions are, above all, the position of a *third-party owner* and the *owners of limited property rights in execution and in bankruptcy*. There are some scattered rules on these questions in old statutes which relate to execution, viz. in the Bankruptcy Code (1868) and the Execution Act (1895). Furthermore, the new Law of Winning Back Assets to the Bankruptcy Estate of 1992 gives bankruptcy creditors, subject to conditions prescribed more closely in law, the possibility to revert otherwise valid and legal actions made by a bankrupt before bankruptcy, if they violate creditors' rights. The property that has been reverted belongs to a bankrupt's estate. With the enactment of this law creditors' rights to recovery have been strengthened. The revision is based on principles prepared and accepted by inter-Nordic legislative co-operation and the goal has been to carry it out without waiting for the total reform of bankruptcy legislation, which is under discussion.

4. Objects and Property

4.1 Immovables and Movables

4.1.1 General

By *objects* in property law are meant limited tangible objects that human beings can have power to dispose of. According to this way of thinking, objects are *individually determined tangible objects*. Outside this kind of concept of object remain so-called intangible objects (*res incorporales*), such as inventions, claims, or shares of various kinds of corporations. These intangible objects basically consist of property rights with regard to a certain content, although they might more or less visibly be connected with tangible objects.

An object does not need to have a net asset value. Neither is it presumed that the object should belong to somebody. However, in fact, the economic value of objects in exchange has become increasingly important. From this point of view, as objects should be considered also all rights that have a net asset value, such as rights to a claim mentioned before, or shares. As phenomena physical objects and rights are not on the same level and in creating the concept of an object, drawing a parallel between them is not consistent.

It must be noted that this concept does not preclude the examination of intangible property benefits (i.e. rights) along with objects, for example, in different kinds of conflicts relating to property law in which the question is of a better right to some object. For example, in a conflict between two creditors in which the object of the dispute is a better right to a claim from a third party (right to a claim), this object has been individualized in order to apply the rules relating to property law: the question is of a right to a performance from a certain debtor on certain legal basis.

In property law objects are distinguished on many grounds. The most important distinction in Finnish law is that between immovables and movables. Legal rules relating to these groups of objects differ in many ways from each other. On the other hand, it is precisely the "nature" of immovables and movables, respectively, which accounts for the differences in regulation.

Land is concretely the basis for all social activity. Land remains; on the other hand it is not unlimited. The division of land into separate legal units is always arbitrary in the respect that the boundaries of units could be defined in another way, too. The need for the splitting up of land into legally constituted units has led to the birth of a *registration system for real estates* and the significance of the land presumes a splitting up of a land which is as complete and reliable as possible. The nature of the *registration system of the rights to real estates,* with its requirements for publicity and reliability, is determined to a great extent on the basis of the characteristics of the land and the values it represents. The legal relations concerning the land must be as clear as possible. The factual possession of real estates can not be transferred from "hand to hand" like movable objects. In real estate law the legal effects extending to third parties are attached above all to the registration of rights, which creates publicity more efficiently than actual possession.

The crucial importance of the land is the reason for the inclusion of different kinds of provisions in Finnish real estate law that restrict the power of use and the power of transfer of the holder of the right. These provisions are not known in law relating to movable property. They have been provided to secure both private and public interests. As clarified before, the transfer of a real estate presumes a rather strict specified form which, if disregarded, results in the invalidity of the assignment.

A movable object which is transferable is, on the other hand, easy to forward to somebody else's possession. The possession of movables may also be observed by outsiders and it creates publicity. These matters give reasonable cause to link legal effects to the transfer of possession of movables in various situations which relate to establishing and transferring rights. It is true that the legal significance of registration, even in law relating to movables, has grown in recent times.

Despite the basic differences between the regulations relating to immovables and those relating to movables, there are many situations in which the same rules apply. These include e.g. many matters relating to the legal status of the holder of an object, such as the right to proceeds from an object, or compensation for expenses incurred in connection with an object. Also many of the same contractual legal rules become applicable. Thus rules relating, among other things, to the invalidity of a juridical act and to the adjustment of an unreasonable condition, as provided in Finnish general contract statute, the Legal Transactions Act, are applied in legal acts relating to both immovables and movables. For example, disputes concerning the invalidity of a real estate transaction are not uncommon in practice. Also cases relating to the adjustment of the conditions of a real estate transaction have occurred in Finnish legal practice.

4.1.2 Immovables

As *immovables* in Finland are defined real estates, set forth in Finnish land register legislation and other units of land and water areas. The land register is a list of land and water units. The partition of real estates extends to the whole area of Finland. To be true, the land register is defective for the present, especially as it relates to land owned by the State. A two-part land register system has been employed so far, so that register units have belonged to two different registers, either to the Land Register, or to the List of Plots in town areas. The ADP-based land register, based on the Act on Land Register (1985), will gradually replace these two registers, which have been kept manually. The same register units will be recorded in it as in previous registers. Also differences in the regulations on the formation of a piece of real estate shall remain.

The Land Register is a list which is maintained by each municipality, and the State is responsible for keeping it. The responsibility for keeping the List of Plots, on the other hand, rests with cities and other municipalities. The Land Register is kept also for those real estates which are located in cities but which have not been entered into List of Plots.

In respect of private ownership and exchange, units called pieces of real estate constitute the most important group in the Land Register. New pieces of real estate are formed primarily in two ways. Firstly, a piece of real estate can be divided (partitioned) into two pieces of real estate, according to certain shares of the original estate (1/2, 2/5 and so on). Everybody who owns a specified share of an estate has a right to have it divided by partitioning. Secondly, an area whose boundaries have been set, in other words, a parcel, can be separated (parcelled out) to form a separate piece of real estate. The assignee of a parcel has a right to separation from the estate as long as the estate is in the ownership of the assignor of a parcel, or in the ownership of a new owner who has accepted the transfer, or who has received the estate into his or her ownership knowing about the transfer, or who is the heir of the owner who is bound by the transfer of a parcel. In the last mentioned cases the assignee of a parcel receives third-party protection vis-à-vis the new owner of the estate. This is called protection of exchange in property law.

The formation of estates which are subject to registration in the List of Plots always requires zoning. The formation of a registered plot is associated with a detailed plan called a town plan, and also with another plan, which concerns the subdivision of the area into building plots (site layout plan). Nowadays the formation of a registered plot is possible not only in cities, but also in other municipalities. A plot becomes a real estate after it has been surveyed and entered in a register. Only when a plot has been registered in the List of Plots it can be recorded and only then can mortgages be granted on it. Real estates, entered in the List of Plots, include not only plots, but also public areas, like streets, markets and park areas, which are owned by a municipality. They are not eligible for registration and are not subject to execution.

4.1.3 Movables

All objects except immovables are considered to be *movables*. That is why, the category of movables is broad and incoherent. For example, living animals are objects in the meaning of property law. Movables are also goods that are estimated "by weight, measure or number" as stated in the already repealed provision of the Commercial Code of 1734 Codification. Provisions relating to property law can apply to these kinds of objects after the required specification has taken place.

Certain categories of movable objects have a special status compared to others to the extent that the rules that are applied to them differ in some way from those which apply to other movables. As special categories must be mentioned here securities, registerable movable objects and buildings on some other person's land.

A bond security is a document the possession of which is a necessary precondition for its use. In respect of exchange, significant bond securities are especially 1) negotiable promissory notes that entitle to a performance having monetary value and 2) share certificates, which are issued as an evidence of a right to a share of a company. Finland's general law on securities is based on the provisions on negotiable promissory notes contained in the Promissory Notes Act prepared in Nordic legislative co-operation. These provisions have been deemed to apply to bond security types which have developed in the stock market and which are not regulated by law. In the transfer and pledge of a share certificate to a third party, the same protection pertaining to property law which is accorded to the assignee of a negotiable promissory note under the provisions of the Companies Act is accorded also to the assignee of a share certificate.

Important legal effects are attached to the possession and transfer of a bond security in different situations of third party-protection. This applies, among other things, to the protection against the loss of title and to the protection of exchange of an assignee of a bond security. By protection against the loss of title, as mentioned above, is meant the protection of an assignee acting in good faith, vis-à-vis the real owner or vis-à-vis a third party that is in the same position. By the protection of exchange, on the other hand, is understood the protection of an assignee against assignor's later successors and creditors.

The protection against the loss of title of the assignee of a bond security is stronger than the equivalent protection of the assignee of a movable object. Thus protection is not withdrawn in the event that real owner has been deprived of the ability to dispose over the bond security owing to the commission of such a crime which, in Finnish law, would exclude protection against the loss of title of a movable object. The protection against the loss of title of a bond security cures also the defects based on the lack of power of representation. An essential difference in comparison with protection against the loss of title of a movable object is that protection accorded to the assignee of a bond security against loss of title is not restricted by the real owner's redemption right.

The possession of a bond security gives to an assignee the protection of exchange, in other words, protection in a conflict with either assignor's later creditors or later assignees who act in good faith. In connection with the customary sale of movables, instead, the surrender of possession is not a precondition for the protection of the purchaser against seller's later creditors in execution proceedings or against seller's creditors in bankruptcy, but the purchaser is protected against them already on the basis of a transfer contract.

The new data-based *book-entry system for securities* is bringing changes to the Finnish law of securities. Pertinent legislation was enacted in 1991. The implementation of the book-entry system for securities as a whole will take a couple of years. By book-entry securities are meant shares and rights that are included in the system for which security bonds are no longer issued. Security bonds, including as well rights and restrictions relating to them, are being replaced by entries in the book-entry registers. Book-entry registration of securities is compulsory for a company listed on the Helsinki Stock Exchange. Other shares or other rights can apply for inclusion in the book-entry system for registering securities.

Legal effects relating to the possession and transfer of a traditional security bond are connected to the contents of the book-entry register and changes occurring in it. The new law contains e.g. provisions on protection in a conflict pertaining to property law (protection against the loss of title and the protection of exchange) with regard to book-entry securities. The book-entry system for securities is by nature a system for the registration of rights which has public credibility similar to a modern system of land title registration.

According to Finnish law, *registerable movables* are vessels, aircrafts and vehicles. Registration is necessary owing to administrative supervision, taxation and for other similar reasons. The registration of movables must be distinguished from the *registration of rights relating to movables,* in correspondance to real property law. As mentioned before, the mortgage of vessels, aircrafts and certain vehicles as a security for debt is subject to special provisions in Finland.

The precondition for granting a mortgage on the above-mentioned means of transport is that the means of transport has been duly registered. The register entry also contains information about the owner of the means of transport as well as later changes in ownership. The registration of ownership creates the basis for registration of a right of lien. Legislation makes it possible for the owner to pledge a means of transport without transferring its possession. According to special provisions in law, means of transport that are mortgageable can not be pledged. Registerable means of transport have been defined according to their characteristics and purposes of use so that, in practise, only means of transport that are used in enterprise activity and that are economically significant can be mortgaged.

The provisions relating to the mortgage of a means of transport as a security for a debt is under revision while this article is being written. The goal is a uniform data-based register of mortgages of means of transport with the intent of protecting the good faith of the holder of a right of lien by the public credibility given to the register entries.

The buildings on a real estate can belong to persons other than the owner of the real estate. These kinds of *buildings on somebody else's land* often represent considerable economic values. The right to maintain a building on somebody else's land always presupposes a legal basis. Most commonly it is in a form of a contract between the owner of the real estate and the owner of the building, such as a contract of lease.

In Finnish legislation buildings, unlike real estates, are not an independent object for registration. Thus ownership of or a right of lien to a building can not be registered. Nor is it possible to pledge a building which is on somebody else's land. Instead, a lease on the land, together with the buildings belonging to the leaseholder, can on certain grounds be an object for mortgage rights to real estate established by registration. When the lease, with such buildings, is sold, the seller's and purchaser's obligations are regulated in many regards in the same way as in a real estate transaction. Transfer does not, however, require the form of a real estate transaction.

4.2 Constituent Parts and Appurtenances of an Object

Constituent parts and appurtenances of an object divide the legal designation of an object. As in Finland there is no general legislation on what belongs to an object as a constituent part (*Bestandteil* in German law) or as an appurtenance (*Zubehör*) legal practice and juridical doctrine are of great significance in this issue. Although the concepts of a constituent part and an appurtenance are separated in Finnish law, the applicable legal rules are the same.

The relationship between a constituent part and an appurtenance implies a certain kind of dependent legal relationship with regard to its contents, between the rights relating to constituent parts and those relating to appurtenances of an object. The most significant problems concern the constituent parts and appurtenances of a real estate and constituent parts and appurtenances of buildings on that real estate.

In order for an object (subordinate object) to belong to the main object, a certain kind of *factual annexation* is presumed. Apart from the physical relationship, the permanent use of the object for the needs of the main object is presumed. For example, to the real estate belong as constituent parts, apart from natural substances, objects, such as buildings and equipment, that the owner has permanently attached to the real estate to be used. An appurtenance is a separate object from a real estate but locally connected to it and it is meant to serve its purposes permanently.

Apart from factual annexation, often a *community of ownership* is presumed: the ownership of a subordinate object must belong to the owner of a real estate. If for example the holder of a lease of a real estate or the holder of a lease of a building attaches to the real estate something for his or her own use, these objects do not belong to the real estate, although previously mentioned the factual annexation relationship exists. If, on the other hand, an object belonging to an outsider is attached to the main object in the interest of the main object's owner, it is possible that the constituent part relationship arises although the ownership to the object belongs to an outsider. This is the case e.g. when an object belongs to the seller owing to a provision of reservation of title or, in the case of leasing, to the lessor.

The central legal effects of a constituent part and an appurtenance relationship appear in the voluntary transfer of the object. Everything that is deemed to belong to the object as a constituent part or as an appurtenance transfers to the ownership of the assignee, unless otherwise shown. Secondly, in a compulsory auction of the object the purchaser receives ownership to everything that belongs to the object of a sale as a constituent part or as an appurtenance. Thirdly, the transfer of constituent parts or appurtenances of the object does not, without grounds shown separately, bind the owner's successors and creditors before separating them from the object. In this respect the so-called *non-binding rule* is followed through which the principle of publicity is fulfilled and the interests of exchange and credit granting are protected.

If we see the relationship between constituent part and appurtenance as a relationship between rights and not between objects, it becomes understandable that an object (i.e. ownership of it) can be subject to another right, which is different from that of ownership. Buildings belonging to a leaseholder, for example, belong, in the case of the execution of a lease, to the lease.

4.3 Real Property and Personal Property

According to the established way of thinking in Finnish property law, the concept of *property* is formed *on the level of rights*. This, on the other hand, means that property consists of property rights. These rights are either real property or personal property.

The distinction between real property and personal property has a significance in situations when property rights are legally determined. An essential question is, whether the same rules that regulate real property are applicable to the transfer of a right from one person to another. This applies both to the form of conveyance and to legal rules that restrict the transferability of real property or the right to acquire real property.

The special position of real property in comparison with personal property is based on the significance of the land. Therefore real property comprises above all an owner's right to a real estate. Furthermore, it comprises rights to real estate or other land or water area, which are similar to the right of ownership. Other property rights are personal property.

For example, joint ownership by undivided shares to a real estate – in colloquial language a fraction – is real property. Personal property comprises, apart from ownership of movables, all limited property rights, whether their object is a real estate or a movable. Thus e.g. a leasehold to a real estate is personal property. Personal property includes also all such property rights whose connection with the concrete object is distant or missing, such as incorporeal rights, or shareholders' rights to shares of different types of companies, or the rights to a claim.

The significance of the distinction between real and personal property is the smaller the fewer special rules relating to real property are included in the legislation. For example, the Companies Act in force does not contain these kinds of provisions relating to the conveyance of real property of a company. Finnish matrimonial law no longer includes general restrictions on the right of disposal of the marital real property in favour of another spouse, either. Restrictions apply to property used as a common home by the spouses whether it is real or personal property.

5. Ownership

5.1 The Concept of Ownership

The concept of ownership is one of the most important concepts in private law. On the basis of German tradition Finnish law has defined ownership in principle as the complete, exclusive right to an object. The objects of ownership are objects, in other words individually determined tangible objects. If some special ground – law, authorized regulation or legal act – does not set restrictions, the owner can exercise full power over the object. Occasionally, reference is also made to the ownership of rights, such as the right of lease or the right to a claim. For the clarity of concepts this kind of use of these terms is not very recommendable.

Ownership is undivided; thus, it can, despite joint ownership, belong only to one subject. All legal entities which have a legal capacity, physical as well as legal entities, can be owners. Public corporations (the State, municipalities, parishes) can be owners like private persons. For example municipalities as land owners conclude many real estate transactions and contracts of lease with many private entities. Such transactions are by nature legal acts of private law despite the fact that they in the first place aim at securing certain public interests relating to land use and housing policy or other similar interests.

As mentioned in the beginning of this chapter, the concept of ownership has been broken up into various elements in new Finnish property law. This kind of division has led to the formulation of a certain kind of "auxiliary figure". It is easier than before with it to understand and describe the situation with respect to the changes of ownership when the object is therefore transferred from one scope of ownership to another. This conception analysis, however, does not give an answer to questions relating to the contents of ownership.

The three basic elements of ownership, according to the way of thinking mentioned in chapter 1.1., are the right of possession of the owner, the competence of the owner and the dynamic protection enjoyed by the owner. The right of possession is the focal point of ownership. It means an exclusive, statically protected freedom to use the object. The owner has, on one hand, the freedom to use the object himself or herself and, on the other hand, the right to demand that outsiders do not disturb the use of the object. The owner is guaranteed so-called static protection against them. The means of the static protection are owner's actions for possession (owner's action for a prohibition and owner's action for the recovery of possession) and the right to claim compensation for damages and punishment for the violation of ownership. The right of possession of the owner has been deemed to transfer to the assignee as a whole immediately on the basis of assignment unless for some special reason otherwise is.

The owner's competence means authorization to determine legally with regard to ownership. Its component parts are the power of alienation, the power of credit and the power of inheritance. The owner has also the right to make a will and the power to establish limited property rights.

A certain kind of dynamic protection is characteristic of the fully developed position of the owner. When an object is transferred, the moment when the assignee receives protection in a conflict vis-à-vis (the protection of exchange) assignor's later creditors in execution proceedings and vis-à-vis assignor's creditors, in bankruptcy has been deemed important for the transfer of ownership. In this phase the transferred object can no longer be executed from the debts of the assignor and it is not part of his or her bankrupt's estate. It has been deemed that only after securing protection of exchange can the assignee be called an owner.

The most important rationale for breaking up the concept of ownership is that the change of ownership can be seen as a successive series of events. From the fact that someone has the owner's possession right can not be concluded the strength of his or her dynamic protection in various third-party relationships. A good example of this is the position of the assignee of a parcel before the formation of a piece of independent real estate. The assignee of a parcel has the owner's possession right, but his or her dynamic protection against assignor's creditors and successors is weaker than equivalent protection of an assignee of a whole piece of a real estate.

5.2 Joint Ownership

An object can belong by joint ownership to two or more persons. Normally joint ownership is determined by specified shares. The Act on Joint Ownership of 1958 governs this kind of ownership. Corporate relationships remain outside the law, apart from the so-called simple or civil-law partnerships. Joint ownership, for example in a general partnership, is undivided.

According to the law mentioned above, joint owners' shares of the object are equal, unless otherwise agreed upon or for some other reason otherwise is. If assignment of the object for compensation occurs, every joint owner receives the portion of the transfer price proportionate to his or her portion of the shares of ownership. Every joint owner has the right to assign his or her share and to dispose of it otherwise. A joint owner may also use the joint object in any way such that his or her actions do not violate the corresponding benefits and rights of other joint owners.

The most important significance of the Act on Joint Ownership is that it gives joint owners recourse after joint ownership has shown to be unsatisfactory. Therefore, the act contains provisions on the dissolution of the joint ownership by selling. If the division of the object is not possible, or if it would cause disproportionately high expenses or would depreciate remarkably the value of the object, the court has the power, at the request of a joint owner, to order the object to be sold for the dissolution of joint ownership. This possibility is important e.g. with respect to the joint ownership of registered plots in the city, which often can not be divided into smaller plots.

6. Principle of Publicity, Possession and the Registration System

6.1 Principle of Publicity and Protection of Good Faith in Property Law

The principle of publicity is a central legal principle in property law. It presupposes that the legal effects extending to outsiders must relate to distinctive marks. In property law these kinds of distinctive marks are, above all, *possession* and *registration*. The aim is that the trust of an outsider relying on these distinctive marks is protected.

The protection of an outsider presupposes that he or she is *in good faith* (*bona fide*). Normally, a *reasonable* good faith is required in Finnish law: an outsider has not known and should not have known the right state of affairs. By securing good faith the aim is to promote exchange and to protect honesty and honour in exchange. The objective criteria are followed in the evaluation of good faith; the degree of care required of an outsider varies depending on the conditions.

The possession of a movable object creates a presumption that the holder owns the object. In regard to real estates a corresponding presumption is connected with the entries made in registers. The presumption created by possession or registration is sometimes wrong. If, in this situation, the outsider's trust in the presumption created by a distinctive mark is protected, the effect of legitimization connected to the distinctive mark has been created.

This kind of legitimation effect relates to the possession of a movable object both *in a positive* and *in a negative sense*. This effect appears in positive sense in situations relating to the protection against the loss of title. One precondition for protection against the loss of title is the assignor's possession. The trust of the assignee, acting in good faith, believing that the holder of the object has a valid title and that he or she is thus entitled to dispose of the object, is protected. In the transfer of securities the starting point is the same.

The legitimation effect of possession in a negative sense appears in double transfer situations. When a movable object is sold to two persons the starting point is the principle of priority of time, as set forth in Commercial Code of 1734 Codification. The Code provides that the first assignee has the preference. This preference can be set aside for the benefit of a later assignee if the first purchaser has not yet obtained possession of the object and possession is still in the hands of a seller. The trust of a later purchaser in the fact that the possessor of the object is still the owner of the object is protected. The same principles have been deemed to apply to the double transfer of securities.

In the so-called book-entry system for securities, which is the new system replacing securities, the public credibility of the entries made in registers has been carried out according to the principles of modern system of registration. It will be examined in the following discussion.

In Finnish real estate law the legal protection of the bona fide acts of an outsider has been rather defective. The matter is different in modern legislation of registration, which has *public credibility*. This system is in force, among other places, in other Nordic countries. The principle of public credibility has been adopted in the new Land Law Code under preparation in Finland. It is one of the basic principles of the proposals for provisions relating to registration.

The *positive public credibility* of the land title register (system of registration) means that an outsider's trust in the validity of the right registered in the land register is protected. This is not the case in Finnish legislation at the moment. If e.g. A has led X to the sell his or her real estate to A through fraudulent misrepresentation and A, after having registered the title (after legal confirmation of the possession of real estate), sells his or her real estate to B who is acting in good faith, B can not trust to the validity of the registration entry concerning A's acquisition. B gets protection against X's action for annulment only according to the provisions concerning the period of enjoyment for a fixed term of the Title Registration Act. These provisions presuppose, in addition to the good faith of the assignee or his or her successors, registration of a title and the elapsing of the period of enjoyment for ten years prescribed by law. In order to secure protection it is not necessary, however, for A to have registered his or her own acquisition. If the right owner's action for annulment is accepted, the rule is, furthermore, that limited property rights relating to the real estate, such as those of the holders of the right of a lien or the holders of the right of lease, are not, despite their good faith, protected vis-à-vis the real owner.

When the system of registration has a *negative public credibility,* an outsider's trust that a right that has not been registered does not exist, is protected. This principle has not been generally implemented in Finland, either. Although C in good faith purchases a real estate from A, in whose name the real estate has been last registered (legally confirming the possession of real estate) C can not trust that the real estate has not already been sold to another (to B). According to law, B has the preference arising from the rule of time priority. C receives protection against B only after the period of enjoyment for one year, which is calculated from the legal confirmation of possession of real estate and from the date of the acquisition of owner possession.

On the other hand, in Finland the protection of the holders of the rights of use and of severance against the later assignee of a real estate is weaker than in systems based on public credibility. The starting point is a non-binding rule: these kinds of rights do not bind the later assignee of a real estate unless a specific basis of validity can be shown, such as a registration as a security for a right or the express approval of the assignee. Validity is not principally created on the ground that the assignee knew of the previous right of another person. An exception is the right of separation of a parcel of real estate, in which case the knowledge of the new owner of the real estate is enough to establish validity according to law. In a proposal for a new Land Law Code all the registrable rights will have equal strength and the starting point in relation to all rights is the rule of time priority. A previous, non-registered right loses its preference only if a later holder of a right having been in good faith, registers his or her right first.

6.2 The Concept of Possession and its Significance Generally

Possession is one of the basic concepts in property law. This is due to the fact that possession is a perceived side of property law. The contents of possession varies. It appears in different ways, depending on the object of the possession and by which property right the object is being possessed. Possession based on ownership (owner-possession) manifests itself to outsiders in a different way than e.g. the possession of the leaseholder that is based on the lease. An object can be in an owner's possession at the same time as another person possesses it by virtue of a limited property right.

As possession usually signifies the right of a holder to the object, possession in itself is protected in many respects. Nobody can deprive a person of possession of an object unless the law so permits. *A general ban on self-help* is effective in Finnish law: nobody can, despite some exceptional cases, rely on self-help in order to rectify a violated legal state and to restore a possession to the person harmed. The Criminal Code provides, on the other hand, that the violation of possession is a punishable act.

In property law, possession appears as a legal fact to which legal effects are attached. Possession as a distinctive mark of publicity was already examined. In addition, it was stated that possession creates the presupposition of a right to an object. The linking of legal effects with possession is reasonable for other reasons, too. Possession signifies the *continuity of the exercise of a right* and the *activity of the holder of a right*. Possession has many functions which can be significant at the same time.

In certain legal acts relating to movable objects, important legal effects are attached to the *transfer* of an object. An object must be separated from the control of the assignor in such a way that he or she does not have any possibility to dispose of it. The transfer can occur also by means of transfer of possession subject to declaration (*traditio longa manu*) as well as by so-called "short hand assignment" (*traditio brevi manu*) when an assignee already has the object in his or her possession on some ground. The requirement of transfer is not considered to be fulfilled by such an indirect transfer of possession (*constitutum possessorium*), the basis of which is a contract that the assignor in the future will possess the object on behalf of the assignee.

In the pledge of a movable object, delivery is a necessary precondition for the creation of the normal legal effects of the pledge. The gift of a movable object is, prior to the actual fulfilment of a gift, invalid in respect to a donor's creditors, even though the donor had given a gift pledge which binds him or her according to the law. The gift of movables and securities is fulfilled only after delivery has taken place. Also in the sale of securities the purchaser's protection against assignor's creditors presupposes delivery. In the sale of a movable object, on the other hand, in Finland as opposed to some other countries the purchaser is already protected on the basis of a contract against the seller's later creditors in execution proceedings or, against later creditors in bankruptcy. However, in the sale of so-called fungibles, in which the object of the sale is defined only by quality and quantity, it is required also that the objects sold have been separated in favour of the purchaser.

Possession and transfer have legal significance also in many of the previously examined legal conflicts relating to movables and securities. Possession has significance also in conflicts relating to rights attaching to real estate, although less than in the exchange of movables. For example, the conflict protection prescribed in the Title Registration Act after a fixed term of enjoyment of a real estate can not be deemed to be in favour of an outsider if the right owner has not lost owner-possession.

Possession has significance also when it comes to the *right to the proceeds of the object* and *compensation for necessary and beneficial expenses put into the object*. The proceeds of the object have been considered to belong to the person who, after the basis for the acquiring of title has turned out to be invalid, has kept the object in his or her possession acting in good faith. It is generally deemed that the possessor of the object always has the right to receive compensation for necessary expenses put into the object for its safekeeping. On the other hand, the holder is entitled to compensation for beneficial expenses incurred in improving the object if the basis for the possession has been a title which is outwardly legal. The good faith of the possessor is generally considered to be an additional condition for compensation in such cases.

6.3 Registration in Real Property Law

6.3.1 General

The registration legislation relating to real estates and the significance of registration for third-party protection has already been briefly examined. The preconditions for registration and effects relating to material law will be observed in the following paragraphs.

Lower courts act as registration authorities. Issues relating to registration are handled in the office of the lower court. Title to real estate is registered to show ownership. Registration creates publicity and strengthens the status of the assignee as owner. The legal significance of registration of other rights to a real estate or mortgage depends whether it involves registration 1) for the right of claim as a security for the payment of a debt 2) for the permanency of a limited property right. Registration as a security for a claim is the necessary precondition for the establishment of a mortgage right on a real estate. Registration as a security for a certain limited property right, such as for the permanence of lease, has not such a constitutive effect. As a matter of fact such registration is close to the registration of title to real estate because in both cases it gives additional protection to the right already established.

The basic principles of the registration procedure are the *principle of speciality* and the *principle of legality*. The principle of speciality contains a requirement that both the objects of registration and the rights to be registered are so exactly individualized that no confusion arises between them and no uncertainty arises as to the contents of the legal relationships that have been registered. The principle of legality presupposes that a registration authority has to examine on one's own initiative the formal preconditions for registration. An entry in a register can be made only as provided by law. The registration procedure is non-contentious jurisdiction which lacks the two-party relationship which is typical in civil cases. Decisions made with respect to registration procedures gain legal force which binds later decisions only in a limited sense.

6.3.2 The Registration of Title to Real Property

Any person who has gained ownership to a real estate is obliged to register his or her title. An obligation to register title to property applies also to the title of a specified share. As regards a parcel of a real estate, the obligation to register title to property begins from the moment the parcel has been made into a piece of real estate. The system relating to the registration of title does not apply to the register units that are outside the normal exchange, such as State-owned forest areas.

The registration of title must occur within a time limit, which according to the reform of the lower courts is six months in the territorial ambit of the former circuit courts and three months in the territorial ambit of city courts. In practice, the period for the registration of the title to property is usually prolonged by the time limits reserved for the right of pre-emption and for the granting of permission to acquire land. An obligation to register title to property begins from the moment when the title is final. If, for example, the seller of a real estate is a minor, a permit from the Guardianship Court is required. The obligation to register title to property begins in this case when the permit has become final. When applying for the registration of a conveyance for compensation the applicant must pay a stamp duty which is a certain amount (4–6 per cent) of the value of the property conveyed. If the registration obligation is neglected, the tax rises gradually until double the original amount of the tax.

The assignee of a real estate can not seek a mortgage as a security for a debt unless his or her title has been registered. Despite the neglect to register the title, a real estate is leviable for the payment of debts of the assignee and it belongs to his or her bankrupt´s estate. He or she may also reasonably convey a real estate to another party. The most significant legal effects of the registration of title to property appear in the dynamic protection of the assignee. It strengthens the position of the assignee in relation to those who claim that they have a better right to the real estate. A legal confirmation of possession of a real estate does not itself prevent the contestation of the title on the grounds of formal error or an error relating to material law. It is required, furthermore, that the assignee has had possession of the real estate for a fixed period of time. In order secure the so-called right of enjoyment, the date of registration of title to property forms one starting point from which the statutory time limits for avoidance begin to elapse.

6.3.3 Registration of Rights other than Ownership

Mortgage as a security for a debt is granted in practice as a security for the payment of a promissory note specified as a sum of money. The registration of a mortgage is a prerequisite for the establishment of mortgage rights to the real estate. In addition, a contract of pledge between a creditor and a debtor is required. It is not subject to formal requirements. Furthermore, a right of lien must have a legal basis, in other words, a claim in favour of the creditor. If the owner of the real estate seeks a mortgage, the transfer of the promissory note which is to be secured by mortgage to the creditor is required for the establishment of mortgage rights to the real estate. The legal effects of the confirmed mortgage start from the day of application. From that day is calculated also the preference that the mortgage receives in the event of foreclosure of a real estate.

Professional credit practice has transferred, on a regular basis, to the *system of two promissory notes*. The current Finnish legislation does not know this system at all. The registration authority marks a certificate of the mortgage on the promissory note which is to be secured by a mortgage. This promissory note is called *a promissory note secured by a pledge*. It is normally a bearer paper. The *real promissory note* (promissory note with collateral security) shows the real claim. When the debtor obtains possession of a promissory note secured by a pledge, he or she gets a right of lien as a security for a claim showed by the actual promissory note to a real estate. When the claim showed by the actual promissory note has been paid, the promissory note secured by a pledge is restored to the debtor. The debtor may transfer it as a security to a new creditor and thus establish a new right of lien with the preferences showed by the promissory note. The mortgage as a security for a debt is effective for ten years from the day of registration, and it must be renewed during this time in order to keep it effective with respect to previous preferences.

The object of a mortgage can be a real estate, the title of which is eligible for registration, as well as a specified share of it, but not a parcel of a real estate. To satisfy the same claim a mortgage may be granted on many real estates owned by the same person. In addition, a leasehold to a real estate owned by another person can be an object for a mortgage if the right is transferable to a third person without the hearing of the landowner. Also a gratuitous right of use of a fixed period of time can be considered the object of a mortgage.

A registration to secure a right in respect of a third party is possible only if the law so allows. The possibility of registration can be said to be based on the consideration of the legislator that the protection of the permanence of the right is justified for public interests.

A registration is possible as a security for a right of use for a fixed term which has been established by the owner of a real estate. In practice, the most important right of this kind is the right of lease. The law provides the possibility to secure the permanence of severance rights of some extractable resources as well as timber felling rights by registration if these rights have been established only for a fixed term. For timber felling rights the required time is only five years. Also a registration for separation of a parcel of real estate is permitted in law.

The legal effects of a registration to secure a right in respect of third parties appear in changes of ownership. The registered right binds the new owner of the real estate. In the foreclosure of a real estate such rights secured by registration in respect of third parties that are in the order of priority before a claim for the payment of which the real estate has been executed, must be kept in force.

VII FAMILY LAW AND INHERITANCE LAW

By Urpo Kangas

1. The Myth of a Uniform Family and Inheritance Law

In Finland, Family and Inheritance Law is a uniform academic discipline and a mandatory part of the law curriculum. However, despite the heavy emphasis in all of its aspects on private family property, the uniformity of Family and Inheritance Law is an illusion. Questions relating to division of property at the dissolution of marriage and the death of the decedent have formed the nucleus of the subject. Guardianship law is a branch of property law taught as an integral part of Family and Inheritance Law. In child law the emphasis has been on the problems of interpretation relative to a child's right to inherit his or her parents. Legal problems having to do with the family other than those relating to matters of property have not been of great interest. For this reason academic Family and Inheritance Law has long been incorrectly perceived as a uniform field of law resting on social judgments relating to the right of property.

The approach of study emphasizing the legal position of the owner has a natural basis in historical developments. Finland was part of Sweden until the year 1809. Family and Inheritance Law developed into an academic discipline within the university that was founded in Finland in 1640. Within Family and Inheritance Law, legal statutes others than the provisions concerning inheritance and marriage did not exist in Swedish common law in the 17th century. When university education was concerned with familiarizing of students with the contents of the existing law, it was natural that the primary emphasis was placed on the legal rules relating to property rights.

This tradition continued during the period from 1809 to 1917, when Finland belonged to the Russian empire as an autonomous grand duchy. It has continued since Finland gained independence in 1917 up until very recently. Today there are three law faculties in the country and they all include Family and Inheritance Law as part of private law. Even as late as in the mid-70's, the teaching of Family and Inheritance Law was integrated with the teaching of property law. Even when teaching and research in Family and Inheritance Law was separated from property law and became a discrete academic discipline, the old tradition was not completely abondoned. In Finland, unlike in many other countries, Family and Inheritance Law is not divided into different subjects in terms of research and teaching, but is taught as an integrated discipile. The determination of the rightful owner continues to be the mother of all questions within Family and Inheritance Law.

The uniformity of Family and Inheritance Law has not always been mere fiction. In 1734 only two significant statutes existed in the field of Family and Inheritance Law, concerning marriage and inheritance respectively. The number of individual provisions was approximately 200. A lawyer in those days could be said to have literally mastered Family and Inheritance Law when he knew the contents of these provisions. Today, in the field of private law alone, nearly 50 different acts or decrees that regulate the legal status of the family are in force. They contain nearly 2 000 individual paragraphs. If all the provisions that regulate the status of the family within the field of public law were to be added to this, the total number of individual legal rules would come to 20 000. Such old legal principles as *"jura novit curia"* and *"ignoratia iuris nocet"* could not have evolved under such extensive legal regulation. The increase of regulation has crushed the dream of a uniform Family and Inheritance Law.

> The hard core of Family and Inheritance Law consists of the marriage law, the child law and the inheritance law. The Marriage Act dates back to 1930. It has later changed in many respects, e.g. the divorce system and the distribution of matrimonial property were renewed in 1988. The predecessor of the Marriage Act, the Spouses' Property Relation Act 1889, is still partly in force. The Illegitimate Children Act was enacted in 1922 and it was in force until 1st October 1976. Since that time the most important legislation in the branch of child law is as follows. The Paternity Act applies to the presumption and establishment of paternity, and it, as well as the Child Maintenance Act, entered into force on 1st October 1976. Some time later the Security of Child Maintenance Act went into effect. Both the Child Welfare Act and Child Custody and Right of Access Act were enacted in 1983. The Adopted Children Act of 1925, was reeplaced by a new Adoption Act, which went into force as early as 1980 and was reenacted in 1985. The difference between the Adoption Acts of 1980 and 1985 is that the latter also contains rules concerning private international law. The Guardianship Act was enacted in 1988, and it is still in force. However, the main content of the guardianship system

was changed in 1983 in the context of the old act. The Code of Inheritance entered into force in 1966, but the main content of the code was written already in the 1930's. In 1983 the code was changed in respect of the surviving spouse, who was given the right to administrate the estate before lineal descendants. At the same time also the distribution of a farm as part of an estate was enacted upon.

The changes that have taken place within society and in the contents of the legal system have raised new questions that cannot be answered by viewing the legal status of the family from the point of view of the law of obligations and the law of property. The myth of a uniform Family and Inheritance Law has been destroyed at the very latest due to the social progress that has taken place since the Second World War. There no longer is a single family law or a single inheritance law – there are only legal problems concerning the family. A number of them have to do with ownership, but by no means all. Questions within Family and Inheritance Law relating directly to issues other than ownership directly are e.g. child maintenance, child welfare and family support.

In spite of the explosive growth of legislation within Family and Inheritance Law, some of the most difficult problems still lack an answer. There is no special statute in Finland regulating the legal relationship of cohabitees that would provide protection at the expiration of the relationship. The legal problems of cohabitation have been left to rest on the general principles of private law.

The history of legal research within the field of Family and Inheritance Law is the best indicator of the nature of the matters regarded as forming the nucleus of the discipline. This trend can to some extent be measured by the themes of doctoral dissertations, which in the Finnish academic tradition are extensive, printed products of reseach corresponding to the German-type doctoral thesis, a written work of exceptionally high quality. In the 20th century, two doctoral dissertations in the field of testamentary law, five within inheritance law, two within marriage law and one within child law have been published in Finland. Ten doctors of Family and Inheritance Law in less than a century is not many, although the population of Finland did not exceed three million at the beginning of this century, and even today is not more than five million.

As a result, an integral part or research within Family and Inheritance Law consists of various other published works of research, commentaries and articles. Within inheritance and marriage law, published written works of this type have reached the extent of approximately 10 000 pages, and within guardianship law and child law the corresponding figures are 2 000 and 2 500 pages respectively. This equals some 10 % of all published research within private law. Legal training has also been built on this foundation. Each student is required to master one written work on inheritance law, one on testamentary law, one on marriage law, one on guardianship law and one on child law. The examination requires a detailed knowledge of nearly 2 000 pages worth of printed text.

2. The Classic Paradigm of Family and Inheritance Law

The goals of research concerned with Family and Inheritance Law have been very practically orientated. The purpose has usually been to formulate the principles of a single legal conflict and its solution. The answer to a problem is the result of research. How marital property is to be distributed, how the creditor of a spouse is protected, what the liability of a minor heir for the debts of the deceased is, in what statutory form an inheritance is to be distributed are only examples of innumerable intertwining questions.

Who, then, needs the answers to questions that are posed this way? Who is the addressee of information relating to Family and Inheritance Law? And how is this information produced? There is not only one consumer of information; there are several of them, usually individuals who are not aware of their rights: someone inquiring whether or not he or she is allowed to dispose of property without spoucal consent, a divorced person inquiring how much alimony must be payed to a former spouse, a father inquiring how he can legally donate property to his child. A lawyer's task is to find answers to these questions. For this reason a student must be able to solve legal cases in an examination. He or she is literally learning the trade of the lawyer.

Family and Inheritance Law is used by the court to find solutions to real-life problems. It must solve the conflicts that emerge between parties. However, in an actual decision-making situation it only rarely has the time to conduct extensive basic research – it has to come to a solution purely relying on its background and experience.

Who, then, produces information concerning Family and Inheritance Law and in what way is this done? Within the framework of the social division of labor, basic research is the task of the university. In theory, a researcher has an earnest ambition to find the answer to a question posed to him and almost limitless time to find it. But answers are not always merely waiting for their discoverer. The researcher has to draw information from several different sources. Finland is one of the countries in which matters are regulated by law. The legal text is the primary source of information. One old oral judge's rule has it that in solving so-called hard cases, the law can be of some use. However, the legal text is seldom unambiguous enough to give a direct answer to an individual legal problem. This is often due to the fact that the set of circumstances of the question at hand does not correspond to the situation described in the law. A total correspondence and isomorphia between the law and the problem is merely a dream. The correspondence that seems to exist between the law and the problem is created by the interpreter opinion that such a relationship exists.

In the field of Family and Inheritance Law – as well as in other legal decision-making – the contents of the written law attempts to clarify with the aid of additional material. In practice, an important source of the law is the legislative history of the written law. The Finnish law-drafting process produces plenty of written text. The instructions of the Government and the ministries, committee reports, Government bills and views brought forward in the Parliament in the end lead to the drafting of a law. A single sentence in a legal text is the proverbial tip of the iceberg – the majority of the whole is covered under the surface. Anyone practicing law must to be familiar with the material produced during the law-drafting process. Often this background material can be used to clarify ambiguous sentences in the law.

But in interpreting legislative history we are faced with the same problem as in interpreting a sentence in the law. Piecing together the comments one finds in legislative history to support a conclusion requires interpretation. The important ingredients must be sifted out and the unimportant must be rejected. For instance, the most important piece of legislative history in view of interpreting the Inheritance Code in force in Finland today can be considered to be a report published in 1935, even though the law itself did not enter into force until 1966. During the intervening thirty years plenty of other, irrelevant pieces of legislative history were produced.

One of the problems of the doctrine of the sources of law within Finnish Family and Inheritance Law concerns the relevance of the legislative history of a foreign country, i.e. that of Finland's neighboring country Sweden. The Finnish Marriage Act in principle conforms to the decisions that were made in the beginning of the century within the framework of general Nordic legislative history in Norway, Sweden and Denmark. Finland renewed her own Marriage Act in 1930, and its basic principles corresponded to those of other Nordic countries. For this reason it is possible to rely also on Nordic legislative material (travailles preparatoires) in solving several basic problems of the interpretation of the Finnish Marriage Act.

A similar situation can be seen in inheritance law. In Swedish legislative history there are considerably more detailed accounts on such statutes that are ad verbitum in force both in Sweden and Finland. In such instances anyone interpreting the law in Finland cannot ignore its factual background.

However, among the abundant number of legal rules of Family and Inheritance Law there are also genuinely more independent legal rules, whose connection to Swedish law is not as direct. For instance, the closest ideological background of the child legislation that was enacted in the 1970's is the American legal discussion. Such material is not given nearly as great an emphasis in the process of solving legal problems as traditional sources of the law. In contrast, international agreements such as the United Nations Declaration of Children's Rights require the interpreter of the law to formulate his or her comment in accordance with their contents.

One traditional part of the sources of law consists of the practice of the courts, the cases. Even though Finland is not a case law country as such, cases may have great weight, especially if a particular matter in the law was previously unclear. The weight that the precedents of the court have as sources of law is indicated by the fact that in basic written works on marriage, inheritance, testamentary and guardianship law there are approximately 700 references to legal precedents. Even though all the precedents referred to are not regarded as correct, in most cases a basic textbool attempts to substantiate an interpretation by citing precedents in the practice of the courts. However, one must remember that an interpreter of the law chooses the cases that he or she wishes to use to justify his or her own point of view.

The answer that a researcher of legal dogmatics, a professional of a certain branch of law (criminal law, administration law, taxation law, family law, labor law etc.) gives to a question is not the sum of fragments of information. The equation of legal dogmatics is not form (legal text + legislative history + judicial literature). An equation requires that its factors are of the same order. In legal dogmatics it is necessary to convert the factors to the same terms with the aid of a background theory and general doctrine. Without these, legal dogmatics is not even possible.

Legal dogmatics concerned with the study of Finnish Family and Inheritance Law could be generally characterized as analytical civil law. The study of analytical civil law has a critical view towards drawing conclusions from concepts; it emphasizes the pragmatism of language and the analysis of legal problems. With each individual case we must first ask what the relationship in which the claim is made is, how the judicial relations are defined ultra partes and inter partes, what the position of the third party is. One can find this line of questioning in all literature concerning the aspect of law of obligations and law of property in Family and Inheritance Law.

But as the myth of uniform Family and Inheritance Law has disintegrated, a similar process has taken place in tendency how to pursue research on Family and Inheritance Law only on the aforementioned basis. The monopoly status of practical legal dogmatics has wavered. The knowledge interests of the welfare state are directed toward the analysis of the functioning of the different systems, the deciphering of the social impact of the law, and the critical evaluation of the value judgments behind the law. The picture of Family and Inheritance Law created by traditional practical legal dogmatics is completed by a critical study of Family and Inheritance Law.

3. The Alternative Paradigms of Family and Inheritance Law

The first signs of the change in paradigm within Finnish Family and Inheritance Law can be found at the beginning of the 1970's. At that time several statistical studies were conducted, whose purpose was to clarify how Family and Inheritance Law operates in society. The object was to study e.g. the amount of alimony payable to the spouse and child, the designation of a provider, the duration of marriage, economic matters concerning divorce, testamentary practices, the age structure of decedents and heirs, the property structure of an estate, and the popularity of cohabitation. This information has not been included in official statistics, which meant that it had to be collected from various sources for the research.

This research provided plenty of such new information that later led to a redefinition of Family and Inheritance Law in terms of its contents. This was also the definite goal of such Family and Inheritance Law research as pursued from the standpoint of an empirical paradigm. The research did not essentially seek to influence the contents of a single legal case in a concrete conflict situation. For this reason the traditional researchers who relied on the paradigm of practical legal dogmatics criticized the research based on statistical data on the grounds that it led to the politicalization of the law. Statistical research was proved to be more clearly value-ridden than legal dogmatics aimed at solving a conflict.

The basic criticism of traditional legal dogmatics directed at researchers representing the empirical paradigm was crystallized into the slogan: "Interesting, but this is not legal dogmatics ! A legal paragraph and a percentage cannot be added up". In the theoretical criticism directed against the empirical paradigm there was also a reference to the Hume Guillotine, according to which "is" (Sein) cannot lead to "ought" (Sollen). Those who criticized legal dogmatics based on statistical data were of the opinion that statistics have no relevance in solving an individual legal problem. The empirists rejected this criticism, claiming that statistical data could better indicate what existing law was than traditional legal dogmatics with its own means of justification.

Research of Family and Inheritance Law based on statistical data could be regarded as a (partly) passing fashion phenomenon of the 1970's. However, it left a void that could not be filled with traditional legal dogmatics. In its stead research began to rely more heavily on legal history. Research with a historical emphasis was interested in – besides a purely descriptive knowledge interest – two questions concerning Family and Inheritance Law.

In the first of these the aim was to clarify the factors leading to the emergence of Family and Inheritance Law. This process moved from an understanding of current practices to the historical and then from the historical back to the modern. The research goal was to observe what had occurred a hundred or two hundred years earlier. With the help of this information was then possibly easier to understand the modernity. These two periods, the past and the present, were then compared, and on the basis of the data acquired in this way an attempt was made to assess how well present-day Family and Inheritance Law corresponds to the needs of society and in what direction the laws should be changed. Legal research with a historical emphasis was conducted in all sectors of Family and Inheritance Law. Its objects were e.g. divorce legislation, inheritance law and child law.

The sources for research of Family and Inheritance Law from the point of view of legal history were often the same as those used from the point of view of someone pursuing traditional legal dogmatics. But the fundamental question that a researcher with a historical emphasis was trying to clarify was not the same as the one being studied by someone working from a more traditional standpoint. Researchers, who used this method, were not so much interested in the existing Family and Inheritance Law in Finland as they were in the questions of which social factors lead at any given time lead to the forming of the contents of Family and Inheritance Law are, as well as the extent to which people's behavior can be directed by changes in the law. The latter question received considerable emphasis in assessing the impact of changes in divorce law on divorce frequency in various time periods.

In the methodological progress of research concerning Family and Inheritance Law a new line of thinking that may be called goal-rational legal dogmatics emerged in the early 1980's. Its goal was to analyze the entire legal system from the point of view of a certain problem and at the same time to consciously strive to develop legal dogmatics as a social science. Its research interests differed from those of traditional legal dogmatics, whose research was based on statistical data and whose interest lay the study of legal history.

Goal-rational legal dogmatics is not only concerned with such questions as "how many" or "how a certain law is to be applied in a particular case", or "what impacts law will have on human behavior". Goal-rational legal dogmatics is interested in the functioning of the legal system in a situation where all mechanisms that are put in place to control any given situation are taken into account. Control of the whole, the coherence and incoherence of the legal system, the bringing together of different legal sub-systems, the random accumulations of interests – these are the kind of issues that goal-rational legal dogmatics seeks to address, and it does this with success.

The study used as an example concerned the legal position of the surviving spouse. Traditional legal dogmatics had only been interested in how surviving spouses position had been arranged from the point of view of inheritance law. Goal-rational legal dogmatics was interested in clarifying what kind of mechanisms had been created to protect surviving spouse and how these various legal arrangements influenced the surviving spouses economic position. In the study, the protective mechanisms within both private and public law were combined. The sphere of traditional Family and Inheritance Law was extended to embrace also the survivor's pension schemes and other forms of protection.

Goal-rational legal dogmatics seeks to study the control structure of the welfare state as a functioning whole. It clearly removes itself from the model of traditional legal dogmatics, but it also differs from studies conducted within the empirical and historical paradigm. The aim of goal-rational Family and Inheritance Law is to systematize the legal system as a functional whole. It focuses a uniform line of examination on all the judicial rules that had been applied to solve problems with similar or identical causes.

A new way of framing questions is providing an opportunity to decipher the legal system in a completely new way. Particularly in research relating to Family and Inheritance Law, it is not possible to gain a complete picture of e.g. the factors affecting the livelihood of a family with a child and the interests of a child if research is only concerned with the rules of child law within private law.

Family and Inheritance Law is a field concerned with the family and the relationships of family members. Traditional research of Family and

Inheritance Law was imbued with emphasized gender neutrality. Family members were individuals without gender. Researchers within women's legal studies have crushed the concept of genderless law. In recent years their research has also reached into the field of Family and Inheritance Law. Several already published and yet unfinished studies are attempting to clarify the gender models included in Family and Inheritance Law. This new point of view is making a valuable contribution to the research of Family and Inheritance Law.

4. The General Doctrine of Family and Inheritance Law

The general methodological development of legal dogmatics has also been visible in research concerning Family and Inheritance Law. It is only natural that research has not differed methodologically from other research within private law at a stage of development when the object was merely interpreted as a category of the law of obligations and property. The same approach, which was also pursued in the study of other questions pertaining to general private law, was also applicable to the analysis of questions concerning Family and Inheritance Law.

Family and Inheritance Law can no longer rely on the system of general doctrine borrowed from the law of obligations and property. As the sphere of legal dogmatics has expanded, so has the field of general doctrine also grown. Within the research of Family and Inheritance Law there is no longer a single system of general doctrine – there are several parallel ones. They are not mutually exclusive, because their justification is based on different knowledge interests.

As a theoretical construction of legal dogmatics, general doctrine consists of two kinds of elements. On the one hand, it is concerned with basic concepts of a certain field of the law, its conceptual systems, and, on the other hand, with general principles of law. As a conceptual system, the general doctrine endeavors to reach the basic structure of a field of law - these basic concepts and generale principles make it specific in terms of its object. As a result we may speak of a special aim-seeking tendency within the general doctrine. For this reason alone Family and Inheritance Law cannot have a single uniform general doctrine because it does not have a single object. The basic concepts of inheritance law and, let us say for example guardianship law differ from each other in terms of the object that the body of concepts seeks to differentiate.

For their part, general principles of law, as part of the general doctrine, seek to reach the basic contents, which are grounded in moral precepts. Autonomy of will within testamentary law, the best interests of the child within child law, and protective principles within guardianship law are typical representatives of the general principles of law which indicate the approach that is to be taken in differentiating the system.

The elements of the general doctrine, conceptual systems and general principles of law make possible the systematizing of the law. This is a central task of legal dogmatics. With its help the law is made into a controllable system, in terms of its contents, upon which the interpretation of the law can rely. From the point of view of legal decision-making the general doctrine is important in at least two respects. That aspect of the general doctrine which concerns the conceptual system makes it possible to locate the legal problem. The general principles, then, direct the contents of the solution in situations of interpretation and gaps in the law.

The success of the general doctrine concerning Family and Inheritance Law is essentially dependent on how it succeeds in differentiating the object. If the general doctrine at hand does not aid in satisfying the knowledge requirement, it must be replaced with others. The general doctrine does not form a closed system in relation to the world outside the normative system - it is influenced by society. Changes of the goals and principles of society have resulted in changes in the legal system. For instance the way that the legal status of the child is perceived has undergone such a thorough change during the recent decades that the traditional corpus of child law is worthless from the point of view of interpreting and systematizing modern law.

This is partly due to a change in the nature of legal control. Previously Family and Inheritance Law had typically attempted to organize the legal problems of the static social phase. This phase was regarded as established, which is why also judicial problems were believed to remain unchanged. Moreover, only a definite number of problems existed.

In the modern market economy the economic and productive basis of society is entirely different. A similar change has also taken place in the political structure of society. The shift from a society based on estates to a representative democracy and politics of interests also immediately influenced the way in which questions within the sphere of Family and Inheritance Law are adjudicated. The family ideology of the secularized welfare state has become alienated from the traditional family ideology based on kin in a nation receiving its daily bread from the land.

5. Principles Pertaining to the Fields of the Law

5.1 The Code of Inheritance 1965

Finland is and has been one of the countries in which private property enjoys the special protection of the State. This is a fundamental principle relating to the economic and political structure of society. Ownership however does not signify an unlimited power of control of the owner over the object. This has been limited, and simultaneously room has been made for a goal-oriented social and economic policy.

In legal language the concept of "owner" is trivialized to that of a "legal subject" who has no privilege over other "owners". In reality, "owner" is often a code name for the power group that makes the central economic decisions in a market economy system. This reality is not addressed by the right of intestate succession. Such ownership that concerns the most important structures and forms of economy is almost invariably transferred from one generation to the next according to other rules than those concerning the law of inheritance.

In Finland for instance the paper industry is the most important of the export trade branches, and the largest paper mills are privately owned. These companies have not been passed on as inheritance from one generation to the next, even though the mills have been owned by the same families since they were founded. The capital stock of limited liability corporations is transferred from one generation to another by means of formal sale agreements and donations. Expressed in a pointed way, it could be said that law of inheritance dictates the transferring of a home, the movable property of a home, bank deposits and a summer cottage from one generation to the next.

The right of intestate succession has a practical function in society. If the legal system did not include rules concerning the address of property after the previous owner's death, a chaos of some degree would occur. Pieces of property with no legitimate owner would drift and wait for someone to seize them. A situation of this would disturbe social tranquility. For this reason rules are needed so that the disposition of property upon death can take place in an orderly fashion.

Culturally there are two models of disposition. The whole property of the owner can be buried with him or her or destroyed upon his or her death. In Finland e.g. among the gypsy minority there is still a custom to burn a woman's festal clothes when she dies. The alternative is to choose a new owner from among several candidates and pass on the property to him or her.

In principle the election of the new owner can rely on any criteria. For instance, upon an owner's death property could be divided among all bald women. But because there are substantially fewer bald women than men, a rule of that kind would favor women at the expense of men. Even this fact might provoke objection. An even greater problem, however, would be presented by the accumulation of property in the possession of bald women.

In every society the fundamental choices within inheritance law must be such that they are acceptable to the majority of the population. Also, they must not have unreasonable social consequences. For this reason decisions concerning the election of a new owner in all societies are based on the existing view of kinship. A person stands to inherit if there is a relationship of kinship, marriage, or adoption between him or her and the decedent. Only a person who was alive at the time of death of the decedent may inherit; however, a child conceived before the said time and delivered alive shall also inherit.

The Code of Inheritance, which entered into force on 1 January 1966 regulates the reciprocal order of priority of relatives. This is roughly as follows. The lineal descendants have the primary right to inherit. Each child receives an equal portion of the inheritance; should a child have died, his or her descendants take his or her place, and each branch receives an equal portion (succesio in stirpes). A lineal descendant and an adopted child, as well as the descendants of such, is entitled to a forced portion of the estate of the decedent. The forced portion is one half of the value of the portion of the estate that, according to the statutory order of succession, devolves the heir.

The forced portion consists partly of the real existing property in the estate and partly of certain previously distributed assets of the estate. In determining the forced portion a calculation is made of the assets of the estate, of any advance distribution made by the decedent and, in the absence of special grounds to the contrary, of any gift given by him or her in such circumstances or under such conditions that, with regard to its intent, the gift is to be equated with a bequest. The same applies to a gift given by the decedent to his or her descendant or adopted child or to a descendant, or to a spouse or to some similar heir with the apparent purpose of favoring its recipient to the detriment of an heir entitled to a forced portion. In the absence of circumstances to the contrary, the value of the property is determined according to its value at the time it was received.

Subject to the demands of lineal descendants for distribution of the estate and, also, subject to the terms of the will left by the descendent, the surviving spouse may administer the estate of his or her former spouse as an undivided whole. Notwithstanding a demand by a lineal descendant for distribution of the estate and the right of a beneficiary under a will, the surviving spouse may retain the residence that was used as the joint home of the spouses or another residence that is part of the estate as one undivided whole in his or her administration. The customary residential chattels in the joint home are always to be left in the administration of the surviving spouse as an undivided whole.

If the decedent was married and he or she is not survived by any lineal descendants, the estate devolves on the surviving spouse. The estate shall not be divided among the descendants of the deceased and the surviving spouse until after the death of the surviving spouse.

If the decedent is not survived by any lineal descendants, his or her parents each receive one half of the inheritance. Should either of these have died, the siblings of the decedent divide the said person's portion. The descendants of a predeceased brother or sister take the place of the said person, and each branch receives an equal portion. If there are no siblings or their descendants, but one of the parents of the decedent is still living, the said person receives the entire inheritance. If no heirs referred to above exist, the parents of the father and mother of the decedent inherit the entire estate. Cousins have no right to inherit. If there are no heirs, the estate devolves to the State.

These rules determine who ultimately has the right to inherit. Seen as a group, the heirs do not, according to Finnish law, constitute an independent juristic person. The parties to the decedent's estate are the heirs, the universal legatees, and the surviving spouse. The inheritance does not pass into the heirs' ownership immediately at the time of death. After death, the decedent's assets and debts require settlement, and this phase can last for a very long time. Only when this stage has been completed can the distribution of the estate commence. The decedent's property does not pass on to the new owner until after the distribution has gained legal force. This process may last for months or years. Therefore succession is a process, not an instantaneous event.

The process is commenced with an inventory of the estate, which is to be made within three months of the date of death unless the court, upon petition made within the same period, extends this period because of the nature of the estate or for some other special reason. The assets and debts of the estate as of the time of death are noted in the inventory document, together with the value of the assets.

The legal status of the heir develops through the administration of a decedent's estate untill its distribution will have been completed. The estate property is not necessarily divided among the heirs per capita. In forming the principles of division the aim has been to take into account the heirs' needs for property, for which reason we may speak of the various functions of inheritance law. The rules of inheritance law can be applied to distribute property in such a way that an heir in need of a dwelling is given priority over his or her co-heir already in possession of one, an heir in need of education is given funds for his or her tuition, an heir in need of support receives funds for his or her maintenance etc. This is pure social policy. The contents of inheritance law are thus not value neutral – they are a result of choices.

The rules of inheritance law also provide for the manner of administration of the estate. Generally speaking, there are two practicies. The heirs may privately settle and distribute the decedent's property. In a private settlement decision-making is based on the consensus principle. The parties jointly administer the property of the estate in order to settle it. In this process, they represent the estate in respect of third parties and can both sue and be sued in matters concerning the estate. Every heir takes part in decision-making and all heirs must agree on the decisions made and steps taken. Only a measure which does not bear delay may be performed if the consent of all the parties cannot be obtained. The majority of ordinary persons' estates are settled in this way because it is an inexpensive way to determine the fate of the property.

Private settling of property may not be successful if problems occur in the relationship between the heirs. This is indeed not rare. Arguments conducted in the nursery are sometimes repeated to honor the death of mother and father. On the petition of a party to the estate, the court may decide that the property of the estate shall be administered by an executor. The court shall appoint as executor a person who can be presumed capable of settling the estate with a skill suitable to the type of the estate and with a willingness to accept the appointment. The executor makes the decisions in matters concerning the estate on behalf of the heirs.

The assignment of the property of an estate to an executor is also the heirs' protection vis-à-vis impending liability for debts. If the estate is not surrendered into the administration of an executor or into bankruptcy upon a petition made within one month of the inventory of the estate, an heir may be held liable for such debts of the decedent as he or she knew of at the time of the inventory.

When the estate has been settled, each party to the estate may request distribution of the estate. The distribution is not to be undertaken contrary to the prohibition of a party until the inventory of the estate has been carried out and all known debts have been paid or the funds needed for their payment have been placed into special escrow.

The parties may distribute the estate in a mutually agreeable manner. This is by far the most popular way to distribute the estate. However, if a party is legally incompetent, or the share of a party has been seized, or if a party so requests, the distribution is carried out by a distributor of the estate. In this case the court shall upon petition appoint a suitable person as distributor of the estate.

The distributor of estate determines the time and place of the distribution of the estate and verifiably invites the parties to this occasion. If all parties are present, the distributor attempts to reach a final, mutually acceptable outcome.

If the distribution of inheritance cannot be carried out in accordance with the agreement of the parties, the distributor of the estate effects the distribution by giving each party a share of all types of property in the estate. However, property which cannot suitably be divided into shares or separated shall, if possible, be allotted into the same portion.

If the estate includes a farm from which the farmer of the farm and his or her family members can obtain their primary livelihood, an heir who stands to inherit at the time of the distribution and who has sufficient vocational qualifications to engage in an agricultural occupation (suitable farming successor) has the right to demand that this farm, together with the agricultural chattels belonging to it, is included in his or her portion undistributed.

The distribution of the inheritance takes place on the basis of a deed of distribution. If the distribution has been carried out by a distributor of the estate, he or she signs the document of distribution. In other cases the document of distribution is signed by the parties in the presence of two competent witnesses.

A party who wants to contest the distribution carried out by a distributor of the estate shall bring action against the other parties within six months of the distribution. The same applies if the parties have carried out the distribution of the inheritance and a party wishes to contest the distribution on the grounds that it was not carried out in the proper form.

5.2 The Law of Wills 1965

The rules concerning intestate succession are based on an assumption of who would inherit if the owner had expressed his or her wishes. This assumption of the legislator may be false. The owner may well deeply resent a person who would inherit according to the rules of intestate succession. In instances where the owner wishes to state how he or she would like the estate to be distributed, the decedent must draw up a will.

The legal rules concerning the will are included in the Law of Wills that entered into force in 1966 as part of the Code of Inheritance. There is a monopoly of the will in Finland: the owner can regulate the distribution of the estate on his or her death only in the form of a will. A person who has reached the age of eighteen years may dispose of his or her property by a will. An agreement pertaining to the estate of a person still living is null and void, and the provisions of a will, which are applied to a promise of a gift not to be fulfilled during the lifetime of the donor are also null and void. According to this rule *donatio mortis causa* is forbidden.

The right to receive property under a will is limited to the extent that a will naming as beneficiary a person other than one surviving the decedent or one who is conceived before his or her death and subsequently delivered alive is null and void. According to this rule it is forbidden to establish a so-called fidei commissum in a will (a rule against perpetuities).

The will need not be drawn up before an official in Finland. It should be made in writing in the simultaneous presence of two individuals who are to witness the will with their signatures after the testator has signed it or acknowledged his or her signature in it. The witnesses are to be aware that the document is a will, but it is in the discretion of the testator whether or not to inform them of the contents of the will. This is the usual form of the will.

A person who, due to an illness or other compelling reason, is prevented from making a will in the normal way, may make it orally in the simultaneous presence of two witnesses or even without a witness in a document that he or she has personally written and signed.

A will may always be revoked prior to the death of the testator. If the testator has revoked his or her will, or has destroyed the will, or otherwise clearly indicated that the disposition no longer corresponds to his or her last will, the disposition is null and void. From this it can be concluded that the testator can always revoke his or her testamentary disposition in free form. A promise not to revoke a will is not binding.

After the death of the testator the will is to be made known to an heir by giving him or her a certified copy of the will. When the will infringes upon the right of an heir to a forced portion, it is invalid in respect of such an heir. However, in order to recover his or her forced portion, the heir must give the beneficiary of the will notice thereof within six months of the date when he or she was informed of the contents of will.

But the whole will may be contested and declared invalid if the testator lacked testamentary capacity, if the will was not made in the form prescribed by the law, if a mental illness, debility or other mental aberration of the testator had influenced the making of the will, or if the testator was forced into making the will or induced to it through abuse of the testator's lack of understanding, weakness of will or position of dependence, or if he or she was deceitfully misled into making the will, or if the testator had in other respects erred in a manner that decisively influenced the contents of the will. If an heir wishes to contest a will on the grounds referred to above, he or she is to bring action within six months after being informed of the contents of will.

Interpretation of a valid will is based on the principle of subjective interpretation. A will is to be construed in accordance with the intention of the testator (so-called armchair principle). This is always the basis of interpretation, but very often the contents of a will are unclear, and, what is more, because of the death of the testator the principle of subjective interpretation is ultimately an empty one. For this reason it has been deemed appropriate to include certain guidelines in the law for construing the contents of a will. These rules are as follows.

If the will has received a meaning other than that intended by the testator due to a clerical error or an erroneous expression, it is nevertheless executed if the true intent can be discovered. A devise is to be executed from the undistributed estate. If all devises cannot be executed, a devise of specific property is to be executed before others. Otherwise a deduction proportional to the value of the devise is made from each.

If a beneficiary under the will dies before his or her right under the will comes into force or if the will for other reasons cannot be executed in his or her respect, his or her descendants shall take his or her place only if they had the right to inherit the testator.

An heir or beneficiary under a will is required to enforce his or her right within ten years of the death of the decedent.

5.3 The Marriage Act

5.3.1 Conclusion and Dissolution of Marriage

A woman and a man who have agreed to marry are considered to be engaged. No formalities are required for an engagement, and it does not create a legal obligation to marry. The breaking of an engagement is also free in form. An engagement is broken when one party informs the other that he or she no longer wishes the engagement to continue.

Marriage is a public institution, and in some cases it is not allowed to take place in the interests of prtotecting the basic values of the society. The impediments to marriage are the following. Persons of the same sex may not marry each other. A person under 18 years of age may not conclude marriage. The Ministry of Justice may for special reasons grant a person under 18 years of age dispensation to conclude marriage. A person who has been placed under guardianship may not conclude marriage without the consent of the guardian.

The absolute impediments to marriage are relationship in the direct line of ascent or descent, relationship of full or half siblings, and a previous, existing marriage. Before the marriage, the Population Register officers examine the required absence of statutory impediments to marriage. When a certificate for marriage has been obtained, the parties may marry either in a religious or a civil ceremony.

According to Finnish law, marriage does not have contractual status. Marriage is concluded by the performative act of a marriage ceremony, which takes place in the presence of relatives or other witnesses and at which the engaged couple is to be simultaneously present. After both of them have given the officiator of the marriage an affirmative answer to his question as to whether he or she wants to conclude marriage with the other person, the officiator pronounces them husband and wife.

The main principles of the Marriage Act are as follows. The spouses are equal. They are to display mutual trust and together strive towards the benefit of the family. Each spouse has the right to decide whether to engage in gainful employment and in social and other activities outside the family. Marriage does not restrict the right of a spouse to conclude contracts. Spouses may also conclude mutual contracts. A spouse's property upon the conclusion of marriage remains in his or her sole possession. He or she also owns what he or she acquires during the marriage.

Upon conclusion of marriage, the prospective spouses may together decide to adopt a common family name. As their common family name the spouses may adopt the name that either of them last had while still unmarried. The common family name is to be declared to the officiator of the marriage before the marriage ceremony. If the spouses have not adopted a common family name, each spouse shall retain the family name that he or she had at the time of the conclusion of marriage.

Marriage is dissolved upon the death of a spouse or upon divorce. Before granting a divorce a court of law may order that the spouses are to end their cohabitation. This may be done upon the joint petition of the spouses or upon the petition of one of them. In the same process, the court may decide, upon petition, that the spouse who is in greater need of a residence has the right to continue to live in the common home. A court may also order the other spouse to vacate the common home and give a spouse the right to use movables which belong to the other spouse and which are part of the household goods intended for common use. The court's decision is immediately enforceable. The decision is in force until further notice but it shall nevertheless lapse in two years from the date of the decision even if no distribution or separation of assets has taken place.

The divorce system in Finland was previously based on guilt on part of the spouse. Grounds for guilt were such as adultery, sodomy, bestiality, a veneral disease, an assault, imprisonment for at least three years, and the habitual abuse of alcohol or drugs. This system was valid until the revision of the Marriage Act in 1988.

The current revised divorce system is based on the principle of divorce on demand. The spouses or, alternatively, one of the spouses has an unconditional right to divorce. The spouses have the right to obtain divorce after a period of reconsideration, which commences on the date of the filing of the joint petition of the spouses for the dissolution of the marriage with the court or the serving of the petition of a spouse upon the other spouse. A minimum duration of marriage is not required before a petition may be requested. After a minimum period of six months intended for reconderation, the spouses are granted a divorce upon their joint request or upon the request of one of the spouses. No additional grounds are required. The request is to be made within one year of the beginning of the period of reconsideration. Normally the divorce proceeds in two stages. After the first petition there is a reconsideration period of six months, and after this time it is possible to obtain a divorce by filing a second petition.

However, the spouses have the right to a divorce without a period of reconsideration if they have continued to live separately for the last two years without interruption or if the marriage was concluded while a prior marriage of one of the spouses was still in force and the said prior marriage has not yet been dissolved.

Upon the granting of a divorce, a spose may change his or her family name acquired through marriage from the other spouse by readopting the name that he or she last had when unmarried.

5.3.2 Property Rights during the Marriage

The fundamental principles of the matrimonial property system in Finland are quite similar to those of the other Nordic countries. The property that a spouse has when concluding marriage remains his or hers. He or she also owns what he or she acquires during the marriage. Marriage does not restrict the right of a spouse to conclude contracts, and spouses may also conclude mutual contracts. Each spouse is alone liable for a debt that he or she has incurred before or during the marriage. Both spouses are, however, jointly and severally liable for a debt incurred by a spouse for the maintenance of the family.

The core of the system is a marital right expressing the doctrine of mutual legal interest of the spouses. Each spouse has a marital right to the property of the other spouse. However, the marital right has reasonably few effects during the marriage. Property subject to the marital right of the other spouse is to be administered in such a way that it does not unnecessarily decrease in value to the detriment of the other spouse.

However, upon dissolution of marriage the spouse's property is usually divided equally between the spouses regardless of individual ownership. This is a modified system of separation of property, and because of this, it might be more appropriate to call it the "system of deferred community of property".

The extent of the marital right is voluntary. A spouse's property is marital property insofar as it is not separate. In a marriage agreement concluded before or during the marriage, the engaged persons or spouses may exclude any property owned or later acquired by a spouse from the marital right. Likewise, they may agree to restore the marital right of a spouse to property previously excluded from the said right by a prior marriage agreement. Such an agreement is to be concluded in writing and filed with the court. It enters into force when this requirement has been fulfilled and the agreement is duly registered.

Also property received by a spouse as a gift or by testamentary disposition on the condition that it be separate property of the recipient is separate. And, finally, also property which has taken the place of separate property is separate.

The difference between marital and separate property is of insignificant importance during the marriage. Totally irrespective of the nature of the property, a spouse (the owner) may not, without the written consent of the other spouse, convey, let, or convey the right to use or possess real property which is solely or mostly meant to be used as the common home of the spouses. A contract contrary to this prohibition is declared void if the other spouse brings action within three months of having gained knowledge of the contract. The protection of the common home is not limited to real property.

Without the consent of the other spouse, a spouse may not convey or transfer a building on the land of a third party if the building and the land are solely or mainly meant to be used as the common home. This also applies to shares of a corporation, tenant's rights or other rights entitling to the possession of a flat which is solely or mainly meant to be used as the common home of the spouses.

The aim of these limitations is to protect the spouse who is not the owner of the property. If he or she, without the consent of the other spouse, conveys or pledges common property or property belonging to the other spouse, the other spouse has the right to redeem it. If the third party was not acting in good faith or if no consideration was paid, the other spouse regains the property without having to redeem it.

5.3.3 Distribution of Matrimonial Property

When a divorce case is pending or when the marriage has been dissolved, a distribution of matrimonial assets is carried out. The general rule is that the net value of the property should be divided equally between the spouses regardless of individual ownership, if both spouses have a marital right to the property. If neither spouse has a marital right to the property of the other spouse, a separation of the assets of the spouses is carried out instead of a distribution.

The principle of equal division in divorce cases results in a spouse being required to hand over property to the other spouse. E.g. if spouse A owns 1 000 000 and B only 200 000, and each spouse has a marital right to the property of the other, A is required to give 400 000 to B. However, in a distribution of matrimonial assets carried out after the death of one spouse, the surviving spouse need not hand over any of his or her property to the heirs of the deceased spouse. Consequently, in this case, if A survives, A is allowed to keep his or her property. The heirs receive only 200 000. But if B survives, the heirs must hand over 400 000 to him or her and A's heirs receive 600 000.

The system of equal division in divorce cases may result in an unjust result. To avoid this, the distribution of matrimonial assets can be adjusted if the distribution otherwise leads to an unreasonable result or to the other spouse´s receiving an unjust financial benefit. When considering the case, special attention is to be given to the duration of the marriage, the activities of the spouses for their common household and for the accumulation and preservation of the property, as well as to other comparable facts regarding the finances of the spouses. If the conditions for an adjustment or modification of the property division are fulfilled, a party's share can be reduced to less than 50 % or even entirely eliminated. The reasons for the breakdown of the marriage or the question of guilt are ignored in this adjustment.

The spouses may distribute their property in a mutually agreeable manner. If a spouse so requests, the distribution is carried out by a distributor appointed by the court. If a spouse is not satisfied with the decision of the distributor on the division of property, he or she may appeal to a court of law within six months of the distribution.

5.3.4 Maintenance of the Spouses

The Marriage Act is an act which concerns only the rights and duties of spouses. The right of a child to receive maintenance from his or her parent is governed by the Act on Child Maintenance (see later p.). Each spouse is, according to his or her abilities, to participate in the common household of the family and the maintenance of the other spouse. The maintenance of the spouses includes fulfilling the common needs of both spouses, as well as the personal needs of each spouse. The amount of maintenance payable to a spouse and the manner of its payment may be confirmed by agreement or by judicial decree.

If a spouse neglects his or her obligation of maintenance or if the spouses are separated, the court may order a spouse to pay maintenance to the other spouse. Maintenance may be ordered to be paid until further notice or until the end of a period determined in the order. It can also be ordered to be paid as a lump sum, if necessary, with a view to the financial and other circumstances of the spouse ordered to pay it. Obligation to pay maintenance lapses if the spouse to whom the maintenance is granted remarries.

5.4 Cohabitation

Marriage is usually preceded by cohabitation: the couple simply lives together, in a shared household. It is a very common institution, with almost 10 % of all families belonging to this group. The customary way to end this form of living arrangement is to enter into matrimony after the birth of the first child. The temporary nature of cohabitation may be one explanation to the absence of any special legislation concerning cohabitation. But surely this is only one of the explanations. The most important reason for this legislative gap lies in the basic values of society.

The legislation concerning financial provisions and financial distribution applicable to divorce does not equally apply to separating cohabitees. The principles of civil law treat such a couple as two separate individuals, as strangers.

5.5 Child Law

5.5.1 Paternity Act 1975

Child law was previously based on the unequality of children. The status of children crucially depended on the status of the presumptive father and mother. If they were married at the time of birth, the child was legitimate – in a situation to the contrary, the child was illegitimate. The fundamental characteristic of the new child law is the abolition of discrimination between children. The old concept of the illegitimate child is unknown to the new child law. All children – formally – have equal rights.

Child law is based on the biological and social relationship between the child and the parent. The starting point is a biological one. There is seldom any doubt of motherhood, and no special legislation on this topic exists in Finland. However, the question of the real father always remains to a certain degree open.

The Paternity Act applies to the presumption of paternity, the establishing of a relationship between a child and his father as well as to the terminating of this relationship. The main rule is the presumption of paternity on the basis of marriage. The husband of the mother is the father of a child born during marriage. If the marriage was dissolved before the birth of the child due to the death of the husband, he is the father of the child if the date of birth of the child is such that the child could have been conceived during the marriage. However, if the mother has entered into a new marriage before the birth of the child, the latter husband is considered the father of the child.

It is possible for a man who was not married to the mother of the child at the time of birth to acknowledge his paternity. The procedural rules of the acknowledgement of paternity are the following. A man wishing to acknowledge his paternity is to notify the child welfare supervisor, a population registrar or a notary public in person that he is the father of the child. The child welfare supervisor is a special child welfare officer in Finland who is responsible for the establishment of paternity and the recovery of maintenance in favor of the child. It is not possible to acknowledge paternity before the child is born nor after the death of the child. The paternity of the husband may also be annulled through acknowledgement.

The acknowledgement of a child is strict in form. A document of acknowledgement and approval is drafted, dated, and duly signed by the male acknowledging his paternity and by the official receiving the acknowledgement. If the acknowledgement is subject to the approval of the child, mother or husband, also they and the recipient of the approval are to sign the document.

When a man has acknowledged his paternity, the child welfare supervisor is to send the documents as well as the record of the investigation of paternity without delay for approval to the territorially competent district court judge. The judge is to verify that there is no cause to assume that the man who has acknowledged his paternity is not the father of the child.

But acknowledgement of paternity is not the only way to establish paternity, even if it is the most common way in cases in which the mother and the father are cohabitees. Both the child and the man have the right of action for the establishment of paternity. An action for the establishment of paternity may not be brought nor continued after the death of the child. An action may not be brought on behalf of a child if the child opposes the action and has the right to file and carry on a lawsuit.

The court establishes paternity if it has been shown that the man in question had intercourse with the mother at the time of conception and if in view of the statements of the man and the mother of the child as well as in view of all other circumstances it is deemed proven that the man conceived the child.

Before the decision of paternity is rendered, an investigation of paternity is to be made. The purpose of the investigation is to obtain information on which paternity may be based and confirmed. If the man or the child welfare supervisor requests the analysis, the child welfare supervisor initiates blood typing of the child, the mother and a man who is the prospective father of the child. The Act on Certain Blood Tests and Tests for Other Inheritable Characteristics contains provisions on the performance of blood typing tests.

On the basis of a formal action, the court may also establish the absence of fatherhood on grounds similar to those for establishing paternity. An action for the annulment of paternity may be brought by the husband, mother or child. The husband and mother are to bring an action within five years of the birth of the child. However, the husband does not have the right to bring an action after having been informed that another man had sexual intercourse with the mother at the time the child was conceived if he has stated in writing after the child's birth that the child is his.

If the husband has died without losing his right to bring an action, his surviving spouse and every nearest heir of the husband in addition to or after the child has the right to bring an action within one year of the husband's death. An action to annul paternity may not be brought if the child has died or if both the husband and the mother have died.

5.5.2 Adoption

The first Adoption Act in Finland, enacted in 1925, was based on the principles of "weak" adoption (*adoptio minus plena*). The legal status of the adopted child in relation to his adoptive parents and the relatives of these parents was in many respects different from the legal status of the children of the adoptive parents born to them in wedlock.

Weak adoption creates a relationship between the adopted child and the adoptive parent similar to that between an acknowledged child and its parent. Guardianship, support and maintenance of the adopted child is transferred through adoption to the adoptive parent. But very important still today is the fact that, according to the principles of weak adoption, adoption does not establish any legal relationship between the adopted child and the relatives of the adoptive parents. One consequence of this is that an adopted child may inherit the relatives of his adoptive parents only through his adoptive parents.

Weak adoption does not completely sever the relationship between the adopted child and his biological relatives. The adopted child retains, among other things, his right to inherit the estate of his biological relative. And the biological parent had earlier also the duty to see to the maintenance and support of his or her child in the event that the adoptive parents were unable to fulfill their duties towards the child.

The new Adoption Act, which entered into force in 1979/1985, is based on the principles of "strong" adoption (*adoptio plena*). After adoption has been granted, the adopted child is regarded as the child of the adoptive parents instead of his former parents. The latter are discharged from their obligation to maintain the child. Through the confirmation of the adoption, the adopted child assumes the full status of a child in regard to his adoptive parents and their relatives.

Regardless of the new Adoption Act of 1979/1985, the Adoption Act of 1925 is still the basic legislation applied to adoptive relationships entered into before January 1, 1980.

The purpose of adoption is to promote the welfare of the child by creating a relationship of child and parent between the adoptee and the adopter. Adoption is always granted by judicial decree. Adoption of a minor child may be granted if it is considered to be in the best interests of the child and if it has been established that the child shall receive good care and upbringing. An adult may be adopted only if it has been established that, while he or she was under 18 of age, he or she was fostered by the adopter. Adoption may not be granted if any remuneration for the adoption has been given or promised.

Adoption may not be granted without the consent of the person to be adopted if this person has attained the age of 12 years. The consent of the adoptee is, however, not necessary if he or she cannot express his or her will due to an illness or a handicap. Nor may adoption be granted against the will of a child under 12 years of age if the child is so mature that his or her will can be taken into consideration.

No person may adopt his or her own child. However, a person may adopt his or her own child previously adopted by someone else. The adopter in normal cases is to have attained the age of 25. Spouses may, according to the main rule, only jointly adopt a child while married. A spouse may alone adopt a child of his or her spouse or his or her own child previously adopted by someone else. Persons other than spouses may not jointly adopt a child.

The adoption of a minor child may not be granted unless his or her parents have consented to it. On exceptional grounds adoption may be granted even if the consent of the parents is not obtained. The consent of the parent or parents is to be given to the Municipal Board of Social Welfare or to an adoption agency.

The legal effects of adoption terminate only if the adopter and the adoptive child marry each other. The dissolution or rescission of an adoption is not, except through readoption or the above mentioned marriage.

The Adoption Act of 1979 did not specifically regulate inter-country adoptions. For this reason a new Adoption Act was enacted in 1985. The contents of the 1979 Act remained unchanged, but the specific provisions on inter-country adoptions were added. These provisions follow the principles of the U.N. Declaration of 3 December 1986 on inter alia inter-country adoptions. Since 1985 it is not permitted for persons domiciled in Finland to arrange inter-country adoptions through private channels. All inter-country adoptions have to be arranged through official channels. The provisions of the Finnish Adoption Act regarding inter-country adoption are based on the notion that the habitual residence of the prospective adoptive parent is the main connecting factor. The nationality of the adopters plays only a secondary role. Finnish courts have jurisdiction over an application for the granting of adoption if the adopters are habitually resident in Finland.

5.5.3 The Child Maintenance Act of 1975

According to the Child Maintenance Act of 1975, a child has the right to sufficient maintenance. Maintenance consists of the satisfaction of the child's material, physical, spiritual and educational needs, care, and of the bearing of the resulting costs. The parents are responsible for the maintenance of the child in accordance with their abilities. In the assessment of the ability of the parents to provide maintenance, consideration is to be given to their age, ability to work and opportunity to take part in gainful employment, the amount of available assets and their other statutory maintenance responsibilities.

The efficiency of the civil law maintenance system depends on factors outside civil law, namely on the financial resources of the parents. Although the legislative intent was to secure sufficient maintenance for the child, this cannot be achieved if the parents are not able to fulfill their obligation, and if society cannot, for economic reasons, fully discharge its share of responsibility. In practice the average maintenance is 10–12 % of the parent's income.

The child's right to maintenance from his parents ends when the child reaches eighteen years of age. However, the parents are responsible for expenses incurred in the education of the child even after the child reaches eighteen years of age if this is deemed reasonable.

An obligation to pay maintenance to the child may be confirmed if a parent does not provide for his or her maintenance in other ways or if the child does not live with his parent on a permanent basis. The amount and manner of the performance of the maintenance is determined by agreement or by court decision. However, an agreement in which the right of the child to maintenance in the future is renounced is null and void.

The maintenance sum is to be paid each month in advance unless otherwise agreed or ordered. The obligation to pay maintenance ends when the child reaches the age of eighteen years unless otherwise agreed or ordered. The payment of maintenance may be made in the form of a lump sum if this is needed to ensure the maintenance of the child in the future and this is deemed reasonable in view of the financial capacity of the person paying the maintenance.

An agreement on maintenance is to be made in writing. The agreement must clearly state personal data concerning the child and his or her parents, the amount of the maintenance, the date from which on the maintenance is to be paid, the final date of the obligation, when the maintenance instalment falls due and to whom the maintenance is to be paid. A maintenance agreement is to be submitted for confirmation to the social welfare board of the municipality.

If the parents cannot agree on maintenance, the court may confirm the amount and form of its payment. The court confirms the responsibility to pay maintenance from the date the action was brought or from a later date specified in the decision.

The amount and method of payment of confirmed maintenance may be amended by agreement or by court decision if the circumstances that are to be taken into consideration in confirming the maintenance have changed to such an extent that an amendment of the maintenance is deemed reasonable in view of the child and if a parent responsible for the payment of the maintenance.

The perennial problem of the child maintenance system is the question of securing the child's right to regular maintenance. The Security of Child Maintenance Act of 1977 enacts measures intended to secure the right of the child to sufficient maintenance. The main measure is the payment of maintenance support from municipal funds, which is a grant for the maintenance of the child paid from municipal funds in lieu of deficient maintenance or in addition to insufficient maintenance.

There are different conditions for the payment of a maintenance grant. A maintenance grant is to be paid to a child if the person liable for the maintenance has defaulted on payment. This is the typical situation. A person liable for maintenance is a parent who has undertaken to pay maintenance to the child on the basis of a confirmed agreement or who has been thus ordered by a court judgment and who cannot fulfill his or her duties. The child however is in need of his or her maintenance, which is in these cases provided in this form.

A maintenance grant is also paid if e.g. no one has been confirmed as the father of a child born out of wedlock, if the obligation of a parent to pay maintenance could not be confirmed at the same time as the confirmation of paternity, or if the responsibility of a parent to pay maintenance has not been confirmed due to the parent's age, diminished working ablility, deficient possibilities of earning of a living, lack of means, or other maintenance responsibility. The amount of the maintenance grant for one child was approximately 610 FIM (nearly 100 ECU) per month at the beginning of 1993. The amount of the maintenance grant is increased or reduced in accordance with an increase or decrease in the cost of living (Act on the Linking of Certain Maintenance Payments to the Cost-of-Living Index 1966).

A maintenance grant is approved by the social welfare board upon application (cf. the Security of Child Maintenance Decree 1977). An application for a maintenance grant may be made by the parent who has custody of the child.

The payment of a maintenance grant does not affect the obligation of the person responsible for maintenance to make full payments. If a maintenance grant is paid on the grounds of default on payment, the right to the maintenance is transferred to the municipality in the amount of the maintenance grant. The child has the right to receive the portion of the maintenance that exceeds the maintenance grant.

If a parent of a child neglects to care for the maintenance of the child and the child for this reason suffers or is in danger of suffering from lack of maintenance, the social welfare board may decide that the employer is to pay a specific share of the wages of such a parent to the social welfare board. Another measure for the enforcement of maintenance liability is to prohibit the issuance of a passport to the said person, when there is reason to suspect that the person responsible for maintenance intends to leave Finland and the departure would endanger the receipt of the child maintenance.

If, having been informed of the granting of a maintenance grant, the person responsible for maintenance deliberately destroys or conceals property in order to evade maintenance payment, favors another creditor, or in another corresponding manner weakens his or her solvency and is for this reason found lacking assets for the payment of a matured maintenance, he or she is sentenced to a fine or to imprisonment for one year at the most for a maintenance security offence.

5.5.4 Child Custody and Right of Access Act 1983

Custody and guardianship have a different purpose in family law. The object of custody is to ensure the well-being and the well balanced development of a child according to his or her individual needs and wishes, and to ensure a close and affectionate relationship between a child and his or her parents in particular. The object of guardianship of a minor has reference to position of the minor as an owner.

The fundamental object of the Child Custody Act is the creation of "heaven on earth" through legislation, with the aid of force if necessary. A child is to be ensured good care and upbringing as well as the supervision and protection appropriate to his or her age and stage of development. A child should be brought up in a secure and stimulating environment, and he or she should receive an education that corresponds to his or her wishes, inclinations, and talents. A child is to be brought up in the spirit of understanding, security, and love. He or she must not be subdued, corporally punished or otherwise humiliated. His or her growth towards independence, responsibility, and adulthood is to be encouraged, supported, and assisted. This is the ideological background of the custodial system.

The objects of the right of access are to ensure a child the right to meet the parent with whom he or she no longer lives and to maintain contact with him or her. A child's parents are to make, in mutual understanding and having the best interests of the child as the first and paramount consideration, every effort to ensure the implementation of the purpose of the right of access in conformity with custodial principles.

The custodians of a child are his or her parents or other persons to whom the custody of a child has been granted. The custodians are to safeguard the child's development and well-being. For this purpose, they are empowered to make decisions concerning the child's care, upbringing, residence, and other matters relating to the child's person. Before a custodian makes a decision of this nature, he or she has the obligation to discuss the matter with the child, whenever possible, taking into account the child's age and maturity and the nature of the matter. In making a decision the custodians are to give due consideration to the feelings, opinions, and wishes of the child. The custodians are jointly responsible for the exercise of custody and are to jointly make all decisions concerning the child. Custody ceases when the child attains the age of eighteen years or concludes marriage before that age.

In cases where the parents of a child are married to each other at the time of birth, custody of the child is vested in both parents. Where the parents are not married to each other at the time of birth, custody is vested in the mother. In cases where one of the parents has sole custody of a child and later marries the other parent, custody is vested in both parents.

Custody problems are frequently connected to divorce cases. In a case regarding divorce or the end of cohabitation, the court may upon its own initiative to consider how the right of access and custody of the child of the spouses should be arranged in the best interests of the child. When considering the custody and access rights of the child, the court is to draw the parties' special attention to the fact that the purpose of the custody and access rights is to ensure the child's positive and close relationship with both parents.

But divorce is only one of the situations in which the problems custody and access presents themself. The other typical situation is the case where the child is born out of wedlock and his or her parents have never lived together. Custody and access must be solved in these situations according to the same principles as in divorce cases, and these same principles must be followed also when the child's parents are cohabitees.

Before the Child Custody and Right of Access Act entered into force in 1983, the most important principles for making decisions in custody matters were giving priority to the mother and the principle of status quo, the meaning of the latter being that a decisive significance had to be given to the established conditions in which the child lives. Since the Act came into force, these principles have been more narrowly interpreted from the perspective of the best interests of the child.

The starting point of the Child Custody Act is joint custody, but this is not an automatic consequence *ipso iure* if the parents are not married. A child's parents may stipulate that they are to have joint custody of the child. The parents may also stipulate that the child is to reside with one of the parents, if they are not living together. The parents may also decide that one parent alone is to have custody and that the child has the right of access to the parent with whom he or she no longer resides, in conformity with the agreement of the parents.

A voluntary settlement regarding child custody and access is to be made in writing and is subject to the approval of the social welfare board of the local authority of the child's habitual residence. In cases where custody is vested in both parents or one of them, a matter of whether to grant custody to both parents or to one parent alone is to be settled as agreed by the parents, provided that there are no reasons to believe that such a settlement would be contrary to the child's interests. A settlement approved by the social welfare board has the same validity and is equally as enforceable as a court order.

In some cases it is not possible to reach a voluntary settlement on custody and rights of access. A court of law may order that the parents are to have joint custody of a child; that a child is to reside with one of the parents, if they are not living together; that one parent alone is to have custody; that one or more consenting persons are to have the custody of a child instead of, or together with, the parent or parents, and that a child is to have the rights of access to the parent with whom he or she no longer resides.

If necessary, a court may issue directions concerning on the attribution of duties, rights, and responsibilities of a person or persons assigned the custody of a child. In deciding on the right of access, a court issues instructions regarding the conditions of access.

In making a decision on child custody and the right of access, a court of law is to consider the best interests of the child and his or her own wishes. The views of the child are to be ascertained tactfully, taking into account his or her stage of development, and in such a way that no harm is caused to the relationship between the child and his or her parents. The best interests of the child are the first and paramount consideration in settling any matter concerning custody and the right of access. For this purpose, special attention is to be paid to the way in which the objects of custody and right of access can best be implemented in the future.

When assessing and defining the best interests of the child, not only legal aspects but also information from a host of other sciences concerning the factors affecting the development of the child need to be taken into account; specifically child psychology, child psychiatry and the social sciences. However, the integration of this information into a juridical study entails problems, because the reasons for gaining knowledge, methods of study, and views of the human being vary greatly from science to science and from school to school.

A settlement on child custody and the right of access approved by the social welfare board as well as by a court order may be amended or revoked where a change in circumstances has occurred or where it is otherwise deemed to be appropriate.

An order relating to child custody or the right of access is immediately enforceable, even though it is subject to appeal. A court decision and an agreement certified by a municipal social welfare board on child custody or on the right of access may be enforced if deemed necessary. (Act on the Enforcement of a Decision on Child Custody and Right of Access 1975).

A request for enforcement is to be made in writing to the executor-in-chief of the locality of the child's residence. Before the case is decided, the executor-in-chief assigns a conciliator appointed by the municipal social welfare board to arrange a conciliation for the enforcement of the decision.

In considering the enforcement, the executor-in-chief may set the threat of a fine or, if the question is of child custody or the surrender of a child to the person awarded the custody of the child, an order that an executor have the child brought. If the child has reached the age of twelve years, the enforcement is not to be undertaken against his or her will.

5.5.5 Child Welfare Act 1983

The Child Welfare Act imposes on public authorities an obligation to intervene in the autonomy of the family in cases where the conditions in the home and the custody of the child are not in conformity with the best interests of the child. A child has a special right to protection under all circumstances.

The social welfare board is to take a child into care and provide substitute care for him or her, if his or her health or development is seriously endangered by lack of care or other conditions of the home, or if the child endangers his or her health or development by the abuse of intoxicants, by committing an illegal act other than a minor offense, or by any other comparable behaviour, if the measures of protective care are not appropriate or have proved to be inadequate, and if substitute care is considered to be in the best interests of the child.

Before taking a child into care, arranging substitute care, or terminating care, the local social welfare board must always, taking the age and the level of development of the child into account whenever possible, ascertain the child's own wishes and opinions and provide a child who has attained the age of twelve, his or her parent and custodians an opportunity to be heard.

When the social welfare board takes a child into care, it is empowered to decide on his or her care, upbringing, supervision, other welfare, and residence. The board is, however, to make every effort to cooperate with the parents or other custodians of the child. The social welfare board is to discharge a child from care when the need for care no longer applies. A care order expires when the child attains the age of eighteen years or concludes marriage.

5.5.6 The Guardianship Act

The original body of the Guardianship Act is very old, but the main contents of the act are from 1893. The connection between custody and guardianship is "logical": guardianship follows custody. Because the custodians of a child are his or her parents and the custody of a child is vested in both parents, they are also the statutory guardians of a minor. The statutory guardians are jointly responsible for the exercise of guardianship. The object of guardianship is the minor's property, the minor's position being that of owner.

A person may be under guardianship either because of minority, i.e. when under 18 years of age, or he or she may be placed under guardianship by a court of law. When a person is placed under guardianship by a court order, a suitable guardian is appointed. An order to place a person under guardianship may be given for a definite or indefinite period of time. If it is not necessary to place a person under guardianship, but his or her affairs must to be looked after, a judicial supervisor may be appointed either for a specific task or a specific group of tasks, at the completion of which the office of the trustee expires. The grounds for placing a person under guardianship are inability to manage one's own affairs and the ensuing danger to that person's economic position.

A person under guardianship lacks legal capacity, but judicial supervision is not as powerful in effect. If a person lacks legal capacity, he or she may not, under the main rule, manage his or her own property nor can he or she enter into legally binding contracts. These are concluded by the guardian on his or her behalf. The guardian and the judicial supervisor are both under the control of the guardianship authorities, and, with certain exceptions, liable to submit an annual account of their acts. In certain cases a person under guardianship may also have legal capacity; for example a child over 15 years of age is entitled to manage any personally earned income.

In all major acts the guardian needs the permission of the guardianship authorities. Conveyance of real property is possible only with the consent of a court of law, while the purchase of real property is to be approved by a lower authority, the Municipal Guardianship Board.

Bibliographical Essay

Drawing up a bibliography on Finnish Family and Inheritance Law for a reader who is not familiar with the Finnish language is a simple task. All the basic written works in the field have been published in Finnish. Some individual works of research may include a short summary, which in most cases is far too short to provide adequately precise information on the contents of the research in question. As this article indicates, research conducted in the field of Family and Inheritance Law has nevertheless been relatively active, and its quality has also been high. For national reasons it is perfectly understandable that this work has been published in Finnish.

The language barrier is lower for Finnish researchers directing their interests abroad than it is for foreign researchers seeking contacts in Finland, and most Finnish researchers have mastered not only the Nordic languages but also at least two of the so called world languages. Consequently, Finnish legal dogmatics has been strongly influenced by the legal dogmatics of certain other countries.

At the turn of the century Finnish legal dogmatics adopted the German tradition of conceptual legal dogmatics. An important reason for this was, among others, the fact that the language used to discuss cultural matters within the educated classes was German. The boundary between the Germanic and Romance languages was also almost invariably the edge of the world of Finnish legal dogmatics. The research conducted in the more southern legal cultures was virtually unknown in Finland. Despite an age-old contact and a shared history with the other Nordic countries, Nordic legal dogmatics as a science was not the ideal that the Finnish academic world adopted. The relationship with the east was even more non-existent. The Russian legal culture has permanently remained alien to the Finns.

After the Second World War, Scandinavian realism and with it an analytical approach towards research gained foothold in Finland. Since the 1970's, the gap between the Continental and the Common Law legal systems has steadily closed. The post-Second World War generation speaks English as its first foreign language. English has taken over the position of German as the language of communication in Finnish legal dogmatics in international discussion groups.

Although Swedish is the second official language in Finland, the position of Swedish-language legal dogmatics has grown considerably weaker compared to the situation of the early 20th century. The former majority language has become the language of the minority. However, official law drafting material and legal texts have continued to be published both in Finnish and Swedish as parallel versions wiht equal standing.

The process of European integration has in many respects signified a challenge not only to the legislator but also to Finnish legal dogmatics. This integration process is said to lead to the internationalization of legal dogmatics. However, Family and Inheritance Law seems to be very much immune to supranational legislative decisions. According to the principle of subsidiarity, the power of decision on fundamental questions will remain on the national level and will do so even in the future. This results in an obligation to interpret national law for the national consumer in his or her native language. In other words, no radical change in the publication language of works of research within Family and Inheritance Law is to be expected even in the near future.

For individuals who are not at all familiar with the Finnish legal system this causes considerable difficulties if they wish to familiarize themselves with the contents of our legal system. The only more extensive work of research that touches upon Finnish Family and Inheritance Law and is possibly more easily read is the French-language doctoral dissertation by Heikki Mattila entitled "Les successions agricoles et la structure de la société", published in 1979. However, it is such an original work of research that one must be careful as not to draw inductive conclusions from it concerning the kind of Family and Inheritance Law that is practiced in Finland from it.

The majority of the articles on Finnish law written in foreign languages are out of date. The legal system described in them belongs to legal history. For instance, the articles "Outlines of Family Law" and "Principles of the Law of Succession" by Martti Rautiala (1966) and "Family Law and the Law of Succession" by Aulis Aarnio (1985), included in the earlier editions of this book only have historical value. Even this article will have the same fate some day.

Readers would be wise to start by familiarizing themselves with Finnish Family and Inheritance Law by acquiring an unofficial translation of the legal text. Although statutes are officially published in Finnish and Swedish in Finland, unofficial translations of the most central statutes of private law exist. They can be obtained from the Ministry of Justice through the local Finnish diplomatic representation.

A complete picture of the legal literature published in Finland can be obtained from the work "Bibliografia Juridica Fennica". It covers all legal literature published in Finland from the year 1809 and ts is updated each year. A general picture of foreign-language legal literature is obtained from the works *Reinikainen, Veikko:* "English, French and German Literature on Finnish Law 1890–1956." Publications of the Library of the Finnish Parliament, nr 2, and *Schauman, Henrik:* "Finnish Legal Publications in English, Franch and German 1957–1977." Scandinavian Studies in Law. 1980, p. 231 et seq. The following fragmentary information on Finnish Family and Inheritance Law is available: *Aulis Aarnio:* "Sufficient Maintenance" in the Finnish Law of Support; in: *Baxter, Ian F. G. – Eberts,*

Mary A. (ed.): "The Child and the Courts". London 1978, p. 169 et seq.; *Aarnio, Aulis:* "Die finnische Ehegesetzgebung heute und morgen". Zeitschrift für Rechtsvergleichung 1978, p. 98 et seq.; *Aarnio, Aulis:* "Changing Concepts of the Family and the Reform of Family Law in Finland"; in: *Eekelaar, John M. – Kats, Sanford N. (eds.):* "Marriage and Cohabitation in Contemporary Societies". Toronto 1980; *Aarnio, Aulis – Kangas, Urpo:* "Le ricerche nel campo del diritto di famiglia e le riforme legislative in Finlandia negli anni settanta"; in: *Pocar, Valeri – Ronfani, Paolo (eds.):* "Famiglia, diritto, mutamento sociale in Europa". Milano 1979.; *Aromaa, Kauko – Cantell, Ilkka – Jaakkola, Risto:* "Cohabitation in Finland in the 1970s." Research Institute of Legal Police nr 63. Helsinki 1983.; *Kangas, Urpo:* "The Functions and the Order of Inheritance." Scandinavian Studies in Law 1985, p. 81 et seq.; *Savolainen, Matti:* "The new marriage act enters into force." Journal of Family Law. 1988, p. 127 et seq.; *Buure-Hägglund, Kaarina:* "International Adoption"; in: The Finnish National Report to the XIIIth Congress of the International Academy of Comparative Law. Helsinki 1990, p. 35 et seq.; *Mattila, Heikki E.S.:* "Recovery of Child Support from Finland to Foreign Countries". Scandinavian Studies in Law. 1988, p. 136 et seq.; *Mahkonen, Sami:* "From Control of the Family to Its Autonomy". Scandinavian Studies in Law. 1988, p. 117 et seq.; *Mahkonen, Sami:* "Orientamenti e tendenze nell'affidamento dei figli di separati". Famiglia e Minori 1991. N. 5–6, p. 123 et seq.; *Mikkola, Matti:* "Supporting Parental Choice"; in: *Kamerman, Sheila B. – Kahn, Alfred J. (eds.):* Child care, parental leave, and the under 3s. Policy Innovation in Europe (ISBN 0-86569-037-5) 1991, p. 145 et seq.

VIII LEGAL PROCEDURE

By Antti Jokela

1. Historical Overview

The earliest form of legal procedure among the ancient Finnish tribes is thought to have been rural court sessions, which were held at special court sites. As a result of Christianity reaching Finland and of the Swedish conquests, the Swedish legal order began to gain status in the country from the 14th century onwards. Separate statutes and lower courts existed for the towns and the countryside respectively. The highest jurisdiction belonged to the king. A centralized court organization was not created in Finland until the 17th century, when appeal courts were created as superior courts in the Kingdom of Sweden (which Finland at this time belonged to).

The 1734 Procedural Code, part of a more extensive body of statutes, has remained in part as the principal source of Finnish legal procedure to this day, albeit not without several amendments. In 1789 jurisdiction was separated from general administration, and a special royal supreme court was established as the court of the highest instance.

When Finland became part of Russia as an autonomous grand duchy in 1809, the western legal system and court organization remained as they had been during Swedish rule, with the exception that the Judicial Department of the Senate became the highest instance and the Finance Department of the Senate became the highest administrative court. In the first part of the 19th century, legislation within the field of procedural law was also at a standstill. Its reforms did not properly commence until the 1860's, when a revival of the national identity began to take place in Finland, and the legal system was consciously and unanimously protected from any attempts at its Russification.

Finland gained independence during the First World War, in 1917. At this time the old national legal system, mainly dating from the era of Swedish rule, and independent courts of law already existed. The highest jurisdiction was transferred to the Supreme Court and Supreme Administrative Court, which were established in 1918.

During her independence, Finland has seen an extensive legislative process. Legal procedure has been revived with several partial revisions. The most significant of these is the reform of the lower court system, entering into force on 1 December 1993, which will introduce a uniform network of lower courts (the district courts) in the entire country and modernize the processing of civil matters to comply with the modern principles of oral, immediate and concentrated procedure.

An active Nordic collaboration and a common cultural background have naturally caused the nearest points of comparison to be found in the other Nordic countries. Closest to Finland, if only for merely historical reasons, is the Swedish legal system, which has often also served as a model for procedural reforms in Finland.

2. The Principal Sources of Procedural Law

Finland, not unlike other countries, follows the rule of lex fori, which is common in international procedural law. According to this rule, the procedural law of the country in question is observed by its courts of law and other authorities. The principal source of Finnish legal procedure is still to this day the Procedural Code of 1734. The same statute was in use also in Sweden until 1948. Even in Finland few significant original provisions remain, because in recent years the legal procedure in Finland has been vigorously updated with partial amendments.

The Procedural Code originally regulated the procedure in courts of law as a whole without differentiating between matters of civil and criminal law. For the most part it is concerned with the procedure in civil cases, but it also contains several purely criminal procedural rules. With the revision of the lower court system entering into force at the end of 1993, some purely civil procedural chapters have been added.

Several newer statutes and decrees supplement the rules of the Procedural Code. These special statutes are concerned with e.g. the organization of the different courts of law and the procedure in the special courts, the prosecutors, the preliminary investigation and coercive means, the advocates, general legal aid, cost-free legal proceedings, the publicity of legal proceedings, the processing of non-contentious civil cases, summary procedure in civil and criminal cases, and arbitration.

The enforcement of civil judgments is regulated by the Execution Act of 1895 and the enforcement of criminal judgments by the 1889 Decree on Execution in Criminal Matters. Both of these statutes have seen numerous changes over the years. The procedure in bankruptcy cases in Finland is also based on the old Bankruptcy Act of 1868. Despite partial amendments and renewals, the bankruptcy law of Finland is to be considered very much out of date.

In recent years Finnish procedural law has been heavily influenced by international legislation, with Finland joining in international agreements on human rights and basic rights. The 1966 United Nations Declaration on Civil and Political Rights has been part of the body of national law in Finland since 1976 and the Human Rights Agreement of the European Council since 1990. The rules included in these agreements have been given the status of law in Finland, and hence in legal practice they are comparable with the written statutes approved by the Parliament. Particularly in criminal procedure they are considered an important source of law, and the courts have begun to cite them in the reasoning of their decisions.

In addition to the written law, unwritten rules (customary law, "the way of the land") have played an important part in the forming of procedural law, due to the datedness of the written law. As a source of procedural law, the way of the land has developed almost entirely from court procedure.

Several of the precedents of the Supreme Court are concerned with procedural law. According to Finnish law, they do not unconditionally bind lower courts, but because of their authoritative status, they have a strong guiding influence, and generally a legal rule included in a Supreme Court precedent is followed in future legal decision-making. A general uniform custom may in turn create new legal rules; thus customs, as unwritten laws, are a source of law manifesting itself in court practice.

Legal dogmatics is not a source of law as such, according to the view adopted in Finland. However, views expressed in legal dogmatics can become customary law if they are followed in the practice of the courts.

The number of written works on legal procedure cannot be considered small today, but the problem in several instances lies in their outdatedness, caused by amendments of the law. Works written in other languages than Finnish or Swedish remain few, although doctoral dissertations usually contain a synopsis in English or German.

3. The Foundation of Procedural Law

The systematic foundation of modern procedural law both in Finland and elsewhere lies in a dualistic differentiation between formal and material law. According to this basic division, procedural law includes the rules that determine the forms of legal protection, i.e. the procedural rules, whereas the main object in the field of material law, or civil, criminal and administrative law, is the contents of the legal relations themselves. This division is generally accepted in written works on procedural law, albeit different views have been presented to support it.

The function of the rules of procedural law is to regulate the application of material law by courts of law and other authorities. Procedural proceedings are not necessary for their own sake, but for the sake of the realization of material law in conflict situations. In a legal process, material law is applied, which has resulted in it also being called application of the law. This function of procedural law results in its legal rules generally being in close contact with material issues. In Anglo-American legal dogmatics, procedural questions are often discussed in connection with material law. Also in Finland with questions of, for example, family, labour and environmental law, the special procedural rules of these fields of law are discussed, even though on the other hand they are also considered to be part of procedural law. However, the administrative procedure is included in the field of administrative law in Finland.

Procedural law is often considered to be a very technical field of law. By this is meant that in interpreting rules of procedural law social values, for instance, would not have as great an emphasis as in many fields of material law. This, however, does not apply, at least to the whole of procedural law, in Finland. For instance, questions relating to court organization and jurisdiction, as well as to the legal safeguards of both the accused and the victim of a crime and the parties in general, have had great social importance. Also with the economic recession of the early 1990s, the rules regarding the insolvency of the debtor and the defects of a dated bankruptcy process have been extensively in the public eye.

Moreover, procedural law is traditionally a field of law in which theory and practice are in close contact – in other words, it is a very practical field of law. For this reason, legal case practices and the following of court proceedings, for instance, have a central part in the curriculum of procedural law in Finnish law schools. It is also one of the most extensive and demanding fields of law included in the law degree, and it is studied at the end of the degree course.

4. Divisions of Procedural Law

On the basis of its principal stages, the legal process can be divided chronologically into three parts: 1) investigation, 2) judgment, and 3) enforcement. The criminal process also includes the consideration of charges by the prosecution, which takes place after the preliminary investigation but before passing judgment. However, a more common way to draw dividing lines within procedural law is according to the object of the procedure at hand. Thus, by its material contents, it can be divided into three parts: 1) the civil procedure, 2) the criminal procedure, and 3) the administrative procedure. Of these, the administrative process applies to proceedings in administrative courts or at other authorities, and, as mentioned above, in Finland it is included in administrative law. This, in other words, leaves the civil and criminal procedure in general courts of law within the sphere of procedural law. In this division, the processing of non-contentious civil cases is included in the civil procedure.

However, the distinction between civil and criminal procedure is not quite clear in Finland: their differences become fewer with the decrease of the degree of gravity of the crime in question. Also compensation in criminal cases can be agreed upon in criminal matters as in civil matters. On the other hand, in some civil cases such a strong public interest is considered to be present that conciliation is not allowed in them. Such cases are called mandatory. The majority of civil cases in Finland, however, are non-mandatory – ones in which conciliation is allowed.

By general civil procedure and general criminal procedure is meant an ordinary, regular procedure that follows the rules laid down in the Procedural Code and that can be applied to all cases for which no particular different procedure has been ordered. The special forms of procedure, on the other hand, are such exceptional procedures as have been decreed to be followed only in certain cases on account of their special quality. Naturally such criteria are to some extent relative. It is not always possible to determine whether a certain procedure belongs to the general process or its particular forms. Generally it can be said that a small deviation is not enough; an essential deviation from the general process is required for the procedure to be included in the special forms of procedure.

In Finnish literature on procedural law, the special forms of procedure in both civil and criminal procedure have included the summary forms of process. Today the earlier summary payment order procedure within the civil process have been abolished and all undisputed demands for payment have been linked with the written preparatory stage of the new lower court procedure in civil cases. In the field of criminal procedure, the summary procedures include summary penal proceedings and petty fine proceedings.

An important group of special forms of procedure are those followed in the special courts. However, even in them, unless otherwise ruled, the general rules of procedure as decreed in the Procedural Code are followed.

A special procedure is followed also in some cases which are tried in general courts, e.g. cases involving bills of exchange, cheques, maritime law, patent, trademark, protection of designs, paternity, tenancy law, and, in the criminal procedure, cases of young offenders, certain offences in office, and the procedure of converting unpaid fines into imprisonment.

5. The Main Principles of Procedural Law

In Finnish textbooks of procedural law, it has been customary to use the phrase "the leading principles of procedural law". Firstly, these include the audiatur et altera pars principle (the contradictory principle), which in Finland is a true legal maxim. It prohibits a court of law from passing judgment before the opposite side has had the opportunity to give his or her rejoinder in the matter. Secondly, leading principles common to both civil and criminal procedure also include the principle of the publicity of the proceedings and the principle of oral, immediate and concentrated court proceedings adopted in the new lower court hearing of a civil case. Occasionally also the principles of an unrestricted evaluation of evidence and the independence of the courts of law are included among the general principles of legal procedure.

The guiding principle of civil procedure in matters in which conciliation is allowed (non-mandatory cases) is considered to be the principle of party disposition. It provides a party with the power to determine whether he or she wishes legal protection (nemo judex sine actore), the extent of this protection (ne eat judex ultra petita partium), and what form of legal protection he or she wishes to use. In criminal matters and in mandatory civil cases, in which conciliation is not allowed, the opposite of party disposition, namely the principle of judicial investigation, is followed. According to this principle, legal protection is given regardless of the wishes of the individual.

The principles regarding the collaboration of the court and the parties have great systematical importance in Finland. In civil procedure, principally the hearing procedure is followed, the importance of which has greatly been emphasized in recent years. It vests in the parties the responsibility to present the relevant facts (the burden of appeal) and to acquire the necessary evidence. The inquiry procedure, on the other hand, leaves these duties for the court to perform. The term "party action" is the primary concept used to denote the principle of party disposition and the hearing procedure, whereas the term "official action" is the concept used to describe the principle of judicial investigation and the inquiry procedure.

In the criminal process, the concepts "accusatorial procedure" and "inquisitorial procedure" correspond to the hearing and inquiry procedures, respectively. In the latter, conducting the procedure is the duty of the court, whereas in the accusatorial procedure this duty has been imposed on a body outside the court of law, usually the prosecutor. In the accusatorial procedure, the court is also tied to the demands of the parties.

In earlier Finnish legal literature it was customary to maintain that the procedure in the case of petty offences was accusatorial, but with more serious crimes inquisitorial in an accusatorial form. Today it can be said that in practice inquisitorial features have disappeared from the Finnish criminal procedure also when serious crimes are in question. In the pending revision of the criminal procedure, an attempt is still made to emphasize the accusatorial nature of the procedure.

Other important procedural principles in Finland include the principle of material truth and the obligation to be truthful imposed on a party. In criminal cases, the latter applies to all other parties except the accused in criminal cases. The principle of favor defensionis has an essential importance in the criminal process, and an important component of this principle is the presumption of innocence and the in dubio pro reo rule. In Finland, as in the other Nordic countries, it is also considered important that laypersons take part in passing judgment, and every attempt is made to ensure that the parties have a factual chance, regardless of their funds and position, to bring their case to court if necessary and to receive professional legal help (cost-free legal proceedings).

In most cases it is not compulsory to follow the procedural principles if they have not been confirmed in the law or in international agreements binding the State. In practice the principles have not usually been applied in their purest forms, but have been more or less modified.

However, some of the procedural principles are unconditional. It has already been mentioned that the contradictory principle is a true legal principle. This is an unconditional rule also in force in Finland, even though it has not been expressed in the law in a general form. Moreover, some of the procedural principles are now included among the human rights, which makes them values in themselves. These include, at least partly, the publicity and immediacy of the court procedure, for instance in the form of the right of the accused to receive an oral hearing and to have witnesses questioned.

Some procedural principles have traditionally been in force in Finland, but some others were not confirmed in the law until after a lengthy legal-political struggle. The written law is still incomplete in terms of certain principles. For instance the important principles of an oral, immediate and concentrated hearing have received confirmation in the law only in connection with the renewal of civil procedure in lower courts as of 1 December 1993. The revision of the procedure in the fields of criminal law and appeal is still pending.

Finland's joining the European Council, the signing of the European Human Rights Convention in 1989 and the ratification of the convention the following year have for their part given an even greater weight to the procedural principles. Upon joining the aforementioned convention, Finland had to make only one reservation: Finland does not for the time being guarantee the right to an oral hearing in the appellate and administrative courts. The intention is to dispose of this reservation as soon as the necessary legal amendments have been made.

6. The Finnish Court Organization

6.1 The Foundations and the Division

The foundations of the way the court system is organized are set in the Constitution. According to the 1919 Constitution Act, jurisdiction in Finland is vested in independent and permanent courts of law, in the highest instance in the Supreme Court and the Supreme Administrative Court. Also in the United Nations General Agreement on Civil and Political Rights and the European Human Rights Agreement, both of which bind Finland, courts of law are required to be legally established, permanent and independent. By independence is meant both the independence of the decision-making and the irremovability of judges.

On the basis of their spheres of authority, the courts of law in Finland can be divided on the one hand into courts with jurisdiction in private civil and criminal cases, and on the other hand into administrative courts, which are mainly concerned with disputes with a public interest between the public authority and private persons. In other words, there is a similar separate administrative court system in Finland as in several other European countries that subscribe to the so-called Continental (or civil) legal system, such as France, Germany and Sweden. In Finland, the supreme administrative jurisdiction is vested in the Supreme Administrative Court, established in 1918. The county administrative courts act as general administrative courts of the first instance.

A significant distinction exists also between general and special courts. The general courts pass judgment in all disputes that have not been specifically ruled to be outside their jurisdiction. The special courts in their part concentrate on cases ordered to them. The general courts hear the majority of legal disputes in Finland, but in terms of the significance of the matters, the special courts have continuously gained more weight in relation to the general courts. The proceedings in the general courts are mainly regulated in the Procedural Act. Particular special statutes, for instance the Partition Act, the Water Act and the labour acts, usually contain rules on both the internal organization and the procedure followed in the special courts.

In general legal matters Finnish courts follow a three-step hierarchy. Courts of the first instance are general lower courts, as of 1 December 1993 known as the district courts. Their decisions can be appealed in the Appeal Courts. For the decisions of the latter, an appeal permit may be requested from the Supreme Court.

6.2 The General Lower Courts

For historical reasons, i.e. mainly as a result of the privileges to organize their own administration and judicial system that the towns received as early as in the Middle Ages, there were different lower courts of law operating in the countryside and in the towns in Finland until 1993. In the countryside and in the so-called new towns (founded after 1959) there were circuit courts, in which the judge decided the cases together with a jury. In the old towns, the lower courts were known as city courts, which consisted of three judges for each case. In the larger towns these were usually legally trained judges, but in the smaller towns there may also have been lay judges.

With the reorganization of the lower court system as of 1 December 1993, the former circuit courts and city courts were abolished and in their stead a network of uniform lower courts (the district court) was established. The model for the reform was the Swedish lower court system (tingsrätt) that has been in operation from 1971. There are 70 district courts in Finland in all.

The composition of the district court varies according to the nature of the case. In criminal cases the basic composition is a legally trained judge and three lay members. In civil and petition cases (non-contentious civil cases) the full composition is otherwise three judges, except in matters of family law and civil disputes that stem from the Tenancy Act, which are heard by a judge and three lay members. The composition can also be enlarged with a second judge and a fourth lay member. Petty offences, undisputed civil cases and non-contentious civil cases can be heard by one judge.

6.3 Appeal Courts

The judgments of the district court can be appealed in the Appeal Courts. There are six Appeal Courts in Finland today, which are situated in the towns of Turku (the oldest appeal court in Finland, founded in 1623), Vaasa (founded in 1776), Kuopio (the Eastern Finland Appeal Court, which prior to the Second World War was situated in Vyborg, at that time part of Finland), Helsinki, Kouvola and Rovaniemi.

The Appeal Courts function in sections. However, certain cases must be heard in a plenary session. There are four justices in each section, three of whom take part at a time in the court proceedings in normal cases. The referendaries present the cases. The President is the chairperson in plenary sessions and in the administrative section.

The Appeal Courts hear cases of high treason and treason as the first instance, as well as any charges against lower court judges and certain civil servants' alleged offences while in office and certain matters ordered to the appeal courts. Moreover, the Appeal Courts supervise the work of the lower courts in their respective precincts and take care of administrative matters.

Cases in the Appeal Courts are nearly always processed in writing, based on documents. Only in rare exceptional cases is an oral hearing arranged. However, the number of these is planned to be increased.

6.4 The Supreme Court

The Supreme Court uses the highest jurisdiction in the land and supervises the work of the judiciary and enforcement authorities. The Supreme Court also has duties relating to legislation and judicial administration. It consists of a president and at least 15 members, or justices. Cases are presented by the deputy chief secretaries and the referendaries. The Supreme Court is situated in Helsinki, the capital of Finland.

The Supreme Court processes cases that it receives via the channel of appeal from the Appeal Courts (civil and criminal matters), the Land Courts (matters of land partition and roads), the Assurance Tribunal (matters of accident insurance and military injuries) and from the Supreme Water Law Court (matters of water rights). The Supreme Court also has the power to annul a judgment that has already gained legal force or to remove such a judgment due to an appeal for nullification, as well as to restore lapsed time. The President of the Republic also obtains an expert opinion from the Supreme Court in matters of pardon.

An important duty of the Supreme Court is supervision of the uniformity of the law and jurisdiction and the work of the lower courts. This is mainly done through precedents, of which the Supreme Court gives approximately 150–200 every year. These precedents are also stored in a computer databank (Finlex).

Nowadays a leave to appeal is required when a judgment given by an Appeal Court as the second instance is appealed, and also in some other cases. A leave can be granted only if it is important to bring the matter to the Supreme Court in order to ensure the consistency of jurisdiction in similar cases (the ground of the precedent), or if it is deemed otherwise necessary due to such an error in the proceedings or otherwise in the case that would lead to the reversal of the particular judgment (the ground of annulment), or for some other weighty reason. In practice the leave to appeal has been granted only in approximately one case in ten.

The composition of the Supreme Court varies according to the nature of the case. In judicial matters, the Supreme Court is competent with five members, unless otherwise ordered for particular cases. The smallest acceptable number is three. If the case is very important or if it has far-reaching consequences, it is processed in a plenary session or in an enforced section with eleven members. Matters relating to judicial administration and legislative initiatives are always heard in a plenary session. The question of the granting of a leave to appeal is decided by a three-member composition.

The proceedings in the Supreme Court are usually written. Oral hearings and inspections have only rarely been held.

6.5 The Special Courts

In the beginning of the 20th century, only one actual special court existed in Finland, the Land Court, which had its foundations in the courts established as early as the late 18th century in connection with the general reparceling of the land. The Land Courts mainly process disputes that arise from land surveys.

During its independence Finland has seen an influx of special courts. The Assurance Tribunal, founded in 1942, has jurisdiction in social security issues. The Labour Court, founded in 1946, hears disputes arising from collective labour agreements. A special feature in Finland as the land of thousands of lakes is the separate Water Rights Courts (the Supreme Water Law Court and the Water Law Courts), which since 1962 have been hearing all matters relating to water rights disputes. The newest civil procedural special court in the country is the Market Court, in operation since 1978, dealing with matters of consumer protection.

The special courts have only limited jurisdiction in criminal cases. Separate military courts were abolished in 1983, and today military cases are, in the first instance, heard in certain lower courts ordered in the law. In such cases these courts include two military members in addition to the legally trained chairperson. As of 1983, special courts in criminal matters are only the High Court of Impeachment and partly the aforementioned Water Law Courts. To the jurisdiction of the High Court of Impeachment belongs the hearing of allegations of illegal conduct in office by members of Government and some high-ranking justices and judicial officials. By 1993, only four cases had been tried in the High Court of Impeachment.

Only the Turnover Tax Court operates today as a purely administrative special court. Also the Water Law Courts are partly to be regarded as administrative special courts because they hear not only cases relating to water disputes of civil and criminal nature, but also questions of permits, which are to be considered administrative in nature.

A dispersed court organization also poses problems, and for this reason the model for the future should be a more uniform court organization. One option is incorporating the special courts as particular sections of the general courts, where cases would be tried in a special composition. A system of this kind is in use in Finland in military cases, as well as in certain other matters. In the larger towns, disputes in tenancy cases are heard in the Housing Courts, which operate as special sections of the general courts. Maritime law cases are concentrated in certain lower courts, located in the coastal areas, that have been appointed as maritime courts. Patent cases from the whole country are heard in the Helsinki district court.

7. The Advocates

7.1 The Use of an Attorney and Trial Counsel

It is not compulsory to use an advocate in Finland, nor does the advocate have the sole right to appear in court: a party to a case has a legal right to represent him- or herself in a court of law. In practice, at least in the more complex matters, anyone faced with a court appearance would be wise to rely on professional legal help.

The law makes a distinction between an attorney and a trial counsellor. A party who has not been ordered to make a personal court appearance is allowed to use a representative, an attorney, in court, who draws his or her authority to represent the party from a letter of appointment and on this ground acts on his or her client's behalf in court.

A trial counsellor, on the other hand, acts by his or her client's side in court assisting him or her. The parties in civil cases and the complainant and the accused in criminal cases are always entitled to a trial counsellor's assistance.

Only an advocate or an otherwise honest, suitable and able person who has full legal capacity is qualified to function as an attorney or as a trial counsellor. In other words, besides advocates, also other lawyers and even laypersons may be qualified; however, they must be sufficiently familiar with the case and the task at hand. Earlier it was common in Finland, due to the small number of lawyers, that also persons without a law degree appeared as attorneys in lower courts, but today, with a wider selection of advocate services and a more complex body of legislation, it is rare. Today also the majority of professional advocates are members of the Finnish Bar Association, which is divided into regional associations.

7.2 The Qualifications and Duties of an Advocate

Only those members of the Finnish Bar Association who have been registered in the list of attorneys are entitled to call themselves advocates. An advocate is to be a citizen of Finland or of some other European Economic Area Member State who has reached the age of 25 years and obtained a law degree. He or she is also to have full legal capacity and be known to be honest and otherwise suitable to the work of an advocate. He or she is also required to pass an examination in advocacy law given by the Finnish Bar Association, and he or she must also have worked within the field of judicature for a minimum of four years, of which time at least two years as an advocate's assistant or in similar assignments. Anyone in an office or position lacking the necessary freedom of action is not accepted.

After Finland becomes a party to the EEA agreement, a person who is qualified to function as an advocate in some other EEA Member State can also be accepted as an advocate. Such a person is required to participate in an examination given by the Finnish Bar Association and thus indicate that he or she is sufficiently familiar with Finnish legislation and advocacy.

The majority of Finnish advocates still operate on their own or in two-partner partnerships. However, in the larger towns larger firms have emerged, consisting of several lawyers, some of whom have been able to specialize in certain types of cases. In Finland advocates are not tied to only certain courts, nor have they been divided into different groups by their assignments, but all advocates have a formal competence to attend to all kinds of legal commissions. After an amendment of the law in 1992, it is now possible to also take on assignments in the form of a limited company. Some of the largest firms have sub-offices or partner firms abroad.

Advocates and judges in Finland do not carry any outer signs of rank. The normal attire in court is a suit and a tie.

The number of advocates in Finland has always been relatively small in relation to the population, but in recent years it has clearly risen. For instance, statistics show that in 1992 in Finland there were 1,055 advocates serving a population of Finland was approximately five million. This number of advocates does not include the assisting lawyers who are not advocates.

7.3 The Advocates' Duties and their Supervision

An advocate is to fulfill the duties bestowed upon him or her with integrity and conscienciousness and to observe a code of professional ethics in all his or her activities. The outlines of these universal rules are included in the 1958 Advocates Act and in the rules of the Finnish Bar Association. More detailed regulations are included in the conventional guidelines of the advocates and elsewhere. If an advocate from some other EEA Member State conducts advocacy in Finland, he or she is to comply not only with the professional rules of Finland, but also with the obligations of the country of his or her origin.

It is the obligation of the board of directors of the Finnish Bar Association to supervise that the advocates fulfill their duties. Any complaints that may be made concerning the work of the advocates are dealt with by a special disciplinary board that consists of two outside members besides the advocate members. All members of the disciplinary board function with the responsibility of a judge. The disciplinary measures are, from the most lenient to the most severe, admonition, caution, public caution and disbarment. In practice, the latter has been ordered only in some few rare cases.

7.4 The Advocate's Fee

An advocate has the right to a reasonable fee for carrying out a commission. The basis of determining the fee is usually the amount and quality of work that the commission has required. Also the degree of difficulty of the commission and the value and importance of the interest in question are taken into account. In practice the advocate's success in carrying out the commission also has an effect on the fee. In exceptional cases the fee is agreed in advance as a specified share of the sum gained to the client through the act of advocacy. Persons lacking in funds have a right to cost-free legal proceedings, in which case the attorney's fee is paid by the State.

The Finnish Bar Association used to regularly affirm a particular schedule of fees, but with the introduction of the 1992 Competition Act, special fee recommendations have been abolished.

If a client wishes to challenge the fee that an advocate charges, the Finnish Bar Association board of directors can on the client's request set a body of arbitrators to hear the dispute. As an alternative, the client can also take the dispute to a lower court.

7.5 General Legal Aid

General legal aid, enacted by law in 1973 to supplement cost-free legal proceedings, covers most of Finland's municipalities. Persons that are entitled to it are those citizens who are lacking in funds, and it is provided free of charge or for a partial fee. Subject to the conditions set in the Hague General Agreement on Facilitating Trials of International Nature, signed on 25th October 1980, general legal aid can also be given to a foreign person. Attorneys providing general legal aid, some of whom are members of the Finnish Bar Association, are supervised by the Association in carrying out their work.

8. The Procedure in a Civil Case in the Lower Court

8.1 The General Contents of the Lower Court Reform

Formerly, civil cases were not prepared by the court before the actual hearing, which often resulted in the postponing of cases from session to session. However, as of 1 December 1993, the provision relating to the hearing of civil cases has been revised on the basis of the principles generally in use in other modern rules of procedure. Now the processing of cases in a trial is divided into two parts: the preparation and the main hearing. The purpose of the preparation is to clarify the object of the trial and to gather material to be presented in the trial. In form the preparatory stage is partly written and partly oral, and, under certain conditions, the case can already be decided at this stage. In other cases, the preparatory stage is followed by an oral, immediate and concentrated main hearing, in which the parties' statements and presentation of evidence are given orally and immediately to the court deciding the case. The composition of this court must not change during the hearing. The main hearing is to take place usually in one continuous procedure.

8.2 The Institution and Preparation of a Civil Action

A civil case is initiated with a written application for a summons sent to the office of a lower court. Already in this application, certain information is required: 1) the plaintiff's detailed demand, 2) a detailed account of the basis of the demand, 3) as extensively as possible, the evidence the plaintiff intends to present and what he or she intends to establish with each piece of evidence, and 4) a demand for the compensation of litigation expenses. If such a demand is based on a written document or piece of evidence, this must be enclosed as an original or a copy. In certain uncomplicated cases that can be solved in a summary procedure, the application can be simpler in content.

If the application for a summons is incomplete, the court is to invite the plaintiff to complete it. If the invitation is not followed, the application may be dismissed.

In the usual case the court grants a summons on the basis of the application. In the summons, the defendant is invited to respond in writing and send the document to the court within a time limit or, in special cases, present his or her response orally in a court session.

In the new procedure it is the duty of the court, according to the main rule, to attend ex officio to the service of the summons. It is generally served by post against an acknowledgement of receipt, but also bailiffs can serve summons if necessary. In exceptional cases a summons can be delivered as a substitute service, for instance to someone living in the same household as the party or employed in his or her business, or by announcing the summons in newspapers.

Already in his or her first response the defendant is to let his or her view on the plaintiff's demand be known, and, if he or she denies it, the grounds for doing so. The defendant is also already at this stage to make his or her plea of bar, if any, and any demands of litigation expenses, and, as far as possible, let his or her own evidence be known.

If the case cannot be decided already at this stage on the basis of written documents, the preparation of the case is continued orally in a session chaired by a single judge. In this court session, no briefs are allowed to be read or given to the court, apart from certain exceptions.

The role of the judge in the preparation is important in achieving its aim. When necessary, the judge is to pursue an active material conduct of the proceedings in order to clarify the demands of the parties and their grounds. During the preparatory stage, it is also to be clarified whether conditions for a conciliation exist. The new lower court procedure also requires careful preparatory work by the advocates.

On certain conditions, a clear case can be decided already at the stage of the oral preparation. Usually the form of judgment in such cases is judgment by default, which today has more extensive use than before. Also a conciliation reached by the parties can be confirmed at this stage.

8.3 The Main Hearing

If it has not been possible to decide the case during the preparatory stage, the main hearing follows, either in connection with the preparatory work or separately. In the first instance, also the main hearing takes place in a single-judge composition, before the same judge conducting the preparatory work. A separate main hearing is conducted in a lower court composed of several judges.

A main hearing conducted in connection with the preparatory stage is to be conducted either immediately after the preparatory session or within 14 days at the latest. Any issue can be heard in a main hearing of this kind with the consent of the parties or even without it if the case is clear. In other cases, the main hearing is to be conducted separately from the preparatory stage by a composition of several judges.

In a main hearing conducted during the preparatory stage, it is not necessary to present the trial documents, which are presented already in the last oral preparation session, for a second time, unless the court otherwise orders. However, in a separate main hearing, the whole trial material is, according to the principle of immediacy, to be presented again, even if some of it has already been presented during the preparation.

The main hearing is, not unlike the preparatory stage session, oral. The parties are not allowed to read out written statements, but they may use written notes to support their memory. They may read their claims from a document, and they may make direct references to legal practice, judicial literature and any documents that contain technical data that is not easily understood.

The new civil procedure also includes a rule of preclusion, which can lead to the loss of a right. In the main hearing of a non-mandatory civil case, the party is not allowed to refer to a new circumstance or a piece of evidence that he or she has not brought forward during the preparatory stage, unless he or she makes it probable that he or she had an acceptable reason for doing so. The aim of this is to eliminate the surprising of the opposite party in the main hearing with such new facts, the responding to which would require the postponing of the main hearing.

The main hearing consists of three main stages: 1) the opening discussion, 2) the presenting of the evidence, and 3) the closing discussion. However, the main hearing is to be conducted continuously, observing the principle of concentration. The postponing of proceedings, which used to be common in civil matters, is possible in the new system only exceptionally, when 1) it is necessary due to a party's absence or some other impediment, 2) when, after the commencing of the main hearing, a new important piece of evidence has come into the court's knowledge and it can only be received later, or 3) if it is necessary due to some unexpected circumstance or for some other important reason. If the main hearing has been postponed for a period of more than 45 days, a new main hearing must always be held. The interruption of a hearing, however, has to be differentiated from its postponement. This may become relevant in such extensive and demanding cases that cannot be decided in one day or in which preparations are to be made for a final oral statement.

8.4 The Minutes of the Proceedings and the Judgment

The revision of the lower court procedures also embraces the rules concerning the minutes and the judgment. For the time being the new procedure of keeping the minutes shall only apply to civil cases, but after the revision of the criminal procedure, the same principles shall be applied also in criminal cases.

The preparation and main hearing of a civil case are such different proceedings that the minutes have different requirements. For the preparatory stage to serve as well as possible as a prologue to the main hearing, it is important that accurate details on the course of the preparatory stage be recorded in the minutes. However, the minutes of the main proceedings do not have the same weight, and the decision is not based on the information in the minutes but directly on what was presented in the main hearing. For this reason, the minutes that are kept in the main hearing need not be as detailed as during the preparatory stage.

In most cases the oral statements of the parties and witnesses in the main hearing are recorded using audio equipment. If this cannot be done, for instance due to the malfunction of the recording equipment, the statement is to be included in the minutes ad verbatim. The recording need not be transcribed into written form, unless a party or the Appeal Court so demand.

The recordings are to be kept for at least six months after the rendering of the judgment, but at least until it has gained legal force.

Earlier the judgment was included in the minutes as part of them. In the new civil procedure, a separate document on the judgment is drafted. It is to include for instance a report on the demands and responses of the parties and the grounds on which they are based. The report is to be sufficiently extensive as to permit enforcement on the basis of the judgment. The most important items in the judgment are naturally the judgment itself and its grounds. The importance of the grounds has been emphasized, compared with the old system. The grounds are to state which facts and legal reasoning the judgment is based on. They must also include information on the basis of which a question under dispute has been decided.

9. The Processing of Non-contentious Civil Cases

By a non-contentious civil case is meant a case that the lower court can process on the basis of a petition, notice or its own initiative. The beginning of lis pendens in civil and criminal cases, on the other hand, requires the serving of a summons. The majority of non-contentious civil cases are taken under consideration either on the basis of a petition or a notice. On its own initiative the court may start proceedings only in exceptional cases, such as in certain matters of guardianship.

The scope of non-contentious civil cases has noticeably expanded during the last ten years and now exceeds by many times the number of civil and criminal cases. Non-contentious civil cases today include for instance matters of a child's care and visiting rights and divorce cases, which formerly were processed as civil cases.

The processing of non-contentious civil cases in courts of law is non-contentious jurisdiction, which is also called jurisdictio voluntaria and preventive procedure. In non-contentious civil cases the petitioner(s) usually does not have an adverse party as in civil cases. Some non-contentious civil cases, however, may be paralleled with civil cases, and in a wide meaning non-contentious jurisdiction is included within civil procedure.

The rules concerning the processing of non-contentious civil cases are included in a law enacted in 1986 that enables flexible and speedy processing. The petition and other necessary documents may be delivered to the office of the court also by post or messenger. If the case cannot be processed in the office, it is transferred ex officio to a court session. A defect in the petition does not cause its dismissal, but the petitioner is urged to supplement it. If persons other than the petitioner have an interest in the case, the court is to present them ex officio with an opportunity to be heard. Non-contentious civil cases are processed in the office of a lower court, and partly also in court session before one judge. A disputed non-contentious civil case is to be heard in a full lower court session, with the exception that the parties so request or the court considers the case clear, even a disputed non-contentious civil case can be processed before one judge.

The general statute on the processing of non-contentious civil cases is however not applied to all cases of this nature. There are special statutes on, for instance, the procedure in matters of the registration of title and the mortgaging of real property, which are the most numerous cases in the offices of the lower courts.

10. The Processing of Criminal Cases

10.1 Preliminary Investigation and Coercive Means

At the beginning of 1989, new statutes on the preliminary investigation and coercive means in criminal matters entered into force in Finland. The reform was significant especially in terms of the preliminary investigation, because prior to the enactment of the law, mainly only administrative rules on the preliminary investigation of crimes existed.

By preliminary investigation is meant the gathering of information on whether sufficient cause exists for the instigating of a regular trial against the suspect. The aim is also to clarify which person can be suspected of a crime and who are the other parties, such as complainants. The preliminary investigation is to be carried out without unwarranted delay, and facts and evidence against as well as in favour of the suspect are to be taken into account in it. An important principle is the presumption of innocence confirmed in the law: the suspect is to be regarded as not guilty during the preliminary investigation. Also in other respects the principles of equality, or objectivity, and discretion and the least inconvenience are to be respected in the preliminary investigation.

A person who is questioned is to be informed of his or her position as soon as possible. A suspect of a crime has no duty to collaborate in the confirmation of his or her guilt. He or she has no obligation to confess or even a duty to give a statement on the matter. However, the aim of questioning even the suspect is to produce evidence, and everyone has the duty of submitting him- or herself to questioning in the preliminary investigation, with the exception of some restrictions concerning acting as witness. The investigation of a complainant offence, according to the main rule, requires that the complainant notifies the authorities that he or she demands a punishment for the offender.

The conducting of the preliminary investigation is the duty of the police, unless otherwise ruled. Usually the preliminary investigation is conducted by the police officials of the locality of the crime. The Central Criminal Police assist the police forces in the whole country and also conduct independent investigations. Nowadays the preliminary investigation is directed by a commander of investigations, who is usually an official with the right to arrest. In the proposal for new lower court proceedings in criminal matters, the command in other than simple criminal matters is transferred from the police to the prosecutor at the point in time when the person can already be suspected of a crime.

A party to a criminal matter has the right to counsel in the preliminary investigation. A suspect of a crime who has been captured, arrested or imprisoned has the right to stay in contact with his or her counsellor. There is a special rule concerning the competence of the counsellor: an advocate or a person providing general legal aid or an other person qualified to function as an attorney who has a law degree or generally conducts matters of advocacy in court is qualified to counsel a party in the preliminary investigation.

Minutes are kept at the interrogation. The report recorded in the minutes is to be read out to the person interrogated immediately after the interrogation and given to him or her for inspection. The report may also be recorded using audio or video equipment. The official is to have the report interpreted, if the person interrogated is not familiar with the language being used. A restricted preliminary investigation may be conducted in minor offences that are simple and clear. Only the main contents of such interrogations are recorded.

Coercive means in criminal procedures can be grouped into those that are directed at a person's freedom and those that are directed at other objects of legal protection. The former include apprehension, arresting a suspect, imprisonment and a prohibition to travel. The latter in turn include a prohibition of transfer and confiscation as security, seizure, the isolation of the investigation site, and a search of premises. At the time of writing, the police do not have the right of telephone surveillance, but allowing it with a court's permission when the most serious crimes are in question has been discussed.

The authorities with the power to use coercive means are usually high-ranking police officers, prosecutors and certain members of the military, border guard and customs. In urgent cases, other members of the police forces also have the right to conduct e.g. capture, search and the seizure of an item to be confiscated. The same general principles as in the preliminary investigation in general are followed in the use of coercive means.

To ensure legal safety and respect for human rights, the authority to use some of the most severe coercive means was exclusively bestowed upon the courts of law from the beginning of 1989. This particularly concerned the right to imprison. The decision on the use of certain coercive means, such as prohibition to travel and confiscation, may be brought to a court of law, which may also extend the time limits of certain coercive means.

In an amendment to the Coercive Means Act made in 1990, the maximum time of arrest was made to correspond with the practice of the European Human Rights Agreement, which requires a demand for the imprisonment of an arrested person to be made to a court without delay and at the latest on the third day after capture. A demand for imprisonment is also to be brought up before the court without delay and within four days (96 hours) of capture at the latest. Matters of imprisonment are processed in court in a single-judge composition, and the publicity of the proceedings in these cases has been limited, compared with those of normal criminal cases.

10.2 The Complainants, the Prosecutors and the Consideration of Charges

The initiation of a criminal process is, according to the main rule, the duty of the public prosecutor. A crime is subject to public prosecution, unless the crime or the type of crime in question has specifically been designated as a complainant offence. The latter crime requires a request of prosecution from the complainant. In some cases, the requirement for prosecution is a request made by a certain supervising official. Certain crimes classified as complainant offences may in exceptional cases become subject to public prosecution if an important general interest so requires.

Generally complainant offences are minor offences and, on the other hand, crimes that may cause considerable harm to the complainant if brought to trial. In other words, the grounds are procedural-economical and the respect of a private person's autonomy.

In an international comparison, the complainant's position in terms of his or her right of prosecution is strong. He or she has an independent and primary right of prosecution parallel to that of the public prosecutor. In practice, however, independent charges brought by the complainants themselves have been rare. The public prosecutor also has a duty to be present in the court proceedings of a charge brought by the complainant. In the preparation of the new lower court procedure, it has been suggested that the complainant's independent right of prosecution be limited in such a way that he or she could only bring charges if the public prosecutor does not do so.

The public prosecutor generally has the duty of compulsory, or absolute, prosecution (the criminal procedural principle of legality): the public prosecutor is obliged to bring charges whenever the evidence is sufficient and the act in question fulfills the conditions for punishability. However, in recent years the public prosecutor's right not to take legal action has been extended. Grounds for the use of this right include the insignificance of the crime and the youth of the offender, as well as reasons of expediency and equity, to a certain degree.

Until now, the public prosecutor organization has been decentralized. Before the lower court reform, public prosecutors in the circuit courts were the rural police chiefs and the deputy rural police chiefs, and in the city courts the city public prosecutors. When the lower court reform enters into force, public prosecutors in the district courts will continue to be the rural police chiefs and deputy rural police chiefs of their respective districts, and the city public prosecutors. Of these, the rural police chiefs are also police officials, and they have additional administrative duties. However, the office of the public prosecutor will be reorganized with the reform of the state local administration. It is intended to establish special population register district offices in the entire country in which prosecutors, police officials and enforcement officials (bailiffs) would operate as independent units. In view of this, a Government decision of dividing the entire country into population register districts replacing the former police districts, which will enter into force on 1 January 1995, has already been given.

Prosecutors are under the supervision of the Chancellor of Justice. In the counties, the superiors of the public prosecutors are the county prosecutors, who are the police inspectors of the county governments and the deputy police inspectors.

10.3 The Regular Criminal Procedure

In the former criminal procedure, the public prosecutor or the complainant could make a request to summon the accused to court directly to the bailiff. The accused was however notified on the summons document drawn up by the public prosecutor to enable his or her preparation for the trial.

In the proposed new criminal procedure, the trial commences with a request for summons drawn up by the public prosecutor and with a summons served to the accused by the district court on the basis of the request. In certain cases the summons could also, with the court's permission, be served by the prosecutor. In the request for summons, the criminal act, as well as the evidence the public prosecutor intends to present in trial, must be specified and detailed. This way the accused is provided with a better chance than before to prepare his or her defence and to acquire the evidence he or she intends to present in the case. Formerly the accused often had to request the adjournment of the case for this reason.

No particular preparatory measures are usually taken in the criminal procedure, apart from the preliminary investigation. The trial material acquired in the preliminary investigation is recorded in the preliminary investigation minutes, on the basis of which the prosecutor and the other parties can consider presenting additional material in court. The public prosecutor sends the preliminary investigation minutes to the court in advance, with the indictment and possible other documents, and the other parties have the right to receive a copy of it. In the proposal for a criminal procedural reform, it is suggested that in complex and extensive cases it would be possible, according to the consideration of the court, to arrange a special preparatory session before the main hearing and also to perform certain other acts to ensure a continuous main hearing.

Also, the accusatorial rather than the inquisitorial principle is nowadays followed in the criminal procedure where serious crimes are concerned; the investigation of the crime is principally the duty of the public prosecutor instead of that of the court. The main hearing follows the same pattern as the civil procedure, and it normally consists of three parts: 1) the preliminary discussion, 2) the presenting of the evidence, and 3) the closing discussion. The main hearing will be oral in the reformed criminal procedure also. According to the main rule, the parties may not read out or present to the lower court a pre-written trial document nor otherwise present their case in writing.

Immediately at the beginning of the trial the public prosecutor is to present a charge based on the request for summons and also its grounds. The public prosecutor need not specify his or her demand for punishment, this being the duty of the court ex officio. However, an accurate account of the criminal act is to be presented in the charge. In this case the public prosecutor has the burden of proving an allegation, and this also sets the limits of the court's investigation. The court may not regard anything not mentioned in the charge as the fault of the accused.

After the public prosecutor has presented the charge, it is the complainant's turn to present his or her demands. According to the principle of adhesion, also civil demands based on a crime may be investigated in the criminal procedure. The most common of these in practice are claims for damages.

After this, the accused has a chance to submit his or her reply to the demands presented against him or her, which he or she can admit or deny. The admitting of the charge or a fact is not sufficient grounds for a verdict in the criminal proceedings, although the accused's own testimony may have substantial weight in the evaluation of evidence. The accused has nevertheless no duty to adhere to the truth, unlike the other parties, nor is he or she heard under oath. This complies with the right of the accused of not having to contribute to the substantiating of his or her own guilt or lack thereof, as guaranteed in international human rights conventions.

The presentation of evidence in the criminal procedure is immediate, and witnesses are to be heard in court in person. According to the main rule, prior to being heard they are to take an oath or corresponding affirmation to tell the truth prior to being heard. Witness testimony recorded in the preliminary investigation minutes is not to be used as such as evidence or read out in court, other than in certain exceptional cases. Likewise, the presenting of pre-written testimonies is generally prohibited.

In the verdict ending the criminal proceedings, the charges are either to be dismissed or considered to be substantiated. A dismissing verdict must not include any references to the accused in reality possibly being guilty of a criminal act, although full evidence thereof does not exist.

10.4 The Reform of Lower Court Proceedings in Criminal Matters

The lower court reform entering into force on 1 December 1993 shall also have an effect on criminal proceedings: the composition of the lower court in criminal matters has been changed in such a way that criminal cases, unless they can be decided by a single-judge court, are heard in a court of one legally trained judge and three lay members. However, the procedure itself has not yet been revised.

However, in connection with the lower court reform in civil proceedings it was presumed already in the Government proposal and during its reading in the Parliament that the criminal procedure will be revised according to the same principles – the orality, immediacy and concentration of the proceedings. A memo of a committee created to prepare the reform of court proceedings in criminal matters was published in early 1993 (Publication of the Legislative Department of the Ministry of Justice 1/93). An effort will be made to bring the reform into force as soon as possible, but this cannot take place sooner than during 1994 at the earliest.

A proposal has been made to include the most important rules concerning criminal procedure in a special act on procedure in criminal matters. The central feature in the new criminal procedure will be the processing of criminal matters in one continuous main hearing, in which all the evidence is received. An effort is being made thereby to avoid the previously frequent adjournment of cases in criminal proceedings. Also, the membership of the court may not change during the proceedings. The main hearing in the criminal procedure will be oral. The purpose of the reform is to dispose of the old custom of reading out preliminary investigation minutes and advocates' briefs in court. The preliminary investigation minutes as such will no longer be included in trial documents.

With the reform an effort is also made to improve the complainant's – the victim's – position. In the memorandum of the committee, particular attention has been given to the victims of sexual offences and to those whom a person they intimately know has assaulted. These victims could be assigned a trial counsellor or a support person at the state's expense, who would help them both in the preliminary investigation and the trial.

It would no longer be compulsory to serve summons to the complainant, unless he or she has a demand for punishment or a claim for damages that differs from that stated in the charge. The complainant's demands would be established already during the preliminary investigation, and after this, the prosecutor's duty would be to present the demands on his or her behalf in court.

A recommendation has been made to partially introduce a system of public defense, presently lacking in Finland. In serious offences the accused could be assigned a public defender, who would usually be an advocate or another person with a law degree. The public defender could be assigned for instance to persons whose income is not low enough to qualify them for cost-free trial proceedings or who have not themselves taken steps to acquire a necessary trial counsellor. After the trial, the accused could be obligated to reimburse either partially or wholly the expenses caused to the State by his or her public defense, if he or she is not eligible for cost-free trial proceedings.

10.5 The Special Forms of the Criminal Procedure

Among the cases heard in general courts, pursuant to a particular order, are cases concerning maritime law and patents, young offenders, the conversion of fines into imprisonment, military crimes and crimes processed with the Appeal Court as the first instance concerning e.g. certain officials' offences in office. The only special courts that can hear criminal matters are the High Court of Impeachment and the Water Rights Courts.

Minor and clear offences are processed in summary procedures (summary penal proceedings and petty fine proceedings). These procedures take place outside the normal court procedure, and, due to their large number, they have great significance. At the time of this writing the passing of a summary penal judgment is still the duty of the lower court judge, but in the criminal procedural reform this task shall be transferred to the public prosecutor. A party however has the right to oppose a petty fine, in which case the matter is processed observing an ordinary criminal procedure. The imposing of a petty fine, on the other hand, is in the jurisdiction of a police official, but the offender has the right to request that the case be investigated by a district court.

11. Appeal

It is considered an essential part of a party's legal safeguards in Finland that he or she has the possibility to seek remedy at least once. A regular channel of doing so in both civil and criminal matters is the appeal. It is a comprehensive means of remedy, and it can be used to contest all kinds of errors in the judgment. It can result in the deletion, annulment or alteration of the decision in question and also to the transfer of the case to the correct court of law.

It is generally possible to seek remedy at the Court of Appeal to the decision of a lower court, with some minor exceptions. In an appeal, the matter can be examined with respect to both questions of evidence and questions of law. An appeal is however only possible regarding so-called defended judgments. If the matter concerns a default judgment in a civil case, the party can have recourse to an appeal against judgment by default, a particular type of appeal, which is made via an action bringing up the case for a second time in the lower court that gave the original judgment.

At the time when a lower court delivers its judgment, it is also to give the parties appeal instructions. If a party wishes to seek remedy, he or she is to register his or her intent to appeal the jugdment within seven days of its pronouncement or deliverance, and after this, he or she is to send a letter of complaint to the office of the lower court within 30 days of the said event. The opposing party has the right to ensure the defendant's right to defense and respond in writing to the appeal within 14 days of the expiration of the appeal period. The lower court sends the documents of appeal and its appendices delivered to it to the Appeal Court when the time period for responding has expired.

Up to the present time, the procedure in the courts of appeal has mainly taken place in writing. Oral hearings have been rare, and judgments have been rendered almost entirely on the basis of the documents provided by the complainant and the defendant and the trial materials obtained by the lower court. The verdict is given on the submission of the referandary on the basis of his or her proposed decision and a possible memo.

The judgments and decisions of the Appeal Court can be further appealed at the Supreme Court. As of 1980, a leave to appeal has been required for this when the case concerns matters that the Court of Appeal has processed as the second instance. A permission can be granted only if it is important to bring the matter to the Supreme Court in order to ensure the consistency of jurisdiction in similar cases (the ground of the precedent), or if it is deemed otherwise necessary due to such an error in the proceedings or otherwise in the case that would lead to the reversal of the particular judgment (the ground of annulment), or for some other weighty reason. In practice, a leave to appeal has been granted in approximately one case in ten.

The procedure in the Supreme Court takes place, as in the Appeal Court, usually in writing. Oral hearings and inspections have been arranged only seldom. Upon joining the European Human Rights Convention Finland made a reservation: for the time being Finland does not guarantee the right to an oral hearing in the appellate and administrative courts. The intention is to dispose of the said reservation as soon as possible, when the necessary legal amendments have been made.

In 1992 a committee preparing an Appeal Court reform suggested an increase in the number of oral hearings in the Appeal Court. It was suggested that an oral hearing be held if reaching a decision depends on the trustworthiness of the witnesses. Moreover, an oral hearing should normally be held if one of the parties in a civil case or the accused or victim of a crime in a criminal case should so demand.

The committee also suggested the introduction of a leave to appeal in minor civil and criminal cases already when seeking remedy at the Appeal Court. On the other hand, it was also suggested that the separate registering of an intent to appeal be abandoned.

Extarordinary channels of appeal in Finland include complaint on the basis of a grave procedural error, annulment of a judgment and restoration of lapsed time. The first channel can be used against a judgment which has gained legal force in situations specifically listed in the law in which procedural provisions have been violated. The annulment of a judgment is used when a material error in the verdict has occurred. With the restoration of lapsed time a party can have a procedural time limit extended that he or she has not observed without fault of his or her own.

The extraordinary channels of appeal are at a party's disposal when the time limit for the use of the ordinary appeal channels has lapsed. Typical for Finland is the partial overlapping of the different channels of appeal. It is however not generally allowed to resort to the extraordinary channels of appeal, except on fairly exact grounds as provided for in the law. In practice the extraordinary channels of appeal are used with restraint.

12. The Compensation of Litigation Expenses

12.1 The Imposing of Expenses

Litigation expenses include the various expenses that the trial causes the parties. These can include both general fees for court proceedings payable to the State and actual party expenses. Litigation expenses are relatively low in Finland. The largest proportion of the actual party expenses is usually taken by the fees charged by the attorney or trial counsel. Other party expenses include e.g. witnesses' and experts' fees, travel and accommodation costs caused by appearances in court, and the loss of earnings. On the basis of preconditions set in the law, the party that loses the trial is obliged to compensate the opposing party for expenses incurred in the case.

The main rules on the duty to repay litigation expenses are still those included in Chapter 21 of the Procedural Code of the Law of 1734. Basically these rules apply to all matters heard in a court of law. However, they were originally drawn up exclusively for civil cases. In cases brought to court by a public prosecutor, the rules on litigation expenses in the Procedural Code have scarcely been applied at all, other than in cases of the complainant's expenses. The rules are also not easily applicable to non-contentious civil cases, because these usually, unlike civil cases, do not have two opposing parties.

As far as the procedure is concerned, it is to be noted that compensation for litigation expenses is not to be ordered ex officio, but a party is obliged to specifically so request. Such a request is to be made before the principal claim is left to the decision of the court.

12.2 Liability to Recompensate in Civil Matters

According to the main rule, the losing party of a case is to provide compensation for all the necessary litigation costs of his or her opposing party. This main rule however has several exceptions that oblige the parties to bear their own damages. In legal language this is known as offsetting them. In practice this usually takes place when the judge considers the case to have been so confusing that the losing party has had justified cause for a trial.

Special rules exist outside the Procedural Code on the compensation for litigation expenses in matters of tenancy and paternity. These rules oblige the parties in principle to see to their own expenses. As an exception, however, when weighty reasons exist, a party can be obliged to recompense the reasonable litigation expenses of the opposing party partly or wholly.

12.3 Liability to Provide Compensation in Criminal Matters

In criminal matters, the question of compensation for litigation expenses arises mainly in the relationship between the complainant and the accused. If only the complainant in the case has demanded a punishment, the same rules as in civil matters are applied. If the complainant has joined the public prosecutor's demand for punishment and/or presented claims for damages to the accused, the complainant has the right to receive compensation for his or her litigation expenses from the accused. But in a case in which a charge brought by a public prosecutor has been dismissed the accused does not – apart from certain exceptional cases – have the right for compensation from either the complainant who has joined the charge, nor from the public prosecutor, nor the State.

12.4 Liability to Provide Compensation in Non-contentious Civil Cases

No rule on compensation for litigation expenses has been included in the act on the processing of non-contentious civil cases in lower courts. For this reason, the same rules as in ordinary civil cases are applied in non-contentious civil cases.

Earlier some confusion on the obligation to provide compensation in non-contentious civil cases existed, and different courts pursued different practices. The Supreme Court published several precedents in the early 1990s that unified the court procedure. The starting point nowadays is that an applicant is to cover his or her own costs that are caused by the hearing of such a case that is brought to court in order to attend to the applicant's own interests and in which only a court of law has the authority to provide a decision. A person that, according to the law, is to be heard in the case is not liable for the applicant's necessary first hearing expenses regardless of whether he or she opposes the application or not. However, the person to be heard is liable for any additional costs that his or her claims may have cost the applicant. The applicant may however be liable for expenses caused by an unwarranted application already in the first hearing.

12.5 Plans of Reform

A proposal for new rules on compensation for litigation costs was made by a committee of the Ministry of Justice in 1989 in connection with the lower court reform in civil matters. According to the proposal, separate rules on compensation for litigation expenses in civil and criminal matters would be included in chapter 21 of the Procedural Code.

The new rules concerning civil cases are more extensive and detailed than their predecessors. Their aim is to enable the winning party to receive compensation in more cases than before, to reduce the numbers of unnecessary trials and to centralize the new civil proceedings and ensure their prompt progress.

In criminal matters the new rules would improve the legal safeguards of a person who has been unjustifiably accused or suspected of a crime. If the charges are dismissed or abandoned, the accused would have the right to receive compensation from State funds. An unjustifiably accused person would have the right to receive compensation for expenses caused by the preliminary investigation. The proposal also includes rules on the obligation of a person sentenced to a punishment or other penal sanction to pay compensation to the State.

The reform is intended to be introduced with the revision of the court procedure in civil matters.

13. Cost-free Legal Proceedings

13.1. The Scope of Cost-free Legal Proceedings

By cost-free legal proceedings is meant an exemption from the payments required by the proceedings, such as various procedural costs and costs incurred in the hearing of witnesses, that the court grants to a party in a case. Such a person is also eligible for the assistance of a counsellor, whose fee and expenses are paid for by the State.

The first act on cost-free legal proceedings in Finland entered into force in the beginning of 1956. It ruled that cost-free legal proceedings could initially only be granted in civil and criminal cases in the general courts of law and in the military court. The present act on cost-free legal proceedings was enacted in 1973. Simultaneously an act on general legal aid became law, in which the scope of application of cost-free legal proceedings was expanded from general civil and criminal cases to include also cases in the Water Rights Courts, the Water Rights High Court and the Land Courts, as well as cases of non-contentious jurisdiction processed in general courts in which the nature of the case and the safeguarding of a party's legal rights for special reasons so required.

The next reform to expand the scope of the application of cost-free legal proceedings was an amendment of the relevant act that entered into force in the beginning of 1989. According to this amendment, eligibility for cost-free legal proceedings in non-contentious civil cases no longer requires special reasons. Cost-free legal proceedings have become possible in the preliminary investigation of criminal matters and in cases concerning treatment or committing someone to a welfare home, the taking into care or placing into surrogate care of a child, or the expiration of custody processed in county courts and the Supreme Administrative Court, and in matters concerning the Aliens Act heard in the Supreme Administrative Court. These amendments for their part have made it possible for Finland to join the European Human Rights Convention.

13.2 Persons Eligible for the Benefits and their Material Qualifications

Cost-free legal proceedings may be granted to a Finnish or a foreign citizen, and thus all natural persons regardless of their nationality are eligible. However, it cannot be granted to juristic persons.

The qualification for the granting of cost-free legal proceedings is the person's inability to pay entirely and without difficulty for the expenses incurred as a party to a case. In considering the matter, the circumstances to be observed are the person's income and assets, maintenance obligation and other matters affecting his or her financial situation. Cost-free legal proceedings may also be granted partially, if the party is reasonably considered to be able to assume liability for the expenses of the proceedings. Cost-free legal proceedings are not granted if the object of the procedure has only minor significance to the party. Annually, approximately 30,000 cost-free legal proceedings have been granted in Finland, and the majority of these have been cases in lower courts.

13.3 Applying for the Benefit and the Procedure

A person seeking cost-free legal proceedings is to submit an application thereof to a court of law. Usually this takes place at the beginning of the proceedings, but it can also be done even before the trial or at any stage of the proceedings. Cost-free legal proceedings may also be granted retroactively, to apply to acts already performed in the case. In a criminal case, cost-free legal proceedings may be granted already during the preliminary investigation regardless of whether the case is eventually brought to court.

An application is to be made in writing, or, in connection with oral proceedings, it can also be made orally. With the application the applicant is also to present a written affirmation of his or her financial situation and maintenance obligations and other necessary reports. According to the main rule, the social authority of the applicant's locality is to verify the affirmation. The required application and affirmation forms are available free of charge at social offices and courts.

13.4 The Appointment of a Counsellor

The benefit of cost-free legal proceedings does not as such include the right to counsel at the expense of the State. The granting of cost-free counsel requires that the person who is to be granted the benefit of cost-free legal proceedings is not capable of appropriately monitoring his or her interests and rights in the case without counsel.

For the purpose of saving the State's funds, it has been ruled that counsel is to be granted neither 1) in non-contentious civil cases, unless particularly significant grounds exist, nor 2) in minor criminal cases in which no more severe punishment than a fine is to be expected or in which otherwise the accused's legal safeguards do not, in view of the expected punishment and the state of the settled case, so require. In interpreting this rule, however, also the provisions of international human rights conventions on the free legal aid granted to an accused are to be observed (The Supreme Court 1992:81).

The person appointed as counsellor is to be an advocate or another person suited to act as an attorney. However, in a criminal matter an imprisoned person, a person sentenced to be imprisoned, or anyone under 18 years of age is to be provided with an advocate or, for a special reason, another legally trained person, if the question is of an offence punishable by imprisonment. A qualified person suggested by the party him- or herself is to be appointed, unless special circumstances otherwise require.

The court grants the counsellor (apart from the general legal counsellor), from State funds, a reasonable fee for his or her work and loss of time, as well as compensation for necessary expenses. Such a counsellor is not allowed to accept remuneration from his or her client. According to the main rule, if the opposing party of a person who has been granted cost-free legal proceedings loses the case, he or she is to be obligated to compensate the State for the expenses that have been paid from its funds.

13.5 The Relationship to General Legal Aid

The present acts on cost-free legal proceedings and general legal aid were enacted simultaneously in 1973. The acts are parallel and they complement each other in terms of their scope of application. The essential difference between them is that cost-free legal proceedings may be granted only in matters listed in the law, whereas general legal aid may be granted to all natural persons in all legal matters, including those matters not involving an actual trial (see above 7.5.).

14. Arbitration

A new, modern act on arbitration entered into force in Finland on 1 December 1992 and thus replaced the earlier act of 1928. The new act was necessitated by the social, economic and technical changes that had taken place in Finland. Also the continually expanding internalization and the expansion of foreign trade caused a need to modernize the law of arbitration and to bring it into compliance with internationally accepted attempts at unification. In the new law the UNCITRAL Arbitration Rules (1976) and the Model Law of Arbitration in International Trade (1985) have been taken into account.

The subject of the new act is mainly arbitration that takes place in Finland. The adoption of the principle of territory indicates thus a change from the earlier situation. Separate rules on arbitration taking place abroad, in particular on the validity and effect of a foreign arbitration award in Finland, have been placed at the end of the act (51–55 §).

An arbitration agreement is to be made in writing. This requirement is filled either by signing the agreement or by concluding it in the correspondence between two parties, or also by agreeing on the use of arbitration by exchanging telegrams, telex messages or other documents produced in a similar way. An arbitration agreement may also be lawfully made by a reference to standard conditions of contract or to some other document that includes a provision on arbitration in an agreement signed by the parties.

The parties themselves have the power to stipulate as to the composition of the arbitration court. Three arbitrators are required, unless the parties have otherwise agreed. It is also possible to use one arbitrator, and this has in fact become more common than before in Finland.

Rules on procedure in arbitration court included in the law are more detailed than before. Most of them, however, are non-mandatory, and thus the parties still have the right to agree on the procedure in the matter, unless the new act otherwise stipulates. But the rule of audiatur et altera pars (the right to be heard) is absolute even in arbitration court: the arbitrators are to reserve the parties a chance to plead their case. Unlike the courts, arbitrators cannot order the parties to act under the penalty of a fine, nor give orders on other coercive means nor require an oath or a corresponding assertation from the parties. The arbitrators can hear the parties, witnesses and experts (without an oath) and arrange inspections even outside the locality of the hearing, also outside Finland. The arbitrators prescribe the language of the proceedings, if the parties have not done so.

According to the former law, the arbitrators were obliged to base their judgment on what they considered to be the requirements of justice and reason. In practice they endeavoured to follow the same rules as the State courts. This has a significance in business life in increasing predictability. Therefore the new act stipulates that arbitrators are to base their judgments on the law, which corresponds to the UNCITRAL rules. The parties may agree that in solving a dispute, the law of a certain country is to be observed, in which case the arbitrators are to base their judgment on this law. The parties may further agree that the arbitration award is based on what the arbitrators consider to be reasonable (ex aequo et bono), instead of on the law.

At the parties' request the arbitrators may confirm a conciliation. Such a conciliation confirmed by an arbitration award is considered an arbitration award as intended in the New York General Agreement on the Acknowledgement And Execution of Foreign Arbitration Awards. The arbitrators can also render a partial award or an interim award, which, particularly in extensive cases, is occasionally appropriate.

An arbitration award is always to be drawn up in writing, and it is to be signed by all arbitrators. An arbitration award does not need to be orally declared to the parties – it is sufficient that a copy of the arbitration award is given to them in the session of the arbitration court or verifiably delivered to them. An arbitration award is no longer recorded in the archives of the general lower court.

The arbitrators may correct a clerical or an accounting error in the arbitration award either on their own initiative or by a request made by a party within 30 days of receiving the arbitration award. A party may also request an additional award on a question that the arbitrators have overlooked in their award.

An arbitration award is final and immediately enforceable, as a judgment which has gained legal force. An arbitration award cannot be appealed at a State court on the grounds of a material fault. However, in certain cases in which material requirements set in order to guarantee the realization of legal safeguards have been violated, the arbitration award is void or voidable. These actions are to be brought in the lower court of the locality where the arbitration award was given.

The lower court decides on the execution of an arbitration award and ensures that it is not void or that it has not been repealed by a court decision. The arbitration agreement and the arbitration award, as originals or verified copies, are to be enclosed with an application of the execution of an arbitration award, which is to be addressed to the general lower court. In the event that a document is drawn up in a language other than Finnish or Swedish, a verified translation into either of these languages is also to be enclosed, unless the court grants an exceptional permission to the contrary. The execution itself takes place as that of a court judgment that has gained legal force; in other words, it is performed by an execution officer (bailiff).

The parties are jointly responsible for the costs of the arbitration proceedings. The arbitrators may set their own fee in the arbitration award, unless otherwise bindingly ordered. The fee is to be reasonable in view of the performed task. A party has the right to appeal the amount of the fee at the court.

A foreign arbitration award is enforceable also in Finland. In such a case, the rules of the New York General Agreement on the Recognition and Execution of Foreign Arbitration Awards from 1958 are observed. According to the new act on arbitration, foreign arbitration awards may be executed even with more lenient conditions than those prescribed in the general agreement. An application for execution is, as with a domestic arbitration award, to be addressed to the general lower court.

15. Enforcement

15.1 The Administrative Organization

Unless the losing party voluntarily fulfills the obligation imposed upon him or her in the judgment, the winning party has to separately apply for the enforcement of the judgment. Enforcement in civil matters is known as the recovery proceedings. In Finland, the duty of enforcement belongs to special recovery authorities. The primary executioner is the bailiff, whose duties are performed by the rural police chief in the countryside and in the new towns and by the city bailiff in the old towns. At a second instance above the bailiff, enforcement matters are processed and examined by the executor-in-chief, whose tasks are limited to certain specified case types and the processing of appeals made on the bailiff's decisions.

When the lower court reform enters into force on 1 December 1993, those tasks of the executor-in-chief that are comparable to passing judgment will have already been transferred to general lower courts. Such tasks include debt recovery, the restoration of possession and a previous situation, eviction and precautionary measures, the equivalents of which are processed in a summary procedure in the reformed lower court system. At the same time the city administrative courts that formerly performed the duties of the executor-in-chief in the old towns will have been abolished. From that time on the only regional execution authorities are the county administrative boards, which also process and examine execution matters in the role of the executor-in-chief. With the reform of the Execution Act, however, it is intended to dispose of executors-in-chief wholly and transfer their duties, according to their nature, to lower courts, bailiffs or other authorities.

With the reform of the regional administration of the State, the presently decentralized execution organization will also be harmonized. The duties of the bailiffs will be separated from the actions of the police in the entire country, and the bailiffs will perform their duties regionally in the new district offices that will be determined on the basis of a division into districts that enters into force on 1 January 1995.

15.2 The Enforcement of Domestic Judgments

Enforcement requires legal grounds. These can be e.g. a court judgment, a conciliation confirmed by the court, or an arbitration award. Principally the principle of judicial investigation is observed in the enforcement, and the principle of contentious action is not applied as unconditionally as in actual court proceedings. It is typical that the procedure takes place in writing and has a summary nature. A guiding principle in enforcement is to avoid causing the debtor greater damage than the fulfilling of the purpose of the execution necessarily requires.

Usually enforcement may be requested directly from the bailiff, to whom an application may also be presented orally or sent by post. A request for enforcement should be made to a bailiff with territorial competence, but he can transfer the matter ex officio to another bailiff if he is unable to perform the enforcement himself. The applicant may expedite and make the collecting of his or her receivables more effective by providing the official with as accurate information as possible on the debtor and his or her funds. With the application, the bailiff is to be given at least the relevant grounds for enforcement and, according to the nature of the case, any additional reports that are required for enforcement. If an attorney submits the application, he or she is to have proper authorization to do so.

The most important type of enforcement is distrainment, which is used when collecting a monetary debt or one consisting of goods. The most common form of enforcement is the withholding of the debtor's wages and their subsequent distrainment. For social reasons, the distrainment can also be directed at only a part of the wages, and a sum that the debtor is considered to require for the support of him- or herself and his or her family is to be excluded. The debtor also has the right to separate property that is essential for his or her livelihood, such as necessary tools, from the scope of the execution. The distrained property is converted into money usually by the of a compulsory auction.

In the enforced collection of taxes and other public payments as well as fines and other claims based on a crime, a procedure is followed that partly departs from civil procedural enforcement. Taxes and certain other public payments are subject to execution without a judgment and even without a decision, but the party liable to pay taxes has the power to make a material appeal as late as during the execution. However, fines, conditional impositions of fines and confiscations by the State in criminal matters are not subject to execution without a judgment. The collecting of these is considered to be enforcement of a punishment, even if it is performed by an execution official. If fines cannot be levied, the person sentenced to pay them can be summoned to a procedure of conversion of unpaid fines into imprisonment.

The bailiff's procedure may be appealed, in writing, at the executor-in-chief. For instance when appealing an execution, the time period allowed is 20 days. The decisions of the executor-in-chief may in turn be appealed (within 30 days) at the Appeal Court and the decisions of the Appeal Court on execution matters at the Supreme Court. Executors-in-chief are however to be abolished in connection with the reform of the Execution Act. According to the reform proposal concerning appeal in execution matters issued by the Ministry of Justice in 1989, the decisions of the bailiff on claims for correction made to him and the performance of such a correction could be appealed directly at the Appeal Court.

15.3 The Enforcement of Foreign Judgments

In Finland, as well as in the other Nordic countries, the main rule is observed: foreign judgments in civil matters are not – unlike arbitration awards – recognized or enforced, unless specifically otherwise stated in the law. On the other hand, Finnish legislation contains several provisions on the international competence of the courts and the effect of foreign judgments. Usually these provisions are based on international agreements.

For instance, in 1932 and 1977 the Nordic countries (Finland, Sweden, Norway, Denmark and Iceland) signed agreements on the recognition and enforcement of judgments concerning civil claims. These agreements regulate the recognition and enforcement in the Nordic countries of judgments passed in one of them. Also an agreement on the recognition and enforcement in civil matters was signed in Vienna in 1986 between Finland and Austria.

Finland has also joined certain international general agreements on the recognition and enforcement of foreign judgments. These include for instance the General Agreement On The Recognition And Enforcement Of

Judgments Concerning The Maintenance Of a Child, signed in the Hague in 1958, and the General Agreement On The Recognition And Enforcement Of Decisions Concerning Maintenance, signed in the Hague in 1973. Provisions relating to the recognition of matters within mainly family law are also included in certain bilateral agreements on juridical assistance.

Finland has from the first of July 1993 joined the General Agreement On The Competence Of The Court And The Enforcement Of Judgments Within Civil Law signed in Lugano in 1988. The aim of this general agreement is to facilitate the reciprocal recognition and enforcement of judgments in the member states of the EC and EFTA, and its provisions correspond to those of an earlier general agreement of the same title signed in Brussels in 1968 by the EC Member States.

16. Bankruptcy Law and the Regulation of the Debtor's Insolvency

16.1 Bankruptcy Procedure

Bankruptcy is a procedure regulated by law in which a person's entire property is handed over in order to satisfy all of his or her creditors. This makes bankruptcy general enforcement. According to Finnish law, bankruptcy largely consists of proceedings in the court. Enforcement authorities usually do not take any part in the bankruptcy procedure; instead, it is performed by administration organs of the bankrupt's estate itself. The court appoints agents for the care of the estate. A significant role in the care of the matters of the estate is also played by the meeting of creditors, in which votes are cast on the basis of the size of the claim. Expenses incurred through the administration of the bankrupt's estate are paid from the estate's own funds. The main provisions on bankruptcy procedure are included in the old Bankruptcy Act of 1868, which however has been later significantly amended. A comprehensive reform of the bankruptcy procedure in Finland is currently being prepared.

Both a natural and a juridical person can be declared bankrupt. An initiative can be taken by either by the debtor him- or herself or the creditor, who is to submit a written application to the court of the debtor's locality. If the applicant is the debtor, the court does not examine the material requirements for bankruptcy but appoints a temporary administrator and summons a meeting of creditors. If, however, a creditor seeks the debtor to be declared bankrupt, the debtor is summoned to be heard. For a creditor's application to be successful, his or her claim is required to be clear and uncontested. The creditor also has to show the existence of legal grounds for bankruptcy proceedings, which usually means the debtor's insolvency. If the creditor's application is accepted, the court declares the debtor bankrupt and appoints a temporary administrator and summons a meeting of creditors.

The task of the temporary administrator is to draw up an estate inventory, which the debtor confirms by oath in the meeting of creditors. If it is deemed worth continuing the proceedings, the court orders the date of appearance and appoints trustees chosen by the creditors to administer the estate. All creditors who wish to receive payment for their claim from the funds of the estate are to file their claim in writing at the bankruptcy court by noon on the last date of appearance. The filing of claims can also be performed by post before the date of appearance.

After the filing of claims, one or two hearings of creditors are held for the purpose of receiving objections. After these hearings, the court declares the bankruptcy judgment, in which the receivables that are paid from the funds of the estate and their mutual order of priority are confirmed. It is possible to appeal this judgment in the regular order at the Appeal Court. The distribution of the funds to the creditors in accordance with the bankruptcy judgment is the duty of the receiver.

Linking with the revision of the court system in civil matters the bankruptcy procedure too are tried to simplify by the change of the Bankruptcy Act, that is intended to be introduced at the end of the year 1993. At that time the date of appearance and the hearings of creditors in their present form stay away. In future they are cared wholly written. The needed material is sended to the court. A person also can be declared bankrupt without the presence of the parties involved in court. The meeting of creditors stay the only stage, in which the presence of the parties involved is necessary. In this occasion among other things the estate inventory is confirmed by oath.

16.2 The Creditors' Order of Priority to Receive Payment

Formerly the bankruptcy law of Finland contained several preferences, such as those of wages and the taxes payable to the State, municipality and church. This usually resulted in ordinary, non-privileged creditors having no funds left to collect after the preferential claims had been satisfied.

At the beginning of 1993, a new act on the order of payments entered into force in Finland. This act sets aside nearly all former privileges in bankruptcy and execution. The main rule in the new act is the equal right of the creditors to receive payment in bankruptcy and execution. Pledge claims and mortgages however are to be satisfied prior to others. Also a child's maintenance claims from the last year before the bankruptcy or execution and the holders of a business mortgage up to 50 % of the value of the mortgaged property have retained their privilege. The abolition of the privilege of wages has not had a direct effect on the position of employees, because in Finland the state remunerates the wage claims of employees in the case of the employer's bankruptcy.

16.3 The Rearrangement of Private Persons' Debts

The universal economic recession of the early 1990s also influenced Finland, as the result of which many debtors, without fault of their own, have found it difficult to repay debts. To facilitate the situation of private persons, a law on the rearranging of private persons' debts was enacted at the beginning of 1993, and it entered into force in February 1993. It enables the court to rule on arrangements concerning an insolvent private person's (the debtor) debts in order to provide a remedy to his or her economic situation and to confirm a programme of payment that corresponds with his or her ability to pay.

The rearrangement of debts supersedes enforcement and bankruptcy directed at the debtor. The duration of the programme of payment confirmed for the debtor is usually five years. In certain cases the court may appoint a special administrator to be in charge of the realization of the rearrangement of debts.

16.4 The Reorganization of an Enterprise

Simultaneously with the law on the rearrangement of private persons' debts, a law on the reorganization of an enterprise was enacted and came into force in 1993. The purpose of this act is to provide conditions for the reorganizing of enterprises in financial difficulties but with potential for survival to avoid unnecessary bankruptcies. The model for the law was to a great extent the procedure for the reorganization of enterprises as set forth in chapter 11 of the United States Bankruptcy Code (1978). The act on the reorganization of an enterprise can be applied to all business enterprises, such as private enterprises and corporations, as well as to professionals, farmers and fishermen. The commencement of reorganization proceedings may be applied for at a court of law by the enterprise itself, a creditor or a probable creditor, such as a guarantor. The proceedings concerning the reorganization of an enterprise have been concentrated in 19 lower courts listed in the act.

At the initiation of reorganization proceedings, the court appoints one or more administrators and, if necessary, a committee of creditors to assist him or her/them. The central task of the administrator is to draw up a suggestion for a reorganization programme in collaboration with the parties. An important part of the programme is the payment arrangements of debts. The reorganization programme is confirmed by the court, prior to which the creditors are to be provided with a chance to express their views on the proposal, and the confirmation of the programme requires that a majority of the creditors determined in the law are in favour of it.

The court's decision on the commencement of reorganization arrangements results in a general prohibition of payment, collection and execution of debts, which applies to all creditors. The prohibition is in force until the reorganization programme is confirmed or the reorganization proceedings are finished.

Bibliography

Ekelöf, Per Olof: Scandinavian Countries. International Encyclopedia of Comparative Law, Volume XVI, Civil Procedure, Chapter 6. Tübingen 1984, p. 189–210.

Klami, Hannu Tapani & Hämäläinen, Merva: Lawyers and Laymen on the Bench. A Study of Comparative Legal Sociology. Annales Academiae Scientiarum Fennicae. B:262. Helsinki 1992.

Klami, Hannu Tapani – Hatakka, Minna – Sorvettula, Johanna: Burden of Proof. Truth or Law? Scandinavian Studies in Law 1990 p. 115–149.

Lager, Irma: Landesbericht Finnland. Professional Ethics and Procedural Fairness, Gerhard Walter (Hrsg.). Bern; Stuttgart 1991, p. 299–310.

Möller, Gustaf: Pre-trial Procedure to Expedite Judicial Proceedings. Defensor Legis (Helsinki) 1989 p. 264–272.

Tirkkonen, Tauno: Das Zivilprozessrecht Finnlands. Helsinki 1958. Publikationen des Finnischen Juristenvereins Serie D 3.

IX ADMINISTRATIVE LAW

By Olli Mäenpää

1. Introduction

1.1 Theoretical and Conceptual Evolution

The theoretical basis for administrative law doctrine was established in France and in Germany in the 19th century. The French theory emphasized the role of administration as a producer of public services and as an entity which acts in the public interest. The German theory, on the other hand, emphasized administration as a holder of public authority and the conformity of administration to law.

Administrative law emerged as an independent branch of Finnish jurisprudence towards the end of the last century. German administrative law served as a predominant doctrinal model whereas the French doctrine exercised only modest influence. The doctrinal premises of this emerging administrative law were based on the ideology of Rechtstaat. It corresponded, among other things, to Finland's state-oriented administrative traditions and to the requirement of strict legality emphasized at the end of the oppressive Russian rule.

Under this model, administrative law was regarded predominately as a mechanism for preventing administrative authorities from making unlawful intrusions into the sphere of private interests. Administrative law played mainly a passive role; its main function was to define legal limits to trespass on private autonomy when such incursions had not been authorized by the legislature.

Given this background, it is understandable that the doctrine was focused on the notion of public authority, the administrative methods of exercising that authority and the legality of administrative activity.

Administrative activity within this doctrine was mainly conceived of as the use of power, the concrete form of it being an administrative act in the form of a written administrative decision, which actualizes the use of power. Administrative acts interfere with the legal status of citizens by defining their rights or by imposing obligations. Besides, the conformity of administration to law presumes that legislation defines and protects the legal status of citizens, firstly, by defining the competence of authorities applying the law and secondly, by securing adequate means of legal safeguards which can be resorted to, if authorities exceed their authority or otherwise act illegally.

Public administration has expanded and strengthened in all Western countries during the last four decades by the formation and development of the welfare state. At the same time the formal framework and the contents of administrative activity have changed to a great extent.

For administrative law, the most important of these changes are 1) the broader interpretation given to the conformity of administration to law, 2) the essential decrease in the enforcement nature of the administration, 3) the gradual dissolution of the uniform state machinery, and 4) the increasing symmetry, as opposed to unilaterality, in the use of public authority.

Although public administration continues to conform to law, special attention should be paid to the increase of flexible and goal-oriented norms, as well as of norms providing a framework or other competence norms, which allow broad discretionary power to the authorities. At the same time the significance of legal principles as a source of administrative law is increasing. Instead of non-independent enforcement of legislation, public administration is acting more freely and more on its own initiative than before. It is also more common for authorities to establish norms independently, the emphasis of internal planning and supervision systems has increased, and the activity of administration in the preparation of legislation and in the determination of the details of its implementation has become stronger.

Legal, qualitative and quantitative changes of this kind require a re-evaluation of the classical doctrine of administrative law. For many parts, it is sufficient only to supplement the principles and concepts of administrative law, based on the ideology of the Rechtstaat. To a considerable extent the new features of administration, which are produced by the expansion of the welfare state, require also the review of the general doctrine of administrative law based on the ideology of Rechtstaat.

However, the central area of general doctrine relating to administrative law still comprises the legal regulations relating to administrative activity and to the structure of public administration. They deal with the whole administration or, at least with the essential part of it. They can be analyzed in terms of the following categories, among others: 1) administrative procedure,

2) administrative legal safeguards, 3) administrative structure 4) internal administrative supervision systems and 5) the status of administration in the State machinery.

1.2 Sources of Administrative Law

The nucleus of administrative law consists of general administrative law. It includes general rules relating to various forms of administrative activity, as well as general rules applying to official authorities in common. Also the general doctrine, developed in legal dogmatics and the general principles of administrative law, which are formulated partly by legal dogmatics and partly by legal praxis, have an essential status in general administrative law.

The principally most important sources of law in general administrative law are contained in the Constitution Act (1919). Its provisions on basic rights define the general limits of the activities of authorities. The provisions relating to the organizational structure of administration and the supervision of legality, as well as, those relating to public finance and official machinery, to the conformity of administration to law, and to the responsibility of authorities have an important principal significance, as well.

Essential sources of administrative law are also the Administrative Procedure Act (1982), the Access to Public Documents Act (1951), the Administrative Appeals Act (1950), and the Administrative Annulments Act (1966). General administrative principles, on the other hand, are the prohibition of the abuse of power and the principles of equality, objectivity, and proportionality.

As stated before, administrative law includes also branches whose rules have been formed in a relatively differentiated manner and which might have principles of their own to follow. The most differentiated of these branches are Municipal Law and the Law of Civil Cervants. Special legal features are connected to the legal regulation of social, environmental, and police administration, as well.

The basic rule in municipal law is Section 51 paragraph 2 of the Constitution Act, which requires that the administration of municipalities must be based on the principle of self-government by the citizens. The Municipal Act (1976) contains more specific rules on the organization of municipal administration and its activity. The most important source of the law concerning civil cervants is The Act on State Officials (1986). On the other hand, specific staff regulations determine the rights and duties of the holders of municipal offices.

International aspects of administrative law are also having a growing significance in public administration. This is due to the fact that international treaties and co-operation with authorities from other countries are becoming increasingly important in national administration. If an international convention has been implemented in Finland, it can also contain legal rules which are immediately applicable or otherwise binding on administrative authorities. As a consequence, individuals may also invoke such provisions in their dealings with the authorities.

The rule of law. The basic rule emphasizing the conformity of administration to law is in Section 92 of the Constitution Act: "Under the threat of a legal consequence, in all official functioning the law shall be strictly observed. If a provision in a statutory order conflicts with a constitutional act or another act of Parliament, a judge or other civil servant shall not apply it". Literally understood, the contents of the regulation is a relatively formal requirement of conformity to law. According to it, the duty of authorities and officials is to strictly obey the provisions that are in force. This requirement applies to all activities of public administration. It is binding not only on the decision maker and the drafter of an administrative decision, but also on any official responsible for providing services.

Various hierarchical levels in the sources of administrative law must also be taken into consideration in the "strict" application of different provisions. The duty, and at the same time, the right of an authority, is to not apply provisions of a decree which are clearly inconsistent with a law enacted by the Parliament. In this connection other regulations of lower standing are comparable with decrees. These kinds of regulations are primarily the decisions of the Council of State, the normative decisions of administrative authorities subordinate to the Council of State, the decisions of municipal organs and various implementing provisions issued by administrative authorities. If they are inconsistent with law they must not be applied.

In addition to the formal requirement of conformity to law it has, on a regular basis, been deemed that section 92 of the Form of Government contains also a broader and more substantive principle of conformity to law. According to it, the competence of an authority must be based on law and be justified on the grounds laid down by law. This principle applies, at least, when an authority makes decisions or other acts that directly affect the rights and obligations of a person, in other words, when an authority exercises official authority.

In practice this means, among other things, that public authorities have no general competence to perform their duties. Although the main duty of the police force is to keep public order and security, any intervention by the police in the sphere of private activities must have a legal basis in each individual case. The principle of conformity to law also denotes that the decision-making power can not be based solely on administrative regulations, guidelines or plans. It is the duty of an authority within its sphere of competence to apply law, not internal administrative supervision. However, decision-making can be supervised by administrative regulations and instructions, provided that this kind of supervision is based on a sufficiently precise rule of competence.

In the administration of the welfare state the requirement and principle of conformity to law can still be problematic. On one hand, the law can not be "strictly" observed, if the applicable provisions are broad and if they entitle an authority to use discretionary power. In these kinds of situations general administrative principles supplement the formal liability to legal norms.

On the other hand, the requirement of strict adherence to law applies directly only to the exercise of public authority, which in the administration of the welfare state often remains in the background. For this part, it has been considered a goal that administrative activity which offers citizens rights and benefits also must be based on law. Among other things, the anticipation and binding force of administrative activity, as well as the equality between citizens presume the ability to know in advance, for example, on which conditions a social benefit or right can be granted or denied.

The hierarchy of norms has gained new significance even for administrative activity with an emerging doctrine that is more prone to place emphasis on the substantive, rather than the abstract character of normative hierarchy. The new doctrine stresses the importance of giving the applicable statutes in each case an interpretation which best conforms with the superior norms. Such an interpretation tends to avoid potential normative conflicts and aims at facilitating the implementation of the objectives of especially basic and human rights.

The prohibition on authorities exercising their authority and discretion in a manner conflicting with basic rights provisions is a well-established principle in legal doctrine and legal practice. That prohibition has gradually been extended to imply a positive obligation as well, and is now commonly described as an authority´s general duty, when interpreting and applying statute, to give to it, where possible, an interpretation which favors the requirements of basic and human rights. That positive interpretative principle requires that in a situation calling for statutory construction, the choice made from a range of justifiable alternative should be one conducive to the implementation of human rights.

Principles. In addition to the rule of law expressly prescribed in Section 92 of the Constitution Act there are four well-established legal principles which must be observed in administrative implementation and decision-making. These are the principles of equality, proportionality, objectivity, and the prohibition of the abuse of power. They have acquired their legally binding quality in the judicial praxis of the Supreme Administrative Court.

The principles function mainly as legally binding guidelines and constraints in using discretionary administrative powers. As a result, decisions taken in breach of one of these principles may be annulled or revoked by judicial organs, provided of course that the decision is reviewable. The principles are invocable by individuals in administrative procedure and as such they can be asserted in legal proceedings related to administrative matters.

For these principles have been established:

Objectivity means that only the factors relevant to the case may be taken into account. The decision-making and the other official activities of an authority must also otherwise be impartial and objectively justified. This principle has acquired concrete form e.g. in bias provisions and in the prohibition of section 21 of the law of Civil Cervants to accept a benefit "if it can diminish the trust in an official or in an authority". In legal practice, a decision concerning the appointment of a social worker was annulled because it was based on party favoritism.

The principle of *proportionality* requires that a reasonable relationship must be observed in all circumstances between the relative importance of the ends pursued and the means put into operation. The activity of an authority must be determined in a right way in relation to the ends pursued. Such a determination can usually be made on the basis of the reasonableness of the activity. For example, when using administrative coercive means or disciplinary punishments, their severity must be determined reasonable in relation to the quality and blameworthiness of an act or a failure to act. On the other hand, also the benefits granted by an authority should not be disproportionate. In legal practice, on one hand, a fine imposed with excessively high conditions has been reduced and, on the other hand, the municipal decision to sell a plot far more cheaply than a current price has been annulled.

Abuse of power is prohibited. According to this principle administration must not pursue a purpose other than for what the corresponding power has been conferred. If a decision is taken for purposes other than those stated, it may constitute abuse of power, even if the decision as such stays within the powers of the authority. As, for example, offices are established to perform certain official duties, it may amount to a misuse of power to establish an office especially for a certain person. Neither must the granting of financial support be made conditional to the performance of a duty that is not related to the use of such support.

The general principle of *equality* is connected with section 5 of the Constitution Act, which states that "All citizens are equal before the law". This provision applies also to the activity of authorities. Similar situations shall not be treated differently, unless there is an objectively justified cause for such treatment. Discrimination or favoritism, for example, on the basis of origin, religion, sex, age, political or social view, trade union activity or for other similar reason is prohibited. A similar procedure and a consistent approach must also be complied with in similar cases, although for a justified reason an authority may also change its practice if this practice will be followed consistently.

Any procedure or decision which is against general administrative principles can be challenged as involving misuse of power, especially in connection with an appeal. The misuse of power has established to be an independent legal ground, which in itself makes it possible to annul or revoke an administrative decision. The observance of these principles can also be deemed to belong to official duties. The establishment of legal responsibility for a public act is, thus, possible as a consequence of a procedure which violates one of these principles.

2. Scope and Forms of Administrative Action

2.1 The Duties of Public Administration and their Fulfillment

The duties and the powers of administrative organs vary by their contents and their nature in different fields of administration and in different activities. As late as at the beginning of this century, the main duty of authorities was the implementation of legislation through administrative regulation. It has still an essential significance in the activity of authorities, but in the welfare state the quantitative emphasis of the activities has shifted to providing social benefits and public services. At the same time the administrative machinery has grown considerably and become more complicated. To this change is attached also an increasing emphasis on the internal activity of administration.

The forms and procedure used and the lines of action applied by administrative organs depend greatly on what kind of administrative duty is concerned. Administrative regulation, especially, most often takes the form of written administrative decisions. On the other hand, administrative bodies which provide services may do so in many forms. Instead of written decisions, they provide, for example, care and education services. The internal activities of administration, for their part, have usually not had as immediate an influence on the status of individuals as the first two mentioned.

There are many other differences in the ways and forms in which the duties of administrative bodies are carried out. Differences – as well as similarities – are examined in a more detailed way in the following paragraphs.

Regarding the applicability of the most basic rules and principles of administrative law it must be kept in mind that, despite differences, it is official activity that is concerned. Thus, those rules and principles must be taken into consideration although, for example, the legal regulation of a specific area of administrative activity would be meagre.

Administrative regulation. By administrative regulation is decided what a private person, whether natural or legal, is entitled to or obliged to do. In their regulatory activity, authorities, among other things, grant licenses to build and trade, impose the payment of public fees or taxes, and set limits or prohibitions e.g. to activity, which is dangerous for the environment. Administrative regulation often includes limitations or obligations but also decision-making concerning the conditions of rights and benefits is common.

In addition, the supervision of the fulfillment of the aims of regulation, which generally is the duty of administrative organs, is an essential part of regulation. For example, in the areas of employment and environmental protection, authorities have an essential role to play in supervising the effectivity of the applicable legislation.

The legislation determining the competence of an authority is the basis for administrative regulation, in accordance with the principle of the conformity of administration to law. Typical of the regulating activity is the enforcement of legislation by an administrative decision made in each individual case. The discretionary powers, vested in an authority by legislation can vary a great deal.

The decision-making, which includes administrative regulation, can be relatively unilateral. An authority makes a determination independently and only bound by the applicable legislation. The preconditions for the application of law are evaluated separately in each individual case. Others than authorities may usually not make decisions concerning regulation. Moreover, administrative regulation is usually backed by the possibility to exercise public powers. It should be noted, however, that in actual practice that unilaterality is modified considerably by the procedure which precedes the administrative decision-making, during which the parties concerned have a right to state their views and claims.

Public services. One of the most important tasks of the welfare state is to provide services and different kinds of benefits. The services provided by administrative organs of the welfare state comprise, for example, education, health care, social welfare and support to cultural activity. The economic benefits provided by the welfare state, on the other hand, consist especially of different kinds of income transfers, such as social benefits and aids to business activity. Apart from providing services and benefits, the administrative machinery oversees the construction and maintenance of public roads and means of public transportation, and it also in other ways makes various public utilities and commodities available for use.

Quite little written decision-making is used, especially in providing and producing welfare services. In service administration the actual one-sided exercise of public authority is also unusual. As a matter of fact, authorities often exercise similar functions as private entities – for example through different kinds of contracts and other legal acts relating to private law. Likewise similar tasks can be taken care of, and in practice are being taken care of, both by public and by private organizations (among other things medical centers or telephone systems). On the other hand, public utilities companies have been established by governmental or municipal authorities, especially to provide transportation and communication services (for example Post and Telecommunications Service).

To a large extent, service administration can still be characterized as a typical administrative activity although the typical features of public law are lacking in the activity of administrative bodies or they are, at least, in the background. It is a question of administrative activity because a public body takes care of it and its aims, contents and forms are governed, although quite broadly, by legislation.

In the distribution and provision of different kinds of services and benefits administrative bodies make decisions concerning the entitlements and rights of citizens - often also concerning their obligations. Features comparable to administrative regulation, such as the administrative supervision relating to the use of benefits are also involved. The primary aim of the activity, however, is the improvement of the position of beneficiaries and the amelioration of their legal status – and not so much interference with their rights or setting up limits, as often in the actual exercise of public authority.

Internal administration. Internal administration comprises the activity of authorities, the immediate or primary object of which are other administrative bodies. This kind of activity does thus not directly affect the rights and obligations of those who are outside administration, although, it can indirectly be quite significant to them. Control, supervision and planning form an important part of it. Also preparation and investigation are formally internal, as well as presentation, which is based on preparation and investigation, but which immediately proceeds decision-making. All of these include technical functions which vary as to their contents (for example ADP and registration procedures).

The basic forms of internal administrative control are rules and instructions. Authorities at higher levels may issue them to their subordinates in accordance with law and subject to the limits of internal administrative competence. The most common forms of supervision are circulars, implementing provisions and instructions. They have, in practice, a considerable influence on the decision-making of the authorities in each individual case. Their contents is usually the supervision of enforcement, the use of funds and the supervision of the procedural form of an activity.

Also planning affects decision-making, however, more indirectly than rules and instructions. Planning has been organized in several broad and centralized planning systems. They can extend to the entire administrative machinery, but planning defined by the scope of functions is also common. Usually, these systems are statutory and they relate to the functions of service administration. The contents of the plans are decided by administrative authorities, ultimately most often by the Council of State.

Planning, investigation and presenting, on the other hand, are connected most often with the making of an administrative decision. For these functions the most important thing is to acquire, process and interpret information. Various procedures and methods of a technical nature are usually used to carry out these functions.

Some other duties belonging to administrative bodies. Finland has adopted a rather clear division of state powers. According to it, legislative power is exercised by the Parliament and the President of the Republic, whilst judicial power is vested in independent courts. However, also administrative bodies can, within certain limits, exercise both quasi-legislative and adjudicatory power.

Legislative power may, in practice, be conferred primarily to the Council of State, ministries and central administrative boards. Under express provisions of law the power to give more specific regulations concerning its enforcement has often been entrusted to one of these bodies. Such provisions can also include a partial transfer of legislative power to the administrative machinery. It must, though, be observed that also the executive power can be used in the form of a norm. For example, the circulars and application directives mentioned above are most often the enforcement of legislation by their nature – and not the independent use of legislative power. In practice the distinction between executive and legislative norms has proven to be quite difficult to maintain.

Also adjudicatory power in administrative matters rests to some extent with the authorities themselves, although the aim has been to strengthen the system of administrative courts as a system which is separate and independent from administrative machinery. Especially central administrative boards may still act as appeal instances in state administration. The corresponding task in municipal administration often rests with the municipal executive board. To some extent also the Council of State and ministries function as appeal bodies in the first instance.

2.2 Administrative Law Relationships

Typical of administrative law relationships is that an immediate party of it is an administrative authority and that the contents of the relationship are defined by administrative law. The other party of an administrative relationship may be another administrative body, in which case it concerns an administrative organizational relationship. In most cases the other party is a legal entity outside administration, e.g. a private person or an undertaking.

Special features relate to the legal relationships in the field of administration, which separate them especially from private law relationships. Such special features include a strict conformity to law of the legal relationship and often also its unilaterality, which is based on law. Therefore binding contracts relating to rights and obligations can be made in the field of administration only in a quite limited framework.

The general objective of administrative activity is to carry out the public interest, and the activity of authorities is by virtue of its contents bound to the observance of general administrative principles. Also an emphasized obligation to comply with specified procedures, an especially organized public liability and legal safeguards under administrative law separate administrative activity from private law proceedings.

Administrative law relationships are most often created through an administrative act and with an administrative act legal relationships can also be modified or concluded, as provided for by law. Usually the creation of an administrative law relationship presupposes the co-operation of the other party, such as an application or a consent. For example, the granting of a building permit, appointment to an office or granting a social benefit establishes an administrative law relationship, the contents of which is determined according to the pertinent legislation. In some cases the creation of an administrative law relationship is based on the one-sided decision of the authority imposing e.g. different kinds of obligations.

2.3 The Use of Decision-making Power and Decision-making

Administrative acts are usually decided on the basis of presentation. The main aim of presentation is to secure that the decision to be made is legal and proper. The presentation procedure is subject to few regulations. In any case, the general duty of the presenter is to prepare the matter and propose a decision. The presenter is responsible both for the legality of the presentation and for the decision made on the basis of it. If the presenter has his or her dissenting opinion recorded in the minutes, it will, however, absolve the presenter from the legal responsibility arising from the decision. According to an established view, only an official can act as a presenter.

According to the rules concerning the allocation of decision-making power, the authority to make an administrative decision rests with either a single official or a collegiate body. In both cases the decision-maker may either accept the draft resolution as such or reformulate the contents of the proposed decision partly or completely.

Many rights and benefits are established and obligations are imposed upon private persons by an administrative act. In practice, the decision-making of an administrative authority may be of a fundamental concern for the legal status of citizens, although the concrete influences of decision-making vary considerably in different situations. The legal effects of an administrative act can be generally classified as being to some extent weaker than the effects of a legal act under private law. This applies especially to acts relating to granting of benefits by administrative authorities.

The general legal qualities, the nature and the strength of an administrative act are defined primarily in terms of the formal force of law, enforceability and the material force of law (res judicata).

Formal force of law. A decision has acquired a formal force of law when it is no longer appealable by regular remedies. If there are provisions prohibiting an appeal against the decision, the decision immediately acquires the force of law. On the other hand, an appeal made within the term of appeal postpones the force of law. Even a decision having acquired the force of law is, however, appealable by special legal remedies, and then it is also possible to apply for a stay of execution. The force of law does not, by itself, prevent an authority from taking steps to correct an error itself, if the other prerequisites exist (see Ch. 4.6).

Enforceability. As a general rule, an appeal made during the term of appeal has a suspensive effect on the enforceability of an administrative decision. There are several exceptions from this main rule, however. A decision may usually be implemented despite an appeal, first, if there are specific provisions to this effect in a law or a decree, second, if the decision is of such character that it must be executed immediately, and, third, if the entering into force of the decision cannot be postponed for the sake of public interest. According to the Municipal Act the decision of a municipal authority can be executed before it has acquired the formal force of law, unless an appeal against the decision becomes useless if it is executed or unless the appeal court prohibits the execution.

Res judicata. In a matter already settled by a decision with the force of law, a new decision cannot generally be given on the merits of the matter. The extension and applicability of the material force of law depend on the case law of the Supreme Administrative Court and on legal theory. Generally, a decision acquires the material force of law, when notification thereof has been duly communicated to the parties. After this, the authority may not unilaterally amend its own decision without an express basis in law or the consent of the parties. Thus the decision is stable and binding in relation to future decisions within the deciding authority as well as within other authorities.

The scope of material legal force is of great significance in administrative activity. Arguments for the *res judicata* effect emphasize legal certainty and the protection of legitimate interests. The citizens must be able to trust the authorities' standpoint and these must to a certain extent be foreseeable. On the other hand the *res judicata* effect should not act as an absolute obstacle to the demands of public interest and flexibility. In this regard it is important that it is possible to account for new and changed circumstances; the authorities should also be allowed a certain amount of flexibility in their decision-making.

All decisions do not acquire the material force of law. One reason is the character of the decision. Applications for various kinds of permits can be made and handled anew, although an earlier application has been rejected. Also decisions concerning prohibitions, restrictions and obligations are often less permanent than decisions granting rights or benefits. Thus the rejection by a final decision of two applications exempt from charge would not preclude the examination of a third application with the same content. A previous obligation may also be amended to the advantage of the party.

There is no general statutory basis for amending a *res judicata* decision on the grounds that the circumstances have changed, unless the factors on the basis of which the circumstances were considered did not exist when the decision was made. In this respect, administrative decisions are characterized by a considerable permanence. But there are certain exceptions to this rule, as well. Especially where environmental permits are concerned the case law and legal doctrine allow for more flexibility. If there has been an essential change in the circumstances or if a very important public interest so requires, a permit which has been granted for an unlimited time can be limited or a permit can otherwise be limited by issuing stricter regulations concerning the harmful effects of the activity.

The permanence of a decision can be limited already when it is made by e.g. setting a time limit or by including a possibility of revocation or a condition concerning repayment. In these cases the authority shall usually be based on an express provision. In some cases a decision can also be amended or corrected with the consent of the party concerned.

3. Public Administration

3.1. Structural Elements and Principles

In Finland public administration is divided into state and municipal administration. It is customary to distinguish even a third distinct sphere of administrative activity, namely indirect public administration. Located squarely between the public sphere and private activity it consists of both structurally and functionally heterogenous bodies.

Independent legal personality within the area of public administration belongs to the State, the municipalities, and the municipal corporations. In addition, certain bodies, such as the Bank of Finland, have legal personality on the basis of express legal provisions. As organs of the State or the municipalities, the various administrative bodies do not possess independent legal personality. In practice, however, they may appear to be fairly independent as parties in legal relationships.

As a rule, the division of functions and decision-making powers among the administrative authorities is well-defined. The areas of jurisdiction of the various administrative authorities are in accordance with fixed general norms. Each authority enjoys a relatively independent position within the administrative organization. Superior authorities may issue only general guidelines to the subordinate bodies. They are not authorized to give specific instructions on how an individual case must be solved; neither can they take over the obligations of a subordinate authority or use its competence. As a consequence of such characteristic features, the general structure of the state and municipal administration may be characterized as fairly inflexible.

3.2. State Administration

Central Administration. Executive power in the highest instance is exercised by the President of the Republic. The most important administrative functions of the President include decision-making regarding Finland's relations with foreign powers, appointing the highest civil servants, issuing administrative regulations, granting exemptions and pardons, and supervising the functioning of the State administration.

Although the President's powers within the field of public administration are formally quite extensive, the administration is actually directed by the sitting government, the Council of State. The Council is composed of the ministers, who act as heads of the respective ministries (departments), and it is headed by the Prime Minister. The Council makes its most significant decisions collectively, in plenary session. Its main functions consist of putting into effect the decisions of the Parliament and the President, making proposals to the Parliament and directing the administration.

The powers of the Council of State do not extend beyond the limits of governmental and administrative business, except in so far as it has, in special cases and by express authorization, the right to issue statutory provisions which concern a specific matter or which regulate specific legal relationships.

The actual core of the central administration has traditionally been formed by a combination of the ministries and the some twenty central administrative boards. It is the general responsibility of the ministries to supervise and control the subordinate administration, but their duties also include the making of individual decisions of major importance in a number of administrative activities.

The administrative boards, e.g. Board of Education, Board of Taxation, act under the direction of the ministries although they have always enjoyed considerable functional independence. However, in the 1990's, the focus of administrative reorganization has shifted towards a simplification and even a partial dissolution of the board system. Their decision-making powers have, to a large extent, been transferred to the ministries and their duties have been decentralized, principally to the municipal level. Boards that previously were mainly responsible for administering public utilities, e.g. The Railway Board and the Board of Post and Telecommunications, have been reorganized as public corporations.

In addition to the central administrative boards there are various agencies and institutions with a more limited sphere of activities. Their functions are either administrative in character or their activities are more or less analogous to business activities.

District and local administration. Art. 50, sec. 1 of the Constitution Act defines the basic organizational structure of regional and local administration: "For the purpose of general administration Finland shall remain divided into provinces, districts and municipalities." The provinces and districts are state organs at the regional and local level, respectively.

The provinces form an integral part of the state administrative hierarchy. The provincial government functions as the highest executive and police authority of the province. As such, it is responsible for maintaining general order and security as well as for putting into effect decisions and judgments. As a result of the growth of the central administration, the provincial and regional levels have recently been losing much of their earlier significance. At present, however, more powers and duties are being delegated to these levels.

In general, the administrative system lacks autonomy at the provincial level although there exist certain constitutional features that would allow for its establishment. The most prominent of these features is the fact that the Constitution Act contains a provision allowing the establishment of autonomous provincial bodies by law. So far no general laws providing regional autonomy have been passed, however, although there has, from time to time, been considerable interest in expanding the scope of autonomy at the provincial level, as well.

The unique kind of autonomy of the Åland Islands should be mentioned, however. It is guaranteed by international agreements and a special law that has a specific constitutional status. The municipal corporations formed by municipalities possess certain features of self-government, as well, but their status and functions are not equivalent to that of properly autonomous regional bodies.

The functions of state administration at the local level are fairly restricted. The state has actually exempted itself from keeping an extensive local administration by conferring administrative tasks on local self-government units. As a consequence, it is the municipalities that are responsible for most of the local administration. Yet, the State has certain local administrative units, as well. Their main functions have to do with the control of public order and certain jurisdictional execution. In general, state local administration plays clearly a secondary role compared with the autonomous municipalities.

3.3 Municipal Administration

Local autonomy in the Finnish system is a concept referring basically to municipal self-government and administration through the municipalities. At present there are about 460 municipalities, and the local autonomous bodies hold a prominent place in public administration. In addition, there are some two hundred municipal joint authorities that constitute the basic form of cooperation between the autonomous municipalities. The scope, competence, and detailed structure of the municipal administration are determined by the uniform Municipal Act of 1976.

During recent decades the municipal activities have greatly expanded. This has led to a remarkable increase in the tasks the municipalities have taken upon themselves as well as in the specific functions that have been assigned to them through special legislation. Simultaneously, even the municipal administrative machinery has expanded and become more complex. The part of the local administration for which autonomous municipalities are responsible for forms today actually quantitatively the largest section of all public administration.

Municipal autonomy. The principle of municipal autonomy is expressed in the first sentence of Art. 51, sec. 2 of the Constitution Act: "The administration of the municipalities shall rest on the principle of popular self-government as prescribed by special laws." Since the constitutional provision prescribing the scope of municipal autonomy is rather elastic and open-ended, supplementary procedures are essential in providing an authoritative definition. In the Finnish constitutional system it has mainly been the parliamentary Committee on Constitutional Issues that in practice has been vested with the task of determining the the content of municipal self-government. (It should be noted that Finland has no constitutional court, and the ordinary courts, as a rule, lack the power to control the constitutionality of laws passed by the Parliament.)

In the established practice of the constitutional committee the following features may be distinguished as the fundamental characteristics of municipal self-government:

- The right to conduct the municipality's own administration and finances independently. State organs are competent to interfere only to a limited extent specifically provided by law.

- Decision-making powers are wielded by organs elected by direct ballot in municipal elections. The municipality may, however, delegate these powers within the municipal organization.
- Municipal authority is general and broadly based. New functions and financial obligations may be imposed on the municipalities only by act of Parliament. The same procedure is required in cases where the municipality is deprived of its existing functions.
- The municipalities have the right to levy taxes from their members and other local bodies subject to taxation. The tax rate is determined by each municipality independently.

General and Special Competence. The basic ambit of municipal competence is determined by the Municipal Act of 1976. Under Art. 5 it is the responsibility of the municipality to carry out functions falling within the sphere of its autonomy as well as other functions entrusted to it by law. Accordingly, it is conventional to distinguish two spheres of municipal competence: the general competence is based solely on the principle of municipal autonomy, whereas the special competence is based on and defined by special laws.

There is no neat borderline between the general and special competence of the municipality, nor are there any stable grounds for determining how the functions should be distributed between the central government and the autonomous municipal authorities. The constitution remains silent on this issue although it is generally accepted that in order for the municipal autonomy to have a real and substantial meaning, a municipality is, in principle, competent to handle all matters of common local interest.

The specific limits of these municipal functions are basically determined by law, executive state organs, and administrative courts. The limits of the special functions – functions entrusted to the municipality separately by law – are determined by law and, in detail, by the state organs supervising and controlling the execution of those laws. On the other hand, the limits of the general competence – functions within the sphere of local autonomy – are defined in the praxis of the Supreme Administrative Court.

Regarding the scope of the special competence, the problem from a constitutional point of view is not so much the fact that executive organs may be in a position to control and possibly even to limit the scope of the municipal competence. The problem is rather the vast expansion of the special competence regulated by sectoral laws.

As a result, it is the municipalities that are mainly responsible for such vital public functions as basic education, health care, housing, and social welfare services. To a considerable extent, this has transformed the municipalities from autonomous local bodies to local executive extensions of the central government. The local autonomy may, in fact, be effectively curtailed through the widening of the municipal functions. This paradox has caused much criticism and in recent years a structural change has taken place in the legislation.

In principle, the scope of the functions within the sphere of local autonomy is decided by the municipality itself. In final analysis, however, it is determined by administrative jurisdiction, which shows considerable continuity on certain recurring issues. Some of the basic limits are set, first, by the municipal territory. The functions of the municipality are generally limited to its own area but this does not prevent cooperation between municipalities.

Second, it is within the general competence of the municipality to take responsibility for all matters of common interest, provided that they are not entrusted by law to a special body, and that they do not fall under the competence of a state agency. As for the use of municipal funds for supporting political parties or sponsoring the activity of local companies the scope of the general competence has been construed strictly. With certain limited exceptions the support of political parties has been found *ultra vires*. Direct support of private economic activity has been found acceptable for the reasons of maintaining local employment. No specific restrictions apply to more indirect support in the form of generally facilitating local economic activity. Furthermore, the municipality can itself engage in economic activity, for instance to provide different kinds of local services.

The Municipal Organization. The Municipal Act presupposes a somewhat modified division of powers within the municipal organization. The decision-making powers are exercised by the council whose members are directly elected in municipal elections. The executive functions are carried out by the municipal board and the administrative organs controlled by it. The judicial control of the decision-making is the task of non-municipal bodies and the Provincial Courts.

Such a balance of powers envisaged by the drafters of the Municipal Act has proven to be highly idealistic, however. The exigencies of the practical implementation of shifting administrative programs and public policies have molded the municipal organization considerably. From a constitutional viewpoint such a transformation of the municipal organization has gradually grown in significance since it affects one of the basic components of municipal autonomy – the democratic basis of municipal functions.

The representative organ of the municipality is the council. The members of the council (the municipal delegates) are elected every four years. Its main duties include making all politically important decisions in municipal affairs, adopting a budget, general steering and controlling of other municipal organs, and passing local by-laws. It is competent to decide on all issues of municipal concern unless otherwise expressly prescribed.

Responsible for the administration in general, as well as the implementation of municipal decisions, are the municipal board, the committees, and the administrative staff. The municipal board is composed of persons elected proportionally by the council. Its main duties include supervising and steering the activity of the committees and municipal staff, drafting the council's decisions, and implementing them. Among its functions is even the preliminary review of the legality of the decisions passed by the council.

Each one of the committees is responsible for the administration of one of the main areas of municipal activity. Even the committees are elected by the council by proportional vote. The principal committees are statutory but the council may also set up ad hoc committees to carry out specific tasks. All the committees are formally subordinate to the board but especially the statutory committees enjoy considerable freedom in their decision-making within the municipal organization.

Some committees – especially those responsible for health services, education, social care, housing, and environmental protection – have a large quantity of significant administrative decisions to make. These relatively wide decision-making powers pertain partly to various executive functions within the municipal administration. To a large extent, however, the powers are assigned to them through legislation. In fact, the activity of the main committees is regulated quite closely by general legislation and controlled fairly intensely by the central government units.

The significance of the administrative personnel has grown considerably along with the increase in statutory municipal functions. The administrative and executive personnel is subordinate to the council, the board, and the committees. Under the Municipal Act, it is possible to delegate decision-making powers also to the administrative functionaries. In practice the position of the administrative staff has grown stronger due to a quite liberal use of the delegation powers.

The Exercise of the Municipal Competence. The guarantees of autonomy within the sphere of municipal finance have gained considerably in importance in the last few decades. This is mainly due to a rapid increase in the relative share of municipal finance as a part of the public sector. The municipal sector produces and provides most of the basic health, education, and social welfare services. In fact, it has a statutory duty to provide such basic services. As a result, the municipal sector accounts for about 2/3 of public sector consumption and the local authorities employ about 70 % of public sector work force, which is about 19 % of the whole labor force.

Although municipal taxation brings in about 40 % of revenues, the state subsidies and grants to the municipalities are vital for most local services. Consequently, funding through the state budget plays a significant role in the municipal economy.

Assessed from a constitutional viewpoint it is important to note that the formal provisions guaranteeing municipal autonomy have *de facto* proven to be fairly weak when confronted with the power of the purse exercised by the central authorities. The statutory state subsidies and grants, which generally are earmarked for specific purposes, provide a basis for an extensive state control over municipal decision-making.

Even though the administrative norms, directives, and sectoral plans steering the operation of the subsidy system are not necessarily *de jure* binding on the municipalities, they are, at least in a majority of cases, an obligatory prerequisite for receiving the subsidy. As a result, it is the exigencies of municipal economy that in practice lend them their binding quality. In this sense the subsidy system combines the effects of both the carrot and the stick.

Such a state of affairs has given rise to much criticism and, as a consequence, the state subsidy system been completely reorganized. The aim of the reform is to strengthen and widen the municipalities' independence in making decisions on local investments and services. This is accomplished by an overall simplification of the system by pooling the separate categories of subsidies into larger units, by limiting the discretionary powers in appropriating the funds, and by restructuring the control system so as to allow more autonomy for the local level.

The Control Exercised by Superior Organs. The scope and intensity of the control exercised by superior organs depend, by and large, on the distinction between the general and special competence of the municipality. General control is restricted to an overall supervision of the municipality. It can include recommendations and general guidelines but the central authorities lack the competence to issue binding instructions or commands to the municipal organs. However, in the rare cases of manifestly illegal action or clear neglect to carry out statutory functions the provincial authority has the competence to issue an injunction.

Special control is exercised under specific provisions in law. This guidance may consist of binding directives and instructions of a general character. Such control is usually based on legislation regulating the municipal functions within the field of its special competence. Multi-level sectoral planning systems serve as powerful instruments for policy-steering, as well. Moreover, certain municipal decisions must be submitted to a state authority for sanction or approval. Submission procedures apply to various land-use and sectoral development plans, local ordinances, certain service charges etc.

The revived interest in strengthening the autonomous basis of public administration has resulted in a number of reform plans, some of which have already been realized. The ongoing free commune experiment may be seen as one of the harbingers of the new kind of attitudes. Far-ranging proposals have been made to reduce the level of state supervision by, for instance, constraining the role of regulations and instructions, delimiting the submission procedure, as well as increasing the delegation of independent authority to the municipal level and deregulating the normative framework of local decision-making.

3.4 Indirect Public Administration

Indirect public administration consists of four organizational categories viz. independent public agencies, public associations, state-owned companies and certain private subjects. Common to all of them is that they are empowered to perform public duties or, in several cases, even to exercise public authority. As a rule, their sphere of competence is rather limited and the specific public powers are expressly assigned to them by law.

Whether rules of general administrative law are applicable in indirect public administration must be determined in each case separately. The Administrative Procedure Act, for instance, is applicable in this field only, if so expressly provided, and basically the same rule applies to the Administrative Appeals Act. Access to public documents, by contrast, is held to be applicable to all exercise of public authority regardless of the organizatory form it takes. Similarly, the qualified penal responsibility of civil servants extends to indirect public administration to the extent that a person has been entrusted with public authority.

3.5 The Civil Service and Public Employment

The public sector employs approximately one-third of the total work-force. Most public servants are employed by the municipalities and their duties involve mainly producing and providing public services, especially those related to social welfare, health care and education. Approximately one half of the public servants employed by the State are located in public corporations such as the Postal Service and State Railways. The other half actually discharges traditional public functions involving the exercise of administrative authority.

The persons employed in the public service are classified into two principal groups according to their legal status – public officials and public employees. Public officials are in an employment relationship governed by public law and it is only public officials who may be empowered to exercise the public authority. Accordingly, even the rights and duties of public officials are determined by law, the Act on State Officials. The rights and duties of public employees, on the other hand, are based on a contractual relationship regulated by the same legislation (the Employment Contracts Act) as is applicable in the private sector.

Despite the traditionally dissimilar normative basis of the two types employment, the actual conditions of the employment relationships in the public sector have converged considerably. In both categories, the economic conditions of employment are based on collective agreements. And even though public officials will in most cases be appointed to a tenured position, they may be dismissed on the basis of a good cause. Distinctions between duties based on public authority and other tasks performed by public employees have lost much of their qualifying features, as well. Accordingly, penal responsibility to which previously only public officials were subject for breach of their duties has also been extended to employees discharging similar duties.

The formal differences in public employment relationships thus largely diminished, a need has arisen to reappraise that basic dichotomy. In municipal administration this has led to a decision to integrate both categories into a single form of municipal employment. That employment relationship would be based on the model of private sector employment but it would also incorporate certain elements typical of the status of public officials. In state administration, a similar overhaul has been considered infeasible. At least some of the essentially distinctive features of the status of public officials will be retained in the future.

4. Administrative Procedure

4.1 Basic Principles of Administrative Procedure

Setting the essential ground rules for administrative activity should be neither an end in itself nor, as such, a sufficient guarantee of flawless procedure. While procedural rules do provide the essential, formally uniform framework for administrative activity, they have more substantial functions, as well.

Indeed, common objectives in the implementation of procedural legislation include enhancing preventive legal protection available to the individual dealing with the administrative authorities, guaranteeing impartiality in administrative proceedings, and providing necessary flexibility where appropriate.

Such objectives form a basis for the general guidelines of administrative procedure, as well. Among the most significant of them are openness in administration, the obligation to provide service, procedural equality, and objectivity. The main role of the general guidelines is to inform the interpretation and implementation of the more specific procedural rules.

Openness in administration may be characterized as one of the cornerstones of democratic government and public accountability of the administrative personnel. Transparency of administration makes it possible to publicly monitor its functioning. It also strengthens the public's confidence in the administration. In general, government information should be considered as a public asset with the exception of personal privacy, national security matters and such other legitimate interests as may be prescribed by law.

The methods of guaranteeing openness in administration vary depending on the character and form of administrative activity. Basically three separate methods and areas of openness may be distinguished. First, official documents and information about the working of the administration are subject to the principle of publicity. They are presumed to be publicly accessible, unless express provisions form a restriction.

Second, it is the general obligation of the public authorities to make public information available on equal terms to all individuals requesting it. Should the matter under preparation be of such character that it may have widespread effects the authorities even have an active duty to make known the information concerning it. Third, openness may even extend to the actual business of preparing and handling administrative matters by the authorities. However, the processing of individual matters takes place predominately in written procedure and the general public, consequently, lacks access to this part of it. Legislation concerning access to public documents, sessions and administrative information will be presented in chapter 5.1.

The public administration has a general obligation to provide service to all citizens. In this sense one can speak of a *service principle* governing administrative procedure. One of the principal applications of that principle is the duty to ensure that it is actually possible for the individuals to comply with their procedural duties. The authorities and officials are also obliged to supply necessary guidance and advice concerning the formal requirements in individual cases.

One of the more efficient ways to produce real guarantees for procedural *equality* is to alleviate the actual difficulties that the individuals are confronted with in administrative matters. In this sense the duty to provide appropriate procedural advice to clients can also be regarded as a way to lower the bureaucratic obstacles, taking into account the differences in individual propensity to deal with administrative matters. But even formal equality is important, especially if a matter is subject to joint proceedings or where several parties are involved. In such cases the authorities are under an obligation to ensure that the preparation of the decision is carried out in a way that does not prejudice the equality of the parties.

Objectivity and *neutrality* are indispensable qualitative components of a due procedure in general. Putting the requirements of public interest into effect evenhandedly and without bias forms the basic object of a fair procedure even in administrative cases. Neither undue external standpoints nor personal preferences of the officials should be allowed to influence the conduct in administrative cases. Indeed, the right to impartiality is a basic requisite of fair procedure. It is mainly for these reasons that procedural rules bar ostensibly impartial decision-makers from deciding cases whose outcome directly or substantially affects their own personal interests or the financial concerns of organizations with which they are affiliated.

4.2 Scope and Application of Procedural Rules

Administrative functions are carried out in several different forms. Central among them are public regulation and provision of public services. Regulation is mainly implemented through administrative decision-making which enables the authorities to determine directly, and in most cases unilaterally, the rights and duties of individuals. Public services are usually both produced and provided by administrative bodies but the characteristic features of that activity are to a large extent indistinguishable from those of comparable private activities.

Since administrative regulation usually involves the exercise of public authority, comprehensive legislation prescribing the basic standards and procedural ground rules for administrative decision-making has been deemed necessary. Along with the need to bring together and codify previously diverse or scattered rules, this forms the general reason for enacting the Administrative Procedure Act of 1982. The Act contains the basic procedural norms to be observed in all administrative decision-making and in the preparatory procedure leading up to the decision-making stage.

Characteristic to those procedural provisions is that they regulate primarily the written forms of administrative activity. As a result, such procedural rules are largely inapplicable in the actual production and provision of public services, the internal activities (planning, drafting etc.) of public administration, the proprietary functions of government, and in otherwise less informal administrative functions. While the following presentation will mainly focus on the application of the procedural rules in written administrative procedure, mention should be made of significant new legislation extending even to those heretofore largely unregulated areas of administrative activity. Relevant new legislation includes the Act on Patient's Rights (1992) and the Public Procurement Act (1992) as well as the Act on Executive Instructions and Orders (1989).

4.3 Grounds for Establishing Bias

The specific grounds for disqualifying a public official or employee on the basis of bias are listed in the Administrative Procedure Act. One of the basic aims of expressly defining bias is to ensure that objectivity and impartiality are taken seriously in administrative procedure. Specific emphasis on the importance of unbiased treatment of administrative cases may also function as a vital element ensuring that the legitimacy of administrative activity is being protected.

The grounds of disqualification apply to all persons employed in state or municipal administration regardless of the juridical character of their service relationship. Even lay representatives in municipal organs fall within the scope of application of the grounds, albeit with minor exceptions. Exempt are only the directly elected members of the municipal council. The sole ground of disqualification applicable to them is that the matter to be decided is of direct personal concern to them.

The grounds are applied in a concrete, case-by-case manner. For there to be sufficient basis for disqualification it is necessary that there exists an actual connection between the public employee and the case to be decided. Should the relationship be more remote or of a less specific character, that would be considered insufficient as an independent ground for disqualification. And in technical or standard matters, such as simple registration acts or setting routine charges, the disqualification grounds, understandably, play a minor role because of the nature of the matter.

As a common ground for disqualification the Administrative Procedure Act provides that the confidence in the impartiality of the official is at risk for a particular reason. Such particular reasons may include e.g. firm bonds of friendship, antagonism or association in financial dealings with a party. Prior involvement with the case may also be disqualifying, but not automatically.

Other, more specific grounds are the following:
- The public official or his close relative appears as a party in the case. In such cases, it is apparent that the outcome will also have a direct effect on his rights, obligations or other interests thus forming a potential basis for bias.
- The public official or a close relative has an interest in the case in the sense that they can be expected to derive particular benefit or suffer particular loss as a result of a decision in the matter.
- The public official or a close relative acts as counsel to or as representative of party or a person who has an interest in the case.
- The public official is employed by a party or by a person who has an interest in the case; or they have given the official an assignment related to the case under preparation.
- The public official is a member of the board of directors or of a comparable body or the managing director in a comparable position in an entity, foundation or institution appearing as a party or having an interest in the case.

The procedure of establishing bias is not expressly regulated. However, according to a well-established doctrinal convention, each public official and employee has both the power and the obligation to disqualify himself or herself should the situation so require. In an administrative body consisting of equally empowered members it is up to the whole body to decide on the bias of its individual member in cases where a party raises the issue of disqualification. A disqualified person may not make or participate in the making of the decision in the actual case and is allowed neither to prepare, present or otherwise treat the case nor to be present at the proceedings.

As a breach of the procedural rules, bias occupies a qualified position in the sense that it is regarded as an especially serious error. Even if the decision is correct and valid, as such, bias may render it invalid or at least voidable. Bias is also a ground for subjecting the employee to criminal sanctions for failure to comply with official duties.

4.4 Preconditions for Taking the Case into Consideration

Formal requirements. The procedure may be initiated either by a public authority or a private party. The minimum formal requirements of a correct initiation are that the case is brought before a competent authority, observing the applicable formalities and time limits, and that the case is properly identified. Since these procedural rules basically govern access to administrative procedure their observance is not meant to be an end itself. Flexibility in their implementation is thus essential instead of strict formality.

Based on the general duty to provide guidance the administration should facilitate the initiation of the procedure. The authorities must give advice to the party and other persons on how to bring a case into administrative procedure and how to proceed in matters that fall within its powers. To a certain extent it is also later possible to correct procedural errors or remedy deficiencies.

The procedure is started in writing or, with the consent of the authority, orally. The use of telegram or facsimile transmission is allowed, whereas access by computer is inadmissible. At the initiation of the proceedings, the claim together with its reasons must be stated. During the procedure additional statements or claims may be presented, even orally, and they must be recorded by the authority.

Since the administrative organization structures are very complex it is possible that a case is brought to an authority that lacks the power to decide on it. If the reason for this is an obvious mistake or ignorance, the authority must attempt to determine the competent decision-maker. Where the competent authority is evident, the case must be immediately referred to it. The person who submitted the document must be notified of the transfer.

Locus standi. There exist no express rules on *locus standi* in administrative procedure, perhaps because there has been only meager need for them. In general, access to administrative procedure is quite extensive. The competent authorities are under an obligation to process any case submitted to them in due course. Yet, it is obvious that certain qualifications must apply; not everyone is entitled to demand a decision in any case.

The decisive criterion is whether the case has been brought by a party or someone who has a more remote interest in it. Provided that the case has been brought to it by a party, the authority has also the duty to take an actual and substantial decision on the extent of his or her right, duty or benefit. The most common way of doing this is to submit an application for a benefit or an entitlement.

If the case is brought by somebody other than the actual parties, the authority has the duty to render a formal decision only where it acknowledges that it has received the petition or appeal. It remains at the discretion of the authority whether it will take any further measures in the case. In such cases, the petitioner also lacks the right to challenge the decision by way of judicial appeal.

Remedying deficiencies. Even after a case has been brought to be decided by an authority, formal and factual deficiencies may still be corrected fairly widely. If a document submitted to the authority does not contain the required information or annexes, or if it is not signed or has any other deficiency as to form, the person who submitted the document will be provided an opportunity to remedy that deficiency.

In cases where a time limit for submission applies, such remedy is only possible to the extent that the documents pertain to the time before the expiry of that limit.

4.5 Means of Investigation

It is the decision-making authority that in each case has the duty to ensure that the facts in the matter are established. But the authority is not solely responsible for either finding those facts or establishing the evidence. The party shall, where necessary, produce evidence in support of his or her own claim and it is the authority's duty to obtain any other evidence, especially support for the public interest.

To ensure that all relevant views can be heard and taken into consideration, the authority preparing the matter for decision must in some cases make a public announcement that the case is pending. This duty applies to decisions that may have a considerable effect over a wide area or on the circumstances of a number of people. Even a person who does not occupy the position of a party but who can be identified and on whose living or working conditions or other circumstances the decision is likely to have a considerable effect shall be notified that the matter is pending. Such persons may be e.g. tenants when the decision is made on the landlord´s right to demolish their residence, or factory employees when the decision concerns the safety of factory equipment.

Before a decision is to be made the parties must be heard. The parties shall be afforded an opportunity to reply to the claims put forward by others (including the administrative authorities) as well as to any evidence that may affect the decision. In order for the hearing to be conclusive a party shall be informed also of the pertinent documents which are not public but which may be used by the authority as a basis for its decision. A right to such insight is subject to certain limitations, however.

4.6 Administrative Decision: Formal Requirements

Administrative decisions are usually decided upon a report presented by an official. It is the duty of the reporter (or referendary) to summarize the facts of the case and the legal norms applicable to it as well as to express his or her own opinion on how the case should be decided. The reporter assumes full responsibility for the correctness of the facts and the proposal. Even if the decision differs from the proposal the reporter will share responsibility for it, unless his or her dissenting opinion is put on record. The traditional rationale for the requirement of decision-making upon report are to enhance the correctness of administrative decisions and to extend public accountability even to the preparatory stage.

A decision made by an administrative authority shall clearly specify what rights it grants to the party, what obligations it imposes on the party or in what other manner the case was resolved. The authority also has the duty to give reasons for the decision. The decision must state the reasons for the determination by indicating the principal evidence on which it was based and the statutes and provisions that were applied. The duty to provide reasons is intended to help insure that the administration will act fairly and in this sense it serves as a device for the protection of substantive rights.

Generally, an appeal reference should be given with the decision in which information is given concerning the process of appeal.

4.7 Self-correction

When a decision has been made, the deciding authority may not alter it; at least, not to the detriment of a party. Traditionally, it has been only upon appeal that a superior authority or an administrative court has had the power to amend or overrule a final decision that an authority has made within the limits of its powers. Nowadays, an authority can, even at its own initiative, reconsider and correct its own decision provided that there are obvious technical errors in the decision or the decision is materially defective.

Correction of a materially defective decision is possible if a decision is based on obviously incorrect or insufficient information or on an apparently incorrect application of law. In these cases the authority may correct the error by deleting the incorrect decision and substituting it with a new decision. Reconsideration and correction of such an error in the premises or mistake in the actual application of law may not be corrected without the consent of the parties. *Correction of a formally defective decision* does not necessarily require the consent of the party since plain typing errors and miscalculations must be corrected by the authority who made the decision. However, should such self-correction prove unreasonable for a party, consent is required.

Reconsideration and self-correction on these two grounds leave a certain amount of discretion for the authority. On the other hand, self-correction is not available if the error is not obvious or plain. In such cases the decision should also be challenged by administrative appeal since a request for self-correction does not extend the time-limit for appeal and the decision to refuse self-correction is not appealable.

5. Public Control of Administrative Activity

5.1 Access to Administrative Documents

Principle of public access. The right of free access to administrative documents forms one of the most important guarantees of the transparency of public administration. Basic rules governing access to administrative documents are laid down in the Access to Public Documents Act of 1951. The act is based on the *principle of public access* to official documents, denoting an assumption of openness. According to the general principle stipulated in section 1, all official documents are public, as provided in this act.

Judicially, and particularly from the point of view of the normative hierarchy, it is significant that the principle of public access has not been defined as a basic right. Thus, transparency in government is not, as such, a requirement provided for in constitutional law, even though the freedom of information principle, a vital component of a constitutional state, is adhered to in Finland. It should be added, however, that in 1992 the basic rights committee have proposed an express provision elevating the access principle to the status of a basic right.

The right of access is applicable to a variety of documents regardless of their external configuration. Since the use of the term *document* is not restricted to written texts or pictures only, the Access to Public Documents Act is applicable even to information stored in a specific form such as data disk or files, tapes as well as pictorial presentations, maps or x-ray pictures.

With respect to the organization of the administrative entities, the scope of application of the Act is fairly wide. It comprises all state and municipal bodies; e.g. administrative organs, courts, representative and legislative bodies. But it also extends to formally private bodies to the extent that they are authorized to exercise public authority. This implies that most of the indirect public administration is also covered by the right of access.

Public accessibility may be limited if a document must be kept secret or it is related to the preparation of a particular matter. The accessibility of information contained in such documents is restricted; more so with secret documents than with draft documents. Thus, official documents can be divided into three groups in terms of publicity: 1) public documents, 2) draft documents and 3) secret documents.

Public documents. For a document to be qualified as public, it must have been produced or issued by a public authority. However, even an initially private document is regarded as official when it has been duly received by a public authority.

Everyone is presumed to have a general right to examine the contents of an official document and to obtain information contained therein, subject only to specific exceptions provided in law. The right extends to Finnish citizens and foreigners without distinction. No reason needs to be given when exercising this right. In fact, an authority is expressly forbidden to demand verification either of the identity of the person requesting information, or of the purpose of the information sought, unless knowledge of that purpose is essential to the exercise of discretion by the authority. Such discretion may be necessary if the document is secret or not yet public and the information contained in it may therefore be disclosed only to certain groups of persons or for specific purposes.

An individual may exercise the right of access in several ways. In most cases the document itself is made accessible by allowing the individual to read and copy it on the premises of the authority. The minimum requirement is that the authority supply a copy or an official transcription of the document requested. Should the technical form of the document so require, the applicant must be given the appropriate equipment for reading, seeing or hearing its contents or otherwise retrieving information from it. Such arrangements could, for instance, include providing access to a computer or the use of a CD-ROM reader.

In cases where the right to access has been denied by a public official, the individual who has requested the document may require that the public authority in question take a formal decision. That decision is always reviewable and the applicant has the right to make an administrative appeal according to the rules applicable to ordinary appeals against that authority. The Supreme Administrative Court is the court of last instance in all such appeals.

Draft documents. In actual administrative practice, official documents under preparation, in the process of being drafted, or otherwise incomplete constitute an important category. Because of their formal incompleteness, internal character, or preliminary nature they will not acquire the status of a public document until the issue in question has been decided. As a consequence of such a deferral, draft documents will be subject to the right of access only after the final decision is made. Purely internal documents may remain inaccessible indefinitely.

The reason for the special status of draft documents has been a need to ensure the undisturbed functioning of the administration. Nevertheless, such documents are also significant for the general monitoring of administrative activity and for influencing official action. After all the outcome of an administrative procedure will often be determined already at the drafting stage. The obvious tension between these two conflicting arguments has been resolved by a stipulation to the effect that an authority has been reserved a wide discretionary power to disclose a draft document.

Since it is at the discretion of the authority to disclose a draft document, there is no general right to obtain information in it. In administrative practice draft documents are usually disclosed relatively easily, although attitudes vary concerning the dissemination of information at the drafting stage.

Secret documents and non-disclosure. As such, the principle of public access would require that practically all documents produced or received by the public administration be made publicly available and that the information held by public officials could be disseminated without restrictions. However, such extensive accessibility has been considered unfeasible for various reasons. Therefore access to administrative documents and disclosure of information held by public authorities are subject to certain qualifications.

These qualifications are defined in provisions determining the grounds of official secrecy and providing for the duty not to disclose confidential information.

To protect such legitimate interests as personal integrity or business secrets, access has been restricted with regard to information about e.g. privacy, economic interests and business undertakings. One reason for restrictions is that the personal data obtained in the course of government work need to be protected. The operations of authorities can also not be wholly public in matters dealing with national security or crime prevention. These reasons account for the majority of express secrecy or confidentiality provisions. Furthermore, rapid advances in automatic data processing set new demands on protection of privacy, currently being met by developing data protection.

As a general rule, documents are regarded as secret if this is provided for in an act of Parliament. In general, no particular procedure of specific classification (or de-classification) is necessary, nor is it performed in actual practice. Any document can be declared secret by law. Numerous such provisions of secrecy are included in the legislation concerning e.g. taxation, health care, and social welfare. A document may also be declared secret by presidential decree, but doing so requires a particularly good reason, i.e. a specific and legitimate confidentiality interest.

Such specific interests include, according to art. 9(2) of the Access to Public Documents Act, important personal interests, safeguarding data protection or the external security of the State, prevention or prosecution of crime, the economic interests of the State or the municipalities. The most important and extensive decree defining the scope of secrecy of administrative documents and information is the Decree incorporating certain exceptions to the publicity of official documents (1951). The possibility of circumventing openness under this decree has been criticized heavily, mainly because of the flexibility and ease with which access can be restricted.

In an individual case a document may be declared secret by the President or the Council of State. Other public authorities lack similar power of assigning secrecy to official documents and they are bound by the general secrecy provisions.

Public officials are under the duty not to disclose to any unauthorized person a secret document or information contained in it. That obligation extends also to information which has been proclaimed confidential by a superior official or administrative body pursuant to an express provision in law. The duty not to disclose confidential information is binding on public officials even after leaving the service.

The wrongful disclosure of a secret document or confidential information is subject to disciplinary penalties or criminal liability.

Even official secrecy fails to remain unconditional. Secret documents and confidential information may be disclosed in certain cases, to qualified recipients, and under specific circumstances. The most important of such exceptions are made to guarantee procedural rights and satisfy the maxim 'audi alteram partem'. Secret and draft documents may fall within the purview of 'access to parties', in which case the parties concerned are allowed more extensive access to the documents than the general public. Parties in an administrative procedure or dispute may have access even to a secret document if it either actually has affected or may affect the outcome of the procedure. However, in administrative matters this right is not unconditional, since the relevant authority enjoys a fairly wide margin of discretion in determining whether the disclosure is necessary.

Other exceptions include a special permission issued by the appropriate Ministry to surrender information in an otherwise secret document for special reasons. Inside the public administration, authorities may share secret documents and confidential information in cases where especially imperative reasons require disclosure.

5.2 General Control of Legality

The control of legality in public administration is the duty of specific supervisory organs, the Chancellor of Justice and the Parliamentary Ombudsman, but such control is also exercised by superior administrative organs. Besides legality even adequacy and good administration are in the focus of the control. Within the field of general control interventions are initiated either by the controlling organs *ex officio* or at the request of individuals in the form of an administrative complaint.

The Chancellor of Justice is appointed by the President and must possess "outstanding knowledge of the circumstances in the country related to justice and law". The Chancellor is formally part of the Council of State and is present at its sittings. Moreover he or she is closely connected with the work of the Council by supplying legal counsel and advisory opinions both to the President and the Cabinet on the legality of the government business.

The Chancellor also acts as a general supervisor of legality in public administration, the courts, and in the performance of public duties. It is the duty of the Chancellor to observe and keep an eye on the activities of the public bodies, and to see that the authorities and officials uphold the law and carry out their duties so that no person is adversely affected or suppressed in his or her lawful rights. The Chancellor has the right to be present at the meetings of all courts and public authorities. The Chancellor also combines the duties of attorney general and chief of public prosecutors. As the highest prosecutor his power to observe legality extends to the sphere of private activity, as well.

The Parliamentary Ombudsman is elected by the Parliament for a term of four years. The activity of the Ombudsman focuses more on the general surveillance of legality in administrative matters and in the exercise of public authority, in general. The specific duties of the Ombudsman include the supervision of legality in the defence forces, prison administration and closed institutions. In actual practice the Ombudsman has also proven to be more accessible to ordinary citizens than the Chancellor.

Administrative Complaint. The legality and appropriateness of administrative activity may also be supervised by superior organs. In fact, it is their official duty to see to it that the authorities under their direction observe the law. This, in turn, is considered to entail that anyone has a right to submit a complaint to a hierarchically superior body claiming that the subordinate authority has acted in breach of its duties, that it has in some other manner failed to conform with the law or that other faults or errors have been committed. Such an administrative complaint is the ordinary procedure for an individual to bring an administrative irregularity into the knowledge of the Chancellor of Justice or the Parliamentary Ombudsman, as well.

There exist neither time-limits nor qualifying rules for making an administrative complaint, which makes it very practicable for an ordinary citizen to resort to it. As a collateral, however, it remains relatively ineffective as a remedy for illegal action or administrative inappropriateness.

A decision may not effectively be challenged by an administrative complaint, since such a complaint is incapable of resulting in a reversal or overruling of the decision. It may have other consequences, however. Acting as a public prosecutor the Ombudsman may sue public employees in the general courts and demand punishment. In less grave situations, which are much more common, the Ombudsmen can express their critical opinion to the official or the administrative authority.

5.3 Legal Responsibility of Public Employees

All public employees are subject to legal responsibility, which may be enforced in various different ways. Public officials have traditionally been subject to qualified criminal responsibility which embraces practically all their activities as officials. Practically similar responsibility has recently been extended to public employees, as well. While it is not unusual that public servants are prosecuted, the main thrust of the qualified criminal responsibility probably lies in its preventive effect.

Only public officials are subject to internal administrative responsibility which is enforced by disciplinary punishment. The disciplinary penalties include removal, suspension, and official reproach. This form of responsibility has, however, a rather narrow scope and it is mainly used for minor faults. Public officials and employees are also liable for damages caused to private persons and to the employer.

6. Review of Administrative Action

The right to judicial review has traditionally been regarded as a fundamental part of the system of legal protection in administrative matters. The regular judicial remedy available to the individuals concerned is the administrative appeal. In addition, there are special legal remedies for the annulment of a final decision that is not any more or not at all appealable. While the administrative complaint (see ch. 5.2) does not constitute an actual judicial remedy, it is significant as a general and informal guarantee of legal protection. Self-correction (see ch. 4.6), on the other hand, has a limited scope of application since only obvious errors may be rectified by the authority that made the decision.

6.1 Administrative Appeal

The Administrative Appeals Act (1950) contains general provisions on the right of appeal and the procedure to be followed in instituting the appeal procedure. According to the Act, an administrative decision can be appealed as long as nothing to the contrary is stated in a law or an ordinance. Specific provisions limiting access to appeal procedure are fairly rare, and in practice, there is a general right of appeal in all administrative matters. The right to judicial review in municipal matters is based on separate provisions in the Municipal Act. They, too, are based on a general right to appeal all decisions taken by the municipal authorities.

Administrative and Municipal Appeal. Administrative judicial appeal is the general form of instituting the appeal procedure. It is further divided into two separate forms of appeal. Decisions made by state administrative authorities are subject to an administrative appeal, while decisions made by municipal authorities within the field of municipal self-government may be challenged by a municipal appeal. There are certain significant differences between these two forms of appeal concerning mainly standing, reviewability and the procedure. It is customary, however, to use the term administrative appeal as a generic term for both kinds of appeal. Following this standard, only the distinctive features of the municipal appeal will be specified in this presentation.

The appeal procedure is instituted by a written appeal, which must state the claims and the grounds for them, and to which must be attached the decision being appealed. The appeal must be made within a fixed time-limit, in most cases 30 days. Only formal deficiencies and omissions in the appeal document may be corrected after that. For instance missing signatures and identifying information may be supplemented.

Appeals against decisions by lower authorities are lodged either with the superior administrative authority or with the Provincial Administrative Court. While the traditional appeal to superior administrative authorities still is the formal rule, in practice, it is the independent Provincial Administrative Courts that have general jurisdiction in most administrative matters as the court of first instance, pursuant to express provisions. The Supreme Administrative Court is the appeal court for decisions made by upper level administrative authorities, including the Council of State and the ministries, as well as the Provincial Administrative Court.

Standing. There are only rather general provisions on who has standing in administrative procedure, and the doctrine has evolved in the application of law by the appeal courts. Under a well-established case law, any person whose right or legally protected interest is directly infringed or affected by an administrative decision is considered to have the right to lodge an administrative appeal against that decision.

In the first place, the person to whom the decision is directly addressed and who is affected by the outcome of the decision is entitled to challenge the decision. For example, an applicant whose application for a license or a social benefit has been totally or partially rejected has standing as a party. Gradually, the doctrine concerning standing has been expanded to include even those whose rights or interests are affected by a decision even though they do not occupy the position of a party. Indeed, in modern administration the actual effects of a decision tend to extend further than to the applicant or to others with direct interests.

Thus standing has been extended by express provisions or judicial practice to those who are indirectly but factually affected by a decision, e.g. to competitors and neighbors. Special attention has been paid to the harmful effects of the decisions concerning environmental regulation. For example, a siting permit for a plant or a warehouse which may be hazardous to health may be appealed by the neighbors and those living in the neighborhood. In these and similar cases, a further general requirement is that the interests of the appellants are in some way legally recognized.

Administrative decisions are fairly often appealed by various organizations and associations representing interests which the decision may affect. Their standing has been construed rather narrowly, however. They have generally been granted standing only as ordinary parties and, additionally, when the appeal is directly connected with their statutory tasks. At this point, however, the doctrine has recently shown some signs of expanding. While the State as an applicant enjoys the position of an ordinary party and has standing, the authority whose decision has been reversed or amended is not considered to have a right to appeal that decision.

As for municipal appeals a considerably broader approach is applied. Decisions by municipal authorities may be appealed both by the immediate parties concerned and any member of the municipality, including associations having their domicile in the municipality.

Appealability. Basically, appeal may be directed against any act of an administrative authority whereby a matter has been decided or dismissed without examination. In this respect, no distinction is made between administrative decisions and acts of the State. Decisions by the Cabinet or the ministries may thus be subject to appeal even if they were based on a very wide margin of discretion. The advisability of those decisions cannot be investigated by the Supreme Administrative court, however.

To be ripe for appeal, the decision must contain a final and conclusive settlement of an individual case. This entails that appeal is available neither against initial or tentative decisions made at the preparatory stage nor technical decisions concerning merely the implementation of a decision. Recommendations as well as decisions of a general nature, such as administrative circulars, instructions concerning implementation and project plans, also fall outside the scope of appealability. On the other hand, if an authority remains passive, delays the matter or fails to act completely without making a decision, no appeal is available against such conduct. In such cases the only, albeit ineffective remedy is the informal administrative complaint.

For a limited group of matters, such as some cases concerning taxation and social welfare, a leave of appeal is required from the Supreme Administrative Court. The main ground for granting such a leave is the need to maintain unity of legal praxis. A decision cannot be appealed if there is a specific provision prohibiting this or if the time limit for appeal has expired. Even in these cases special legal remedies are available under certain conditions.

Appeal Procedure. There is no specific legislation to regulate the procedure in the appeal proceedings, although such an act is under preparation. General provisions on judicial remedies are in the Administrative Appeals Act, which regulates the appeal procedure, appeal instances, completion of appeal documents, information to be given about how to appeal (appeal reference), and the the effect of the appeal on the enforceability of the decision subject to appeal. Procedure in the administrative courts is further regulated in provisions concerning the administrative courts. In these provisions specific reference is made to general principles concerning judicial procedure. Such principles include the obligation to hear the parties and to state the reasons for the decision.

The proceedings are characterized by a predominance of written procedure and the main significance is accorded to documentary evidence. Oral hearing is rather rare since the parties are not generally entitled to require their case to be heard in an administrative court. Such hearing is mandatory only if expressly provided for, e.g. in cases directly concerning personal liberty. On the other hand, the courts are under an obligation to actively conduct the procedure and to acquire evidence and factual information *ex officio*. In this sense, the procedure is characterized by the investigation principle, according to which it is the duty of the court to acquire the necessary supplementary information.

As a rule, the administrative authority that has made the decision subject to appeal, is not considered to acquire the status of a party in the proceedings. However, that authority is normally provided an opportunity to communicate and expand the grounds of its decision, but other than that, there is no specific system for attending to the public interest. The actual parties must be heard and they have the right to give their opinions on all the material affecting the decision.

Powers of the Court. By and large the powers of the court depend on the nature of the appeal. They are wider as regards an ordinary administrative appeal and more limited in cases where a municipal appeal is concerned. In all cases the court has the power either to affirm or overrule the decision challenged by an appeal. Decisions subject to an administrative appeal may also be amended, but this is not possible in proceedings initiated by a municipal appeal because it is cassatory by nature. The rationale for the limited jurisdiction in the latter case is to be found in the principle of municipal self-government; the courts are regarded to lack the power to interfere in the material substance of discretion within the sphere of local autonomy.

For the same reason a similar distinction applies to the scope of investigation, as well. The conduct of the procedure is more active in administrative appeals, where the court is empowered to take a more detailed stand on the contents of the case. Generally, new claims cannot be introduced after the appeal period has expired. However, in administrative appeals new grounds may be stated to support the original claim but, on the other hand, in municipal appeals that is not possible.

The administrative appeal has not been limited to certain specific grounds for appeal and in practice the grounds for the appeal vary from case to case. Generally, decisions of state administrative authorities may be appealed on grounds of legality and expediency, but in actual practice appeals based on arguments of expediency are quite rare. Should the decision subject to appeal depend primarily on a consideration of its expediency, the Supreme Administrative Court refers the matter to the Council of State. Decisions of the Council of State and the ministries may be appealed only on legal grounds. A similar restriction applies also to the municipal appeal, which can rest only on legal grounds.

According to an established doctrine, courts are considered to lack the power to investigate the constitutionality of legislation enacted by the Parliament. It is mainly due to this doctrine that administrative courts have tended to be fairly reserved in addressing specific constitutional issues in their deliberations and decision-making. Instead it has been the ombudsmen that have displayed considerably more activity in this respect.

An administrative appeal generally suspends the enforcement of the decision. However, in matters concerning municipal self-government, the appeal usually does not have a suspensive effect. In both cases, the administrative court can, either on application or *ex officio*, prohibit or interrupt the enforcement.

6.2 Special Legal Remedies

Special legal remedies are available if an administrative decision cannot be challenged utilizing the ordinary administrative appeal. This is the case when the prescribed term of appeal has expired or when the ordinary appeal cannot be used, because it has been expressly prohibited. In both cases, the decision has acquired legal force and it must be possible to rely on its continuing to hold good. However, under certain, especially pressing conditions it must be possible to subject such unalterability to certain exceptions in order to satisfy fundamental exigencies of legal protection. The Administrative Annulments Act (1966) contains the express provisions on the availability and use of special legal remedies against such otherwise final and unalterable decisions made by administrative authorities or courts.

Under the Administrative Annulments Act, a final decision can be set aside if there has been a grave procedural error which has materially affected the decision. This is most often the case when a party to the case has not been heard before the decision was made. A closed case may also be reopened and the final decision made in it may be annulled. The grounds for such an annulment are, first, that the decision was based on a manifestly incorrect application of the law, second, that a material error has occurred in the decision-making process, and, third, that essential new evidence has appeared in the case. A further general requirement for setting aside or annulling a final decision is that it violates private rights or its annulment is in the public interest.

Generally the right to apply for the use of special legal remedies is determined on the basis of rules governing standing in administrative appeal. In this respect the special legal remedies have a wider availability since also the authority that has made the decision is considered to have the right to apply for its reconsideration and annulment. Applications for annulment may also be made by supervising authorities as well as by the Chancellor of Justice and the Parliamentary Ombudsman.

The Administrative Annulments Act also provides for the restoration of expired time. The time for lodging an administrative appeal may be restored using this remedy due to, for example, severe illness, delay in the postal delivery of the appeal petition, or if the authority has given erroneous instructions on how to appeal.

Bibliography

Stanley V. Anderson, Public Access to Government Files in Sweden. 21 American Journal of Comparative Law (1973), 419–473.
Edward Andersson, Appeal against Council of State and ministry decisions in Finland. Scandinavian Studies in Law (1972), 11–36.
Simo Hakamäki, An Introduction to Local Government Activities. Tampere 1988.
Nils Herlitz, Elements of Nordic Public Law. Stockholm 1969.
Mikael Hidén, The Ombudsman in Finland: The First Fifty Years. Berkeley: Institute of Governmental Studies 1973.
Indirect Public Administration in Fourteen Countries (Modeen, T. & Rosas, A., eds.) Åbo Academy Press, Åbo 1988.
Kaarlo Tuori, The General Doctrines in Public Law (Scandinavian Studies in Law (1987), 177–199.
Krister Ståhlberg, Finnish Local Government in the Postwar Period. Åbo 1990.
Juha Vartola, Finland in Rowat, D. C. (ed.), Public Administration in Developed Democracies, 117–132. New York: Dekker, 1988.

X ENVIRONMENTAL LAW

By Kari Kuusiniemi

1. Environmental Law as a Legal Discipline

1.1 The Development of Environmental Law in Finland

Internationally as well as in Finland *Environmental Law* is usually defined as a legal discipline regulating the use of the environment. Environmental law covers the acts and statutes which have been made in order to control the use and provide for the conservation of the physical environment. Environmental law is a mechanism to realize environmental policy.

Environmental law is a relatively new legal discipline. Although its roots date back to the nuisance rules of the Roman Law, the appearance of current major environmental problems in the 50's and 60's has given rise to specify environmental regulation as an independent systematic area. What we now call legal environmental regulation was in Finland originally a part of so-called *Economic Law*. Economic law was a branch of particular private law, though some elements of public law were covered as well.

Land and Water Law, as distinguished from economic law, consists, according to the traditional grouping, of four main sectors, viz. Land Law (law related to real estates, parcelling, surveying etc.), Water Law, Planning and Building Law and, a fourth sector identified as "Essential Environmental Law", i.e. mainly Nature Conservation and Pollution Control Law. As an academic subject land and water law covers the essential statute material of modern environmental law, but its point of view is orientated according to the traditional legal structure. *Environmental Law*, which is based on land and water law, has partly displaced this latter term also in the academic world. Environmental law expresses a functional way of thinking. It is defined on the basis of the functions of the statutes. Environmental law consists of rules that have a considerable effect on the state of the environment.

1.2 Characteristics and Structure of Environmental Law

Environmental law is typically *goal-orientated*. Environmental regulation has increased due to the need to protect some aspects of the environment from pollution and landscape-altering activities. For the same reason one of the characteristics of environmental law is *problem-orientation*. Studies of environmental law are concerned with the regulation of certain environmental problems, in spite of traditional law systematic boundaries.

Research of environmental law is *interdisciplinary*. Environmental law includes elements of *Real Estate Law, Administrative Law, Compensation Law* etc. Material rules of environmental law often contain so-called *vague expressions*, such as unreasonable harm or particular reason. Interpretation of these norms must frequently be based on the scientific research of, e. g., the natural sciences (in determining, for example, whether the concentration of a certain pollutant is likely to harm a particular ecosystem) or technical or economic sciences (to determine, for example, whether the emission in question can be reduced by means that are technically feasible and economically reasonable).

Functionally, environmental law can be systematized in three sectors. *Planning of the Use of the Environment* includes mainly general, area-based planning or land use planning, but it covers some parts of sectoral planning systems as well, such as the planning of nature conservation, water management and electricity supply. Also Environmental Impact Assessment can be grouped here. *Regulation of the Use of Natural Resources* aims at solving conflicts between different forms of land use. To this group belong, for example, rules concerning nature conservation and protection of landscape, hunting, fishing, outdoor activities, and different projects of utilizing natural resources, such as soil excavation, water management and road construction. The objective of *Environmental Protection (Pollution Control) Law* is to protect environmental media – air, water, soil – from pollution.

2. General Background

2.1 Development and Structure of Environmental Legislation

Finnish environmental legislation has been enacted during a long period. Legislation on building, public health and water management was in force already in the 19th century. The Nature Conservation Act and the Neighbourhood Relations Act were passed in 1920's. Enactments concerning building (and planning), public health and water management were reformed in 1950's and 1960's. The time of environmental legislation *per se* came in the 70's and 80's. During these decades were enacted, among other statutes, the Waste Management Act, the Air Pollution Control Act, the Noise Abatement Act, the Chemicals Act, and the Soil Excavation Act. The former legislation has subsequently been reformed. Finnish environmental legislation is *sector-based*. A comprehensive code of environmental protection, unlike in the other Scandinavian and in many European countries, does not exist in Finland. Hence, pollution control is built upon legislation related to particular environmental media.

The newest phase of development can be seen in acts and bills that touch on matters regulated in several existing sectoral acts. The environmental permit procedure reform combines permit procedures previously set forth in neighbourhood, public health, air pollution control and waste management legislation. Parliament is currently discussing the proposed Environmental Damages Act. A draft on Environmental Impact Assessment (EIA) is also on the agenda because of the forthcoming obligations in relation to the European Communities (EC) Law. Also enactments concerning environmental criminality are being unified.

2.2 Systems of Regulation

Regulation of the use of the environment is usually dichotomized. *Legal-administrative regulation* is primarily based on decisions of the authorities, including the approval of land use plans and granting environmental permits. The purpose of *economic regulation* is to have an indirect effect on the decisions made by the relevant actors (entrepreneurs, consumers) by either rewarding environmentally sound behaviour (subsidies for environmental investments) or sanctioning harmful behaviour (pollution taxes). *Guidance by information* should also not be forgotten. Consumers' attitudes, for example, are affected by education that makes them realize the environmental relevance of their every-day actions.

The system for legal-administrative regulation places great demands on administrative resources. Finnish sectoral environmental legislation provides for a rich assortment of various *permit procedures*, according to which an authority considers – in advance – whether the project can be permitted or not and what kind of provisions should be included in the permit decision. The authority makes its decision *case-by-case*, based on general provisions and, where applicable, administrative guidelines.

> The permit system of the Water Act is the most orthodox example of case-by-case judgments. The decision is made on the basis of vague legal norms, mainly by weighing the pros and cons of the project (balancing of interests); general regulations or guidelines on maximum concentrations of different emissions are missing. A revision of the Water Act made necessary by the Treaty of the European Economic Area (EEA) granting the Council of State (the Cabinet) the authority to issue general regulations based on the EC directives, has, however, recently been passed by the Parliament.

Pressure to lighten administrative regulation can clearly be felt for economic reasons as well as the need to be reasonable. Permit control should be reduced by covering small scale, technically standardized plants (e.g. small power stations, stone crushing and asphalt plants) by general administrative regulations; compliance with the regulations would be controlled afterwards, while the operation of the plant goes on. If the EEA Treaty comes into force or if Finland becomes a member of the EC, environmental directives of the Community must be implemented. This alleviates, to some extent, case-by-case decision-making, but, on the other hand, many of the directives presuppose existence of a system of permits. The Finnish control system does not differ from that of the EC in as radical a manner as is sometimes thought. So far, administrative regulations and guidelines are not very numerous.

Advocates of economic regulation have pointed out the rigidity of the legal-administrative system. In a pure economic model a certain behaviour, such as an emission into the environment, is not forbidden, but the right to emit costs money. This is how the external production costs can be internalized in the price of the product. The polluter pays principle (PPP) is put into practice, and the market takes care of the regulation. The environmentally soundest product is the cheapest.

Every type of regulation has, to my mind, its own function to fulfil the goals concerning the quality of the environment. In Finland the most clearly predominant legal-administrative regulation has been especially designed to address major polluting activities. Everything must not be left at the mercy of the market.

Economic regulation has found increasing interest as a supplement or, in part, also as a substitute for the legal-administrative control system. The price model is well-suited to reduce emissions whose effects are global, irrespective of the site of the plant (carbon dioxide, CFC compounds). Only the total reduction of the emissions is relevant, not the concrete surroundings of the actual plant. Economic means can also be applied to control diffuse loading (thus, for example, water pollution through overfertilizing emissions from agriculture is "paid for" by fertilizer taxes). Administrative regulation has gradually been supplemented by taxes and fees.

2.3 Landowner's Position and the Environment

Private ownership is well safeguarded in Finland. According to the Constitution the property of every Finnish citizen is guaranteed by the law. *Expropriation* (compulsory purchase) for "public need" is allowed by a provision of a Parliamentary act, if fully compensated. An act regulating the use of the environment that prevents the normal and reasonable use of the property must be enacted by a qualified majority. Proposals to revise the Constitution by, e.g., an amendment that would guarantee the citizens' basic constitutional right to a decent environment, have been made, but they are highly controversial.

General prohibitions applicble to all citizens in the same manner, such as bans on deforestation, on private nuisance and on water pollution, have naturally been enacted in the normal legislative process, without any duties of compensation. Conversely, the regulation concerning building activities and utilization of natural resources frequently causes debate on the community's duty to compensate the losses caused by the restrictions or to purchase a property that can no longer be used in a rational manner.

The system of *planning law* is based on the so-called "freedom to form a sparse population settlement" (about the concepts of dense and sparse population settlements, see 3.1.3 below). Therefore a building permit, for example, cannot be rejected solely on the grounds that the site belongs to the National Shore Area Protection Programme. However, the minimum size of the site or its unsuitability because of danger of flood are possible grounds to reject the application. A general prohibition to build closer than a certain distance to the coast-line, unlike, for example, in Sweden and Denmark, does not exist. Sometimes the only way to prevent such a project is to expropriate the site. The compensation is determined according to the Expropriation Act. When the piece of land is compulsorily purchased, the starting-point of the compensation is the going price, based on a comparison of prices actually paid for voluntary purchases in the area. If only the "building rights" are expropriated, the owner will be compensated the loss of so many building sites as could have been formed according to the Building Act.

Restrictions based on the *Soil Excavation Act* (see 4.2 below) safeguard on one hand the landscapes, but on the other hand they guarantee the applicant's claim to be issued a permit for extraction, to the extent that no significant adverse effects on landscape or nature arise. If the permit is not granted, the State or the municipality in question is liable to purchase the area if the owner cannot use it for agriculture or forestry, building or other comparable purposes bringing reasonable profit. In practice, however, the liability is hardly ever actualized. The debate concerning the constitutionality of this act is still going on.

The *Rapids Protection Act* provides for the protection of 53 rapids against the construction of new hydroelectric plants. The owners of hydroelectric power capacity had a claim to apply for compensation for their losses. The Act, including rules about compensation, was enacted even though the construction of power plants in these rapids could have been rejected on the basis of case-by-case permit decisions rendered by the Water Courts pursuant to the Water Act. In such cases, no compensation would have been paid.

The guarantee of ownership does not contradict the principle of pollution control, and no conflicts have arisen in this respect. The expropriation of private property has, in constitutional states where the rule of law is reigning, as a prerequisite that a sufficient compensation is paid. On the other hand, particular, territorially determined restrictions of use that concretize the general law-based rules create real problems. According to the principles of social ownership an owner's freedom of use can be restricted. Finnish legislation has in this respect been very cautious. The protection of nature may have to be paid for dearly, as the most restrictions of use must be inflicted by expropriatory means, requiring the payment of full compensation.

2.4 Citizens' Influence and the *Locus Standi*

The opportunities of interested groups and citizens to have an effect on environmental decision-making is gradually broadening. When examining the forms of participation from a legal standpoint, citizens are divided into parties and other interested persons.

The *parties*, i.e. persons, whose legally relevant interest may be concerned, must be heard before the decision is made. The parties have also the *locus standi*; they have the right to appeal against the decision. Nowadays several acts, such as the Environmental Permit Procedure Act and the Water Act, provide that other interested persons are also given the opportunity to express their view on the project. They do not have the *locus standi*, however. In environmental matters administrative agencies are frequently treated like parties and may appeal against decisions contrary to the public interests they are in charge of (e.g. the National Board of Waters and Environment in water cases, Provincial Offices and some municipal boards in cases concerning environmental permits).

An exception to the narrow, interest-based *locus standi* can be found in cases where the rules of appeal are based on the Municipalities Act (e.g., cases on land use planning and soil excavation permits). In these cases an appeal on grounds of illegality may be made by any of the "members" of the municipality, i.e. inhabitants, persons who own land, or associations registered in the municipality in question. Hence, the right to appeal belongs to environmental associations or inhabitants' associations. In cases involving the Administrative Appeals Act, in contrast, appeals of these kinds of associations are not examined because of the lack of a relevant interest if they do not coincidently own a piece of land in the vicinity of the plant. This tradition of such a restrictive interpretation of the relevant interest has been criticized, but a comprehensive review of the rules is not in sight.

3. Planning of the Use of the Environment

3.1 Land Use Planning

3.1.1 The Bases of the Planning System

Land use planning is *general physical planning*. In plans at various levels, areas are reserved for different purposes (population, industry, traffic, recreation, conservation) to fulfil the needs of various social functions. A (land use) plan is a scheme concerning the future use of an area, drawn in a form of a map. The map is completed by a written statement describing the starting-points of the planning task, its aims, alternatives etc. Besides the area reservations, a plan includes additional provisions about the planned use of each piece of land (plan provisions). The rules concerning land use planning are set forth in the Building Act of 1958.

The planning system based on the Building Act is hierarchical. No rules about general planning at the *national level* can be found in the Act; neither does Finland have a system comparable to the Swedish Natural Resources Act. The Building Act nevertheless presupposes the existence of nation-wide planning by referring to it in the rules concerning the regional plan. The *regional plan* is a general plan on an area covering more than just one municipality. The *master plan* is a general plan of a municipality. It may be mentioned that Finland, with its 338 000 sq. km is divided into 20 regional plan areas and 460 municipalities. Detailed plans are 1) *town plans* (in towns and cities), 2) *population centre plans* (in other municipalities than towns and cities) and 3) *shore area plans* (on densely built shore areas). *The principle of the plan hierarchy* is expressed in the fact that a more general plan guides the drafting of a more detailed one, and a confirmed, more detailed plan takes the place of the more general one in the relevant area.

> A commission appointed by the Minister of the Environment and charged with the reform of land use planning, completed its work in April 1993. The proposals would, among other things, restrict State control over the municipalities, tighten up the control over building activities outside the detailed plan areas and emphasize the position of master plans in controlling building activity on shore areas. In order to protect national interests the Ministry of the Environment or the Provincial Office would, however, have the power to control municipal planning decisions.

3.1.2 General Planning

The *regional plan* is an intermunicipal plan covering usually an area somewhat smaller than a province. Planning has in practice proceeded in phases. The plans of the first phase identified areas for nature conservation and recreation, those of the second phase areas for densely populated communities. The plan shall include sufficient areas for various purposes that the development of the region presupposes. The plan shall pay attention to the particular needs of the region. It shall be co-ordinated with the nation-wide planning and with the regional planning of the neighbouring areas. The regional plan may not be unreasonable to a land owner (e.g. by reserving his entire land property for recreational or conservation purposes).

The regional plan guides master and detailed planning. Its effects reach also other activities of public authorities: plans or decisions endangering the realization of the regional plan are not to be made. The plan has only a so-called relative restriction of the right of a landowner to build. The building activity may not endanger the realization of the plan. But, if the refusal of the building permit would cause the applicant considerable harm, and the State or the municipality will not purchase the land or otherwise compensate for the harm, a permit for *a sparse population settlement* must be granted (money or permit -principle).

Master plans can, according to their legal effects, be classified into three categories. A master plan of the first degree, or a plan approved only by the municipality, is the basis of the physical planning in the municipality; it has a kind of self-realizing effect. A master plan of the second degree must be confirmed by either the Ministry or the Provincial Office after approval on the municipal level. A plan of the third degree is a confirmed master plan with some more far-reaching restrictions on building or works activities. Rules about drafting a master plan and the legal effects of a confirmed plan correspond to those concerning the drafting and effects of a regional plan.

3.1.3 Detailed Planning

The Building Act is based on an old-fashioned dichotomy, in which rules concerning towns are separated from those concerning other municipalities. This can be seen in detailed planning, too. The detailed plan for towns and cities is the town plan, for other municipalities it is the population centre plan. The rules concerning the respective type of plan are somewhat different but in drawing up a plan in practice, the need and aims of planning obviously are more relevant than the name of the plan type.

Detailed plans are drawn up for a dense population settlement. One of the leading principles of the Building Act is the ban on permitting dense population settlement outside a detailed planned area. A dense population settlement is, by definition, a uniform settlement that calls for certain common measures for public utilities (roads, water pipes, sewers etc.). Every other kind of settlement is called a sparse population settlement. A group of at least five single-family houses, where the distance between houses is not more than roughly 200 metres, has in practice been interpreted as a dense population settlement.

The plan must be drawn up so that the area will be appropriately used. Areas shall be reserved for future development. A uniform building code and the requirements of beauty, health, comfort, fire-safety and traffic are to be taken into account. Sites of cultural interest etc. shall be protected and preserved. Landowners may not be burdened with unreasonable restrictions in the use of their property that could be avoided without undermining the primary requirement-appropriate planning.

A specification of building restrictions is attached to detailed plans. Building activities or other land use contrary to the plan is forbidden: a building permit may not be granted unless the applicant has received an exceptional permit. The plan also gives the municipality certain rights and duties concerning the purchase of areas reserved for streets, parks etc.

3.1.4 Shore Area Planning

Increasing cottage building at the end of the 60's worried the people who were afraid of excessive construction in areas valuable for recreation, nature conservation and landscape protection. The so-called "common right of access" recognized in Nordic law grants the freedom to move about on somebody else's land and pick mushrooms and berries. This freedom does not, however, extend to the yard, and this is why dense cottage building on the shore prevents recreational use in the area.

> Because a 1967 bill, drafted after a Swedish model with a general ban on building near to the coast line, did not gain sufficient support, the Building Act was amended by rules on shore area planning in 1969. The shore area plan, as opposed to other plans, may be called a "landowner's plan". Drawing up the plan has been left to the landowner – or to an authorized consultant – naturally within the terms of the rules. Planning is in the interest of the owner, because a shore area, where the plan, according to the Building Act, shall be drawn up, is under a kind of a building prohibition. A building permit may not be granted until a shore area plan has been confirmed for the area, unless the applicant has received an exceptional permit.

The need for a shore area plan has been linked to five criteria: 1) the area shall be in the vicinity of a lake or a river or the sea etc.; 2) land use planning is needed in the area; 3) the need is for the most part caused by cottage building; 4) the area shall, judging by the sale, rental or parcelling of real estates for leisure use, be subject to the pressure of building activity; and 5) a town plan or a population centre plan is not needed in the area.

A shore area plan must satisfy the terms that reasonably may be set for organized building activity. The area shall be large enough to form an appropriate whole for planning. Land use shall be appropriate to the shore landscape and to the use of the neighbouring areas. Areas needed for building activity and common use, such as for bathing, and, if necessary, for public areas, for example for public road or for a public bathing place, shall be reserved.

3.1.5 The Authorities and the Procedure

The starting-point of the Building Act is *the Municipal Planning Monopoly*. It is the duty of municipal bodies to draw up plans and to decide the contents of plans within the rules of planning law. During the planning procedure the parties shall be heard in several stages. Other interested persons also have an opportunity to express their opinion about the draft. The municipality has also a duty to publicize information about significant planning projects. The plans are normally approved by the Municipal Council (a body consisting of trustees). This is also true of the shore area plan.

The provisions of the Building Act concerning e.g. nation-wide interests or the landowners' position, have long been controlled by submitting the plans to a State authority (Provincial Office or the Ministry) for confirmation. The current trend is to strengthen municipal decision-making, and some procedures of confirmation have been withdrawn. A reform of 1990 introduced a so-called delegating master plan. When confirming the master plan the State authority may decide that changes in town or population centre plans do not have to be submitted. Thus, decisions about regional plans and shore area plans must in every case be submitted for confirmation but the confirming authority must not make any relevant changes in the plan; it is a municipal task to decide the contents of the plan. In any case the plan may be left totally or partially unconfirmed.

Every member of the municipality has the *right to appeal* against the plan decision on legal grounds (see 2.4 above). The appeal is directed to the authority confirming the plan or, when no confirmation is needed, to the authority who would be competent, if the plan should be submitted

(Provincial Office/the Ministry). A further appeal to the Supreme Administrative Court is allowed. Interpreting rules with vague expressions about planning is considered to be left exclusively to legal discretion.

3.2 Sectoral Planning Affecting Land Use

Nation-wide *nature conservation planning* is based on national protection programmes approved by the Council of State. These programmes have included inventories of nationally valuable ecosystems etc. Programmes concerning e.g. national and natural parks and the protection of peatlands, eskers, shore areas, and groves have been approved thus far.

Legal rules about the drafting and approving of nature protection programmes or about their juridical relevance do not exist. However, the Government's general competence covers planning activity concerning nation-wide inventories of natural resources and areas worth protecting. The programmes do not have any direct legal effects on a single landowner. For example, a building permit may not be refused solely on the base of a programme, and the programme as such does not restrict the landowner's otherwise permissible freedom of use. To carry out the programmes the authorities may, either according to the Nature Conservation Act (see 4.1 below) or the Building Act, temporarily prohibit all land use that could endanger the purpose of the programme. The approval of the programme directs, in fact, a threat of expropriation to the landowner. The programme may also have an indirect legal effect on interpreting the vague norms of environmental law (e.g., the esker protection programme when judging whether soil excavation damages a beautiful landscape, see 4.2 below).

> The practice of governmental protection programmes has been criticized by the landowners. But the realization of nature conservation on the basis of informal programmes is also far from certain. A commission recently published its proposals to amend the Nature Conservation Act (rules on drafting, on the legal effect of programmes, and on the landowner's initiative).

In spite of some proposals, the Water Act contains no rules about *the planning of water management*. Land use plans may, however, extend to include wetlands. The National Board of Waters and Environment has, especially in the 70's, made water management plans for greater river basins. This kind of planning lacks direct legal effects. In permit procedures under the Water Act, these water management plans have served as a kind of background material.

Some other sectoral planning systems may also have significant effects on land use. According to the Electricity Act environmental impacts must be taken into account in *electricity supply* planning at the regional level, but the goals of planning refer to electricity supply. The plans do not give legal force to the judgments of the environmental authorities, but these kinds of plans, nevertheless, have certain factual effects on land use in the plan area.

3.3 Environmental Impact Assessment

From the international viewpoint environmental impact assessment (EIA) is one of the most important questions of environmental law. The roots of EIA date back to the United States' National Environmental Policy Act of 1969 that presupposes an EIA of significant federal projects. In European environmental law, the common principles of EIA can be found in the EC Directive on Environmental Impact Assessment (85/337). EIA has been mentioned as one of the most important tools of the strategy towards *sustainable development*. Also its role as a channel of citizens' influence on decision-making has been emphasized.

At the present time, an integrated act on impact assessment procedure is lacking. In the sectoral system of decision-making, environmental impacts are naturally assessed as a part of the permit evaluation process, e.g. according to the Water Act and the Environmental Permit Procedure Act. This assessment is, however, only directed to one environmental sector, and no other options or alternative ways of projecting are provided for. The assessment that is made late, as a part of the permit procedure, cannot serve as to remedy the project planning, as the EIA procedure is supposed to.

The EEA Treaty imposes an obligation on Finland to implement the EIA Directive. A commission that was set up to propose such rules completed its work on summer 1992. It proposed the enactment of special legislation on EIA procedure. The complexity of the proposed procedure, the relation of this procedure to existing sectoral permit systems, and the great number of projects that should undergo an EIA have raised critical discussion. On the basis of the proposal, a draft bill was prepared in April 1993, but the Government has not yet passed it to the Parliament.

According to the draft the EIA procedure should be obligatory in all projects or installations specifically listed in a Decree that may have significant environmental impacts. The Ministry of the Environment is to decide on a case-by-case basis whether the procedure shall be applied also to a project, whose environmental impacts are likely to be significant, taking into account the project's location and its impacts on important natural and cultural values, vulnerable objects and human health, living conditions and comfort, as well as the extent of the impact area of the project and the potential cumulative effects of the project and other installations on the environment.

> The project list of the draft decree includes 18 sections, dealing with among others, oil refineries, power plants with a capacity of over 300 megawatt, significant plants for management of hazardous waste, paper mills, motorways, railroads and airports for heavy traffic, pipelines for natural gas etc., certain waterways, significant dams, man-made lakes and water-level regulations, large and permanent drainage and deforestation projects, and nuclear power plants.

Environmental impacts shall be assessed before environmentally essential measures are taken to complete the project. In any case, an impact statement shall be at hand before the project is approved, e.g. prior to a permit decision. The developer is in charge of initiating the assessment procedure. The developer shall deliver to the liaison authority an *assessment programme*, i.e. a plan about reports, information etc. needed and about organization the assessment procedure.

If necessary, the liaison authority suggests adjustments in the programme to the developer. At the same time, the hearing procedure is co-ordinated with the party hearings according to the various permit procedures required by the project. On the basis of the assessment programme the developer shall clarify environmental impacts of the project and its alternatives. The results of the assessment are recorded in the *environmental impact statement*, which shall be delivered to the liaison authority. The statement includes information about the project and its alternatives and an integrated assessment of their environmental impacts.

The impact statement will be made available in the area in question, and opinions of the relevant authorities will be solicited. A public hearing may be arranged, as well. Hearings may also be held in connection with procedures contained in other acts, such as the Water Act. The liaison authority gives its opinion about the statement, and asks for other opinions and viewpoints. The assessment procedure is completed when the authority delivers all the material to the developer and to the authorities overseeing the project.

The EIA procedure is a method for gathering information and viewpoints. During the procedure no legally binding decisions on the project will be made, but its goal is to have an effect on the project planning. On the basis of the procedure the developer is able to make necessary changes on the plan and, hence, to avoid conflicts with the inhabitants of the affected area. The results of the assessment have, naturally, an effect on decision-making. A permit may not be granted or a corresponding decision may not be made, unless the relevant authority has received the impact statement and the opinion of the liaison authority. The authority shall indicate how the assessment has been taken into account in the permit decision.

4. Regulation of the Use of Natural Resources

4.1 Nature Conservation

The protection of nature is regulated in the Nature Conservation Act (1923). Need to reform the Act has long been recognized, but the amendments have been limited to partial adjustments. The Act includes rules about *conservation areas*, as well about the *protection of the habitats of endangered species*. Procedures on establishing nature conservation areas vary, depending on whether the relevant area is state-owned or belongs to another owner ("private owners", which would mean in this context, in addition to private landowners also municipalities, the Church and different associations).

On *state-owned land* either a *general* or a *special conservation area* may be established. A general conservation area is preserved in an entirely natural condition. A special conservation area, in contrast, is designated to preserve an area of outstanding natural beauty or otherwise significant natural properties or to protect an animal or a plant species. The decision to establish a conservation area of special significance is made through a special act of Parliament, in other cases by a decree. General conservation areas established by an act are called natural parks. A national park is a special conservation area established through an act.

> A commission has proposed the Nature Conservation Act to be amended by the addition of a rule about the aims of the Act. The purpose of the Act would be, to protect biological diversity, to protect and preserve species and natural areas, and to promote the care for natural beauty and to support the research of nature. A conservation area should fulfil the preconditions of representativeness, typicality or valuableness (presence of rare animals or plants, natural beauty, unusual traditional milieus etc.). These rules would specify and modernize the present regulation, but no change of principle would occur.

A special conservation area can be established by the decision of the Provincial Office on *privately owned land* if the area is exceptionally remarkable from the point of view of nature conservation. This kind of a decision presupposes an application from the landowner; a conservation area cannot be established by compulsory means on a private land (cf. about expropriation below). The landowner is entitled to compensation because of the restrictions on the freedom of use. The reduction of value of the area is not compensated, however.

The conservation programmes approved by the Council of State (see 3.2 above) cover a great deal of privately owned land, too. If under the Nature Conservation Act a conservation area is intended to be established on that kind of an area (e.g., the Esker Protection Programme is implemented in the permit procedure according to the Soil Excavation Act; see 4.2 below), the area must be purchased by the State or the landowner should be persuaded to apply for the special conservation area. The area can be purchased either voluntarily (by buying or exchanging) or compulsorily (expropriation). The State has right to expropriate real estates or specific rights to meet the public need for conservation, paying full compensation.

The purchase of land by the State is often a burdensome and, at the same time, a costly means to protect nature. Increasing international and national stress on the preservation of biodiversity presupposes an integrated survey of the enactments protecting nature (e.g. protection safeguarded by general or particular restrictions of land use, a more effective system of protecting nature in the decision-making concerning nature altering projects).

Endangered species can be protected either by banning the harm or removal of individual plants or animals or by protecting their habitats. A proper biotope protection regulation is not included in the Nature Conservation Act, but a special conservation area can, as mentioned above, be established in order to protect species. A great number of birds and some mammals are expressly protected in the Act. In addition, based on the Act, a species of animals or plants may be protected by decree, if its existence is endangered. The hunting of game animals – in Finland the largest beasts of prey, such as the bear and the wolf, are regarded as game animals – is regulated in the Hunting Act. Nature conservationists have been critical of the rules concerning protection of game animals, based on the Hunting Act. The Act, which has now been revised, is administered by the Ministry of Agriculture and Forestry, not by the Ministry of the Environment.

A kind of an intermediate form between the protection of species and area-based preservation is represented by the rules concerning the protection of endangered or specially protected species. The Council of State may declare an endangered species or a population to be specially protected if the threat of extinction is evident. Where necessary, the Ministry of the Environment is obliged to make a plan to protect the habitats of the species. The Provincial Office shall, if a plan has been made, inform landowners about the existence of specially protected species on their properties and about activities endangering the presence of the species. Hence, the landowner is obliged to inform the authorities of any activies which might endanger the presence of the species. Having received the notice, the Provincial Office shall negotiate with the owner about the protection. Alternatives to protect the habitat are, e.g., the purchase of the property by the State, the landowner's refraining from some activities, temporary prohibition of land use which could endanger the protection or expropriation.

Natural monuments are individual, extraordinary natural objects, such as trees, glacial potholes and large separate rock formations. On state-owned land the authority in charge of the area may protect a monument which is significant because of its peculiar character or of its scientific importance. On other areas the decision is made by the municipality in question.

4.2 Soil Excavation

Soil excavation is regulated in two parallel acts that are mutually exclusive on the basis of areal criteria. Excavation on certain areas for which *detailed planning exists* or for which a *building prohibition* has been issued is covered by the provisions of section 124 a of the Building Act, including a ban on excavation, quarrying, ground levelling, earth filling, cutting of trees and similar activities that alter the landscape, without a permit ("activity prohibition"). *Elsewhere* soil – stone, gravel, sand, mould, clay, but not peat – excavation is regulated in the Soil Excavation Act. As far as soil excavation activities are concerned, the rules of the Soil Excavation Act and the Building Act regarding procedures, permit provisions etc. are mostly uniform.

According to the Soil Excavation Act, soil extraction may not damage a beautiful landscape, destroy significant aesthetic values of nature, damage natural formations of special character or have significant or far-reaching detrimental impacts on natural conditions. The preconditions of the permit are thus connected with the protection of landscapes and nature. According to the Building Act an activity permit may not be granted if the drafting or implementation of a plan will be made difficult or hindered, respectively, or if the landscape or the townscape will be spoilt. The permit judgment concentrates on aspects concerning planning and the landscape.

Soil excavation is generally prohibited without *a permit*. Only extraction for ordinary household use (e.g. for building activities or the maintenance of private roads) is allowed without a permit. The purpose of the legislation concerning soil excavation is, above all, to restrict damage to the landscape and ground water pollution caused by large-scale professional and commercial gravel extraction. The competence to grant the permit is vested in municipal authorities. The permit is granted for a fixed time, usually for not more than ten years at a time. In certain cases (involving e.g. a nationally significant area; the State or a municipality etc. as the applicant; or where the effects extend beyond the boundaries of a municipality) the permit decision shall, according to the Soil Excavation Act, be submitted to the Provincial Office for confirmation.

> According to the Soil Excavation Act the permit shall be granted, when a proper extraction plan has been presented and the project does not violate the restrictions prescribed in the Act. *No discretionary powers* are left to the authority: the landowner has right to obtain the permit, if the protection of landscapes and nature is not jeopardized by the project. This was in practice a very important precondition which made it possible to pass the Act according to the normal legislative procedures, without violating the guarantee of ownership in the Constitution.

Through various *permit provisions* the permit authority strives to make sure that the negative effects of the extraction on nature and landscape are minimized. The activity may not cause a near-by settlement or the environment danger or such harm that could be avoided with reasonable cost. The provisions may regulate for example the boundaries of the extraction area, the depth of the excavations (especially in relation to the ground water surface), and the restoration measures, such as landscape management and planting of trees after the activities have been completed.

The supervisory authority may order the excavation to be ceased if it has been undertaken contrary to the rules of the Act or the permit, or without a permit. The permit provisions can be revised or the permit withdrawn if the provisions have been gravely violated, if harmful effects that could not be foreseen have been caused to the environment, settlement or natural conditions, or if false information has been given in the permit application. Naturally, actions contrary to the law may be punished.

4.3 Water Management Projects

The Water Act of 1961, consisting of approximately 500 sections, is the most extensive act in Finland. The Act, which aims at a comprehensive system of water management, provides for various forms of water management and water pollution control, permits as well as damage compensations and expropriation, punishments and the system of authorities and procedures. The Act includes rules of both public and private law. The most important issues handled by the special Water Courts concern permit applications for different projects of water management or construction.

The Act is based on a system of *general bans*: the bans on closing off, altering, and polluting bodies of water (about the ban on polluting see 5.4 below). These bans are complemented by bans on altering and polluting of so-called small water areas and ground water. The general bans define the necessity for a permit. Measures contrary to the bans are prohibited without a permit from the Water Court – a special court of first instance deciding cases according to the Water Act. The ban on polluting ground water is unconditional; not even the Water Court can grant a permit to deviate from this ban.

Constructing in water areas means generally construction of various structures (hydroelectric plants, cables, bridges etc.) in a water area or across it, clearing of or filling of water areas, making a new bed, etc. These projects presuppose, as a rule, a permit if the construction project may violate public or private interests safeguarded by the bans on closing off or altering bodies of water (e.g. damage or harm to a water area owned by somebody else or to somebody's fishing, building or other property, danger of flood, detrimental impacts on water ecology, or danger to health). Common rules concerning construction in water areas are, for the most part, also applied to water-level regulation, lowering the water surface, or water intake.

The construction project shall be carried out in a manner that restricts the other forms of water management as little as possible, not increasing the costs unreasonably (a rule of minimizing the harm, implementing the principle of "manifold use" of the waters). The project may not cause damage or harm that could be avoided to the owner of the water area or the shore, the fish stocks must not be damaged, the project shall not, more than is necessary, hamper boating or timber floating, use of hydroelectric power, fisheries, land drainage or water intake, damage water ecology, impair the suitability of the water area for recreational use, or infringe natural beauty, cultural values or comfort.

There is a rule in the Water Act which provides for *an absolute prohibition on granting a permit* if a threat to public health, substantial and far-reaching ecological changes or essential deterioration in the conditions of local people or economic life would result. This rule has, in practice, been applied extremely seldom.

At any rate, the interests of environmental protection are to be taken into account in applying the most essential *precondition of the permit*, the weighing of interests. If, on one hand, the construction causes more harm than is allowed by the so-called harmlessness precondition that is applied in minor projects only, and, on the other hand, if the project is not required by the public interest, the permit is granted if the benefits from the project are significant compared to damages and inconveniences caused by it. As inconveniences are counted also immaterial environmental and similar effects, taking account of which presupposes, among other things, comparing the utility of the project with its negative effects from the public point of view. Rather unique, on the contrary, is the provision that neither the costs of the project nor the damages that have been agreed with the victims are considered as inconveniences. It is a question of weighing of interests, not of a cost-benefit analysis on a national economic basis.

In Finland water areas are privately owned, which has a remarkable effect on its water law system. In practice, water areas are not usually parcelled out; they belong jointly to a shareholders' association for common areas. Damages caused by a water management project shall be compensated. Compensations may be paid, in addition to the water area owners (and their associations) and shore owners, also, e.g., to professional fishermen, who carry out their trade on the basis of the common right of fishing. Carrying out construction and other projects may presuppose expropriation of land or covering a land area with water and so on. These rights may, under certain conditions, be granted the developer in connection with the permit. In the permit decision damages are provided *ex officio*.

4.4 Road Construction Projects

4.4.1 Public Roads

According to the Public Roads Act (1954) the construction and the maintenance of roads for public traffic is a public function. The construction of a road is based on the road plan approved by the Ministry of Traffic or the road authorities. Before the plan is approved, landowners concerned have to be heard. The decision to construct the road is made on the basis of a valid road plan. After this the State or the municipality is empowered to take possession of the needed road area by invoking the so-called road right. The road right is a permanent right to use the area for road purposes; it is question of a measure similiar to expropriation.

The construction of the road shall be necessary from the public point of view either for long-distance or local traffic. A public need of traffic is thus presupposed. In developing the road net the requirements of settlement, industry and trade shall be taken into account. When locating and constructing the road, the principle of minimizing harm shall be observed: the road shall, as to its direction and width, be constructed so that its purpose is achieved as favourably as possible without causing anybody more damage or harm than is necessary. According to an explicit rule, environmental viewpoints are to be taken into account. Road planning may not contradict land use planning.

4.4.2 Private Roads

The Private Roads Act of 1962 is applied to private roads which may be used also by others besides the owner (i.e. not to roads a property owner constructs in his own area for his own purposes). The constructing and the maintenance of private roads are the responsibility of the association of the shareholders. Constructing a private road serves a private interest, and therefore the road right according to the Act, which is a permanent right to use an other property's area for road purposes, is a servitude by nature.

The prerequisites of the road right are, on one hand, attached to the appropriate use of the dominant real estate, and, on the other hand, to the reasonableness of the harm inflicted to the serving property. The harmful effects of the road shall be minimized and land use planning taken into account in the same way as for locating and constructing public roads. Also an explicit criterium of environmental protection has been set: the road must not be constructed if significant deterioration of nature or decrease of the cultural values of the environment or other comparable violation of the public interest may result.

5. Environmental Protection (Pollution Control)

5.1 The Structure of the System

Finnish legislation concerning pollution control is divided into sectors. Instead of being treated in a unified code of environmental protection, pollution control is regulated separately from the viewpoints of air and water pollution control, noise abatement, waste management and so on.

Air pollution control is mostly vested in the provisions of three acts. The most important is clearly the *Air Pollution Control Act* of 1982, but also the *Public Health Act* (1965) still has relevance, especially concerning health risks caused by atmospheric pollution from small-scale plants. Of minor importance are the nuisance rules in the *Neighbourhood Relations Act* (1920) that regulate the private relations of adjacent real estate owners.

After coming into force the Air Pollution Control Act has narrowed the territory of the two earlier Acts, but, in spite of the recent Noise Abatement Act (1988), see 5.3. below, the Public Health Act and the Neighbourhood Relations Act still have a considerable effect on abating *noise* from stationary sources. The permit decisions both on the basis of the Air Pollution Control Act and the Public Health Act and the Neighbourhood Relations Act are nowadays made in the combined *environmental permit procedure* (see 5.6 below).

5.2 Air Pollution Control

5.2.1 The System of the Air Pollution Control Act

The purpose of the Air Pollution Control Act is to prevent pollution of the air. *Pollution* has been defined as a change of the composition or properties of the air caused by human activity that either directly or indirectly leads to

1) threat to health,
2) significant harm to the functions of the biotic nature,
3) other significant detrimental alteration of the environment,
4) significant economic damage or
5) significant decrease in the quality of life or
6) other comparable violation of public or private interests.

Threat to health may appear as risks to the public health or to vulnerable groups of people or as acute health effects on pollution victims. Significant ecological harm may be seen as, e.g., the death of trees or injuries weakening their growth. Significant economic damage may be caused by the corrosion of materials. Significant decrease in the quality of life is most often caused by emissions of particles or of odourous gases.

The most essential means of air pollution control are the *general guidelines or regulations* issued by the Council of State. Guidelines and regulations may refer, *inter alia*, to maximum limits for the concentration of a substance in the air or in fallout, the maximum limit for the concentration of a substance in an emission or for the maximum amount of a substance in an emission, or the composition of a substance or a product. A general regulation is directly binding (on plant operators, importers of fuel etc.). General guidelines, in turn, direct the decision-making of the environmental permit authorities when they apply the Act. Guidelines serve as a basis for provisions issued to the plant, but they are not binding as such – neither to the plant operators nor the authorities. In practice the impact of the general guidelines on case-by-case decisions is significant.

Guidelines on airquality standards contain standards on maximum concentrations in the air of certain pollutants, viz. sulphur dioxide, particles, nitrogen dioxide and carbon monoxide. The Council of State has as well laid down a large number of general emission guidelines, also some regulations, for the fulfilment of the national air pollution control policy. Most of the guidelines and regulations are based on the work of the governmental sulphur commission, however NO_x-emissions of power production and use of CFC compounds have also been reduced.

The *notification procedure* of the Act has now been incorporated in the environmental permit procedure (5.6 below). The notification system compares functionally to the permit procedure except in one respect: it was possible to start or continue the operation of the plant, even though the notification procedure was still going on. Plants under the notification system (about 20 types of plants) are, e.g., cellulose mills, cement industries, power plants with a capacity over 5 MW, fertilizer factories, stone crushing or asphalt plants which are permanently located or which will exist on one location for at least one year, and plants in which at least one ton per annum of CFC compounds are used for production. The obligation to notify covers some 2,000 plants in Finland.

The obligation to notify is of great importance. The Act is namely rather weak against plants not under this requirement. Binding provisions concerning air pollution control can (in the environmental permit procedure) be issued only to plants that are under the notification duty, in the event that general regulations issued by the Council of State are not applied to the plant in question. The plant operator cannot be forced to observe general guidelines or to fulfil the obligation of reasonable care outside the environmental permit procedure.

Air pollution is not directly prohibited in the Act. The environmental permit can, however, include *specific provisions* (permit provisions) to achieve the acceptable air quality. These provisions are binding to the operator. They may relate to the reduction of emissions, other protection measures concerning emissions, and monitoring of emissions and their impacts. In practice, such specific provisions are often issued concerning the sulphur concentration of industrial fuel oil, the stack height of the plant, and various monitoring and reporting arrangements.

Specific provisions can be included to implement general regulations or guidelines of the Council of State or to prevent apparent pollution of the air. When considering if specific provisions are needed and deciding their contents, the plant operator's *duty to take reasonable measures to prevent air pollution* shall be taken into account. The operator shall also be sufficiently aware of the impacts of the activity on the quality of the air. What is reasonable is decided case-by-case, paying attention, e.g., to characteristics of the target area, impacts of the plant on air quality, technical and economic conditions of air pollution control measures, and the activity's importance to the public interest.

>Both area-based and plant-specific considerations have an effect on the plant operator's duties. General guidelines of the Council of State direct the national air pollution control policy, but these general guidelines cannot take local circumstances into account. The aim of the Act is to achieve or to maintain an acceptable quality of the air. This level is described in air quality standards. In the environmental permit procedure provisions to prevent air pollution can be issued according to the cicumstances. Specific provisions reflect the quality of the air around the plant and the vulnerability of the environment, as well as the technical and economic ramifications of air pollution control measures. The Act does not presuppose that the so-called best available technology is used in all cases, but the provisions for major new plants shall usually be dimensioned on the basis of the best emission reduction or process technology.

5.2.2 The Control System According to the Public Health Act

The Public Health Act is in practice one of the most important environmental acts in Finland. Especially in the 1970's the importance of the so-called location consent system increased substantially, while proper legislation on environmental protection was lacking. The Act contains relatively broad powers to control sanitary nuisances of noise or air pollution caused by stationary plants. The Air Pollution Control Act has, to be sure, diminished the scope of the location consent system in air pollution control. The Public Health Act is at present under reform, but the draft Health Protection Act would not fundamentally deviate from the present Act in questions of noise abatement and air pollution control.

The Act applies solely to prevention of *sanitary nuisances*. It does not extend to issues irrelevant for human health (e.g. the aesthetical damage of a landfill to a landscape, lowering of real estate values). Neither have changes in the stratosphere caused by CFC compounds and their effects on earth been considered as sanitary nuisances.

Plants specified in the Public Health Decree that may cause sanitary nuisance to the environment presuppose in advance an approval of the site of the plant (location consent). The issue of the consent is handled in the environmental permit procedure. The number of plants that require such consent is much greater than of those that should be notified according to the Air Pollution Control Act (maybe 15,000). Location consent is needed, among others, for a mine, cellulose mill, dairy, pig farm for more than 50 pigs, brewery, fertilizer factory, nuclear reactor, fur farm, stone crushing or asphalt plant, and numerous comparable plants which may cause sanitary nuisance by emissions into the air and water and by noise. If the site of the plant is individually reserved in a detailed plan, the consent is not necessary.

Sanitary nuisance caused by trades and industries shall be prevented as far as possible. The site of the plant shall be appropriate from the sanitary viewpoint, taking account of the character of the activity, the neighbouring settlement, the risks of air and water pollution and noise. The permit judgment is guided by the instructions of the national sanitary authorities. The importance of the instructions is great in decisions of administrative permit authorities and also administrative courts, even though the formal legal relevance of these instructions is doubtful. Instructions have been issued about maximum values of noise and air pollutants, air pollution control of minor power plants, and hygienic arrangements of fur farms (including distance from neighbours).

The Act includes, as well, an effective mechanism for supervision. A municipal health board may issue injunctive prescriptions in order to prevent hazards to health or sanitary nuisances to the environment, regardless of whether the plant concerned needs a consent or not. The prescriptions may be issued, even if the provisions of the location consent (or environmental permit) are complied with, if harmful sanitary impacts occur later. A conditional fine etc. renders the prescriptions more effective.

5.2.3 The Nuisance Rules of Neighbourhood Law

The Neighbourhood Relations Act including the *nuisance prohibition rule* is, by its foundations, an act referring to private law, regulating interrelationships of neighbours. Private nuisance ("immission") in the Act means a potentially harmful effect, felt on a real estate, that may be brought about by gas, smoke, soot, odours, vibrations, noise etc. substance or energy moving from one real estate to another. An effect is considered as a (forbidden) nuisance if permanent, unreasonable harm is caused to the neighbour. The harm is not seen as unreasonable, if it is, paying attention to the circumstances, frequent or anticipated (e.g. normal smell from cattle farming in rural areas). Neither is harm that is common under comparable circumstances elsewhere defined unreasonable. Harm caused by a land use which predates the neighbourhood relation is not considered unreasonable, either (*the priority principle*).

The Act contains two parallel systems implementing the nuisance prohibition, a system based on administrative rules and a system based on private law. The decision of a municipal building board to approve the site of the plant in advance is called a *nuisance consent*. Normally the consent decision is nowadays made in the environmental permit procedure. The consent protects the plant operator from the neighbours' *nuisance actions* based on private law. The ordinary court of first instance may not order the operation of a consented plant to be ceased, even though harm exceeding the tolerance level would unexpectedly result. Nevertheless, a neighbour has a claim to have the harm reduced under the tolerance level, and is entitled to compensations for damages.

The aim of the nuisance consent procedure is to confirm the plant's site so that no harm exceeding the tolerance level will result. The intention is not to allow permanent, unreasonable harm, but to prevent such harm in advance. In practice the nuisance consent of a certain plant has, in most cases, materially corresponded to location consent decision of the plant. By virtue of the provisions attached to the location consent it has been considered that no unreasonable harm prohibited in the Neighbourhood Relations Act results.

5.3 Noise Abatement

The Noise Abatement Act followed the tradition of sectoral legislation on environmental protection. The Act attempted to strengthen the status of noise abatement in environmental protection. It includes rules about the cooperation of the authorities, a general obligation to abate noise, and a municipal noise abatement programme. The relevance of the Act in the environmental permit system is small. It does not contain a permit system for stationary plants; noise abatement was, in this respect, left to the Public Health Act and the Neighbourhood Relations Act (about these acts see 5.2.2-3 above).

Noise is defined in the Act as sound or vibrations that may be detrimental to health or significantly diminish the quality of life, or cause significant harm to working. The notion of noise has been concretized in the standards of noise level issued by the Council of State; these guidelines have been differentiated for several types of areas. However, in permit judgments according to the Public Health Act, the previous instructions of the National Board of Health are still used as guidelines. The new standards are more comprehensive than those, but the figures do not substantially deviate from the sanitary instructions.

A noise polluter is obliged to provide for *noise abatement* to a reasonable extent. When implementing this obligation, attention shall be paid to settlement, noise-sensitive areas and activities, local noise levels and the contribution of the activities to it, the relevance of the noise abatement measures on the noise level, and technical and economic conditions for these measures. The rule has only an indirect effect. It is implemented via the general regulations and guidelines of the Council of State.

The Council of State is entitled to issue *general guidelines or regulations* necessary to prevent noise pollution, on acceptable noise levels outdoors and indoors, to reduce noise emissions of devices and vehicles, to prevent the spreading of noise, to promote measures aimed to protect exposed objects, and to prohibit or restrict noisy activities or devices for fixed times.

> The relevance of the general guidelines of the Council of State and the obligation to care for noise abatement is indirect and weak, as is the case with the provisions of the Air Pollution Control Act. These

guidelines and provisions cannot be applied directly in the permit procedure according to the Public Health Act and the Neighbourhood Relations Act. Disobedience of the general regulations, on the contrary, is liable to criminal sanctions.

Noise caused by temporary activities (construction or repair activities, motor races, other sports, entertainment or exhibition occasions) has mostly been left outside the scope of the Public Health Act, as well as of the Neighbourhood Relations Act. In the Noise Abatement Act the noise polluter is obliged to *notify* a municipal environmental board about temporary activities causing particularly disturbing noise. The strength, duration and recurrence of the noise are taken into account when the existence of the obligation to notify is considered. Some acts of emergency and activities of private households (constructing a single-family house) are excluded.

The notification is to be made at least two weeks before the activity takes place. The board has the power to issue the noise polluter reasonable provisions in order to limit the disturbance of the noise. The provisions may include time limits fixed to the activity and orders about positions of noisy device and information to the inhabitants of the neighbourhood, etc.

5.4 Water Pollution Control

Instead of a comprehensive environmental protection act the rules on water pollution control are included in the comprehensive Water Act (see 4.3 above). The ban on polluting bodies of water implies what kind of pollution necessitates the issuance of a permit by the Water Court. A polluting event is defined as the emitting of various substances or energy into waters resulting in a change in the quality of water or bottom that leads to certain detrimental impacts on public or private interests (such as detrimental impact on biotic nature and ecology or apparent damage to fish stocks, danger to health, significant deterioration of the pleasantness of the environment, of cultural values, or of the environment's suitability for water supply or recreation).

> Polluting activities have not been defined in a list of plants, but the necessity of a pollution permit is occassioned by a risk of banned

impacts. The necessity of a permit is defined by material criteria. This fact has given rise to regulate some types of plants which commonly cause risk of pollution in a so-called Water Pollution Control Notification Decree. A notification concerning a listed plant is to be submitted to Water and Environment District Office. The opinion of this authority regarding the conditions under which the activity can take place without violating the ban on polluting waters is in practice very important. The statement does not, however, remove the necessity of a proper pollution permit, and the Water Court may assess the need for anti-pollution measures differently than the above-mentioned supervisory administrative body.

A permit to deviate from the ban on polluting (e.g. an application of an industrial plant or a community to emit effluent water into a body of water) presupposes that the detrimental effects are relatively small as compared with the benefits (weighing of interests). Also a so-called weighing of costs precondition shall apply: it must not be otherwise possible to eliminate the discharge at a reasonable cost. A theoretical ultimate limit for allowing pollution is set in a rule stating an absolute prohibition to grant a permit. A permit shall not be granted if a threat to public health, substantial and far-reaching ecological changes or essential deterioration in the conditions of local people or economic life would result.

As a rule, various provisions (conditions), such as emission limits and different instructions for monitoring and surveillance, are attached to the permit. The damages that can be assessed in advance shall, *ex officio*, be prescribed to be compensated e.g. to professional fishermen and to owners of shores and water areas. The permit decision may include fees as provided for in public law, as well.

5.5 Waste Management

The Waste Management Act regulates generally waste management (collecting, transport and treatment of waste) and its financing. *Waste* is defined as any thing or substance of little or no value that is removed from use. The principles of the Act apply to the recycling and re-use of waste and avoiding harm to the environment of wastes. The Act is being reformed to take better account of the requirements of EC law than the present code. In the draft Waste Act the waste permit would displace the present procedures of approval of the waste management plan and of the hazardous waste processing permit.

When waste from a real estate is not delivered for treatment to a public facility (e.g. a landfill), the owner has a duty to arrange for proper treatment of the waste. If waste of exceptional quality or quantity is either produced or treated on a property, the owner or holder must submit a waste management plan for approval of the authorities. The decisions on these plans are nowadays made in the combined environmental permit procedure (5.6 below). Conditions necessary for waste management, recycling or re-use of waste, or environmental protection can be attached to the approval of the plan. The conditions may refer to collecting, transport, storage and pre-treatment of waste, measures promoting re-use, and monitoring of environmental impacts.

> In practice the number of properties subject to the obligation to submit the plan is great (maybe approximately 20,000). The approving authority can always order the property-holder to submit the plan. The obligation to submit a plan applies to industrial plants, mining, power plants, hospitals, laboratories, pharmacies, depots, waste water treatment plants, and service stations.

The concept *hazardous waste* denotes waste which, due to its toxicity or other properties, is difficult to render harmless, or to handle, or is otherwise especially deleterious to the environment. These wastes were, at one time, defined in a regulation by the Ministry of Interior (now the power is vested in the Ministry of the Environment). As examples of hazardous wastes can be mentioned wastes containing oil, solvents, acids, alkalis, heavy metals, PCB's, pesticides etc.

Treatment of hazardous waste is, with minor exceptions, forbidden without a permit. A *processing permit* may be necessary for many other plants besides those whose express purpose is the treatment of hazardous waste (burning of oil waste to produce heat). The permit decision is made according to the Environmental Permit Procedure Act. The method of processing and the processing site shall, *inter alia*, meet the requirements for environmental protection. Granting the permit presupposes that the activity is considered compatible with the public interest and necessary and expedient for the national development of hazardous waste management.

5.6 Environmental Permit System

Various decisions made pursuant to advance-control procedures, whose intention is to regulate environmentally relevant activities, are widely defined as *environmental permits*. Advance-control systems are, besides permit procedures, various systems presupposing approval of a notification or a plan. The difference between these focuses on the fact that a proper permit is an absolute precondition for putting the activity into operation, while the submitting of a notification or a plan does not prevent the operation. Under the terms of the *Environmental Permit Procedure Act* some former environmental permits were combined in the new environmental permit. The concept "environmental permit" may thus refer to either the wide general denotation or to the concise special denotation stated in the Act.

The *aim* of environmental permits is not to prevent or prohibit activities having an impact on the environment. In the permit judgments an effort is made to make sure in advance that the requirements set in environmental law are observed in the operation of polluting plants. In the permit decision the authority, on the basis of an advance assessment, provides limits for the future operation of a polluting plant. The limits are based on the material rules of the relevant acts etc. On the basis of the application it shall be decided in the procedure whether the activity is acceptable under the applied environmental act. The issuing of permit provisions can guarantee that the preconditions for the permit are fulfilled.

The aim of the Act is to co-ordinate the granting of certain permits etc. based on different acts concerning pollution control, to render supervision more effective, to speed up the permit procedure and to develop a more unified assessment of environmental impacts. A permit granted in the procedure according to the Act is called an environmental permit. The permit comprises the nuisance consent according to the Neighbourhood Relations Act, the location consent according to the Public Health Act, the approval of the operator's notification according to the Air Pollution Control Act, and the approval of the waste management plan and the hazardous waste processing permit according to the Waste Management Act. It is forbidden to start activities without the necessary environmental permit. The notification and planning procedures according to the Air Pollution Control Act and the Waste Management Act respectively were thus included in a permit system.

The permit systems in the Water Act remained untouched. In the Noise Abatement Act there was no permit system that could have been combined with the new procedure. If only the nuisance consent were to be included in the permit, the decision is made, as earlier, in connection with the building permit so that the applicant is able to transact with one authority only.

The Act combined (rather than integrated) some control procedures in a unified process without significantly changing the basics of the system. The criteria applied to determine the necessity of a permit or notification were left as they were before (e.g. the lists of plants in the Public Health Decree and the Air Pollution Control Decree). The Act did not change the material rules concerning the permit jugdments, either. When granting an environmental permit, the authority may apply only those rules according to which the plant in question is under obligation to apply for the environmental permit. If, say, the nuisance consent according to the Neighbourhood Relations Act and the location consent according to the Public Health Act are necessary, the requirements for air pollution control of the plant are set solely on the basis of these acts, not on the basis of the Air Pollution Control Act. The decision is not made on the basis of the Environmental Permit Procedure Act, but according to the procedure stated in the Act, applying the material rules of the relevant sectoral acts.

The permit granting competence is divided between the Provincial Office and a municipal board. A list of plants in the Environmental Permit Procedure Decree points out that some activities of major importance require a permit from the Provincial Office. Other permit applications are decided on the municipal level. In certain cases the municipal environmental permit authority may decline to decide the matter and submit the case to the Provincial Office.

5.7 Compensation for Environmental Damage

Compensation for environmental damage is, on one hand, based on the negligence rules in the general Damages Compensation Act, on the other hand on the strict liability according to the nuisance rules of neighbourhood law. In addition to these, water law and e.g. road construction law have compensation systems of their own.

Parliament is at present discussing a proposal for an Environmental Damages Act. Environmental damage is, according to the bill, personal injury, damage to the property, loss of profit etc. caused by environmental pollution or comparable nuisance, such as noise or radiation, from stationary activities. Losses caused by a nuisance that is fair and reasonable, with regard to the local circumstances and the frequency of the harm, should be tolerated without compensation. The obligation to tolerate would not, however, extend to damages caused intentionally or by crime or to personal injuries or significant damage to property. The starting-point is compatible with the principles of traditional neighbourhood law.

The liability for environmental damage would be strict, i.e. not dependent on negligence. The bill has not embraced the so-called principle of the reverse burden of proof, but from the victim's side sufficient evidence would be sufficient to show a probable causal link between the damage and the activity. The responsibility for the damage would be collective. This rule would still not remedy the problems of compensations attached to pollution damages caused by emissions from unidentifiable sources (e.g. long-range transboundary effects of air pollutants, diffuse loading). In these cases the compensation can probably be obtained only by using secondary arrangements, such as funds or insurance.

5.8 The Impacts of EC Rules on Finnish Environmental Law

Finland has signed the Treaty of European Economic Area. When it comes into force, the environmental EC directives specified in annex XX of the Treaty shall be implemented. Finland has also applied for the membership in the EC; negotiations are in progress. Also the European Council Convention on Human Rights, the articles of which have relevance e.g. in dealing with some environmental cases, has been ratified by Finland.

The pressure created by the Community law to change our environmental legislation is relatively weak. The general material level of the legislation is quite compatible with the European standard. Nevertheless, it is necessary to complete this legislation with rules concerning environmental impact assessment in order to implement the EC directive in question. Drafting of a special act has progressed far (3.3 above).

The EC regulation concerning air pollution control does not necessitate a profound revision of the Finnish legislation. Some details may be changed, however (e.g. supplementing the air quality standards and apparently giving a legally binding status to them).

In water pollution control the necessity of change is greater. The Water Act is based totally on the case-by-case system of decision-making, while EC law employs general regulations concerning certain emissions and plant types. For this reason the Act has been amended with rules which empower the Council of State to issue general regulations to implement some EC directives. These regulations apply within the water law permit system as minimum standards of the level of material requirements. These two systems do not fundamentally contradict with each other, because EC regulation presupposes in many cases the existence of a permit system to guarantee in advance that the requirements are met (both the framework directives on air pollution control and water pollution control).

The Waste Management Act dating back to 1978 is under reform, partly to implement the EC requirements. The proposed Waste Act would be based on the principles of recycling, re-use and the use of best available technology; it would extend the producer's liability over the entire life-cycle of the product. The bill includes relatively broad powers to issue administrative regulations.

The Chemicals Act, which entered into force in September 1990, aims to prevent health and environmental hazards caused by chemicals. The Act requires that the operators etc. exercise reasonable care and be sufficiently aware of the impacts of chemicals, paying attention to the amount and dangerousness of the chemicals and the circumstances of their treatment. Industrial treatment and storing of chemicals dangerous to health or environment is subject to the issuance of a permit or to proper notification, minor cases excluded. The Act has been recently revised in order to adjust it to the EC regulation.

The structure of the environmental permit system would be significantly influenced by an EC Directive on Integrated Pollution Prevention and

Control (IPC Draft Directive). Its purpose would be to minimize emissions from industrial installations, so as to achieve the highest practicable level of protection for the environment as a whole; it should prevent "solving" the pollution problem by transferring it from one environmental medium to another (e.g. transforming by technical means an emission into the air to a water pollution problem). The directive would enter into force on 1 July 1995.

Plants specified in the annex should not be operated without a permit issued in accordance with the directive. It may be a permit granted by a single competent authority or a permit granted on behalf of all competent authorities. Sectoral permit systems regulating a plant's operation woul not necessarily be unified, but in order to facilitate an integrated approach the member states should – if one agency is not a competent authority alone – identify a lead competent authority to co-ordinate the permit procedures. Any permit granted should describe how the integrated environmental protection considerations of air, water and land have been taken into account.

The IPC directive would presuppose more extensive co-ordination also in the Finnish environmental permit system. The permit system concerning water pollution control and decision-making according to the Environmental Permit Procedure Act should be combined, at least procedurally. A step from procedural co-ordination towards Scandinavian-style, unified legislation on environmental protection might still be rather long. The Directive would not presuppose a comprehensive code, but the permit procedures would be co-ordinated. The gap between the Water Courts model based on judicial decision-making and an administrative-based environmental permit model may furthermore be too wide.

Bibliographical Essay

Books about Finnish environmental law are, unfortunately, almost exclusively written in Finnish. A extremely valuable exception is a thorough general survey by *Pekka Vihervuori*: Environmental Law – Suppl. 3 – Finland (Kluwer Law and Taxation Publishers, Deventer – Boston, 1992, 185 pp), published autumn 1992.

A comprehensive outline of Finnish environmental law is provided by *Erkki J. Hollo* in his large book "Ympäristöoikeus" (Environmental Law) (Jyväskylä 1991). The number of monographs and general surveys of different sectors of environmental law during the years has been rather large; nature conservation law is an unfortunate exception.

From the sector of real estate and land law can be mentioned "Kiinteistönmuodostamisoikeus" (Vammala 1974) by *Jorma Pietilä*, not quite of current interest, "Kiinteistöjärjestelmä ja kiinteistönmuodostamisoikeus" (Jyväskylä 1982) by *Veikko O. Hyvönen* and "Erityinen kiinteistöoikeus" (Vammala 1984) concerning, *inter alia*, expropriative measures according to various acts, by *Hollo*.

Extensive textbooks and handbooks on planning and building law are "Kaavoitus- ja rakentamisoikeus" (Jyväskylä 1988) by *Hyvönen*, a commentary of the caselaw based on the Building Act ("Rakennuslaki ja oikeuskäytäntö", Jyväskylä 1989), edited by *Erkki J. Hollo* and *Kari Kuusiniemi*, and the fourth printing of the Building Act commentary by *Otto Larma et al.* ("Rakennuslaki ja -asetus", Jyväskylä 1992). Besides these, a study on the system of exceptional permits contained in the Building Act, "Oikeudesta rakentaa poikkeusluvalla" (Vammala 1981) by *Vesa Majamaa*, should not be forgotten.

A general outline on water law can still be found in *Pietilä's* Water Law ("Vesioikeus", Vammala 1979), even though time has partly passed by the book. A comprehensive monograph about drainage and related projects according to the Water Act is *Vihervuori*: "Vesistön järjestelyn ja ojituksen oikeuskysymykset" (Jyväskylä 1987). Water law has over the course of years proved a favourite topic of doctoral theses on environmental law, e.g. *Hollo's* "Pilaamiskiellon sisältö vesilain mukaan" (Vammala 1976) about water pollution control, *Vihervuori's* monograph on the standing of administrative authorities in the permit procedures at the Water Courts ("Viranomaisen asianosaispuhevallasta vesilain mukaan", Vammala 1981), *Antti Jokela's* "Vesioikeuden ja yleisen alioikeuden asiallisesta toimivallasta" (Vammala 1983) about procedure in water cases, *Matti V. Repo's* thesis about timber floating ("Oikeudesta uittaa puutavaraa", Vammala 1990) and *Hannele Pokka's* "Rakennettujen vesistöjen jälkivalvontajärjestelmät" (Vammala 1991), concerning certain control systems of water construction projects.

Other studies about environmental management are, e.g., a large monograph by *Vihervuori* about soil excavation ("Maa-ainesten ottaminen ja suojelu", Jyväskylä 1989) and *Kyösti Holma's* thesis about road constructing law ("Tieoikeudesta yleiseen tiehen", Vammala 1982).

The research tradition on pollution control law is, if Hollo's above-mentioned thesis is not counted, rather young. In the 1990's two doctoral theses have been published, viz. "Terveydenhoidollinen sijoituslupa" (Tampere 1990) about sanitary nuisances by *Veijo Tarukannel* and "Ympäristönsuojelu ja immissioajattelu" (Jyväskylä 1992), which is concentrated on legal issues of air pollution control and noise abatement, by *Kuusiniemi*. Of the books dealing with environmental permit systems may be mentioned *Olli Mäenpää's* "Hallintolupa" (Vammala 1992, second edition), a book on administrative permits, consents etc. in general, and *Kuusiniemi's* study on interrelationships between different permit systems "Rakentamiseen tarvittavien lupien keskinäisistä suhteista" (Helsinki 1985).

XI TAX LAW

By Timo Viherkenttä

1. Introduction

The Finnish tax system is composed of a large number of taxes and levies, the principal of which being those levied on income and on consumption.[1] The major income taxes are the state (national) income tax, the municipal tax and the corporate income tax. The turnover tax, which has been the principal consumption tax throughout the post-war period, is to be replaced with a value-added tax in 1994. Consumption taxes are state taxes. Apart from the taxes which are levied by the state and the municipalities, taxes and similar contributions are paid to the National Pension Institution as well as to the Evangelical-Lutheran Church and the Orthodox Church.

In international comparisons, the Finnish tax structure is characterised by the high share of revenue which accrues from income taxes and consumption taxes. By contrast, public revenue raised from social security contributions has been relatively low in comparison to most OECD countries as a consequence of the structure and pattern of financing of the social security system. One feature of this system is that the private sector compulsory pension scheme is run by privately owned pension corporations, and the compulsory premiums paid to those corporations have not usually been classified as taxes.

The general level of taxation in Finland has been close to the OECD average when calculated with reference to gross national product. In 1991, the ratio of taxes to GNP was 37.7 per cent in Finland compared to the 1990 figure of 38.8 per cent in the OECD. If, however, the compulsory pension contributions are included, the 1991 tax ratio in Finland rises to 43.4 per cent. In comparison to other Nordic countries, the gross tax ratio has been rather low in Finland.

According to the Finnish Constitution, taxes may be imposed only by law. Until 1992, the imposition of new or increased taxes for more than one year required a two-thirds majority vote in Parliament. On several occasions, this requirement led to the unsatisfactory state of affairs whereby major tax reforms were enacted on a year-by-year basis until they gained enough support. Now the constitutional rule has been repealed and, from September 1992 on, tax laws can be passed by a simple majority decision in Parliament.

2. Income Taxation

2.1 Background and General Structure

Income taxes have been imposed in Finland without interruption since 1920. During this time, the income tax system has been subject to a number of substantial reforms, not to speak of annual minor modifications. The reforms have often included the adaptation of models found in other countries. In this respect, the Scandinavian, in particular the Swedish, model has been a dominant influence.[2]

In the 1980s, Finland participated in the worldwide tax reform movement with a new policy direction towards broader tax bases and lower rates. This turning point in tax thinking, which was initiated in the United Kingdom and the United States, was incorporated into Finnish tax laws in 1988. In the beginning of the 1990s, this development was followed by the adoption of the newly created *Nordic model* of income taxation, which involved a still more fundamental structural change in the income tax system.[3] Income tax laws based on this model came into force in 1993. The following presentation of the Finnish income taxation is based on this legislation.

The Nordic model of income taxation was adopted first in Sweden where it took effect in 1991. Norway followed suit a year later, and thus Finland was the third country to introduce this kind of tax system. Denmark actually took the first steps in this direction in its tax reform of 1987 but, unlike its Scandinavian neighbours, it did not fully implement the Nordic model.

The three crucial elements of the Nordic model are: 1) a sharp *distinction between capital income and earned income,* and 2) a relatively low *proportional tax on capital income* and 3) a *progressive tax on earned income.* A further element of the model is that the tax value of deductions in capital income taxation, including *interest,* is determined by the capital income tax rate. And finally, in all three countries *the capital income tax rate equals the corporate tax rate.*

There were several reasons for the adoption of the diffentiated income tax structure in Finland. Although the tax reforms in the neighbouring countries clearly served as models, there were strong domestic economic rationales behind the reform. In particular, the low uniform tax rate on capital income has eliminated the alleged needs for various tax preferences for different kinds of income, and thereby substantially increased neutrality in capital income taxation. The low nominal tax rate is also believed to be a strong element in the tax system from the point of view of international competitiveness, perhaps in particular with respect to company taxation. A further advantage of the structure is that opportunities to carry out tax arbitrage are relatively limited in a system where items of income and deductions are dealt with in a symmetrical way. Moreover, the reduction in the tax benefits associated with borrowing is also believed to have a positive impact on the economy.

It is a characteristic feature of the Nordic model that the flat tax rate on capital income is significantly lower than the rates at the upper end of the progressive tax schedule. In Finland, this gap is particularly wide. In 1993, which was the first year the system was applied, the difference was at worst almost 40 percentage points. This is indeed the weak point of the Nordic model in general and the Finnish version in particular.

In Finland, the tax rate for capital income and for corporate income was set at *25 per cent*. This rate is lower than the 30 per cent adopted in Sweden two years earlier and the 28 per cent rate which took effect in Norway one year prior to the Finnish reform. International tax competition was one of the driving forces behind the reforms, and it is hardly a coincidence that first Norway and then Finland lowered their tax rates further than their neighbours had done.

It is complicated to make international comparisons with respect to the tax rates on capital income because of the differences in the tax systems in various countries. As regards the company tax rates, comparisons are easier (of course taking into account the substantial differences in the tax bases). When adopted, Finland's 25 per cent rate was *the lowest general corporate tax rate in the OECD*, although lower rates could be found, e.g., in certain cantons in Switzerland and for qualifying industries in Ireland.

In personal taxation, the operation of the differentiated tax model requires that two taxable incomes are computed for individuals: the *taxable capital income* and the *taxable earned income*. The taxable capital income is then subject to the 25 per cent tax whereas earned income is subject to various taxes and levies, some of which are progressive. This dichotomy is alleviated by a system whereby a *deficit* of capital income, i.e. the excess of deductions over income, can be utilized to offset taxes on earned income (section 2.2.5 below).

The following table presents the general structure of the Finnish individual income taxation. The various items included in the table are discussed in more detail in later subsections.

Earned income	Capital income
+ wages and salaries	+ interest
+ fringe benefits	+ rents
+ pensions	+ proceeds from timber sales
+ social transfers	+ capital gains
+ earned income share of dividends and business and farming income	+ capital income share of dividends and business and farming income
+ imputation credit	+ imputation credit
+ etc.	+ etc.
– deductions for acquiring earned income	– deductions for acquiring capital income
– social deductions	– interest deduction
Taxable earned income	Taxable capital income
Taxes 0–63 %	Tax 25 %
– imputation credit	– imputation credit
– 25 % of the deficit of capital income	If deficit, 25 % credited against taxes on earned income

392

2.2 Capital Income

2.2.1 General Aspects

The capital income of individuals is subject to a 25 per cent tax which goes to the state. Because the tax is considerably lower than the taxes and levies payable on earned income, it is important that the distinction between capital and earned income is clear.

The Income Tax Act of 1992 divides all taxable income of individuals into capital income and earned income. The legislative technique is to define (in rather general terms) capital income and treat all other income as earned income. The 1992 act defines capital income by enumerating a number of typical items of capital income and by classifying as capital income all income produced by capital assets. Items of capital income include, *inter alia*, interest, dividends from a company listed on a stock exchange, rents, the proceeds from timber sales, the yield on certain insurance investments and capital gains. A further item is the capital income share of dividends or of partnership, business or farming income (section 2.5.2 below). Imputed income from owner-occupied housing was taxed in Finland for decades until this form of taxation was replaced with a *property tax* beginning in 1993 (section 3 below).

2.2.2 Interest

Traditionally, interest income has been particularly important in Finland, not least because of its long-standing preferential tax treatment. Interest on bank deposits and various bonds had been tax-exempt for individuals for most of the post-war period, and it was not until 1991 that a considerable share of interest income became subject to taxation. At that time, *a final source tax* of 10 per cent was imposed on individuals' interest income from bank deposits and bonds.

Since then, the source tax has been raised more rapidly than was expected at the outset. The tax was 15 per cent in 1992 and 20 per cent in 1993. In 1994, the tax on interest is due to reach the general capital income tax rate of 25 per cent.

The world of tax-exempt interest has not fully ended, however. An exemption is still granted on interest from qualifying 24-month and 36-month bank deposits. These rules are transitional but it may be noted that exemptions for such interest have several times been extended for a few years "one more time". These exemptions may benefit certain banks rather than those small savers whose primary role has been to justify the tax breaks.

2.2.3 Dividends

The differences between the tax treatment of interest on the one hand and dividends on the other has traditionally played an important role in the debate over Finnish tax policy. Until 1989, the double taxation of distributed corporate income was alleviated both from the point of view of both the distributing company and the dividend recipient. The result was a system where the tax burden varied strongly with little apparent economic justification.

As of 1990, a system of *full imputation* has been applied to dividend distributions. In this system, the tax paid by the company on the distributed profit is fully credited to resident shareholders. In order to make sure that the credit is only given for taxes actually paid, a *compensatory tax* is payable by the distributing company if dividends are distributed out of profits which have not been fully taxed.

Prior to 1993, dividends were subject to progressive taxation, and the marginal tax rates could well exceed 60 per cent. For this reason, the tax burden on dividends was relatively high in spite of the fact that double taxation was eliminated. In comparison to the 15 per cent tax burden on interest in 1992, the tax treatment of dividends was believed to discriminate too heavily against the equity financing of companies.

The imputation system was preserved in the tax reform of 1992 but its economic character changed radically as a result of the introduction of the 25 per cent tax rate for capital income and for corporate income. From 1993 on, dividends received by investors are, as a main rule, subject to the general 25 per cent capital income tax. However, because the creditable company tax paid on distributed profits is also 25 per cent, the result in the standard situation is the same *as if the dividend were tax exempt*. Technically, the system operates so that shareholders must include in their taxable income both the dividend and an imputation credit equal to 1/3 of the dividend. The amount of the credit is then used against the tax payable. This can be illustrated as follows:

COMPANY LEVEL
Profit before taxes	100
Company tax	(25)
Distributed profit	75

SHAREHOLDER LEVEL
Dividend	75
Credit for company tax	25
Taxable income	100
Tentative tax	25
Credit for company tax	(25)
Tax payable	–

The overall tax burden of 25 per cent of distributed corporate income is exceptionally low in international comparisons. When this regime took effect in 1993, no other OECD country could offer its investors equally or more favourable dividend taxation rules in a standard situation. The treatment of foreign investors is dealt with in section 2.6 below.

The dividend tax system described above is fully applicable only in the case of dividends distributed by companies listed on a stock exchange. In other instances, dividends may be partly or fully taxed as earned income under the rules described in section 2.5.2 below.

2.2.4 Capital Gains and Losses

Capital gains enjoyed substantial tax preferences until 1992. As a base-broadening element of the 1992 tax reform, the capital gains tax breaks were strongly curtailed. As a main rule, capital gains are, from 1993 on, fully taxable as capital income and thereby subject to the 25 per cent tax rate.

In general, the full nominal amount of the gain is included in the taxable capital income. However, there are rules which limit the taxable gain by replacing the actual acquisition cost with a higher deemed basis in cases where the actual cost is small. In such cases, instead of deducting the actual acquisition cost, taxpayers are allowed to deduct 30 per cent from the sales proceeds. In the case of property acquired prior to 1989, this presumed cost is 50 per cent, and when real estate is sold to the state or to a municipality, as much as 80 per cent. With the tax rate of 25 per cent, the minimum basis of 30 per cent means that the tax cannot exceed 17.5 per cent of the sale proceeds.

There are also a number of fully tax-exempt capital gains. The most important of these are gains from the sale of a permanent residence. Gains on the sale of farms and companies to the next of kin are also substantially tax-exempt.

Capital losses may only be deducted from capital gains arising in the same year or in the three following years.

2.2.5 Interest Expenses

In a system where different tax rates are applicable to earned income and capital income, deductions must be appropriately allocated to those two categories. In particular, costs for acquiring income obviously have to be deducted in the proper category. The most complicated problems in the area of deductions are generated by interest expenses, primarily because of their mixed character. Loans are used for various purposes, only some of which would appear to justify an interest deduction, but no satisfactory pattern of earmarking the money used by the taxpayers can be found.

In Finland as well as in other Nordic countries, interest deductions have traditionally been one of the major means for taxpayers to reduce their tax bills. This was often rewarding whenever interest was being deducted from income which was subject to very high marginal tax rates. Particular benefits could be reaped in connection with leveraged investments where interest could be deducted while the yield on the investment was received in the form of tax-exempt or lightly taxed items such as capital gains.

This arbitrage, as well as other tax benefits which used to be attached to high leveraging, is counteracted in the post-1992 tax system by the principle that *interest costs are deducted from capital income*. In general, this means that the tax value of the interest deduction is determined by the 25 per cent capital income tax rate so that taxpayers carry three quarters of their interest cost. In comparison to the earlier system where the fisc paid anything up to a half of taxpayers' interest cost, the new system clearly serves to discourage borrowing.

In the drafting of the legislation, it was thought that the relatively low tax value of the interest deduction does enough to limit the amount of the benefit even where the loans are used for purposes which would not actually merit a tax deduction. The idea was to free the tax authorities from the desperate task of differentiating between items of interest with regard to the use of each loan. This line of reasoning, however, upset the moral sensibilities of the members of Parliament, who blamed the Government for equating a high-speed motorboat with the necessary shelter of a family. The result was that interest expenses are divided into a number of categories determined by the use of the corresponding loan. In general, interest paid on loans used for the purchase of permanent residence or for income-generating purposes is deductible, whereas interest paid on consumption loans is not.

In particular because a large number of taxpayers have loans which are used for the purchase of residence while only a relatively small number of taxpayers have substantial capital income, it is common that taxable capital income is negative. If there were no opportunities to use this deficit in the taxation of earned income, only taxpayers with capital income could actually obtain a tax reduction based on their home loan interest. This would hardly be socially acceptable. This effect is eliminated through a credit which is based on the deficit of capital income but which is allowed against taxes payable on earned income.

The credit against earned income taxes is determined by the tax rate on capital income and is thereby 25 per cent of the deficit of capital income. However, to the extent that the deficit stems from interest paid on a loan used to purchase the taxpayer's *first permanent residence*, the credit is 30 per cent. There are also upper limits for the credit; in 1993, the ceiling was FIM 8 000[1]

---

1 FIM 6,60 = 1 ECU (22.7.1993).

(corresponding usually to a deficit of FIM 32 000) for a single taxpayer and FIM 20 000 for a family of four or more. The possible excess of the deficit can be carried forward and deducted from capital income in the following 10 years.

2.3 Earned Income

The greater portion of taxable income in the economy consists of earned income, the most important of which are salaries, wages, pensions and various social transfers. Dividends, partnership income and income from business or agriculture are divided into earned income and capital income according to certain, partially schematic rules (section 2.5.2 below). The calculation of a taxpayer's taxable earned income includes the adding up of his/her various kinds of earned income and subtracting the allowable deductions from the sum.

Taxable earned income of employees includes, apart from wages and salaries, the value of fringe benefits such as cars and luncheon vouchers. The valuation of most common fringe benefits is done on a schematic basis which has been gradually tightened but, which still usually leads to some degree of undervaluation. Certain fringe benefits, including health care provided by the employer and moderate personnel rebates, are tax-exempt.

Allowable deductions include, of course, expenses of acquiring income. As a presumptive deduction for such expenses, employees are allowed to deduct 3 per cent of their taxable wages and salaries up to a maximum of FIM 2 100. Allowable deductions in the taxation of earned income also include various socially motivated items. These include, *inter alia,* a pension income allowance, a disabled person's allowance and an allowance due to reduced taxpaying ability. It is note-worthy that deductions based on a taxpayer's personal circumstances are only made in the taxation of earned income, and they are thus not available to taxpayers with only capital income. There are only minor differences in the calculation of taxable earned income in state taxation and in municipal taxation. Although the municipalities decide on the municipal tax rates, they do not have any discretion over the determination of the taxable income.

Credits against taxes have formerly been of minor significance in Finland, but the situation is different from 1993 on due to the credit based on the deficit of capital income. As noted in section 2.2.5 above, this credit against taxes payable on earned income is an important element in the system because it is common that taxable capital income is negative.

An important deduction is based on pension insurance contributions. Apart from the compulsory contributions, which are 3 per cent of gross income for employees, voluntary contributions are mostly deductible too, although the deduction was cautiously limited in the 1992 tax reform. The deduction of voluntary pension premiums is a useful tax planning device because it may create opportunities to 1) postpone taxable income; 2) realise taxable income in a year with lower income and thereby a lower marginal tax; or 3) deduct the premiums in the taxation of the spouse with a high marginal tax rate and channel the pension to the low-taxed spouse.

2.4 Taxes Payable

The calculation of taxable income is conducted separately for each individual, including each family member, although there are certain interconnections in the taxation of family members. Until the 1992 tax reform, the tax on capital income of children was computed with consideration given to the income of the parents; as of 1993 the adoption of the system of proportional taxation of capital income has rendered this mechanism useless.

Earned income is subject to a number of taxes and levies. The most important of these are the progressive state income tax and the all-but-proportional municipal income tax. A *national pension insurance contribution* and a *sickness insurance contribution* as well as the *church tax* are also based on the taxable earned income as calculated for the purpose of the municipal income tax. The church tax is payable by members of the Evangelical-Lutheran and Orthodox Churches. The majority of the Finnish population belongs to the Evangelical-Lutheran Church and is thereby liable to pay the church tax. In a way, however, the church tax is a voluntary tax since only members of the above-mentioned churches are liable to pay it.

In 1993, two new levies based on gross wages and salaries were introduced. In 1993, the new *employee's pension premium* was 3 per cent and the *unemployment insurance premium* was 0.2 per cent; however, the latter is due to be raised to 1.87 per cent in 1994. These levies are tax deductible.

The state income tax schedule has usually been adjusted annually linked to inflation. But, as a consequence of the heavy deficit in the state budget, the schedule remained unchanged in the tax years of 1991 to 1993. This was the case in spite of the 1993 change whereby earned income alone is subject to the schedule. The state tax schedule for the period 1991-93 has been as follows (FIM):

Taxable income	Tax on lower amount	Tax on excess (%)
40 000– 56 000	50	7
56 000– 70 000	1 170	17
70 000– 98 000	3 550	21
98 000–154 000	9 430	27
154 000–275 000	24 550	33
275 000–	64 480	39

In 1993, the municipal tax rate varied among municipalities between 14.5 and 20 per cent. The church tax rate was most commonly 1 to 1.5 per cent. The national pension premium was 1.8 per cent and the sickness insurance premium 1.9 per cent of taxable income up to FIM 80,000 and 3.4 per cent of the excess. None of these levies is deductible in the computation of taxable income.

The tax calculation for 1993 of an individual living in Helsinki could look like this (FIM):

Earned Income

Salaries	200 000
Compulsory pension premium	– 6 000
Unemployment insurance premium	– 400
Deduction for presumptive expenses	– 2 100
Taxable earned income	191 500
– state tax	– 36 925
– municipal tax 16 %	– 30 640
– church tax 1 %	– 1 950

– national insurance contribution   – 3 447
– sickness insurance contribution   – 5 231

Capital Income
Capital gains   50 000
Interest expenses   – 30 000

Taxable capital income   20 000
– tax 25 %   – 5 000

2.5 Business Taxation

2.5.1 The Calculation of Business Income

Taxable business income is computed according to the Business Income Tax Act of 1968. Business income includes income from trade and profession. The Business Income Tax Act is applied to private firms and partnerships as well as to limited companies and co-operatives. Partnerships and corporations as well as individuals can also carry out activities which are *not* classified as business and which are therefore dealt with under the Income Tax Act.

In business taxation, the concept of income is broadly defined, and there are only few items of income which are tax-exempt. This is particularly the case following the 1992 reform, in which the reduction of the corporate tax rate to 25 per cent was accompanied by a widening of the tax base. One of the base-broadening measures was to repeal the previous tax preferences for capital gains on fixed assets. After the reform, the most important items of tax-exempt income are certain kinds of foreign income, including direct investment corporate dividends from treaty countries.

The broad taxability of items of business income is accompanied by a broad range of deductible expenses. Virtually all expenses necessary for acquiring taxable income are deductible. In company taxation, an important deduction which is internationally uncommon is based on *merger loss*. This is the difference between the purchase cost of the merging company's shares on the one hand and the company's net worth at the time of merger on the other. The deduction of the merger loss is a particularly sought-after tax benefit, and it has made tax-induced mergers between parent companies and their wholly-owned subsidiaries a common phenomenon.

One of the few limitations in the deductiblity of costs in business taxation is that only 50 per cent of entertainment expenses can be deducted. This rule was also introduced as part of the 1992 tax reform.

For decades, Finnish business taxation was characterised by substantial tax-deductible *reserves and provisions*. These benefits were strongly curtailed in the 1992 tax reform. The most important ones, the inventory reserve and the operating reserve based on wages and salaries paid, are no longer available to companies. The operating reserve was, however, maintained in the taxation of partnerships and private firms.

Depreciation allowances on buildings were also reduced in the 1992 tax reform. From 1993 on, the maximum annual depreciation under the declining-balance method is 7 per cent for industrial buildings and 4 per cent for other commercial as well as for residential buildings. Plant, machinery and equipment can be depreciated at the rate of 30 per cent under the declining-balance method. For 1993 to 1994 double allowances are granted for certain qualifying new investments in plant, machinery and buildings used in production.

For *losses* in tax years from 1993 on, the carryforward period has been extended from five to ten years. No carryback is allowed.

2.5.2 The Division of Business Income into Earned Income and Capital Income

It is not overwhelmingly problematic to categorise most kinds of income either as earned income or as capital income. However, substantial difficulties are involved in the classification of income generated by enterprises when the entrepreneur has both worked in and invested capital in his or her business. In economic terms, the income of such a business consists partly of the yield on the invested capital and partly of the value of the work done by the entrepreneur. In a differentiated income tax system of the Finnish kind, the yield on the invested capital should be taxed at the flat rate whereas the yield on the owner's labour should be taxed progressively. The division rules should not result in a substantial disparity in the taxation of entrepreneurs and wage earners; at the same time, however, the rules should ensure that investment in one's own business is not discriminated against vis-à-vis investment in other capital assets.

The solution adopted in Finland is to start by calculating the capital income share of the income and to treat the rest as earned income. The determination of the capital income is schematic, and it is based on the net wealth of the enterprise. Business income is regarded as capital income up to *15 per cent of the taxpayer's share of the net wealth of the enterprise,* and the excess is then treated as earned income. The net wealth computation is based on the values assessed for the purposes of the net wealth tax. These main rules are complemented by a number of modifications.

The problem of distinguishing between earned and capital income comes up in all forms of conducting business, i.e. in private firms, in partnerships and in closely held companies. In private firms and in partnerships, the entire income of the firm is taxed as the owners' earned income and capital income. The income of limited companies is not, by contrast, taxed to the owners until it is distributed. The issue of separating an earned income share from a dividend is a particularly vexed one. In principle, such a separation is needed in the case of shareholders working in their company and receiving the yield of their labour as a dividend; by contrast, in the case of a dividend received by a passive investor, there is no reason to treat the dividend partly as earned income. The policy problem is how to draw the line between such "active" and "passive" shareholders.

In this respect, the Finnish system is based on a bold simplification. Actually, dividends received by *any individual shareholder from any company other than those listed on a stock exchanqe* are subject to the division into earned income and capital income. This solution is not quite orthodox because it may cause a dividend received by a fully passive shareholder to be taxed as earned income. However, this unorthodoxy exists primarily in theory because dividends paid to passive investors seldom exceed 15 per cent of the shareholder's share of the net wealth of the company. Moreover, in the relatively meagre Finnish capital market, there is only a small number of truly outside investors in non-listed companies.

2.5.3 Corporate Tax

Limited companies as well as other corporate taxpayers are liable to pay the 25 per cent *corporate income tax* on their income. There are no other taxes based on the income or net wealth of corporations.

2.6 International Aspects of Income Taxation

2.6.1 Residents and Non-Residents

Finnish residents are taxed on their worldwide income. Non-residents are taxed on income derived from Finland. Individuals are held to be resident in Finland if they have their main abode in Finland or if they stay in Finland for a continuous period of more than six months. These rules are complemented by the so-called *three-year rule*. It provides that Finnish citizens remain resident until such time as three years have elapsed after the end of the year in which they left Finland, unless it is shown that they have not had substantial ties with Finland during the tax year.

There are no provisions concerning the residence of companies, but a company is generally understood to be resident if it is incorporated in Finland. There is no precedent for regarding a company registered in a foreign country as being resident in Finland.

Tax treaties concluded by Finland usually contain provisions of the type included in the OECD Model Treaty concerning residence for the purpose of the application of each treaty.

2.6.2 Tax Treaties

Finland has an extensive income tax treaty network, which in 1993 covered approximately 50 states. The treaties are based on the OECD model treaties, albeit treaties with developing countries often incorporate features of the United Nations model convention, too. The most important is the internationally unique multilateral Nordic tax treaty with Sweden, Norway, Denmark (including the Faroe Islands) and Iceland. In 1993, Finland was among the first countries to sign tax treaties with the Baltic states.

2.6.3 The Taxation of Foreign Income

In domestic tax legislation, there are only few deviations from the taxation of worldwide income. With regard to individual taxation, an important provision is that income derived from employment abroad is tax-exempt if the stay abroad lasts at least six months and certain additional conditions are met.

International double taxation of residents is primarily prevented through *provisions for a foreign tax credit*. Tax treaties concluded since mid-1970s are based on this method, although exemption provisions are also found in these treaties. Tax-sparing credit is also used in most treaties with developing countries. Treaties which date further back than the mid-1970s are based on the exemption method.

In spite of the status of the foreign tax credit as the main method, the Finnish policy is to exempt inter-corporate direct investment dividends in tax treaties. Since not all treaties include such a provision, the Business Income Tax Act also contains an exemption for such dividends from treaty countries.

In the absence of a tax treaty, international double taxation is alleviated under the Foreign Tax Credit Act. The prevention of double taxation is not as complete under this act as under a tax treaty.

2.6.4 The Taxation of Non-Residents

Non-residents are taxed on their income derived from Finland. The Income Tax Act includes a list of items of income which, *inter alia*, are considered to be derived from Finland. An important exception to the general rule is that *interest* derived by non-residents is not taxable in Finland except for a few uncommon cases. The interest income generated by Finnish branches of foreign banks is, of course, still taxable.

Whereas the basic rules on whether income is derived from Finland are found in the Income Tax Act, the provisions for the actual taxation of non-residents are included in the Act on the Taxation of Non-Residents' Income and Wealth. Apart from these statutes, tax treaty provisions often affect the taxation of non-residents in a significant way.

Items of income derived from Finland by non-residents are *either* subject to a final withholding tax *or* taxed on the basis of assessment. The most common types of income are subject to the final withholding tax. These items include salaries, wages and pensions as well as dividends, royalties and interest in the few situations where interest is taxable.

The withholding tax rate for salaries, wages and pensions is 35 per cent for non-residents, and only a limited number of deductions are allowed. Dividends and other items of capital income are taxed at the same 25 per cent rate as the capital income of residents. The actually applicable tax rates on dividends, interest and royalties, however, are usually lower due to tax treaty provisions. Business and farming income, proceeds from timber sales as well as rents and capital gains on real property and on shares of property companies are taxed on the basis of assessment. Business and farming income are divided into capital income and earned income, which are taxed at the rates of 25 and 35 per cent, respectively. Rents, capital gains and proceeds from timber sales are taxed as capital income at the 25 per cent rate.

In contrast to fully domestic settings, dividends received by non-resident shareholders are always dealt with as capital income. The imputation credit is not available to non-residents unless such a credit has been granted within the provisions of a tax treaty. The first treaty with such a provision was the Finland – United Kingdom treaty, which was revised in 1990 with a partial extension of the Finnish imputation credit to U.K. shareholders in Finnish companies. Although some other treaties are to follow suit, the reduction of the company tax rate to 25 per cent may have made Finland less inclined to extend its imputation credit to foreign investors.

2.6.5 The Arm's Length Rule for International Transactions

Like most countries' tax laws, Finland's Taxation Act includes a particular provision stipulating am arm's length rule for transactions between related enterprises. According to this rule, the income of a Finnish enterprise may be adjusted if transactions between the enterprise and a related foreign enterprise differ from those which would have been made between independent parties. The composition of the rule is in effect quite similar to the corresponding provision in other countries and in tax treaties.[4]

There are no detailed regulations concerning the application of the arm's length rule. In general, the interpretation cannot be characterised as strict, although a small number of rather severe court rulings have been given. The practice has been particularly liberal in respect of transactions between Finnish parent companies and their foreign subsidiaries.[5]

2.7 Anti-Avoidance Clause

Finnish income tax legislation contains a general clause against tax avoidance. The provision states that if a circumstance or a transaction has been given a legal form which is not commensurate with its actual character and meaning, taxation takes place as if the correct form had been adopted. The provision also explicitly authorises the tax board to estimate the taxable income and wealth where it is obvious that a sales price or other consideration or agreement has been fixed or some other action taken for the purpose of avoiding the payment of tax.

The anti-avoidance clause has been applied in various situations. For instance, corporate income may have been directly taxed to the shareholder in cases where the corporation has been nothing but a vehicle for the professional activities of the shareholder.[6]

There is no *controlled foreign company* -legislation in Finland, and neither has the general anti-avoidance clause been applied to passive foreign companies owned by Finnish parents.

2.8 Procedure and Appeals

Taxpayers with taxable income during the tax year must file a tax return. The taxable income is then assessed by the tax office or by the municipal tax board. Actually, income taxes are for the most part collected through withholding. Wages, salaries and pensions are subject to a comprehensive with-holding system, and businesses are required to make advance payments in the course of the tax year.

Taxpayers dissatisfied with their assessment may appeal either to the municipal tax appeal board or to the respective provincial administrative court. Decisions of the provincial administrative courts may be appealed before the Supreme Administrative Court. There are, however, substantial restrictions on the right to appeal to the highest instance.

3. The Net Wealth Tax, the Inheritance and Gift Tax and the Property Tax

The *net wealth tax* is payable by individuals with a taxable net wealth in excess of FIM 1.1 million. The tax rate is 0.9 per cent of the excess. Due to the relatively high lower limit and a lenient assessment of certain assets, the number of taxpayers actually liable to pay the tax is rather small. Taxable assets, allowable deductions as well as the valuation of assets and liabilities are dealt with in the Wealth Tax Act of 1992.

Non-residents are liable to pay the net wealth tax on their Finnish assets. The tax is 0.9 per cent of the excess of the net wealth in excess of FIM 800 000. In general, Finnish securities and other financial assets owned by non-residents are not subject to the net wealth tax. Most tax treaties concluded by Finland also cover the net wealth tax.

Inheritances, testamentary dispositions and gifts are subject to the *inheritance and gift tax* under the Inheritance and Gift Tax Act of 1940. The highest marginal tax rate between closest relatives is 14 per cent; this rate is applicable to net amounts in excess of FIM 2.1 million. Various tax preferences are granted to generation shifts of businesses and farms.

The inheritance tax is payable on any property situated in Finland and on personal property situated abroad but belonging to the estate of a Finnish resident. The gift tax is payable on property situated in Finland and on personal property donated to a Finnish resident. Finland has concluded inheritance tax treaties with the Nordic countries, the United States, Switzerland, France and the Netherlands; the Nordic treaty covers gift taxes, too.

A *property tax* was levied for the first time in 1993 according to the

Property Tax Act of 1992. The tax replaced a number of old taxes and levies, including the income tax on owner-occupied housing. All real property is subject to the tax unless a specific statutory exception is applicable; the most important exemptions are granted to forests as well as to land used for agriculture. The property tax is calculated on the basis of the assessment done for the net wealth tax. The property tax is a municipal tax, and each municipality has the right to determine the applicable tax rates within statutory limits. In general, the nominal tax rates vary between 0.1 and 0.8 per cent. The effective tax rates are lower because the assessments usually fall short of full market value.

4. Value-Added Tax

Throughout the post-war period the role of the general tax on consumption has been played by what is referred to as a turnover tax. After several changes, by the early 1990s this tax had come to resemble a value-added tax (VAT) rather closely. However, certain crucial differences remained and, after a thorough drafting process, in 1993 the government submitted a proposal for substituting a VAT for the turnover tax. The new tax is to take effect in 1994.

One reason for the adoption of a VAT was Finland's application for membership in the European Community. The proposed value-added tax will be roughly compatible with the VAT directives of the EC, albeit with minor deviations. In contrast to the turnover tax which, apart from a few exceptions, only covered the sale and rental of goods, the VAT will be widely applicable to services and the construction industry as well. However, the tax does *not* cover, *inter alia*, health and medical services, services related to social welfare, education and training, or banking and insurance services. Agriculture and forestry are also, in the main, tax-exempt.

Another major change is that while taxpayers' right to deduct taxes included in inputs was not consistently applied under the turnover tax system, such deductions are all but completely available in the VAT system. The 'hidden tax', which burdened domestic production and affected prices in a haphazard way, is thereby eliminated. Input taxes included in company cars and entertainment expenses remain as exceptions to the main rule.

The general VAT rate is due to be 22 per cent, which corresponds to the old turnover tax rate. This rate is among the highest in Western Europe. A reduced rate of 12 per cent will be applied to personal transport, accommodation, movies, medicaments and books. A zero rate will continue to apply to subscriptions to newspapers and periodicals. Food is subject to the general tax rate but its effective tax burden is substantially lowered through fixed primary product deductions.

5. Other Taxes and Levies

Although the great part of tax revenues is derived through the general income and consumption taxes, there are several taxes and levies of considerable fiscal significance. Except for the municipal property tax (subsection 3 above), the revenue from these other taxes is received by the state.

A *stamp duty* is payable on sales of real property. The stamp duty is usually 6 per cent of the price paid, and it is payable by the buyer. A stamp duty of 1.6 per cent is to be paid on sales of shares and other securities, with the exception of listed securities, which are tax-exempt.

There are various excise duties and other specific taxes on certain goods. The most important of these are the excises on fuels, alcohol, tobacco and beer in addition to the motor vehicle taxes. Energy and carbon emission taxes have been developed from the early 1990s on; in 1994 these taxes are to be based both on energy ratings and on carbon contents, with the emphasis on the carbon factor.

6. Future Aspects

The future development of the Finnish tax system is more than ever before dependent upon the international tax policy scene. In this setting, the main roles are played (not independently of each other) by other Nordic countries on the one hand and by the European Community on the other. The crucial issue here is whether the international community will take the road of fierce tax competition or the path of cautious harmonisation of tax rules, perhaps with minimum taxes on critical targets.

The vision of the future is very different in respect of direct and indirect taxation. Concerning income taxation, Finland adopted as of 1993 the Nordic model of sharply differentiated taxation of earned income and capital income. This model has several intrinsic points of strength but it has its weaknesses, too. It remains to be seen whether the broad capital income tax base and the 25 per cent tax rate can endure the pressures of the international financial market, where electronic money can be transferred anywhere in the world in an instant. On the other hand, the 25 per cent tax rate is low in comparison to the very high marginal tax rates on earned income. A crucial issue is whether the tax burden on earned income can be and will be lowered in spite of the inevitable budgetary pressures of the coming years.

Concerning company taxation, the base-broadening that was carried out in the 1992 tax reform has moved the Finnish system closer to the international pattern. The 25 per cent company tax rate is very low and it falls short of the minimum rate that was suggested for the EC in the report of the Ruding Committee in 1992.[7] However, the reactions to the committee's proposal have been mixed, and there will hardly be any legal obstacles for Finland to maintain its company tax rate of 25 per cent in the future.

The value-added tax, which is to come into force in 1994, is technically modern. Although some important details may give rise to tension, the adjustments which may be necessary, for example, to facilitate Finland's membership in the EC will not be fundamental in nature.

Actually the most dramatic changes before the year 2000 may be expected in other areas of indirect taxation. The development here, however, is hard to predict because it is strongly dependent upon international aspects. For instance, EC membership would place immense pressure on the traditionally very high taxation of alcohol in Finland. On the other hand, it can be expected that the so-called *green taxes* will play a substantially weightier role than has been witnessed to date.

1 A general description of the Finnish tax system is found in the booklet *Taxation in Finland,* which was published by the Ministry of Financed in 1992. However, due to substantial legislative reforms, large parts of the booklet are already outdated.
2 See *Edward Andersson,* How Swedish Tax Law Affected Finnish Income and Net Wealth Taxation. Scandinavian Studies in Law 1986, 13–28.
3 For the background of the reform, see *Kari S. Tikka,* Taxation of Capital in Finland and International Tax Competition – Survey of the Actual Situation and Development Trends, in *Pekka Timonen* (ed.), Nordic Perspectives on European Financial Integration, 1992, 333–347. For the reform and also more generally for the Nordic model, see *Timo Viherkenttä,* A Flat Rate Tax on Capital Income: The Nordic Model. 6 Tax Notes International (March 15, 1993), 659–670.
4 For a general presentation of the provision and its application, see *Heikki Niskakangas,* Transfer pricing in the absence of comparable market prices, National report Finland. LXXVIIa Cahiers de droit fiscal international, 1992, 371–378.
5 See *Timo Viherkenttä,* Case Law Sheds Light on Transfer Pricing Issues. European Taxation 1988, 135–138.
6 For the application of the anti-avoidance clause, see *Kari S. Tikka,* The Disregard of a Legal Entity for Tax Purposes, National report Finland. LXXIVa Cahiers de droit fiscal international, 1989, 259–268.
7 Report of the Committee of Independent Experts on Company Taxation. Commission of the European Communities. 1992.